MW01230322

Predicting the Winner

Predicting

Potomac Books| *An imprint of the University of Nebraska Press*

the Winner

The Untold Story
of Election Night 1952
and the Dawn of
Computer Forecasting

IRA CHINOY

© 2024 by Ira Chinoy. All rights reserved. Potomac Books is an imprint of the University of Nebraska Press. Manufactured in the United States of America.

∞

Library of Congress Cataloging-in-Publication Data
Names: Chinoy, Ira, author.
Title: Predicting the winner: the untold story of election night 1952 and the dawn of computer forecasting / Ira Chinoy.
Description: [Lincoln, Nebraska]: Potomac Books, an imprint of the University of Nebraska Press, 2024. | Includes bibliographical references and index.
Identifiers: LCCN 2023019342
ISBN 9781640125964 (hardback)
ISBN 9781640126152 (epub)
ISBN 9781640126169 (pdf)
Subjects: LCSH: Presidents—United States—Election—1952. | Presidents—United States—Election—Forecasting. | Election forecasting—United States—Technological innovations. | BISAC: POLITICAL SCIENCE / Political Process / Campaigns & Elections | POLITICAL SCIENCE / History & Theory
Classification: LCC E816 .C456 2024 | DDC 324.6/5097309045—dc23/eng/20231031
LC record available at https://lccn.loc.gov/2023019342

Set in Miller Text by A. Shahan.

For Gail, Molly, and Tyler,
who provide limitless
support and encouragement.

For Sally, who was always a
great comfort,
and for Xena, who provides
no shortage of comic relief.

We look backward for clues
because, the future being on
the other side of a closed door,
we have no place else to look.

—Louis Menand, *American Studies*

Contents

Illustrations

Acknowledgments

The story I have pieced together in this book—and in a PhD dissertation that preceded it—was not told before because the evidence I needed to tell it lay hidden and took years to assemble. Dozens of people helped me along the way to make these finds and to make sense of them—mentors, colleagues, historians, librarians, archivists, friends, and family. There were documents tucked away in archives, in personal collections, and in company records. Old television footage and radio recordings were hard to find. Relevant news articles and ads turned up in databases of historical newspapers with search terms that had to be refined by trial and error. The memories of a few living participants of these long-ago events provided leads and details—not to mention delightful conversations—once I was able to identify them and track them down. Little of what I needed to tell this story was on the open web, though some important pieces were. A bare-bones version of a few parts of this saga had been told and retold before. But these events had not been explored in depth to reveal the surprises, new meanings, and relevance to our time that you will find here. This treasure hunt took me by subway, car, train, and plane to archives and museums in Wisconsin, Delaware, Maryland, New Jersey, California, and Washington DC. I traveled to Alabama and Pennsylvania for interviews with surviving innovators, to the Christie's auction house in Manhattan, and to see records stored on microfilm at the Library of Congress, in boxes of documents at the Smithsonian National Museum of American History, in collections of newsreel footage at the National Archives, in a set of old newsletters at the New York Public Library, and much more. I received records sent by archivists in Wyoming, Michigan, Texas, Georgia, Minnesota, and elsewhere. This is also the only exploration of election night 1952 to piece together the television broadcasts from CBS and NBC—thirteen hours combined.

Help came from many in the form of brainstorming, providing access to records, suggesting leads, reading drafts, or offering encouragement at critical times. They included Tom Rosenstiel, Mike Conway, Jen Golbeck, Margaret Sullivan, Chip Scanlan, Dan Russell, Rafael Lorente, Dan Gerstle, Katie Aunie, Stella Rouse, Michael Hanmer, Josh Davidsburg, Tom Kunkel, Chris Callahan, Maggie Saponaro, Michael Powell, Sarah McGrew, Allison Druin, Chris Hanson, Merrilee Cox, Sandy Banisky, Jennifer Bires, A. R. Hogan, Jim Baxter, Emerson W. Pugh, Thomas J. Bergin, Lucy Dalglish, Jay Kernis, Kevin Klose, Jon Franklin, James Gilbert, Douglas Gomery, Philip Meyer, Jeff McChristian, Jiabao Zhou, Doris Mattingly, Judy Bernard, Kate Pretorius, Mike Chinoy, Kevin Chinoy, David Chinoy, Kathy Chinoy, Marc Chinoy, and three friends and colleagues who passed away while I was working on this project: Haynes Johnson, Lee Thornton, and Michael Gurevitch.

Hunting for treasure in archives around the country was a challenging process made easier by Peggy Kidwell, Paul Ceruzzi, Michael Henry, Chuck Howell, Nancy Cole, Luis Aristondo, Marni Pedorella, David Bushman, Maria Pagano, Carole Parnes, Michael R. Williams, Paula Jabloner, Alexander Magoun, Brecque Keith, Carrie Seib, Stephanie Crowe, Valerie Komor, Paul C. Lasewicz, Dawn Stanford, and Dan Rooney. Richard Roberts, CEO of Monroe Systems for Business, gave me a huge boost early in this research by opening the historical records of the Monroe Calculating Machine Company to me, and one of his successors, VP Jason Marsdale, has also been accommodating.

The research for this book began more than two decades ago and resulted, initially, in the completion of a PhD dissertation in 2010 at the University of Maryland. I am grateful for the guidance of the members of that committee: Maurine Beasley, Robert Friedel, David Sicilia, W. Joseph Campbell, and Mark Feldstein.

A lot happened that slowed my path toward completing this book. Then in mid-2019, Jill Lepore, the Harvard historian and *New Yorker* writer, reached out to me. For an episode in a podcast series she was preparing, *The Last Archive*, Jill and producer Ben Naddaff-Hafrey came to campus to talk about the research she found in my dissertation and to watch some of the video from election night 1952. The podcast's ten episodes were released during the pandemic a few months later, including episode 5, titled "Project X." The title comes from a document I found in an archive in Wisconsin. Meeting Jill was a turning point for me. She urged me to do this book and was enthusiastic about its prospects. She included me in her podcast and gave my research a shout-out in the *New Yorker*, too. Later she provided me with invaluable leads in navigating the process of finding a publisher.

Hundreds of students at every level have offered encouragement over the years that I have worked on this project, even checking in long after they graduated. I am grateful. I know we are in good hands as they become leaders in producing quality journalism and in other paths they are choosing to follow.

As this book neared completion, two people at NBC Universal were immensely helpful: Lynn Carrillo, vice president, and Stephanie Freire, rights and clearance specialist. At CBS I am grateful for invaluable help from Ann Fotiades and Daniel DiPierro, formerly of CBS News Information Resources, and Ray Faiola, formerly of CBS Audience Services.

I owe the publication of this book to Peter Bernstein of the Bernstein Literary Agency. He became my agent for this project and my mentor in the process of developing a proposal and securing a publisher. I am grateful to the terrific team at Potomac Books for taking on this book and bringing it into the world: Tom Swanson, Kayla Moslander, Taylor Gilreath, Ann Baker, Rosemary Sekora, Leif Milliken, Erika Rippeteau, Barbara Townsend, Tish Fobben, Tayler Lord, Terry Boldan, and the design, marketing, and sales specialists, along with this book's ace copyeditor, Jennifer Boardman, and indexer Jessica Freeman.

When my eyesight began to fail during the final year of this project, Dr. Maxwell Helfgott and Dr. Adam Wenick restored it and enabled me to finish.

There are three people who have had to put up with this project, day in and day out, and without whose love and support it would not have seen the light of day: my wife, Gail Chinoy, my daughter, Molly Muldoon, and my son-in-law, Tyler Muldoon.

I value the opportunities I had to talk with some of the people who took part in events you will learn about here. They were generous with their time, records, leads, and recollections. These included Richard LaManna, Vincent Pogorzelski, Morgan Huff, Irving Gardoff, and Reuven Frank. I also want to share here some indelible memories of my encounters with several more.

Forty-eight years after election night 1952, and just two years before the subject of this book first grabbed my attention, William Burkhart passed away after a long illness. He was an inventor who played a pivotal role in the development of the Monrobot computer used on NBC that night. While he was ill, he drafted several autobiographical sketches. He talked about his childhood, his war years, his business endeavors, and his personal philosophy. I saw these writings when I flew across the country to meet his wife, Dorothy, and examine her husband's papers. I was eager to know what he might have said in them about that election night in 1952. But nowhere was it mentioned. The only related artifact among his files was a *Newsweek* magazine from November 1952. It included an article citing him and noting his role in connection with the Monrobot on NBC. I wondered whether he realized back in 1952 that he was doing something of historic importance. I talked this over with Dorothy. She suggested that I pay a visit to Monroe and Frederica Postman, who lived nearby. They had been friends of the Burkharts since the 1950s. Monroe Postman went to work with Bill Burkhart at the Monroe Calculating Machine Company in New Jersey in 1954. I was hopeful for anything the couple would remember of what Burkhart might have said about election night 1952. I asked, but my question was met by puzzled silence. I showed them photographs. They were astonished. They had no recollection of Burkhart ever talking about the events of that night. Burkhart had taken part in a seminal episode at the dawn of the computer age, but its significance, perhaps, was not something he could see in real time.

I was saddened that I had missed him by just a few years. I was also sad to learn that I had missed talking with Marilyn Mason, whose smarts and looks had been highlighted by NBC in connection with her on-air appearance operating the Monrobot on election night. Here was a young woman at the intersection of two domains—computers and election-night broadcasting—where women, let alone young women, were a rarity. I wanted to know more. But in my searches, her trail grew cold shortly after that night in 1952. I suspected she had gotten married, took her husband's name, and left her job at Prudential Insurance—where she was helping that company explore the new world of computers—to raise a family. It turned out I was right. We might tend to think that with the passage of time, more and more of the past is likely to disappear. Certainly, records, photos, and video are discarded or lost or forgotten. But the passage of time can also serve up surprises. One afternoon in February 2014, nearly four years after I wrapped up my dissertation, I received an email from a woman named Wendy Friedman. The message took my breath away. She was Marilyn Mason's daughter. Her mother had passed away a few days earlier. Wendy was searching the web to create a tribute to her mother and came across my dissertation in a digital repository at the University of Maryland. I later met with Wendy and her husband, Bill, and I was able to show them what I had collected that featured Wendy's mom—NBC video, press releases, and photos. Wendy and Bill filled in some gaps for me, too. They shared documents that Marilyn had kept since 1952 from her election-night role at NBC —even her Rockefeller Center ID badge and her pay stub. The check had come with a letter from Bill Burkhart, thanking her for her help. He also sent her a copy of Monroe's *Keynote* magazine featuring her. And he wrote this: "We are still receiving favorable comments and publicity." There was one other striking pair of items in the papers that Wendy showed me. The first was a large black-and-white photograph. Fifteen men in coats and ties are seated at desks in what might be a classroom and another man stands at a lectern, all facing the camera. Marilyn Mason is in the very back of the photo—which was the front of that classroom—where there was also a large diagram of a computer and an easel. A letter provides context. It is from an executive at IBM. He thanked her for what he termed her "exposition" to the "members of the customer 650 school"—a reference to IBM's Model 650 magnetic drum computer. The letter spoke of her "knowledge and grasp" as exceptional, her presentation as "interesting" as well as "very clear and forthright," and her "demonstrated ability." She was just twenty-four years old.

I so wished I had met her. As fate would have it, our paths had crossed, unknowingly, long ago. Wendy told me that I had been in the same graduating class at Harvard with Wendy's brother. His name rang a bell. I dug out my yearbook and sure enough, he had not only graduated in the same year I did, but he had lived in Dunster House, as had I. In those days, after the main commencement in Harvard Yard, graduating seniors and their families repaired to various places around campus for more intimate diploma ceremonies. In my case that was the courtyard at Dunster House. It is not a large space. And so on the day I received my diploma in 1977 and Wendy's brother received his, Marilyn Mason David was right there, too.

I was delighted to meet and hear about other individuals who are not common names in histories of journalism and technology but played important roles in the events I have explored. One was Max Woodbury, a mathematician who worked out the election-night formulas in 1952 for UNIVAC, the Universal Automatic Computer, which was featured on CBS. I spent a pleasant day with him in Birmingham, Alabama. Another was Stephen Wright, a UNIVAC engineer. He led a team that converted Woodbury's ideas into a program for generating forecasts from voting data as it came in on election night. Several months after we spent a day together at his home outside Philadelphia, Wright sent me an announcement by email. There was to be a ceremony dedicating a historical marker in front of 3747 Ridge Avenue in Philadelphia, the site of the former plant where the UNIVAC computers had been built. It had been an unheralded landmark of the early computer age.

When I arrived on the appointed day in the fall of 2006, a large canvas tent had been set up in a lot adjacent to the building. About 150 people had gathered, including Woodbury, who traveled from Alabama for the event, and others who had worked in that brand-new world of computing. After the ceremony began, one of the speakers asked these pioneers to stand. Dozens rose to their feet, some more slowly than others, and they received a hearty ovation. Congratulatory letters were read. There were speeches, including one by Wright. He began by quoting two lines from William Wordsworth's poem about the French Revolution: "Bliss was it in that dawn to be alive, / But to be young was very heaven!" Wright explained, "To those of us who were here at the dawn of the computer revolution [those words recall] the enthusiasm with which we took part in it. We came to work each day with a sense of joy in exploring the challenges of this undiscovered world." He talked about the preparations for that night in 1952. His engaging account was met with laughs, knowing nods, and admiration. Wright said that after that first contest between Eisenhower and Stevenson, he continued to work on election-night computing projects through 1964. "But," he added, "I don't think anything will ever match the thrill of that night in 1952."

Predicting the Winner

1 | Fearsome Contraptions

Nobody saw it in real time. How could they? The history of American elections changed profoundly on the night of November 4, 1952. The candidates were at the center of attention, of course, but they were not central to this change. We can see its significance now with decades of hindsight. Something never tried before was launched live and untested on national television. Viewers witnessed an outside-the-box approach to predicting the winner from early returns using something new—computers. Like exhibits in a freak show, the computers were referred to as "electronic brains" and "mechanical monsters." That's the way it can be with innovations—considered laughable before they become so locked-in that we cannot imagine life before them. This innovation would help fuel an obsession with numbers as a way of understanding—and shaping—politics. It would also engender controversy right down to our own time. And it would herald a future in which the public square would go digital. Yet on that night, this path was in no way guaranteed or even envisioned. Americans did not yet have computers at home or at work. Most had never seen one. The thinking in broadcast news circles was that the flashing lights of these newfangled gizmos as they spit out forecasts might provide an edge. Television news executives hoped to get a jump on the competition both in calling the election and attracting viewers. But the whole enterprise of reaching outside the box with something so new was an enormous gamble. And it is important to understand—especially in our own time—that this gamble was undertaken in response to a crisis of credibility. This crisis was the fallout from election-night forecasts four years earlier that turned out to be upside down. What's more, a lackluster presentation of returns on television in 1948 was at odds with television's promise as a new visual medium for news. What transpired four years later, in 1952, is a complex tale of innovation in response to crisis, along with reactions that ranged from enthusiasm to ridicule to outright resistance. The events surrounding that election night in 1952 also offer us a way to think about another more recent inflection point—the vexing events of 2020—and the future of election nights in America.

At 8:00 p.m. on election night in 1952, CBS launched its coverage from a cavernous studio above Grand Central Terminal, the massive rail hub in Midtown Manhattan. A camera perched aloft on a swivel in the middle of the studio slowly surveyed the scene and zoomed in toward the anchor desk.[1] The zoom lens itself was a recent invention. Viewers found themselves immersed in the hubbub. Walter Cronkite was anchoring his first election night on television. The audience could see for themselves what he described as a teeming beehive.[2] The studio was packed with people, cameras, cables, telephones, typewriters, adding machines, and all manner of other equipment. A massive banner that read "CBS Television Election Headquarters" was installed along one wall. The click-clacking of teletype machines signaled a steady flow of wire service dispatches delivering a rising mass of vote counts. Beneath the banner, and in view for the first few seconds, was an exotic-looking device about the size and shape of an organ console. It had a keyboard and rows of blinking lights. Viewers would learn later in the broadcast that this was the so-called "supervisory control panel" for a Universal Automatic Computer, known simply as UNIVAC, one of the pioneering computer models in a quickly growing field. The control panel was not actually connected to a UNIVAC computer. Rather, the panel had been installed on the CBS set as a prop. Its blinking lights were sleight of hand, produced by something akin to a Christmas tree light circuit.[3] The actual UNIVAC was a behemoth. It weighed in at more than eight tons, too big to move to CBS for the broadcast. So it would be generating forecasts from the place where it was built, one hundred miles away in Philadelphia. Tensions were running high behind the scenes at the UNIVAC home base.[4] And the stress was only going to get more intense. The first predictions soon generated by the computer would be so far from the expected outcome that they would not be released to the network. Instead, the computer's keepers would scramble for a solution to this mystery. How could their eight-ton baby be so wrong, they wondered. The UNIVAC programmers and engineers had built redundancy into their systems to guard against errors in data entry and calculation. But they had not considered what they would do if the computer's first forecast diverged wildly from expectation—as, in fact, it did.

The election program on NBC television got a later start than at CBS. That allowed for a regularly scheduled NBC variety show—the *Buick Circus Hour*—to run in its usual time slot, albeit with a special guest star, the comedian Milton Berle.[5] The NBC election broadcast began at 9:00 p.m. from the legendary Studio 8-H in Rockefeller Center. The studio had been built for the NBC Symphony Orchestra and is known in our own time as the home of *Saturday Night Live*. John Cameron Swayze, familiar to Americans for his radio and television newscasts, appeared on camera to explain the night's main event—the presidential contest.[6] He sat in front of a visual gimmick, a blinking, oddly-shaped United States map in which states were sized based on their number of electoral votes. A centrally located camera provided a slow, 360-degree sweep of a scene as frenetic as the one at CBS a few blocks away. Dozens of guests in formal attire milled about on the studio floor, cordoned off from the radio and television staff. An announcer pointed out several sets, about the size of carnival booths, where running vote totals would be reported for the House and Senate. There was another set to report running tallies in the race for president between Republican Dwight Eisenhower, Democrat Adlai Stevenson, and a raft of third-party candidates. The announcer also spoke of "scientific brains" to be used for the first time. Just as at CBS, NBC had the use of a brand-new computer. But this one was based on an entirely different vision than the UNIVAC. It was named Monrobot. In an age of big and showy—like the rocket ship look of new cars—the Monrobot was diminutive and unassuming. In fact, it was the size of an office desk, small enough to be installed right there on the NBC set. This had the potential to be a public relations bonanza for the Monrobot's manufacturer, the New Jersey-based Monroe Calculating Machine Company. But behind the scenes, the Monrobot team was apprehensive. They were seeing a potential downside of their gamble. Over the weekend, after the computer was shipped to the NBC studio, its top was flipped up—like an untethered desktop—in a touch of showmanship. This would allow television viewers to see lights blinking from hundreds of vacuum tubes in the computer's interior. But flakes of metal—solder from the connections of various components—had fallen onto the surface of a magnetic drum in the guts of the machine, below the vacuum tubes. That drum served as the machine's memory. The debris had to be retrieved, flake by flake, with tweezers.[7] How well the apparatus would work on election night was an open question.

Still, the stage was set for a new election-night formula. There could be bragging rights for the players if all went well. Yet, it was also risky for the computer world's new entrepreneurs, who were eager to turn businesses and government agencies into customers. There had been small demonstrations of these newfangled machines before. But those stunts had been a sure thing, using data and results prepared in advance. Now the computers would be crunching a mountain of data collected and transmitted hastily as the evening wore on. They would be using programs never put to the test under those circumstances. And they would be performing in front of an audience of millions. Glitches could sabotage business prospects at a critical time. This was equally risky for the television news networks. They were trying to attract viewers more accustomed to getting their breaking news from radio. The new medium of television had to be seen as credible, especially in the crucible of election night. The previous presidential election night—1948— carried uncomfortable memories of gaffs by pollsters and journalists. The pollsters had misread public opinion in the run-up to the voting. Then some broadcast and print news organizations infamously screwed up with premature reporting of election-night outcomes that were in line with the pollsters' predictions—and wrong. Most memorable was the *Chicago Daily Tribune*'s infamous headline, "Dewey Defeats Truman." Broadcasters were also skewered for errant conclusions about the outcome. As election night shaped up in 1952, would cbs and nbc have more of a jump on the outcome this time with computers? Maybe. But what if the computers got it wrong?

There was plenty of skepticism about the whole arrangement. *Business Week* magazine had wondered openly whether these "robot brains" had any place in the "Election Night hurlyburly" at broadcast news studios.[8] Notable names in broadcast news were wryly dismissive. At cbs that included two network stars, Edward R. Murrow and Eric Sevareid.[9] Walter Cronkite was on the fence.[10] Bill Henry, a noted sportswriter who would be anchoring for NBC, was dismissive, too, referring to computers before election night as "fearsome contraptions."[11] Executives at ABC, meanwhile, were having none of it, mocking the plans of rival networks. Instead, ABC touted the "human brains" it would feature on air.[12] These were well-known names such as Walter Winchell and Drew Pearson. Following election night, famous television celebrities would weigh in with a laugh at the computers' expense, too. Among them were entertainer Arthur Godfrey and comedian Ernie Kovacs.[13]

That skepticism has not aged well. But no one could know in 1952 what we know now: that computers on television would eventually become an election-night staple—and that computers and television news would become defining features of American life. We are now like the audience of an Alfred Hitchcock thriller, seeing what is just beyond view of the protagonists as we yell at the screen, "Why can't they see it?" But they could not—just as we cannot see now what is down the road. So our excavation of events from 1952 is an opportunity to travel back in time and see what happens when something new comes along. We have the benefit of hindsight, but we should not lose sight of how things seemed then. At CBS the distinguished-looking, somber-toned Eric Sevareid was known to Americans for his daring reports on CBS radio during World War II. On election night in 1952, he gloated after the computer used by his network hiccupped. "I'm delighted," he said as he cracked a smile, "that UNIVAC, our machine competitor, was wrong for a while and we were consistently right with a human voice—or we'd all be victims of technological unemployment pretty soon."[14] It is unlikely that Sevareid feared losing his job to a computer, especially in light of his penetrating analyses that night.[15] But he was among those who treated the computer as an incursion. The computer would make its way into journalism early—and with a great deal of fanfare—but with a lot of pushback and derision, too.

This is the untold and timely story of a critical pivot point in American politics, journalism, and culture. It is not taught in school and has largely slipped from memory. Yet, how we know what we know on election nights would never be the same after November 4, 1952. This is also a story about innovation, undertaken to meet journalistic imperatives of accuracy, timeliness, and engagement. New approaches may not work as well at first as the things they are meant to replace. Or they may work fine, but what they produce might not be trusted. To envision possibilities and traverse barriers, innovators must have more than just bright ideas. They must be willing to take risks. They must challenge widely held assumptions. They must enlist allies. And they must, especially, connect the new with what is not new. This was all true in 1952, when the path of things we now take for granted was in no way certain. A couple of generations later, some news industry leaders got left behind by the digital revolution when they were not willing to question their assumptions, think outside the box, and take risks. Could it have been different? We cannot answer that. But I believe a close study of events in 1952 tells us something worth remembering when the next chance to innovate comes along. That is nowhere more important than the way journalists and Americans will respond—in the near and long term—to challenges raised by the fraught events surrounding election night 2020. We will see in this book that election nights have long mattered as opportunities to innovate—often in the face of serious challenges—and foster new approaches to journalism more broadly.

I did not set out to explore the long-ago history of election nights. I had been a journalist for twenty-five years and was intrigued by the pushback I had seen in journalism—even in the late twentieth century—toward adopting the computer as a tool for discovery in the reporting process. My curiosity led me to wonder when computers and journalism first hooked up, and how. That, in turn, led me to a great surprise. The "when" was 1952—so much earlier than I had imagined—and the "how" was election night.

As I started my research on those historic events, I kept coming across a standard, almost cartoon-like account of the debut of computing for election-night forecasting. That thin thread of a story has varied in the telling, but basically it goes as follows. The CBS news team had the use of a room-sized UNIVAC. It was said to have accurately predicted a landslide early in the evening. That is something no human could have done, as the standard story goes. But since a landslide was at odds with preelection polls, the result was not released until much later in the evening.

By that time, the outcome—an actual landslide—was clear to everyone. There are a variety of omissions and other issues with the typical account. One of the biggest of these omissions took me completely by surprise when I came across it. And this discovery locked me into the quest that turned into this book.

Early in my research, I came across an online newsletter celebrating the history of Unisys. That company was a corporate successor to the UNIVAC's early manufacturer, Remington Rand. The newsletter had a paragraph about the computer's use on election night in 1952. It included this: "Jack Gould, the television writer for the *New York Times*, was not impressed with . . . the UNIVAC." But there was more to that sentence. Here it is in full: "Jack Gould, the television writer for the *New York Times*, was not impressed with either the UNIVAC or the much smaller Monrobot computer used by the NBC network."[16]

Another computer? What? I had not seen this mentioned anywhere else, and I had not yet started my search for contemporary news coverage from 1952. When I did, using various databases of historical newspapers, I quickly learned that the mention of the "Monrobot" in the *New York Times* in 1952 was not some mistake or fluke. Other papers and magazines reported the same thing at the time. I also learned that on my own campus at the University of Maryland, there was an important archive, the Library of American Broadcasting. And on its shelves were so-called "trade releases" from NBC going back decades. These were notices sent to newspaper and magazine writers. A curator helped me find the volume for the fall of 1952. As I leafed through the pages, I came across a release dated October 16. It was astonishing. This was the headline: "Meet Mr. Mike Monrobot, 'Electronic Brain,' Who Will Compute Election Count for NBC Radio and TV; Mechanical Wizard Can Tackle Many Problems at Once."[17] The release went on to tout—with more showmanship than accuracy—the machine's purported qualifications: "Mike is the fastest—not the biggest—electronic computer in the country. From his place in one corner of NBC's election night headquarters . . . Mike will help predict and prove the outcome of presidential and state elections at the earliest possible hour." The release tried to make a virtue out of the dimensions of the desk-sized Monrobot since "small" was not yet a virtue for the new world of computing. "Unlike earlier style computers that bulk so large that they can hardly be moved from the place where they were originally built," said the release, "Mike will ride over from New Jersey and be installed in NBC election headquarters." That release also touted the Monrobot's ease of use—replete with 1950s-era stereotypes meant to grab a reader's attention: "He's fond of pretty girl secretaries, who can be readily trained to operate him, but on election night Mike will have a beautiful woman PhD for his companion." And there was more: "Like any well-oiled brain, he makes no noise and needs only a bit of electricity for his nourishment, and perhaps a wee bit of affection from his operator." If the Monrobot would not look like much in the circus-like atmosphere of election night in a TV studio, so be it. NBC would just have to generate the hype as best it could. I would learn more later about the woman. Although she was not a PhD, she was a recent college graduate talented in mathematics. And she was adept at operating the Monrobot, making her a young pioneer in a young field. That unconventional role made for good TV on election night, just as the computers themselves did.

The trade releases were the first of what would turn out to be a treasure trove of thousands of primary sources I would find over the next few years as I learned more, bit by bit, about what happened on that night in 1952. But I am getting ahead of myself and will come back to all of that. I do not want to lose sight here of what that night was ostensibly all about—the election. It was packed with drama and would draw record crowds to voting places. While the presidency was the most high-profile race, there was a rich array of other political offices and ballot questions to be decided. They intersected with hot-button issues—race, war, taxes, corruption, and communism. And they contributed, in turn, to an intense interest in the fall elections and to a lack of certainty about who would be moving into the White House in January.[18]

The race for president featured a large cast of characters. In addition to the dominant Democratic and Republican parties, all sorts of minor parties nominated candidates. These were dubbed "serious, sinister, or silly" by *Time* magazine.[19] There were nominees from the Socialist Party, the Socialist Workers Party, and the Industrial Government Party, operating in some states as the Socialist Labor Party. The candidate of the Progressive Party, Vincent Hallinan, was a well-heeled, Harvard-educated lawyer, who favored cooperation with Russia. He was serving a prison sentence for contempt of court at the time of his nomination. He was also the candidate of the American Labor Party in New York and the People's Party in Connecticut. His running mate, Charlotta Bass, was the former publisher of a feisty Black newspaper in Los Angeles. Three fringe parties each nominated the same military hero without his consent—General of the Army Douglas MacArthur. These were the Christian Nationalist, Constitution, and America First parties. The Prohibition Party also tried to sign up General MacArthur as its candidate. When he declined, the party nominated Carl Stuart Hamblen, a singer, actor, and host of *Cowboy Church of the Air*. On election night an NBC radio commentator said of Hamblin that he had "had a bout with the booze habit and came out the winner."[20] The Greenback Party, its name harking back to an earlier era, was represented by a Seattle grocer. The Vegetarian Party had a candidate but not the one whom the party most wanted. Its first choice, a retired brigadier general, ran instead as the candidate of the American Rally Party. And on the other end of the dietary spectrum, the standard bearer of the Poor Man's Party was a pig farmer from New Jersey. A photo of him posing next to a young woman with a handheld campaign sign appeared in *Cosmopolitan* magazine under the headline, "Presidential Candidates that Won't Get Elected." The Church of God Bible Party fielded a candidate, as did the American Party. The Washington Peace Party had the season's only female candidate for president, an astrologer who claimed to be in touch with George Washington.

None of these minor-party candidates were expected to draw enough voters to sway the election. Still, as recently as 1948, some thirty-nine electoral votes had gone to a third-party candidate, Sen. Strom Thurmond, the segregationist leader of a group of disaffected southern Democrats. A story in the *New York Times* on the day before the 1952 election did not rule out the possibility of a minor candidate siphoning off enough votes in a state here or there to alter the outcome of a tight race between Eisenhower and Stevenson. But this was a long shot.

At center stage were the major party candidates and their running mates, both of whom were U.S. senators. Richard M. Nixon was a Republican from California. John J. Sparkman was a Democrat from Alabama. This was the first time in a generation—since 1928—that neither a sitting president nor a sitting vice president was running in the general election. The sitting president was bogged down in an unpopular war, and this did not help his party. Republicans were hoping to get back into the White House after two decades of Democratic occupancy, first by Franklin Delano Roosevelt, and then, after his death, by his vice president, Harry S. Truman. The Republicans were also hoping to break the Democratic majorities in the House and Senate. Out of ninety-eight million Americans of voting age, some seven-five million were registered to vote.[21] Women slightly outnumbered men among potential voters, a gap most pronounced in the cities and in the East. Non-white voters, as they were called, represented just 10 percent of the pool. They had been shifting out of the South and into the North and West. The farm population continued to shrink. By 1952 it accounted for less than one in eight potential voters. But voters could be parsed in ways other than easy-to-spot demographics. War, communism, scandals, civil rights, pocketbook issues, and parochial affairs would factor into divisive stands, charges, and counter charges in what began as a contest between two men widely perceived to be highbrow candidates.

In the Senate, Democrats held a narrow two-seat majority.[22] In the House, Democrats had more of a majority, but they were still vulnerable. The fall elections, including races already decided in Maine, featured 35 Senate contests, 435 House contests, and races for governor in 30 states. Balloting at the state, county, and local levels would also encompass a host of other offices. On the ballots in thirty-seven states were more than two hundred proposed constitutional amendments and other questions to be decided by the voters.[23] Some attracted national attention and became tricky issues for the candidates, especially in matters of race and civil rights. South Carolina's system of free public schools would be in jeopardy under a proposed amendment to the state constitution. That measure was intended to bypass any future order from the U.S. Supreme Court banning school segregation. Proponents included the state's governor, James F. Byrnes, a Democrat who was backing the Republican candidate for president. Race was behind a contentious ballot question in Mississippi, too. A proposed amendment to the state constitution would make voting rights contingent on literacy and on a prospective voter's ability to interpret any section of the U.S. and Mississippi constitutions. The measure's opponents alleged it was racially motivated and would be used to suppress the Black vote.[24] In California, communist sympathizers were the target of a measure that would require loyalty oaths of a half million public officials and employees.[25]

Television and politics became a potent mixture during the 1952 campaign. One of the most iconic events in the twentieth century politics of scandal—Richard Nixon's infamous "Checkers Speech"—was aired in the run-up to the election. Nixon faced allegations that money from donors went into a slush fund for personal expenses. He turned to television in his defense, an event widely seen as helping to establish the medium's place in the culture of American politics. During the same campaign season, political figures were making unprecedented use of television for advertising and for broadcasting speeches and appearances.[26]

Besides computers, 1952 also marked the debut of something else that has since become commonplace at the intersection of politics and television. A Madison Avenue advertising guru, Rosser Reeves, conceived of a new model of campaigning to replace long-winded speeches.[27] He focused on the kind of snappy "value proposition" featured in advertising products—like M&M's candy that "melts in your mouth, not in your hands." He thought that approach could work in politics, too, and produced ads for Eisenhower. There were also campaign jingles on both sides that, by today's standards, look painfully naïve. But by the time Election Day rolled around, the Associated Press would summarize the politicking in 1952 as an increasingly dark affair. Americans heard Republicans claim that "the Democrats have bungled the Korean War, have condoned corruption, have been cozy with the Communists, and have been responsible for higher prices." Americans heard Democrats claim that "the nation's economy is safer in their hands, that the GOP is cozy with big business and forgets the working man, that the real test of the Republicans is not what they say but how they have voted in Congress these twenty years." The presidential campaign, which had "started out on a high plane, fell into the more familiar name-calling pattern as one taunting word led to a worse one," per the Associated Press. "At the end, many were calling it one of the most vicious in memory."[28]

There were other forms of ugliness not referenced in the news that most Americans would read, hear, or see. Black reporters were filing stories for the Black press—generally the only places where they could find work as journalists in that era—and they were writing about challenges facing them in reporting from the Jim Crow South. While the atmosphere they found in Dixie was deemed to be an improvement from the past, there were still instances like the one in New Orleans when Black reporters following Stevenson were denied accommodations at the "swanky" Hotel Roosevelt.[29] Indeed, elections in the 1950s were a high-stakes affair for Black Americans. The epidemic of lynching that had raged in Dixie and border states since the Civil War was declining by then. But other forms of intimidation were intended to suppress the Black vote. There were overt threats, efforts to institutionalize suppression in law, and the arrangement of voting districts for a similar effect. Black Americans would certainly have had a keen interest on election night in following returns on television if they had access to one.

More and more Americans did have access to television. While fewer than one in ten homes had a TV set in 1950, that number jumped to more than one in three by 1952 and would keep rising.[30] Radio, which had been a commercial medium since the 1920s, was still the dominant platform for broadcast news in 1952 and could be found in almost every home. But pressure on television to perform on occasions like election night was ramping up. So it is no surprise that the networks were touting their strengths in the run-up to election night. Their experts in news and commentary were household names, and they had large crews who would gather returns and other election news. Computers fit into that mix now for the first time. The NBC trade release touting "Mike Monrobot" was issued on October 16. It came one day after CBS revealed its own big plan for computer use on election night. That plan was dubbed "Project X." I stumbled across this in a script for *Report to the West*, a CBS radio news program, in records of famed CBS correspondent Charles Collingwood.[31] He referred to the UNIVAC as a "prodigious monster of electronic thought." He marveled that it could do in seconds what would take hours for dozens of mathematicians to do with adding machines and slide rules—comparing the results of past elections with the early returns on election night.

Meanwhile, the television news director at ABC "professed disdain for such electronic gimmicks," as *Time* magazine put it.[32] Instead, he said, ABC had its well-known "human brains." ABC would also use some technology from IBM, an archrival of Remington Rand, the UNIVAC's manufacturer. But the IBM equipment was of the precomputer type that depended on hand wiring algorithms to count, sort, and tabulate data fed in on punched cards. This was not one of the cutting-edge "stored program" computers that could modify its instructions on the fly. IBM was working on one of those, but the company was not quite ready to debut it. After election night in 1952, IBM's internal documents show that the company brass would start scheming to get their own computer in on the next presidential election in 1956.[33] But in 1952 they most likely watched in anguish as makers of the UNIVAC and Monrobot got their pioneering electronic brains on air.

Competition between "brains" was not limited to computers. I came to see this after the most striking finds in my research—the complete election-night footage from NBC and CBS. The broadcasts make clear that the networks were not gambling everything on computer projections. There would be a reputational price if the electronic brains choked. So there were human brains aplenty on both networks. They did what journalists had been doing for more than a century—detecting trends by eyeballing early returns from key areas and comparing them to the way the same places had voted in the past. The banter at CBS and NBC made clear that those human brains were not delighted to have machines doing that, too.

The election-night competition did not end there. A culture-wide free-for-all was underway to keep television from eating away at other things people might be doing. As had been the case for generations, this election night would offer up a rich confection of news, performance, promotion, and technology. In Albuquerque, New Mexico, where the evangelist Billy Graham had just launched a month-long crusade, the public was assured that returns would be announced both before Graham's sermon and after the service.[34] In Oneonta, New York, an American Legion post was promoting a dance with old-time music—and election returns.[35] In Manhattan, ads for the National Horse Show in Madison Square Garden promised jumping contests, teams of giant Clydesdales, and "ELECTION RETURNS announced frequently."[36] In Lincoln, Arkansas, a women's basketball team that toured small towns playing—and beating—men's teams would be at a local high school gymnasium, with election returns to be announced every ten minutes.[37] Across the nation movie theaters also promised that patrons would not miss out on the day's political theater. In Helena, Montana, for example, the Marlow Theater advertised a "last chance" to see its feature, *The Greatest Show on Earth*, Cecile B. DeMille's 1952 hit about life in the Ringling Brothers and Barnum & Bailey Circus.[38] But the biggest, boldest letters in the ad were reserved for another attraction: "ELECTION RETURNS." The entertainment trade publication *Variety* reported that theaters around the country were "set to fight the TV bid for attention on Election Day" in two ways—by pitching the idea that the outcome would not be known until after theaters closed and by keeping patrons posted on trends.[39] The International News Service had made a deal with theaters to install teletype machines for $130 to $150 apiece.

Not every theater offered returns. One in Oshkosh, Wisconsin, made a point of advertising *that* fact: "Got the Election Day Jitters about Who Is Going to Win Tonight?" asked its ad. "Relax and Forget for a Few Hours."[40] But another Oshkosh theater was going all out. Patrons could see five movies for the price of one. Featured was *Don't Bother to Knock*, a thriller starring Marilyn Monroe as a disturbed former mental patient working as a babysitter. The theater's ad linked Monroe's status as a sex symbol with the election-night theme: "Meet the new Secretary of the Exterior! Every Inch a Woman." The theater promised "ROUND-THE-CLOCK ENTERTAINMENT WHILE YOU GET ELECTION RETURNS."[41]

Meanwhile, some theaters tried to have it both ways. In and around Oakland, California, where several theaters were promising returns, the Paramount—featuring a screen adaptation of Ernest Hemingway's *The Snows of Kilimanjaro*—offered election news in a special "television lounge."[42] At a time when most American homes did not have television, other businesses offered a place to watch, too. In Massachusetts the La Conca d'Ora restaurant invited readers of the *Fitchburg Sentinel* to watch the election returns while enjoying their favorite Italian and American foods.[43] In Greeley, Colorado, a home-furnishings store placed an ad that read, "Democrats and Republicans—We cordially invite you to watch the election returns on our television sets."[44] In Modesto, California, two stores promised "facilities for 'drive-in' television."[45] And in New York City, commuters who would be heading home from Penn Station on the Chesapeake and Ohio Railway learned from an ad in the *New York Times* that they would not be left out of the election-night excitement. Trains would carry "up-to-the-minute" returns by way of speakers in "special lounge cars and coaches."[46]

New synergies were being conjured up, but old practices persisted, too. Years after radio became the dominant medium for disseminating the vote count after polls closed, newspapers in towns across America were still holding themselves out as prime venues for live election-night news. In Pocatello, Idaho, "election tally sheets" were to be displayed in the lobby of the *Idaho State Journal*.[47] In Rhode Island the *Newport Daily News* ran a front-page story letting readers know that the local vote would be "posted on a huge board in the newspaper's counting room window."[48] The paper also promised to announce returns "over an amplifying system to those gathered in the street." In Flagstaff, Arizona, readers got a page-one invitation: "If you want to be in on the fun tonight, come on down to the sun office."[49] In addition to the party atmosphere promised by some papers, one in Oxnard, California, cast the newsroom activity itself as worthy of drawing spectators: "The Press-Courier invites the public to drop in at its office at any time of the night to watch the gathering of returns."[50] Some papers invited calls.[51] And some promised to hold deadlines as long as possible or put out extra editions.[52]

If television were going to win the battle for attention on election night, it needed all the flash it could muster. So apart from whatever the computers might end up doing as a technology, they also offered another sort of utility. At least some network executives were counting on the visual allure of just seeing these new inventions in action—regardless of whatever results the computers might produce—to attract what the digital age would later call "eyeballs." The univac and Monrobot were clickbait, 1952-style.

It would be easy to dismiss the race to report returns on television as showmanship, what some scholars have termed "media events."[53] Wasn't this, after all, just a lot of hype over something that would be known soon enough anyway? But it is important to remember that aside from the work of journalists—especially before the internet era—the news media, and increasingly the broadcast media, were the only place Americans could get live updates, trends, and outcomes. Beyond the obvious interest to journalists, politicians, bureaucrats, and voters at large, the detailed outcomes of these infrequent events are also of vital importance to researchers from a range of academic disciplines. For decades now the counting of votes has offered scholars and pollsters a rare opportunity to test the accuracy of their methods. Elections are occasions when political scientists, sociologists, and practitioners of statistical and quantitative methodologies can evaluate their means of measuring public opinion. Statistical sampling, after all, is often involved in measuring that which cannot be precisely or effectively known in any other way. That includes the opinions of large groups and the factors best able to predict group behavior. Elections provide a way to test the adequacy of sampling algorithms. On election night, students of human nature can find out—often quickly—whether their methods hold up. In the wake of the 1936 presidential election, a popular magazine, the *Literary Digest*, was famously wounded by fatal flaws in its massive nationwide straw poll. At the same time, the more scientific selection of smaller samples vindicated some of the rising stars in survey research. The *New York Times* took note, explaining that the outcome of the 1936 election was important in demonstrating the value of scientific polling to business leaders who might use it for market research.[54] In 1952 the importance of election results in testing scholarly theories was recognized in an academic study. It was published by Mississippi State College with assistance from heavyweights in the still-evolving field of public-opinion measurement. These included Hadley Cantril, director of the Office of Public Opinion Research at Princeton University, and George Gallup, director of the American Institute of Public Opinion.[55] The study focused on the election-forecasting abilities of the chairmen of county political parties. Here was an opportunity to examine how the subjective judgments of partisans, based on personal experience, would match up against the objective, quantitative judgments of impartial outsiders. The question was deemed to have important repercussions for the application of social science to the formulation of government policy.[56] Election-night reporting might be dismissed in some quarters as a trivial sideshow in the political process. But it is likely that scholars who study public opinion are among those watching the returns most closely, election night after election night, for a verdict on some of their own work.

In the business of polling, financial success depended on making a case for reliability. In 1948 the three leading pollsters—Gallup, Roper, and Crossley—had forecast that incumbent president Harry Truman would lose to his Republican challenger, New York governor Thomas E. Dewey. The pollsters were wrong. Their shortcomings were the subject first of postelection news stories and then studies by both pollsters and scholars. These post-mortems were fueled by fears of damage that might be done not only to the reputation of survey professionals but to social science research in general. In 1948 the errant polls had affected print and broadcast journalists, whose early forecasts of a Dewey victory on election night were wrong and were a source of embarrassment. What the journalists expected to see had colored what they saw. The culture-wide ribbing—from candidates, cartoons, and even barbs on Broadway—was merciless. Pollsters wanted to avoid that in 1952. George Gallup penned reassurances in *Cosmopolitan* magazine under the headline, "We Won't be Red-Faced This Time!"[57]

Yet as Election Day neared, the pollsters went overboard with caution. The Gallup poll on Election Day was so noncommittal that an Associated Press story about it appeared on front pages around the country with completely divergent headlines. In Bismarck, North Dakota, the headline said, "Gallup Says Ike Has Edge." In Brainerd, Minnesota, readers of the same AP story saw this: "Stevenson May Hold Lead—Gallup." And in Fayetteville, Arkansas, the headline was in between: "Gallup Poll Notes Possibility of 50–50 Popular Vote." Eisenhower was said to have a slight lead but with Stevenson gaining. Gallup gave 47 percent of likely voters to Eisenhower and 40 percent to Stevenson, but a whopping 13 percent were identified as undecided.[58] Three other polls released the day before the election gave Eisenhower the advantage but not enough to prompt prediction of win. A United Press story said pollsters were seeing a "photo-finish."[59]

The race would not turn out to be neck-and-neck. Rather, it would be a landslide for Eisenhower. Yet once again, expectations would color perceptions. In 1952 those expectations would affect decisions by the computer gurus whether to trust what their "electronic brains" were telling them on election night and whether to release forecasts from early returns. The computer programmers and managers would only be able to see their flawed perceptions in retrospect.

So as night fell and the television studios were readied for live broadcasts, the stakes could not have been higher for the players in this drama. When CBS went on air at 8:00 p.m., Walter Cronkite told viewers that long lines at polling places might translate into sixty million votes, outstripping the previous record of under fifty million in 1940. When NBC went on air at 9:00 p.m., the CBS viewers had already been introduced to the UNIVAC and seen it by remote screen from Philadelphia. The NBC announcer boasted with dramatic flourish that right there in Studio 8-H were "amazing new machines, scientific brains rallied by NBC television to bring you the most accurate picture with split-second timing."[60]

Game on.

Inventors of earlier, less sophisticated computers had staged demonstrations in the past, but election night would be different. With data pouring in live and computers processing it in real time, the television journalists and their collaborators would be performing a high-wire act. There was so much at stake. Computers had a largely unformed place in the American mind. And television news, which lived inside a relatively new entertainment medium, needed to prove itself as a serious endeavor. Why take big risks when there was so much at stake? We will try to answer that question as we go. But one thing I had not expected to find was this: rolling out wondrous innovations—and using them to compete for an audience—had a long and colorful history dating to the 1800s in efforts of newspapers and later radio to place themselves at the center of attention on election night. There was also a long history to refinements in figuring out who was winning when the count was incomplete. Computers on television would be new only in detail. The sort of wonder attached to them would not be new in the history of election nights and neither would the fundamental theory on which the computer programs were based. These things were a century in the making. The new rested on a large and solid foundation of what was not new at all. When, as pioneers in the first generation of commercial electronic computers, the UNIVAC and Monrobot sat poised for their debut as election-night tools, they were continuing a very old election-night story.

2 | We Wanted to Do Something Unusual

Who's winning?

It's a simple enough question. And after all, on election night, it's the question we want answered.

As for answering that question in the murky hours after the polls start closing—and attracting an audience—that's another matter altogether. Yet, by 1952 American news organizations had more than a century of practice at both. There were well-established forecasting methods. There was also a prominent place, election after election, for technological novelty—used to disseminate news and attract a crowd. In fact, well before 1952, the drama of reporting the election-night story had long been *part* of that story. So had collaboration between journalists and outside "experts" of all sorts. Even in the decades before radio and television, newspapers did not wait until the next day to get out word of election results. They experimented with kites trailing color-coded lights and a steamship whistle tooting out coded bursts of sound. Images were projected on the sides of buildings using something called a "magic lantern." Commentary on the size of newspapers' election-night audiences became part of the story, too, and this came with bragging rights. In a competitive environment, election night had long been a chance for journalists to shine. Touting their technologically enhanced efforts had long been a feature of pre- and postelection reporting by 1952. There were well-known risks of course. One risk was the very real possibility of embarrassment from a wayward forecast in the rush to get the news out. Another risk was making a tardy call and being beaten by a competitor. So there was a special place for any innovative tool, practice, or outside-the-box collaboration that could help.

Today, we are used to the idea of a uniform nationwide election night with news organizations as the hub for information. And we are used to elections with massive public participation and interest. But we must forget for a moment that we know this so we can understand the constellation of forces that got us to election night in 1952. Though the United States was founded as a democracy, voting rights were far from universal at the outset. With exclusions based on gender, race, and property ownership, voting tended to be an elite affair.[1] In some states the voting for president was indirect. State legislatures picked electors who would meet with the electors from other states to choose a president. Change came in stages. By the early decades of the 1800s, most white males had voting rights. Along the way there were signs of increasing public interest in the outcome of elections. Election night would take shape as a complex social phenomenon. In a nation where powerful and privileged interests held sway, popular elections, by their very nature, turned the de facto hierarchy of American society on its head. For one day, at least, ordinary Americans—or at least those to whom suffrage had been extended—had a say in the affairs of public life. In a mid-nineteenth-century poem titled "The Poor Voter on Election Day," John Greenleaf Whittier captured this notion in his opening lines. "The proudest now is but my peer, / The highest not more high," he wrote. "To-day, of all the weary year, / A king of men am I."[2] After the polls closed, public celebrations could be rowdy affairs, with bonfires, the spirited collection of wagers, and disputes verging over into violence.[3]

Until 1848 there could be no single, nationwide election night. States held their balloting for president during a window of thirty-four days in the fall. That changed when Congress enacted in 1845 a uniform voting day for president.[4] But the evolution of election night as a phenomenon with newspapers at center stage would also depend on the ever-speedier movement of news from place to place. As early as the 1830s and 1840s, Americans would marvel at new technologies that fostered what some then called an "annihilation of space and time." Steamships crossed the Atlantic in just weeks. Locomotives traveled at a wondrous thirty miles per hour. Later, telegraph messages traversed hundreds of miles at lightning speed for the times.[5] Even so, weeks and even months might elapse as returns dribbled in from distant places before and after the arrival of the telegraph. Newspapers also made use of trains, horse relays, steamboats, rowboats, messenger pigeons, and signal flags.[6] But savvy editors knew, even then, to be wary of making too much of early returns. On November 10, 1840, the editor of a newspaper in the Wisconsin Territory was underwhelmed by the adequacy of election news.[7] Although vote counts were trickling in, they were, in his words, "not sufficient to tell how any one state has gone." The stakes in making a judgment from insufficient data were deemed serious. The editor was quite open about that and put it this way: "We should not like to risk our reputation for prophecy by venturing an opinion."

The first presidential election involving the telegraph took place in 1848.[8] The wonders of technology quickly became part of the story that newspapers told about their efforts. A newspaper in southwest Illinois reported the astounding fact that returns from as far away as New York, Richmond, and Vermont had arrived hours before the newspaper got returns from a nearby village.[9] Still, even after 1861 marked the first coast-to-coast telegraph link, it would take years as the system expanded for a critical mass of votes to be available on election night. In 1882 an Atlanta editor's efforts to speed up reporting from two mountainous congressional districts included couriers on horseback and chartered trains in addition to running special telegraph and telephone wires.[10] As late as 1904 the Associated Press was still relying on couriers bringing returns by horse and bicycle from remote areas.[11] The need for speed even kept homing pigeons in service as late as the 1890s to transmit some returns.[12]

Advances often precipitated new problems. The more rapid flow of returns meant that a deluge of information had to be compiled and published on a tight deadline.[13] Crises of this sort fostered novel solutions. The newly formed Associated Press would come to play a pivotal role in organizing the flow of returns. But that system would take years to evolve. Along the way a plaintive appeal shortly before the 1852 election gives a hint of the challenges. Reprinted on the front page of the *New York Daily Times* under the headline "Telegraphic Election Returns," an Associated Press circular evidenced an ambitious goal, nothing less than making it possible for newspapers nationwide to report the election's outcome on their pages the next morning.[14] "Confusion" was the enemy. The news service was asking telegraph operators, correspondents, and newspaper agents to follow a few rules. Only "reliable individuals" were to be trusted to supply returns. Rumors were to be avoided. As it was, the *Times* reported a week after the election, "Returns dribble in slowly."[15] Eight years later complete news of the election of Abraham Lincoln in 1860 would still require a combination of means—from the telegraph where it existed to the pony express elsewhere.[16] In December the vote was still coming in.[17]

The significance of election night for newspapers increased as a constellation of requisite parts came together—expanded suffrage, a common voting date, rapid transmission of returns, and systems for collating those returns in a meaningful way. As for predicting winners when the count was incomplete, that presented a special sort of mathematical problem. This problem could only be solved with details about the source of the votes and historical knowledge of voting in those places. Nineteenth-century newspaper editors came to understand this just as well as twenty-first-century television news producers do. As early as 1848, a newspaper in Wisconsin showed this sensibility in praising the telegraph for "relieving" the populace "of that long suspense which formerly followed elections." Though results were not available from all locations—in fact, the paper noted, telegraphed results had been "meager"—they had come "from such points as would serve as a basis of calculations for other places."[18] After the same election, readers of the *Massachusetts Ploughman and Journal of Agriculture* were advised to hold on to newspapers listing election returns in order to consult them again at the next election.[19] And in an 1892 article about election-night methods and practices, Willis John Abbot, managing editor of the *Chicago Times*, wrote, "Comparison is the prime factor in the solution of the election problem."[20] Newspapers could also generate income from the sale of voting data. Before the 1860 election, the *New York Tribune* assembled returns back to 1824 and combined that with "historical matter" in a 254-page volume, *The Political Text Book*. The price: one dollar.[21] An advertisement suggested that "as the Election returns come in, politicians will want to compare the result with the votes of former years."

Data points for future use could also be generated from fine-grained analyses linking location, ethnicity, and vote counts in the days following elections—albeit tinged with biases of the day. One example appeared in the *New York Times* following Lincoln's 1864 reelection victory over the Democratic challenger, Gen. George B. McClellan.[22] The *Times* concluded that "from Maine to Kansas," though with "marked exceptions," the "vicious and ignorant population of the cities and manufacturing villages has been for McClellan, while the strength of Lincoln lay in the farming class, and the intelligent class of the towns." A ward-by-ward dissection of the New York City returns followed. There was heavy support for McClellan in areas characterized this way: "all the most crowded and wretched of the 'tenement house' districts"—as in the First Ward, where there "are nearly as many rum-holes as houses," or in the Eleventh Ward, home to "immense multitudes of ignorant Germans" and "the rag-pickers and bone-gatherers of New York." Lincoln's support, on the other hand, could be pegged to specific city blocks with "separate houses and a well-off or intelligent class."

Some editors developed legendary methods of election-night analysis and a special reputation for accuracy. By 1883 Charles H. Taylor, the *Boston Globe*'s iconic publisher and editor, had worked out a system for election-night forecasting using precinct-level data.[23] The *Globe* was able to tame the mass of information flowing through the newsroom with specially designed tools, including figures captured on duplicate sheets of paper that were color-coded. Returns were compiled by general geographical area—Boston, the other Massachusetts cities, and the towns—with knowledge of how much a candidate would need in one to overcome a deficit elsewhere. Political writers might also be asked to make sense of anomalies. Forecasts could thus be made by methods the *Globe* had come to trust. In 1892 the incumbent Massachusetts governor, behind in the early count, waited through the night at the *Globe* as the paper correctly forecast his narrow reelection.[24] In the presidential race of 1916, Taylor resisted joining the tide of papers making an erroneous call before the California vote was known.

The *Globe* system used what would later be known as "key precincts" to make judgments from early returns. This approach has been described by Thomas Littlewood, a historian of the "horse-race" style of political reporting, as "the single most important methodological advance in the history of electoral journalism."[25] Using votes coming in from specially selected areas and comparing the results to historical data for the same areas was the basis of widespread election-night forecasting practices that survived to 1952 and beyond.[26] By then, what was once an innovation had become "common sense," in the words of an architect of the forecasting algorithm used at CBS in 1952.[27]

Well before 1952 and computers, the use of experts outside the newsroom—together with various mathematical tools—was a recurrent feature of the culture of election-night journalism. The *Boston Globe* newsroom borrowed the services of bookkeepers and accountants from the newspaper's business office—known at the *Globe* as the "slide-rule men," or, less formally, the "slide-rule boys."[28] A Chicago newspaper editor wrote in 1892 that "election night finds a newspaper office equipped with skilled accountants like a bank."[29] The source of the mathematical corps employed at the *New York Herald* on election night in 1890 was not specified, but they were described as "lightning calculators" and the best "expert accountants" in the city.[30] Ten were employed, along with sixty "tally clerks," arranged at long tables in a cavernous, block-long room at the *Herald* building. A detailed drawing of them—formally attired, their heads down in concentration as they did their work on paper—was featured prominently in the *Herald*'s extensive report on its election-night exploits. The presence of such experts served multiple purposes, just as computers would later—doing the job at hand while adding both to the mystique of the election-night process and the prestige of the journalists who organized it.

A succession of devices that served as increasingly sophisticated aids to calculation appeared throughout the nineteenth and twentieth centuries before the advent of computers.[31] Along with experts these devices might also be borrowed on election night for newsroom calculations. A manager of the Associated Press wrote in 1905 about using an army of correspondents on Election Day, along with accountants and adding machines supplied by local banks.[32] In 1911 a manufacturer of adding machines, Burroughs, asserted their infallibility in an ad.[33] As evidence, the ad touted the performance of these machines on election night in Buffalo. In a similar display of the linked agendas of newsrooms and technologists, the *Illinois State Journal* gave a nod in 1912 to the Remington Typewriter Company for providing a typewriter with an adding machine attachment.[34] That wondrous device, it was said, allowed the newspaper to provide tables with vote totals on the morning after the election. In 1913 the *Duluth News-Tribune* in Minnesota reported that as returns came in from a hotly contested ballot question on liquor control, a Remington salesman used the same sort of equipment to furnish "rapid fire" results.[35]

Election-night advances always seemed to lead to new challenges. One was disseminating the returns and forecasts in a timely way to ever larger masses of voters eager to know who was winning. Well before radio and television, newspapers employed ingenious means for getting the word out, allowing them to remain at the center of attention on election night even if they did not gain financially. The size of waiting crowds was celebrated in print, demonstrating a newspaper's importance in the community. The practice of posting vote counts on newspaper bulletin boards as returns dribbled in began before the telegraph.[36] But the new technology made it possible by the middle of the nineteenth century to get news from many far-flung places on election night. That in turn helped establish the streets outside local newspaper offices as places to get the latest returns. In communities with more than one newspaper, there was fierce competition to get the word out first.[37] The stage was set for an era of remarkable inventiveness and showmanship, forging and strengthening a link between election-night news, technology, and entertainment.

Before the electric light, newspapers employed devices that went by the names "magic lantern" and "stereopticon." They projected images or photographs made on plates of glass. A powerful light beam, typically produced by heating a block of calcium, was passed through these plates. Aided by lenses, these projectors cast a magnified image on a large surface.[38] The use of such systems to dazzle election-night crowds dates back to at least 1860, when references appear to a display outside the *New York Herald*.[39] In early October 1872, the *New York Times* recounted in a front-page article how crowds intensely interested in the elections taking place in Pennsylvania, Indiana, and Ohio gathered on a New York street corner where the newspaper's returns were to be projected. The *Times* did this by collaborating with a technology provider, the Stereopticon Advertising Company.[40] Images and sayings were projected, too. At the end of the night these were said to include "Washington, Lincoln, patriotic mottoes, and the Goddess of Liberty." The well-behaved crowd was deemed to reflect well on the *Times*. They were of "the best classes," and police were only needed to watch for pickpockets. On election night that November, the *Times* and its collaborator arranged for a display with cartoons of notable people and incidents from the campaign.[41] This kept the crowd in what the *Times* described as "excellent humor."

At Park Row in lower Manhattan, the center of the city's newspaper world in the latter nineteenth century, New Yorkers found papers vying with each other through competing election-night displays and next-day accounts.[42] Newspapers also established outposts around the city for displaying returns, as the *Herald* did in 1890.[43] In 1895 the *Times* boasted that it provided the most accurate and prompt returns, using five stereopticons casting images on a massive screen mounted on the front of the New York Times Building and poaching the crowd from another paper.[44] The *Times* had prepared what it called "a pictorial entertainment," including portraits of political figures, reproductions of artworks, and cartoons.

Starting in the late nineteenth century, publishers showed an increasing desire to draw election-night audiences more distant than those who could see the stereopticon displays. Well before the advent of radio, news seekers in some cities no longer found it necessary to turn out on a cold November night to find out who had won. An election-night free-for-all had developed between newspapers, press associations, telegraph companies, telephone companies, and even the manufacturers of powerful electric lights. Historian Carolyn Marvin found that "the distribution of presidential election returns in the late nineteenth century was the most ambitiously organized American effort to use new electric technologies to deliver the news."[45] In 1888 the president of American Bell Telephone Company and his guests heard election news via a special line at his home in Boston. Arrangements were more elaborate in 1896 as long-distance telephone lines spread to more parts of the country. In advance of the elections, the *New York Times* described in detail what it was calling a "contest of the wires."[46] The telegraph and telephone companies, reported the *Times*, were "going to greater expense" than before "to keep pace with popular demand for news." In addition to special wires that would be run to clubs, hotels, cafés, theaters, and bars, the well-heeled were planning private election parties and arranging to run special wires to their homes. While the telegraph companies were not newcomers to the gathering and transmission of election news, doing so by long-distance telephone was a novelty. Not to be outdone, newspapers were experimenting with visual means of transmitting returns for miles around. Powerful new electric lights were adapted for use on election night both as means of communication and as symbols of status. As early as 1891, newspapers were using searchlights mounted atop their own buildings or other tall structures. The practice continued into the twentieth century and right up to the 1952 election.[47]

The audiences for these returns were not just passive recipients of news by searchlight. Codes were published in advance for deciphering the bulletins. These codes might involve the direction in which a light was cast, its duration, its frequency, or its color. Typical were the codes published in the run-up to the 1904 election by the *New York Times*. From the summit of its new tower in Times Square, the *Times* claimed that its pronouncement of the outcome would be visible for thirty miles.[48] Steady lights to the east or west would signal the victor in the presidential contest, while steady lights to the north or south would flash the outcome of the governor's race. A light moving up and down to the west or east would announce which party would control Congress. "With this code before him," wrote the *Times*, a voter "can don his negligée and from an advantageous window in his flat or his house ascertain the important results."[49] Two years later the *Times* claimed to have installed atop its tower a type of powerful light used by battleships at war and gave a plug to the manufacturer.[50]

One of the most ambitious displays was that of the *New York Tribune* in 1896.[51] Readers were advised to keep the necessary codes handy. They were not simple.[52] A string of colored lights was to be hoisted aloft to five hundred feet above the *Tribune* building by a set of specially built kites, with a nod in print to the manufacturer. There were dozens of codes to indicate which of the three candidates was ahead in each of the forty-five states and New York City. The *Tribune* left no doubt that both technological showmanship and timely transmission of news were paramount values. On the Sunday before the election, in a front-page announcement, the *Tribune* boasted that no other election-night innovation would attract more attention than what it was calling its "signals in the sky." On the afternoon of Election Day, the *Tribune* launched nine kites on a single line that hauled up a massive American flag. But then the weather ceased to cooperate. The kites came down. Instead, the coded strings of lights were raised above the building on halyards.

Elsewhere, the transmission of coded returns was not limited to visual displays. Although thousands gathered around competing newspapers in downtown St. Paul, Minnesota, on election night 1896, far greater numbers may have learned of the results by *hearing* them from miles away.[53] The *St. Paul Dispatch* arranged with the Northern Steamship Company to borrow a whistle system from the forward stack of a behemoth Great Lakes passenger liner, the *North West*. The fog whistle was said to be almost as big as a man and could be heard from fifteen miles away. While the ship was berthed for the winter, the whistle was transported to St. Paul for election night. A notice in the pro-McKinley *Dispatch* provided the codes: "Succession of Sharp, Short Toots If Returns Favor McKinley. A Long, Dismal Wail If Returns Favor Bryan."

In a tumultuous combination of technological enthusiasm, national development, commercial boosterism, and showmanship that marked the latter nineteenth and early twentieth centuries, newspapers were not alone in seeing the possibilities presented by election night.[54] A range of establishments that provided public amusements also hitched themselves to election night's main event. In 1876 an ad for "The Great New-York Aquarium" boasted that in addition to a long list of attractions, from "six rare sea-horses" to "the living white whale," patrons would be updated on election returns.[55] On the same day, an ad for the "New and Greatest Show on Earth" assured prospective patrons of the circus in New York that showman P. T. Barnum had arranged for them to get returns.[56] Twenty years later, on election night 1896, another famous showman, Oscar Hammerstein, operating from a complex on Broadway, was featuring comic opera, vaudeville, acrobats, dancing girls from Paris—and returns to be read every half hour on all stages and shown on a "gigantic" screen.[57] Theaters, in fact, were common venues for returns. Their ads typically did not specify the source of the election news beyond the mention of a "special wire."[58] Theaters also touted their election-night plans on large sheets pasted alongside campaign posters. In 1916 a sheet for the Standard, an establishment in St. Louis, promised "Parisian Flirts," "2 Big Shows," and "Election Returns by Special Wire."[59]

Against this backdrop of culture-wide competition for attention on election night, newspapers showcased technological innovations of all sorts—not just for transmitting news, but as means of entertainment and as objects of wonder. In 1896, for example, a new device for projecting moving images—called a "vitascope"—was used to amaze crowds in New York and Chicago in between the presentation of returns.[60] In 1906 the *New York Times* announced that among its election-night offerings—which included better projection of bulletins, a new searchlight for coded returns, moving pictures, and a live band—there would be something called the "Auxetophone." It was described as an improvement on the phonograph.[61] Two years later the *Times* was promoting its use of another new device called the "telautograph." This would allow crowds to watch a cartoonist at work, projecting drawings as he made them.[62] And in 1920 the *St. Louis Post-Dispatch* orchestrated a rich confection of news, entertainment, and technology, to assert its social role as an essential player on election night.[63] While many of the city's theaters and burlesque houses were advertising that election returns would be provided, the *Post-Dispatch* used its front page to promise the first public showing of X-ray motion pictures of human joints in action—knee, wrist, jaw, elbow, and more.[64] Another innovation, called the "Magnavox telemegaphone," proved so effective on election night, according to the *Post-Dispatch*, that the massive crowd had been "startled" to hear the returns "clearly and distinctly . . . above all street noises."[65]

On the day after that 1920 election, the *Post-Dispatch* devoted at least three news stories to itself—including one on the front page—illustrated by a full page of photographs: how it had attracted the largest outdoor election-night crowd in St. Louis history despite temperatures that fell to forty degrees; how it provided news and amusements to an estimated thirty thousand people at twenty-three indoor venues; and how educational and civic leaders praised the *Post-Dispatch*—mentioned by name seven times in one story—for an election-night role that was a "forward step in community service."[66] The *Post-Dispatch* also claimed a place for itself in communications history. The city's first use of a wireless telephone—an early term for radio—had been to transmit *Post-Dispatch* election returns to a region stretching from North Dakota down to Arkansas, states where returns were then relayed by wireless telegraph to recipients from Canada to the Gulf of Mexico.[67]

As far back as the early decades of the telegraph era, journalists had been telling what might be called "the story of the story" about their election-night exploits, foreshadowing the way television news networks would proudly describe their efforts in 1952.[68] I found the evidence of this phenomenon from the 1800s hiding in plain sight in microfilmed copies of old newspapers and in searchable databases of historical papers and magazines. Key features included dramatic accounts of newspapers' efforts to assemble, analyze, and disseminate election news in a timely fashion, aided by organizational systems, technology, and political expertise. One of the more elaborate accounts appeared in the *New York Herald* on the Sunday after the 1890 election.[69] The *Herald* ran an ad ahead of that promising to reveal "the Inside Mysteries and Mechanism of a Great Newspaper in Action."[70] The Sunday article occupied two thirds of a page.[71] It was accompanied by six illustrations: a police station where reporters recorded the vote counts on color-coded forms; uniformed messengers delivering those forms to the newspaper; the expansive newsroom where vote totals were computed by dozens of clerks and accountants; the stereopticon room for display of returns to crowds in the street; the massive composing room where the paper was set in type, including dozens of columns of results arranged in tables; and a host of delivery men as they hastened away from the *Herald* with bundles of newspapers. If lavishing so much space on a story about itself did not send a clear enough message, the six-deck headline left no doubt about the point—that a newspaper could and should be judged by the quality and content of its election-night performance.

HOW THE HERALD GETS ELECTION RETURNS.
Workings of a System that Insures the Most Complete
and Accurate Printed in Any Newspaper.

ANOTHER TRIUMPH LAST WEEK.
In the Herald Alone Was To Be Found Correct Pluralities
and the Vote Tabulated by Election Districts.

NO EXPENSE SPARED AND AN ARMY OF EXPERTS.
Such a Scene at the Compiling of the Vast Mass of Figures
and Such Intricate but Smooth Working System as Were
Never Duplicated or Attempted.

Themes that would later define election-night broadcasting in the mid-twentieth century could be seen at work here. The headline and story boasted of innovation. Both called forth a sense of wonder at the integration of people, systems, and technology on deadline. Readers were getting a behind-the-scenes look. The writer expected they would be impressed, asking, "What do you think of it now that you have seen it from the inside?" The story also left no doubt that immediate profit was not the supreme motive. The preparation and election-night operations were expensive. But the willingness to incur that cost became a virtue in the *Herald's* telling—what the writer described as "the first and fundamental secret" of the paper's system. The paper's enhanced reputation would be the reward—even internationally. The *Herald* reported that two years earlier, its election coverage, loaded with tables of voting data, was said to have created a "news sensation" in London.

Newspaper reporters also wrote articles for magazines about newsroom drama on election night. One of the most detailed of these "story of the story" accounts—fourteen pages in all—was penned in November 1894 for *Scribner's Magazine* by Julian Ralph, a notable journalist and author of his day.[72] Except for the experiences of "soldiers at war," he wrote that newsrooms on election night churn with a fever pitch, strain, and excitement more intense than any other human endeavor: "This is the night when a few men sit down at six o'clock before virgin sheets of paper, with the knowledge that before two o'clock the next morning they must cover those sheets with the election returns of a nation, digesting mountains of figures and apprising the public of the results in the most condensed forms." And he added, "These results must stand the test of comparison with . . . rival newspapers." Ralph's account communicates a sense of wonder about those taking part, from the managing editor, who remains focused amidst the chaos, to the well-paid, elegantly attired, and well-connected Washington correspondent in town for the occasion. While the first edition is being printed, Ralph wrote, there are a few minutes to take a break: "Hot coffee is brought up from a near-by restaurant, bottles of beer are being opened with a pop and a splash, grapes and sandwiches are being devoured by men who are all on their legs, relieving the strain of long sitting." Competing papers are examined, and then the work of the next edition gets underway. The best papers were said to avoid being swayed by political bias in gathering and presenting the news. They prized accuracy. And, he wrote, they "throw economy to the dogs."

In a magazine article in 1892, Willis John Abbot of the *Chicago Times* voiced another theme that would later be a hallmark of the election-night broadcasts of 1952.[73] With all the preparation, all the work to be done, all the forces to be marshaled, all the deadlines to be met, and all the pressure to turn out a timely and accurate report, the stress on a managing editor was extraordinary. And there was no guarantee of a satisfying outcome. Abbot began his account on this very theme: "When, on election morning, the managing editor lets himself into the cubby-hole of an office in which gentlemen of his profession are usually ensconced, he feels that the error of his career was made when he failed to resign the day before." By 6:00 a.m. the next day, having worked through the night to pull off an accurate report, Abbot wrote, "The managing editor will still feel that he has fallen short." This variation on the behind-the-scenes story presages in 1892 some of the angst that those involved in election-night broadcasts would feel sixty years later.

Some "story of the story" accounts included florid descriptions of the street scene outside newspaper buildings. The crowds that gathered around newspapers' displays grew increasingly massive and so became, themselves, an object of wonder. In 1860 the *New York Herald*'s account noted that the "living mass . . . presented such a spectacle that it must be witnessed to be fairly understood; and the sounds that arose therefrom more resembled the 'rumbling of distant thunder' than aught else we can think of at present."[74] A writer for the *New-York Daily Tribune* was carried away by emotion when describing, in no fewer than eighty-two lines of copy, the street scenes on election night in 1896.[75] They represented, to the writer, the wonder of an entire nation acting in concert. "Merely as a sublime spectacle New-York wore the aspect of a great force of nature last night," the *Tribune* reported. "Poets have written of the sea in its might," the story continued. Traditional objects of wonder—the Hanging Gardens of Babylon, the pyramids, the Alps—could not match the scene. Anyone present, the *Tribune* suggested, got "a glimpse of the glorious attributes of immortality."

Newspaper reporters were not alone in remarking on the awesome nature of collective activity in the service of democracy as a feature of elections. Consider the Walt Whitman poem, "Election Day, November 1884."[76] "If I should need to name, O Western World, your powerfulest scene and show," he wrote, it would not be Niagara, the vast prairies, the Colorado canyons, Yellowstone's geysers, or more. It would be what he called "America's choosing day." And he added this in parentheses: "(The heart of it not the chosen—the act itself the main, the quadrennial choosing)." The wonder for Whitman was not *who* was elected president but *how*. Nineteenth-century journalists understood—just as twentieth-century journalists did—that they were at the center of this activity, key players on election night in drawing the democratic mass together. During the Civil War, the *New York Herald*'s postelection story in 1864 left no doubt about the paper's place in the saga of election night: "A similar scene cannot perhaps be witnessed in any other country than democratic America, nor in any other city of the Union than New York, and nowhere else in the metropolis than around the Herald office."[77] Four years later an even more theatrical account reported that "the sun had scarcely set—long, indeed, ere the dusk had spread its gloomy wings— the multitude, as if by instinct, moved *en masse* towards the Herald building."[78] And once there the "multitude" could behold a technological wonder akin to a "new moon," bulletins projected by "brilliant calcium light" that "shed its rays upon the transparency." Three days after the voting in the disputed 1876 presidential contest between Rutherford B. Hayes and Samuel Tilden, the *New York Times* reported "few signs of decrease," despite rain, in the "surging mobs of eager citizens clustered in front of the bulletin-boards" on which newspapers were posting fresh dispatches from the states with uncertain results.[79] Newspapers eventually used photography to provide evidence of massive crowds drawn to the displays on election night. One such photograph in the *St. Louis Post-Dispatch* is the full width of a newspaper page. It shows a sea of formally attired men and women, their upturned faces captured in a "flashlight" photograph as they watch the newspaper's display in 1920. Even from the distance of more than a century, the scene is striking.[80]

Over the course of several generations, there had developed several powerful lines of continuity in the culture of election-night journalism—with the journalists themselves painted into the center of these wondrous events. All of this would continue into the era of broadcast news and set the stage for the computers' election-night debut on television in 1952.

For the next leg of our journey in the run-up to 1952, let's consider three events in the early twentieth century at the intersection of news and technology.

In 1916 at his laboratory in the Bronx, inventor Lee de Forest had been experimenting with something new in the world—the wireless transmission of sound. He was using a device variously known as a "wireless telephone," "radiotelephone," or "radiophone" before the technology became known as just "radio." On November 7 he broadcast for six hours in what he described as "the first use of radiotelephone for broadcasting news of general interest."[81] At a time when few could imagine how commonplace radio would become, de Forest proclaimed the dawn of "a very significant epoch in the distribution of news."[82]

In 1920 at the Westinghouse Electric and Manufacturing Company in East Pittsburgh, the vice president, Harry P. Davis, had become intrigued by the possibility that "radio telephony" could become a mass medium. He figured Westinghouse could cash in with the sale of receiving devices—that is, radios. Davis thought it was time for a regularly scheduled news service over the air. He commissioned one of his engineers to do that and carefully selected November 2 as an auspicious launch date.[83] The station, licensed as KDKA, is still on air more than a century after its debut at the dawn of commercial radio.

In 1928 the *New York Times* was also experimenting with new ways to reach the public. The *Times* commissioned a wondrous display dubbed the "Motograph News Bulletin." It was a five-foot-tall panel that encircled the Times Tower at one end of Times Square. The "zipper," as it came to be known, featured moving messages with hundreds of letters and numbers spelled out using nearly 14,800 light bulbs.[84] The *Times* rolled out the zipper on November 6, 1928, as the debut of a new medium for breaking news in one of the busiest spots in a busy city.[85]

What do these three innovations in the application of new technology to news have in common? The innovators reached a shared conclusion about just when to launch. They chose the same event—albeit in 1916, 1920, and 1928. They chose election night. This was no coincidence. Certainly, there were risks in rolling out a new technology on election night. For one thing de Forest got the outcome wrong, as he would recall years later, though he was not alone in doing that. Key newspapers initially made the wrong call, too. They assigned victory not to the eventual winner, incumbent Woodrow Wilson, but to his Republican challenger, Charles Evans Hughes.[86] But by picking election night for these debuts, the innovators got what they wanted—attention. As with past election-night innovations, this one also set in motion an entirely new problem to be solved. The problem was this: how to keep the transmission of election news in real time from being just a string of names and numbers that might be hard for listeners to follow. Even if news delivered over the air made the right call, inviting attention to a product that might frustrate the audience was also a risk. Still, the chance for bragging rights was a powerful lure.

The larger historical importance of the de Forest broadcast was not lost on either the inventor or the journalists with whom he collaborated. Each framed it in a way that highlighted their separate but intersecting interests—and put themselves at the center of the election-night drama. Two days after the election, the *New York American* ran an article featuring a letter de Forest wrote to the editor, thanking the newspaper for providing the returns that he broadcast.[87] From de Forest's perspective, the journalists were cooperating parties in his own grand vision—commonplace now but wildly futuristic at the time. Not many people then had assembled receiving sets that would allow them to hear the broadcast. But de Forest was not daunted. He wrote, "I believe you will recognize the fact that the time will come when from large wireless telephone stations scattered throughout the country literally hundreds of thousands of listeners, provided with a simple receiver, will be able to get the latest news, combined with music and entertainment, in their homes."

For its part the *American* provided breathless accounts of its own role in the unprecedented broadcast. This innovation was part of an elaborate set of multimedia and multivenue arrangements whereby, the paper claimed, "more than a million persons received their first news of the returns through the American service."[88] The *American* made these returns available in at least 180 locations around greater New York. Its returns were shown at movie theaters, read from the stage at popular shows including the *Ziegfeld Follies*, displayed in famous hotels including the Waldorf-Astoria, announced to diners at "fashionable" restaurants, projected on outdoor screens, and flashed on what the *American* described as "The Newspaper in the Sky," an electric sign some sixty-four feet long and twenty feet high that could publish news bulletins in letters four feet tall.[89] As for the broadcast, this was the newspaper's headline: "American's Returns Sent 200 Miles by Wireless Telephone; This Newspaper First to Use New De Forest Method for This Purpose." With dramatic flourish the story described the way the newspaper staff had "worked like dynamos" to generate election bulletins. The paper gave this florid description of the broadcast: "To tossing ships beyond the bay, beyond the end of Long Island, across the northern tier of New Jersey, far up the rolling Hudson, leaping far above the rugged palisades, topping the crests of the Catskill foothills and charging above the glowing towns and villages, farms and valleys swept the news." "For the first time," the *American* declared, "the wireless telephone had been demonstrated as a practical, serviceable carrier of election news and comment."[90] Bragging rights. Status. Never mind the paper's errant calls on the outcome. For the collaborating technologists and journalists, they saw their use of election night to roll out a new technology for news as a big win of great historical significance.

After the United States entered World War I in 1917, President Wilson exercised his authority to commandeer wireless stations or shut them down.[91] But with the end of the war, promoters—including newspaper publishers and entrepreneurs with an interest in selling radio equipment—began to see opportunities in the commercial broadcasting of voice and music. The question of who was "first" to do one thing or another in the early history of radio has been a contentious one.[92] But for nascent broadcasting concerns looking to debut with a splash, the public appetite for election news represented an ideal target—and one worth scrambling to meet. In time for the 1920 campaign season, primaries and election night would be seen as perfect opportunities to launch.

One of these debuts took place in Detroit. William E. Scripps, publisher of the *Detroit News*, was intrigued by radio. After hearing voice received via a radio receiver that he assembled at home from parts, Scripps bought a de Forest "radiophone" transmitter and had it installed at the newspaper.[93] The amateur station was licensed as "8MK." By some accounts it represented a collaboration between the newspaper publisher and a group of de Forest associates looking to sell radio equipment.[94] A period of testing ended with a front-page announcement on August 31, the day of the Michigan primary. All but one story across the top of the front page rated single-column headlines, from news of early voting in Detroit to the declaration of martial law in Belfast. But the newspaper reserved for itself a larger, two-column headline: "The News Radiophone to Give Vote Results."[95] Amateurs were urged to hold wireless parties so they could hear "voices in the night." This would be "epochal," the *Detroit News* declared, and there was speculation that "a hundred years from now, perhaps, all news will be transmitted by wireless telephone: who knows?" Indeed. On the day after the primary, the biggest display across the top of the *Detroit News* front page was not the outcome of the voting but the newspaper's successful broadcast of returns.[96] The story also announced a regular nightly service offering news and music. The sentiment in that report was nothing less than euphoric, framing the election-night launch as the culmination of human imagination. It began this way, with the same sort of dramatic language that the *New York American* had used to describe the historic dimensions of de Forest's election-night broadcast four years earlier. "One by one the novelists and poets of the ages have watched their dreams come true," the *Detroit News* proclaimed. "Cold, hard, practical science seems always to follow the dream trail through the primeval forests of man's desires, broken first by the dwellers in fiction-land, bringing up in the rear with the paving stone with which to lay the broad highway to the ultimate conquest of all nature." To be sure the radio crowd was not large. By the newspaper's estimates, listeners measured in the hundreds. But in an event that helps mark the beginning of radio journalism, election night provided an opportunity to make the case for news over the air.[97]

The fall elections in 1920 featured a battle for the presidency between two Ohio newspaper publishers—Republican Sen. Warren G. Harding of the *Marion Daily Star* and Democratic Gov. James M. Cox of the *Dayton Daily News*. The Detroit station, 8MK, broadcast returns again on election night. And in one of the most iconic events in the early history of broadcasting, so did station KDKA in East Pittsburgh. Outlines of the KDKA story are frequently recounted in histories of broadcasting.[98] The broadcast is typically seen as a pioneering and revolutionary event in the context of radio's transition from a curiosity to something commonplace and essential. But with the choice of election night as a debut, the KDKA episode is also part of a story of cultural continuity: the reporting of election-night news as an important showcase for new technology. In a speech recounting the process of choosing election night as the occasion to launch the radio news service, the Westinghouse vice president recalled, "We wanted to do something unusual—we wanted to make it spectacular; we wanted it to attract attention."[99]

By the next presidential election, the KDKA broadcast in 1920 had come to assume legendary status. In a celebratory account, the *New York Times* reported that the four-year anniversary of that broadcast was witnessing something "unique" in the "long history of invention."[100] In just four years, radio was seen as accomplishing what it had taken the steam engine, the steamboat, the telephone, and the airplane "a generation or more" to do, becoming "so much a part of our national life." Indeed, radio was all the rage by 1924. Newspapers owned radio stations. So did churches, schools, theaters, hardware stores, radio clubs, factories, civic organizations, police departments, and utility companies.[101] Candidates advertised on radio. And in the run-up to election night in 1924, purveyors of the new medium engaged in a free-for-all vying for listeners. Plans for returns by radio were announced in newspaper ads. Radio stations would provide both election news and entertainment. News venues would seek to entertain. Entertainment venues would seek to inform. Other entities were hitching themselves both to widespread interest in election returns and widespread excitement over radio by inviting the public in to come hear the news over the airwaves. These ranged from a seller of radio equipment in Fitchburg, Massachusetts, to a high school in Marysville, Ohio.[102] In New York the *Ziegfeld Follies* promised that patrons who came to watch the new show—titled "Glorifying the American Girl"—would get to hear returns by radio.[103]

Also in New York, where the third annual National Radio Exposition was drawing thousands of visitors, celebrity entertainer Eddie Cantor would host an election-night "frolic" mixing returns and an on-air variety show.[104] The *New York Times* estimated that crowds of radio listeners on election night could number twenty million.[105] The strongest of the American stations had a reach of hundreds of miles. Election night would also provide an opportunity for coast-to-coast broadcasting by radio stations linked together—a precursor to national network broadcasting. Humorist Will Rogers was among the celebrities keeping that virtual audience entertained between news bulletins.[106]

Decades earlier the telegraph had created new election-night opportunities even as it generated a chaotic flood of rapidly available returns. The arrival of radio prompted a new crisis for a new medium. How could stations organize and present the numbers-driven election-night reports in a comprehensible way to listeners? In 1924 a *New York Times* critique noted that "the gathering and distribution of election returns was a wholly unfamiliar task for most of the radio managers and their announcers."[107] The *Times* did note one exception—a station that "had the wisdom, or perhaps it was the good fortune, to secure the services as announcer of an experienced journalist who had lived through election nights before." That announcer, the *Times* explained, "knew both that early returns are valueless as they stand and that when skillfully interpreted they may be a fairly safe basis for prophecy as to final results of the voting." So, there was that timeless theme again, as important in 1924 as it had been in 1848 and would be in 2020. Early returns could be either a curse or a blessing: perilous without context but valuable when compared to the right historical data.

In trying to understand what was going on behind the scenes in the radio world to meet this new election-night dilemma, I learned of a trove of nearly century-old NBC records archived at the Wisconsin Historical Society, and I traveled to Madison to have a look. Memos that NBC executives sent to each other in the 1920s and 1930s recounted the challenges of making election-night broadcasts appealing. One described those early attempts as a jumble of returns that were hard for listeners to follow.[108] The message was clear. Broadcasters attempting to supply election-night news risked embarrassment if they operated their wondrous new technology without adopting an established set of journalistic practices. These were the practices that newspapers had worked out over time to derive meaning from a stream of early returns. "The election night broadcaster of the future," the *Times* declared in 1924, "will be a man who can perform the computation of averages 'in his head' and very rapidly."[109] This broadcaster would have to be cautious in declaring winners. Returns must be read in round figures rather than all the digits of large numbers. And competence in interpretation would be more important than the numbers themselves. At stake would be the gratitude of listeners.

By 1928 *New York Times* coverage of radio provides evidence of evolving standards for broadcasting returns and the importance of professionalism.[110] Blessed with sometimes elaborate broadcasting facilities but lacking the stables of reporters and analysts needed on election night, radio stations and networks would recruit help and collaborate with newspapers and wire services. Previewing plans for covering the 1928 election on radio, the *New York Times* described the ambient sound that would be captured for the audience, lending gravity to the broadcast. "The clatter of adding machines and typewriters, alien sounds in a broadcasting studio, will replace symphonies and solos in large studios of the National Broadcasting Company Tuesday night," the *Times* explained. A "staff of writers, analysts and tabulators in the studio would act as a human sieve." Their job was to make sense of returns arriving from a newsgathering force of one hundred thousand people—an estimate of the corps who would be harvesting complete nationwide returns for three wire services cooperating with NBC. The *Times* noted that CBS would be employing its own experts, including statisticians and analysts.

Four years later in 1932, NBC executive Avery Marks circulated an internal memo suggesting that 1928 met with only mixed success in providing listener-friendly reports.[111] "Experience of eight years in election night broadcasting has convinced me," he wrote, "that the average broadcast is a mere hodgepodge of unintelligible returns." He reported limited success with an alternative way of giving vote counts, reporting comparative percentages for the candidates' running totals. This condensation of information would eventually become a prevailing philosophy for election-night broadcasting.[112] In a 1968 study—one of the rare

scholarly explorations of the early history of election-night broadcasting—
Thomas W. Bohn concluded that the reporting of returns had provided an
important "testing ground" for radio.[113] Working primarily from accounts
in the *New York Times* and the trade publication *Broadcasting* between
1916 and 1948, Bohn found that election-night practices on radio took
decades to evolve into full-time, hard-news coverage featuring expert
interpretation and analysis. Along the way there was a realization that
the listening public would be receptive to such broadcasts. Broadcasters
grew more aware that sponsors, too, were game to support an election-
night format in which news predominated rather than entertainment.

From the 1920s to the 1940s, radio established a durable hold in American culture. But the idea that radio could, should, or would be a venue
for the live broadcasting of complex news events was not at all obvious
at the start. And as early as 1924, efforts by broadcasters to disseminate
election returns were among the precipitating events in what came to be
known as the Press-Radio War.[114] A central issue in this battle between
purveyors of old and new media was whether wire service bulletins should
be made available to radio stations. Newspaper publishers were certainly
not uniform at first in their resistance to radio news, especially those who
saw radio as a tool to help position them at center stage in the political
theater of election night. The stakes for newspapers seeking to retard
the growth of radio news was not just economic. Publishers sought to
maintain their power and influence in the flow of information. Election
night in 1932 was a pivotal point in the darkening relationship between
radio and print. Networks were cut off from their sources of wire bulletins. An association of newspaper publishers resolved to stop carrying
radio schedules. As battle lines hardened, broadcasters began investing
in their own news operations. A truce was in place in advance of the next
election in 1936, featuring radio news reports by a short-lived collaborative enterprise known as the Press Radio Bureau. Across the country
the worlds of newspaper and radio, between them, engaged two hundred thousand people in efforts to bring election returns to the public.[115]
While the landscape of election-night journalism had shifted yet again,
a transcript of NBC's offering shows the continuation of practices that
predated radio. On radio the "story of the story" included calling attention, as an on-air commentator did, to what the audience was hearing in

the background: "machines, Morse Code operators, typewriters, newspaper men, rewrite men getting together the greatest story of the year." Radio continued to carry entertainment programs on election night, interrupting them for election news.[116] But by 1944 the all-news format would prevail in election-night broadcasting, with sponsors paying up and going along for the ride.[117]

Still, the values associated with entertainment—including showmanship, storytelling, drama, and wonders—remained part of the news-laden broadcasts on election nights, with some unusual twists. In 1932 WABC radio—the flagship station of the Columbia Broadcasting System—turned the proverbial man-versus-machine trope upside down in its choice of an outside expert for the tabulation of returns. Producers retained and promoted the services of one Salo Finkelstein to add up the numbers— not by machine but in his head.[118] Finkelstein, then in his mid-thirties, was one of those rare "mental calculators," celebrated for remembering long sequences of numbers to carry out complex calculations.[119] Their wondrous work was done not only without the aid of equipment but faster. After Finkelstein came to the United States from his native Poland in 1932, he captured the attention of the *New Yorker*, where he was profiled in a "Talk of the Town" piece titled simply, "Magician."[120] He wowed scholars at Harvard and Yale. After his American election-night debut on radio in 1932, Finkelstein continued to be a curiosity, itinerant showman, and subject of news stories.[121] He also continued his role as an election-night whiz on radio as late as 1944 and figured in a "story of the story" retrospective by veteran broadcasters Robert Trout and Paul W. White.[122] "Dr. Finkelstein was a lightning calculator of the highest voltage," they wrote in 1952. "It was his gift to be able, after a glance at a blackboard crammed with figures, to write a summary such as: 'Roosevelt: 3,656,789, now leading in 19 states having 277 electoral votes; Dewey, 2,991,654, leading in seven states with 95 electoral votes.'" Then, wrote Trout and White, "when the last word had been spoken and the microphones turned off, he would collect his fee in cash and promptly vanish." From his first election-night broadcast, Finkelstein lent an air of wonder and celebrity, and for a time he gained exposure in return. But what television viewers would see instead in 1952, wrote Trout and White, was an "ultramodern 'mechanical brain'"—that is, the computer.

While radio was ascendant as an election-night medium, newspapers did not concede their own demise as important players in the dissemination of returns before their first print editions hit the streets. Crowds continued to gather around newspaper buildings looking for bulletins. Print reporters and editors appeared on air as experts. Newspapers also published prediction guides and blank score sheets ahead of the election, evidence that journalists were coming to see readers and listeners as an active audience. There are accounts from 1892 of a telephone company in New York providing customers with printed cards for use on election night, complete with historical data and room to jot down returns.[123] Ahead of the 1924 election, the *New York Sun* ran ads offering tabulation forms to help radio listeners keep track of returns and "add zest" to the evening.[124] Newspapers' publication of blank score sheets, historic data, and the expert knowledge needed to make sense of returns as they rolled in would become regular features of preelection editions. In 1936 the *Morning News* in Florence, South Carolina, invited readers to "Test Your Skill In Election Forecasting."[125] In 1940 a guide titled "The ABC of Interpreting Election Bulletins" was circulated widely by the Associated Press Feature Service.[126] It included an electoral map with state-by-state data from the 1936 election, stars by the states that had voted with the majority for the past forty years, and economic and demographic considerations. Radio stations also printed score sheets in advance, such as NBC affiliates KECA and KFI in Los Angeles.[127] Their sheet included a chart with spaces to record the party ahead in each state for every hour from 10:00 p.m. to 3:00 a.m.

Score sheets were just one way in which news organizations sought to take center stage by addressing a robust public appetite for excitement on election night. In the era of broadcasting, radio studios continued to be places to show off, further evidence of the unique place of election-night journalism in American culture. Special guests—celebrities, political figures, business leaders, and advertisers—were invited to see the inner workings of the broadcast operations. In 1928 officials of NBC and affiliated entities brought their wives and guests to watch an election broadcast in action. An internal network memo described the scene.[128] The guests crowded around a news announcer in the control room as he ad-libbed his coverage from "meagre information provided by cold hard fact." Four years later an NBC executive would call for changes in this arrangement to make it easier for the news staff to work—and get fed. In 1928, it was recalled, the guests scarfed up the food and drink intended to sustain those producing the election-night broadcast.[129] By 1940 NBC's election-night party was a huge production, worthy of being detailed in a postelection story in the *New York Times*. "The famous Studio 8-H, from which Arturo Toscanini directs the NBC symphony orchestra, was converted into a huge receiving room for wire and telephone reports of the returns," the *Times* reported. "An audience of about four thousand gathered in the studio as the guests of [Niles] Trammell, president of NBC, to hear the broadcasts and see the tabulations of the returns posted on a large scoreboard on the stage. . . . A buffet supper was served."[130] Four years later, in 1944, a photograph taken at the cavernous CBS election-night headquarters in New York shows that NBC's chief competitor had rallied, at least in terms of having high-profile guests. Frank Sinatra, then a twenty-eight-year-old singing and acting sensation, occupied a front-row seat with other celebrities. All were just a few feet from the action—reporters and assistants working at their desks and announcers broadcasting returns from a raised platform.[131] This practice of using election night to show off for celebrities—and using the celebrities to confer status on the news operation—continued into the era of television. Ahead of the 1949 state and local elections, WCBS in New York issued a press release describing in detail how it would cover the returns on radio and television. Special guests, it was noted, had been "invited to watch the returns in the CBS television studios," and they would be interviewed for both radio and television broadcasts.[132] Arthur Godfrey, a popular CBS radio and television entertainer, was among them. So was Eleanor Roosevelt, the widow of Pres. Franklin D. Roosevelt and a public figure in her own right, and Margaret Truman, Pres. Harry S. Truman's daughter and a singer.

Before the days of radio, newspaper publishers and editors could be found admitting select guests to watch the newsroom excitement on election night.[133] This practice continued at newspapers into the era of broadcasting. At the *New York Times*, a copy boy named Arthur Gelb watched in 1944 as publisher Arthur Hays Sulzberger and his wife, Iphigene, brought their after-dinner guests to watch the action.[134] Gelb, who would go on to become managing editor of the *Times*, described the scene in a memoir. "The Sulzbergers enjoyed showing off the city room when it was operating at full tilt, and their guests seemed delighted to witness the making of the newspaper they would read at breakfast a few hours later," Gelb recalled. The level of activity must have been quite a sight, judging from the food consumed, which the newsroom aides documented in their own publication, *Timesweek*: "1,800 sandwiches, made of liverwurst, bologna, salami, Spam, roast beef, chicken, and egg salad." Generations after journalists first came to see their newsrooms as a wonder to behold on election night, the habit had not abated.

Running through decades that witnessed changes in technology, society, and journalism, one of the abiding features of election night was its importance as a venue for news organizations to plant themselves at center stage in the national political drama. Hosting parties was one way. The ever-present trope of the "story of the story" was another. Technological wizardry, too, remained an important element. That there would be tremendous public interest was not in doubt as radio reached maturity and television became the newest player. But holding an audience on election night was as much an issue for broadcasters as it had been for competitive newspaper publishers in the century before. Even as an era of the all-news format arrived—at least for one night—the values of entertainment and showmanship did not disappear.

In 1948 television broadcasters began making detailed election-night plans at least as early as September.[135] The news was to be packaged with glitz. A planning memo for a collaborative effort between NBC and *Life* magazine envisioned kicking off the broadcast at 9:00 p.m. by "televising all the hubbub and clatter of the huge room in which NBC gathers its election returns and originates most of its broadcasting of election results." Radio had long done the same thing, conveying the excitement of reporting an election by positioning microphones to capture the sounds of a busy newsroom.[136] Now in plans for election night in the early years of television, the newsroom would still be part of the story.[137] Even calculation could be deployed not only for its value in generating content, but as a visible indicator of the evening's heroic acts of aggregating returns under intense pressure for timeliness and accuracy. The visual appeal of the scene, per the planning memo, would include "milling guests," "clattering news tickers," and "huge wall charts upon which clerks are changing tallies as the latest returns come in." Also featured would be the human and mechanical machinery of election-night number-crunching: "rows of operators of calculating machines." There was even a proposal for something referred to as "black magic presentation" of returns. Later in the planning process, the concepts for visual gimmickry became more elaborate.[138] As the election drew closer, the list of "gadgets" grew longer.[139] There was to be a tug-of-war between images of an elephant and donkey. There would be cash registers described as "raze-ma-taze" for the "wind-up of the show," bearing the names of eleven major- and minor-party presidential candidates.[140] These devices were explicitly referenced in minute-by-minute plans for the program.[141] While the news itself could not be scripted, there were six pages of details about who would be on camera, when, and where. Instructions for the first few minutes called for the use of "gadgets for visualization," and there was a call to "pan [the] floor showing gimmicks" at a point early on when there would be "few returns" to report. With the passage of time, these arrangements may now seem primitive. But they reveal a marked attention to the importance of visual appeal in the use of this new technology for transmitting election returns, a practice that had already evolved a great deal since 1932. In that year an early television station operated by CBS in New York broadcast returns in a way that simply mimicked the long tradition of outdoor bulletins—training the camera's "electrical eye" on placards with lettered returns.[142] A newspaper account referred to the arrangement, in fact, as an "ethereal bulletin board."[143] Entertainers and pictures of candidates filled in the gaps between fresh news of the election.[144]

At NBC, plans in 1948 for gadgets to be featured in the television studio included one bearing some similarity to the display of election-night news outside the Times Tower. That was certainly not a random or lightly considered idea. In the battle for attention on election night—in which broadcasting would eventually win an absolute victory over outdoor displays—that outcome was in no way guaranteed. Times Square on election night occupied an enviable place not only in the physical landscape but in the nation's mental landscape. While radio quickly commanded a nationwide audience of listeners, election night at Times Square continued to produce some of the very largest gatherings of people anywhere in the United States. This was a storied location that figured prominently in broadcasters' conceptions of their own election-night performance. Even the notion of performance was not remote from the calculus that produced these crowds. Times Square was in the heart of the nation's most famous entertainment district, and that meant a ready supply of people. Just as the vaudeville of an earlier generation had made patrons in the seats feel like they were part of the show, crowds in Times Square could count on being part of the show on election night.[145]

The *New York Times* did not take these crowds for granted. Although the newspaper operation had outgrown the Times Tower and moved a half block away in 1913, publisher Adolph S. Ochs held on to the original building for its public relations value.[146] Located at the southern end of Times Square, it had become an iconic structure in the heart of the brightly lit entertainment capital of the nation, with impressive sight-lines where Seventh Avenue and the "Great White Way" of Broadway converged. The advent of radio and its audience of listeners promised to dwarf the size of election-night gatherings in Times Square. But the *Times*, as noted earlier, used election night in 1928 as a venue to roll out its attention-getting innovation in the delivery of news, the "Moto-graph News Bulletin."[147] The "zipper," as it was known, featured brief news reports that moved across a panel of light bulbs circling the building and could be updated as news broke.[148] This was Twitter decades before Twitter. The *Times* celebrated the motograph's "publication" of election returns as the debut of a nightly news service, declaring that "the apparatus is not merely an electric sign but in one sense a newspaper as well."[149] The moving display of news would go on to be one of the most distinctive features of Times Square, "printing" headlines for the "teeming midtown throng," as one writer put it, "in the medium the crowd knows best—electric light."[150] But the motograph itself was just one element in the *Times*'s imaginative presentation of news on election night in 1928, generations before the term "multimedia" would come to embody both the challenges and opportunities facing traditional print journalism. Even as the *Times* was enthusiastically reporting on nationwide efforts to broadcast the election results by radio, the paper's efforts to engage a crowd in Times Square and beyond continued to include searchlight signals, coded colored lights, and stereopticon projections, plus a new sound system technology.[151] For those listening to radio at home—such as "Mr. Citizen," envisioned as having "drawn up before him a table with paper and figures"—the *Times* had published a half-page packed with election data back to 1916 and a place to record the state-by-state vote.[152]

To be sure, radio might have had more listeners and was being celebrated in *Times* headlines as "The New Instrument of Democracy."[153] But Times Square continued to draw crowds of astonishing proportions—in the tens and hundreds of thousands—well into the era of broadcasting.[154] It is not hard to understand why broadcasters would want in on that Times Square action in the battle for election-night legitimacy. At first getting in on the action meant bringing Times Square to the rest of the nation. In 1932 the "hubbub" of Times Square was captured by radio microphones positioned in hotel windows above the crowd.[155] In 1936 NBC sent radio announcer and news reporter Ben Grauer to Times Square with the NBC Mobile Unit to describe the scene.[156] Here was a new medium, radio, achieving some sort of ironic authenticity as an election-night news source by capturing the excitement of the crowd getting their bulletins the old-fashioned way—packed shoulder-to-shoulder in the street. A few minutes after NBC radio began reporting that President Roosevelt was widely viewed as the victor with just a fraction of the vote counted, Grauer described what he called "a sea of humanity" jammed into Times Square. He let his radio audience hear the jubilation of the crowd in the street as a searchlight displayed the code they had been waiting for, swinging, he said, in "a long and low semi-circle in the heavens."

While reporting from Times Square, NBC was also trying to draw a street crowd to its own enormous outdoor display. Thirty feet wide by thirty feet tall, a map of the United States contained colored glass for each state capable of flashing green for Roosevelt or amber for his opponent, Alf Landon. About an hour and a half after the report from Times Square, there was a report from NBC's mobile unit on the scene around the NBC display, where nearly all states were now flashing Roosevelt's green from coast to coast. The eight to ten thousand who stood watching were admitted to be, per NBC, "not as vast a crowd as we brought to you from Times Square."[157]

Whether officials at NBC were explicitly trying in 1936 to outdo Times Square is not made clear in the broadcast. But internal NBC documents leave no doubt that is just what the network and its parent company, RCA, hoped to do in 1948.[158] It was not enough that NBC's combined radio and television audience would have dwarfed any crowd turning up in Times Square. The broadcasters wanted to be at center stage in the street, too—visible proof of the network's election-night importance. The idea of drawing street crowds to watch large NBC television monitors surfaced by the early fall of 1948 in a memo from a senior editor at *Life* magazine to the publisher.[159] *Life* had collaborated with NBC in coverage of the 1948 political conventions and would do so again on election night.[160] Three weeks after that *Life* memo, an NBC memo shows the network planning for a display in the street.[161] This was nothing less than a declaration of war on the preeminent position of Times Square as the nation's symbolic gathering place on election night. Using technological novelty as a draw, a big-screen outdoor television was envisioned as a way to engage crowds around Rockefeller Center's famed skating rink. The hoped-for result was explicit—and would be made plain for NBC viewers at home. "The whole idea is to take the play away from Times Square," per the NBC memo. "We would of course turn the camera out the window and make a pickup of the crowd and the big screen demonstration and put it on the television network." Television was going to show street crowds watching television. Two weeks later detailed plans included construction of a screen and frame with outside dimensions of precisely 17 feet-3 inches by 21 feet-11½ inches, sitting exactly 9 feet above the sidewalk. It would receive images from a 2,200-pound projector operating 40 feet away.[162] The plan was carried out in time for the election, and *New York Times* reporter Meyer Berger would take note. He referred to the setup in Rockefeller Plaza as "the new trend in Election Night customs."[163]

The approach at CBS also offered intentionally reflexive coverage on election night—that is, reporting on the excitement of its own efforts to report the election. Norman Brokenshire, a CBS radio reporter, was sent out into the crowded streets of Midtown Manhattan in a mobile unit, which he described as "a great big, beautiful Plexiglass bubble."[164] When he came on air shortly before 6:30 p.m., his report quickly turned to a description of his own reporting as the center of attention on the streets. "It's a good thing we're moving," he said, "for the minute we come to a stop, this ultramodern mobile studio gets more attention from the men and women on the streets than the skaters in the plaza or the blimp that flies overhead." There it was again—the story of the story—with a featured place for innovation. A CBS news release from late October—found in the files of a competing NBC executive—promised that its television broadcast would capture the "gala mood of the Great White Way," the storied section of Broadway that includes Times Square.[165] The intent at CBS was also to generate visual excitement in its newsroom. Three cameras would be sweeping a "vast arena of activity," per the memo, immersing the audience in what the network called its "nerve center." There would be "interviews with celebrities and political personalities" and "tally boards in operation."

Despite the networks' enthusiasm for creating a journalistically sound and visually exciting experience, one important viewer in 1948 expressed disappointment. He was Jack Gould, television critic for the *New York Times*. In his estimation, "Radio had much the best of it over television, the video art fumbling rather badly in its first full-dress effort to cover the outcome of a presidential election."[166] Gould suggested that while counting ballots might not be inherently exciting as a visual affair, television could have done better with more effective preparation. Large wall charts were hard to read instead of being simplified and presented in bigger letters. Gould was not alone in noticing the shortcomings of the studio setup. One of the CBS newscasters had to resort to binoculars as he looked across the expansive election-night studio—an auditorium—to read a tally board with the returns he needed to report on air.[167] Gould's critique went beyond the visuals.[168] He felt too much attention was drawn to the on-air broadcasters rather than the news. He deemed the presentation on one network to be pretentious. On another he was disturbed by what he called "altogether too much 'experting.'" And one of the biggest flubs was missing the concession speech of the Republican candidate, New York Gov. Thomas E. Dewey. "Whatever their alibis," Gould wrote, "the television boys were caught napping."

For Gould, it would seem, some of the classic values of election-night reporting that we have seen in play over the prior decades—including attention-getting gimmicks and the story of the story—had interfered with the purported role of a news operation: transmitting the results of the election in an intelligent and comprehensible way. To be sure, by 1948 the broadcasting of election returns on television had come a long way from early attempts. But when the curtain closed on the last presidential election before 1952, the jury was still out on whether television could prove itself a respectable venue for election-night reporting. This reputational crisis would set the stage, once again, for the networks' efforts to innovate.

This tour of election-night journalism during the century leading up to 1952 is not meant to be exhaustive. My initial interest in that history had to do with this question: If computer analysis as a tool to aid in news reporting was slow to be widely adopted during the early decades of the computer age, how could we explain the use of these so-called "electronic brains" as tools for election-night reporting on television in 1952—so early in the history of both television news and computers? While it is tempting to view that episode as entirely revolutionary, the approach here has been to consider ways in which this use of computing on television might also be consistent with well-established journalistic practices on election nights to that point.

In our tour the evident linkage between election night and the wonders of technology also calls to mind the work of David Nye, who has explored in detail across two centuries what he referred to as the "American technological sublime."[169] In Nye's usage the awe-inspiring wonders of technology have been an important and durable American trope. The celebration of technology has intertwined with celebrations of holidays such as Independence Day, and the debuts of new technologies and systems have drawn crowds and tourists.[170] As this chapter suggests, election nights also have a place among the events in which Americans have mixed celebrations of technology and democracy, brought about by the intersecting agendas of journalists and their technological collaborators.

The ultimate wonder on election night may be the spectacle of mass action—starting with the election itself, democracy's main event. We may tend to take this for granted now—or at least we did before the disturbing events on and after election night 2020. But with so few democracies elsewhere during much of the history of the United States, and with perpetual deep and strident conflict in the run-up to voting, the wonder may have been that elections spanning a city or a continent could take place at all. This was not lost on reporters of the election-night scene for that century up to 1952. The language of the sublime weaves in and out of their descriptions of the crowd itself. In 1860 a writer for the *New York Herald*, in trying to convey the "spectacle" of the "living mass," asserted that "it must be witnessed to be fairly understood."[171] In 1896 a writer for the *New York Tribune* described the street scene as a "sublime spectacle" that called to mind poets' descriptions of "the sea in its might" and Milton's rendition of the "gigantic splendors of hell."[172] Photographs of the election-night crowds outside one paper or another conveyed the same sort of impression—what a 1920 caption in the *St. Louis Post-Dispatch* called the "immense throngs."[173] Or consider NBC's Ben Grauer, dispatched in a mobile unit to report by radio from Times Square on election night in 1936. He found "excitement" and "bedlam" in what he termed a "humanity-jammed" place, "choked with people."[174] Here was wonder suffused with a hint of terror, challenging one's ability to adequately capture the scene in words, all elements of the sublime that inform his report. Unlike newspaper reporters recounting such scenes in the past, Grauer was in a location away from the network studio. But he was, in effect, an extension of the studio. As young men climbed all over his mobile unit, he told the radio audience, "The mob is absolutely terrific. There is no other word to express it."

What we have here, then, might be called the "sublime of the crowd"— and, as manifest on election night, perhaps the "American democratic sublime." The story on election night, as much as it is about the victory of one side over the other, is about mass action. When crowds gathered outside newspapers to wait for returns, they became the visible manifestation of this mass action. When they turned to radio and then television, the crowd did not disappear. Some of them, in fact, were still gathering outside and could be heard or shown. Some were invited into the studio and became part of the action there. Most of the crowd was at home. They numbered, eventually, in the tens of millions, a crowd both imagined and unimaginable. And in telling the "story of the story" of election night, journalists made a habit of positioning themselves at ground zero in the act of assembling these crowds—whether by the agency of newspaper writers of the nineteenth century or broadcasters of the twentieth. These real and virtual assemblies would become, in fact, elements of what might even be called an "election-night sublime," election after election.

Still, for any one purveyor of election-night news, there was no guarantee of an audience. It had to be attracted and held. So, the dissemination of returns was suffused with entertainment values. The stakes were high in being right—and being early—so sound methods for doing both were also critical. Technologies of all sorts—the ones for getting the job done and the ones for attracting attention—were often one and the same, and they would find a perpetually important place in the election-night mix up to 1952.

3 | Are Computers Newsworthy?

Election night 1952 would bring together two worlds—the world of people who produced computers and the world of people who produced television news. We can see now, looking back, that each was at a pivot point in its history. To understand what happened next, you must forget what you know—that television news and computers would become defining features of American life. Collaboration on election night would help each gain more of a purchase in public consciousness. Their future paths—the ones we now know about—could not be known then. There were grand visions, certainly. But there was also great peril. The election-night experiments could go either way. The players in both television news and commercial computing wanted to be taken seriously in the society around them. And inside each of these worlds—the world of computer makers and the world of news broadcasters—there were intense battles for supremacy, too. Nothing was certain. Even the collaboration of journalists and technologists that played out on November 4, 1952—while continuing century-old election-night patterns—was nothing that the computer people and the television news people had foreseen very far in advance.

Four years earlier, television had covered the 1948 election. But just a fraction of one percent of U.S. households were equipped with TV sets. The election-night audience was certainly expanded considering the early TV-era custom of "guest viewing" and "television visiting" by friends, family, and neighbors, plus TV watching at bars and other public venues.[1] But the television audience was dwarfed in 1948 by those following the returns on radio, which was found in tens of millions of homes and cars.[2] The technology of television was not entirely new then. Experiments had been underway in earnest since the 1920s. Some regularly scheduled programming began before World War II. But television ownership and television broadcasting had both been limited by the war and were still in their infancy.[3] Even as sales of TV sets picked up in the late 1940s, a variety of issues, including broadcast signals that interfered with each other, prompted a freeze on the licensing of new television stations in late 1948. Then the early 1950s would see an explosion in the world of television—more stations, more sets, more programming, and ever-larger networks. The first television signal to be seen by audiences simultaneously from one end of the country to the other would be broadcast in September 1951.[4] The freeze on new stations would be lifted in April 1952.[5] And November 1952 would see the first coast-to-coast network broadcasts of election returns. The ownership of television sets had grown markedly—to more than a third of all households in 1952.[6] The way this story turns out—with television reaching more than 90 percent of households by the early 1960s and becoming a dominant medium in American culture—can only be seen in retrospect. But the signs were there. In many communities with television, other venues for leisure were taking a hit—movie theaters, sporting events, night clubs, bookstores, even libraries. Americans spent less time listening to radio—and jukeboxes, too.[7] Still, for the parties involved in television in the early 1950s, there were no guarantees—either about the future of their medium or about their own place in it. Even C. E. Hooper, a leader in measuring ratings of the radio audience in the 1940s, saw limited potential for television broadcasting as late as 1950, when he sold his national radio and television ratings service to competitor A. C. Nielsen.[8]

One of the fixtures of the nascent world of television was intense competition between the networks—especially between NBC and CBS. This carried over from their rivalries in radio. NBC was owned by RCA, the Radio Corporation of America, which was involved in television as both a broadcaster and a manufacturer of TV sets. NBC had the largest number of affiliated television stations.[9] And in the early years of television, NBC also had bragging rights to a majority of programs with the highest audience ratings. But the network faced a fierce challenger in CBS, which overtook NBC in the early 1950s for largest number of top-rated programs.[10] Farther back in the competition were ABC, which also had a radio network, and DuMont, which had none. The DuMont Television Network, founded by a pioneer in the manufacture of TV sets, would sign off for the last time in the mid-1950s, evidence that not reaching the largest possible audience could have devastating consequences. Ratings were of intense interest to advertisers. So, for the networks, ratings were a key to financial success.

The threats faced by broadcasters did not just come from competition with each other. The airwaves were regulated by the government. Fear of regulation was not merely an exercise in the hypothetical. ABC itself was created as an independent network after NBC, which had two radio networks, was forced by the Federal Communication Commission and the U.S. Supreme Court to divest itself of one in 1943.[11] In the foreword to her biography of Edward R. Murrow, A. M. Sperber laid out a set of questions to frame her study, including one that was by no means unique to the legendary figure from radio and the early years of television: "How does a responsible broadcaster function in an industry caught between government licensing and the marketplace?"[12]

In addition to the specter of aggravating powerful forces in government, broadcasters also faced perpetual criticism from various self-appointed guardians of the nation's moral, cultural, and ideological well-being. Concerns about deleterious effects of television on young people and home life were voiced as early as the 1940s and then heard forever after. These concerns prompted constant scrutiny of television programming, especially for dramas featuring crime and violence.[13] In 1951 a different sort of protest came from members of the National Association for the Advancement of Colored People, offended by negative stereotypes of Black people in the CBS television situation comedy *Amos 'n' Andy*.[14] A southern governor, meanwhile, complained about the "mixing and mingling of races" on other CBS television programs, including Black men said to be dancing "in juxtaposition to scantily clad white females."[15] He deemed this at odds with southern segregation laws and suggested a firm response: pressure by southern newspapers on the television industry, action by southern congressmen, and perhaps a boycott of products made by advertisers on nonsegregated shows. In mid-1952 a broadcasting trade magazine, *Sponsor*, declared public relations to be television's "hottest problem."[16]

One response to perpetual criticism, a desire for respectability, and the fear of regulation was the TV industry's adoption of a so-called "Television Code" that promoted self-regulation.[17] Internal memos at NBC also show that the network armed itself with examples of programs that were primarily educational, cultural, or informational.[18] The networks positioned the broadcasting of news as an antidote to critical scrutiny of all sorts, framing their journalistic operations as a public service. That included coverage of political conventions and elections.[19] On election night in 1952, NBC radio would open its coverage with a pledge to "render a public service of trust" in reporting the returns.[20] The corporate sponsors of network election broadcasts staked a similar claim to serving democracy. A thirty-two-page guide to the NBC coverage of the 1952 conventions and elections was published "in the public interest" by Philco, a maker of television sets, radios, and other appliances that were touted in the printed guide and during the on-air radio and television reports.[21]

To be sure, the role of television news in American culture was on the rise. By the end of the 1952 campaign season, television received the highest score when Americans were surveyed about the medium that provided them with the most information—even though access to radio and daily newspapers was more common.[22] Still, television news faced its own battles for respect within the realms of broadcasting and journalism. Little time on air was devoted to news.[23] And it took a while for TV news to move beyond the idea of "radio with pictures" by developing practices that would make the most of the medium. In a 1951 column praising *See It Now*, a new television news program featuring CBS star Edward R. Murrow, *New York Times* critic Jack Gould argued that television to that point had not been very successful as a news medium "on a day-to-day basis."[24] Murrow himself gave a nod to the strangeness of the transition as a veteran radio broadcaster who had not been eager to embrace television. At the debut of *See It Now*, he declared, "This is an old team trying to learn a new trade."[25] Television news of the era was described by broadcast historian Erik Barnouw as "an unpromising child"—"the schizophrenic offspring of the theater newsreel and the radio newscast."[26] As late as 1954 a radio and television writer for the *New York Daily News*, Ben Gross, was suggesting that television might be okay for covering planned events but was too ephemeral for breaking news.[27] Television executives, meanwhile, worried whether news was destined to be a money loser.[28] Journalists from radio—which had won public respect as an important news medium during World War II—worried in the late 1940s and early 1950s that making the jump to television might be a poor career move.[29]

At the intersection of news, broadcasting, and politics in 1952, managers and reporters in television news were engaged in a "struggle for parity" with journalists from other media, said Sig Mickelson, director of television news and public affairs for CBS.[30] A notable skirmish took place inside a movie theater in Abilene, Kansas. Eisenhower held a press conference there a day after announcing his candidacy. It was not customary at the time for television cameras to be admitted to such gatherings. The more prestigious circle of print reporters leaned on the Eisenhower camp to keep up the practice. "To much of the printed press," Mickelson later observed, television "was an intruder with its roots in show business, not in journalism."[31] Just before the press conference started, a CBS crew moved into position in the theater and let it be known that they would not leave unless thrown out by force. Eisenhower consented to letting them stay.[32] Gavel-to-gavel coverage of the political nominating conventions further enhanced the efforts of television news pioneers to be taken seriously.[33]

The November elections would offer another chance to shine. But it did not take a long memory to understand that there was peril, too. Jack Gould at the *New York Times* was among those who had panned the election-night broadcasts in 1948.[34] The recitation of vote counts was not good television. Attempts to provide the numbers visually were a bust. And there was an even more embarrassing problem—for TV news and a variety of other players on election night in 1948. For starters there were the three leading pollsters: Gallup, Roper, and Crossley. They stumbled badly with their prediction that New York Gov. Thomas E. Dewey, the Republican challenger, would unseat Pres. Harry Truman. Those wayward polls later unleashed a wave of studies to figure out what went wrong.[35] The polls had also colored the expectations and reporting of journalists. One of the most iconic images in the history of American politics is Truman beaming as he holds up a copy of the postelection *Chicago Daily Tribune* with the famously faulty headline, "Dewey Defeats Truman."[36] The *New York Times* ran a postmortem on its own erroneous preelection forecast—a mea culpa in which *Times* correspondents from each of the forty-eight states were asked to explain what went wrong.[37] Many had been influenced by the very same polls or by local newspaper surveys. One of the best-known radio broadcasters of the day, NBC's H. V. Kaltenborn, was among those who would be ridiculed—by no less a figure than Truman himself—for hanging on too long on election night to the belief that Dewey would emerge the victor.[38] The reluctance at NBC to believe what the incoming returns were showing also rated a ribbing in Gould's *New York Times* review. CBS did not cover itself in glory, either, as far as identifying the big story of the night in a timely way. Edward Bliss Jr., an editor at CBS, later described what he witnessed that night. After Truman pulled ahead in the vote count—but with results still incomplete from several key states that were thought to be in the Dewey column— Bliss wrote that "CBS called it a night and closed down." A fine breakfast was served for the CBS staff, but they were unhappy. Murrow protested, said Bliss, and John Charles Daly, also then at CBS, later referred to the episode as "that unpleasant night."[39]

Four years later on election night 1952, Murrow, Kaltenborn, and Daly would again be key figures in the competing networks' television coverage, with Daly by then at ABC. Avoiding the kinks of 1948 would have been an important goal for each man as well as for other reporters, commentators, and planners of the election-night broadcasts. It is not hard to imagine a common agenda: getting attention, getting the numbers right, and providing those numbers in a timely and visually engaging way with an accurate assessment of their meaning. But it would be wrong to assume that the memory of 1948 was destined to play out as an aversion to any sort of risk. Reuven Frank, who would later become president of NBC News, describes the period between 1948 and 1958 as a time when the people involved in television news "stumbled along, devising ways of presenting news and methods of using pictures as news that have become standard, accepted American fare. All were arrived at by trial and error."[40] Sig Mickelson, the CBS TV news chief, described the early 1950s as a period when "*innovation* and *imagination* were watchwords in the newsroom."[41] At the time, the existing model for stories told in moving images was the newsreel—a news magazine on film that moviegoers would see before the main feature. The whole idea of a television news story that was live—or could be filmed, processed, and presented to viewers on a tight deadline—was itself an innovation. Car batteries were adapted for use as power sources in the field. On occasion, film was hastily processed in a restroom or aboard an airplane.[42] Television graphics had to be imagined and invented—or at least cobbled together in surprising ways from materials meant for other uses. To identify speakers on the television screen for viewers at home watching the Republican National Convention from Chicago in 1952, an enterprising young CBS producer-director, Don Hewitt, arranged to buy the menu board from a nearby diner. It had movable white letters and a black background that would not show up on screen. Hewitt, who would go on to create one of the most successful television news programs, *60 Minutes*, said of those early years, "We were still feeling our way and making it up as we went along."[43] Mickelson characterized the early history of television news as one of "gambling with untested techniques, of daring to defy convention and laws of probability, of flaunting established procedures."[44] For election night in 1952, amidst promotion of what the networks would do to distinguish themselves, one sort of gadget was singled out for special mention. It was the "electronic brain," common lingo at the time for computers. As would be the case in decades to follow, the computer was already invested with multiple meanings. Its place in the world of science, business, and engineering was far from fixed, not to mention its place in journalism and the culture at large. Election night would play a role in working that out.

Since trotting out a new technology on election night carried risks, network news managers would have to wrestle with how to contain those risks. But using that new technology would also address at least one imperative for this new platform for news, situated as television news was inside a medium best known for entertainment and showmanship. When the computer came to Sig Mickelson's attention as a possible addition to election-night gadgetry, he thought it could satisfy a variety of needs for CBS. They could beat the competition in identifying the next occupant of the White House. They could do this with a tool to be touted prominently in advance. They could grab the attention of the print media. And if all went well, they could boost audience ratings.[45] At least that was the idea. Driving these possibilities was what Mickelson described as the "novelty value" of computers. To most people, these machines were invested with mystery. "I knew just enough about computers," he wrote in a memoir, "to know that they could perform mathematical miracles."

During World War II, in the early years of experimentation with the design of machines that would come to be known as "computers," the demands of wartime secrecy limited what the public might know. With the end of the war, there was more freedom to circulate information and ideas. There were enthusiastic accounts from scientists, mathematicians, and business leaders in the late 1940s and early 1950s about the promise that computers held for advances in knowledge, productivity, and human relations.[46] There were concerns, too, such as the ones given voice in Kurt Vonnegut's first novel, *Player Piano*. Published in 1952, it painted a troubling picture of technology managers teamed up with computers and running the world. But among visions both glorious and dark, the use of computers on election night was not what sprang to mind before 1952 when technologists and non-technologists alike pondered the future of these strange new devices. The fact that an election night became a way for computing to enter journalism and find itself at center stage before the American public was in no way preordained.[47]

This is not to say that practical ideas about uses for computers were lacking. Behind the new machines that would come to play a role on election night in 1952 were inventors with fertile imaginations and big dreams. In 1946 two pioneers of computing, John W. Mauchly and J. Presper Eckert Jr., decided to leave their positions at the University of Pennsylvania and set out to create a new kind of business, one that would focus exclusively on the manufacture and marketing of electronic computers and related devices. This was a bold idea. Up to that point, there was no established "market" for computers—nor agreement that there would be much of a market. The military was a critical source of funds for the development of these expensive and complicated machines. In the mid-1940s, while still at the university, Mauchly and Eckert worked on one such project they had proposed to the Army—the design and construction of ENIAC, short for Electronic Numerical Integrator and Computer.[48] As ideas about computers were taking shape, ENIAC was a seminal machine. For one thing, it worked. After its completion in 1945, it would be used on atomic and conventional weapons projects. ENIAC was electronic as opposed to earlier "electromechanical" computing machines that relied on moving parts. Constructed with about eighteen thousand vacuum tubes, weighing thirty tons, and built at a cost of nearly half a million dollars, ENIAC relied on the manipulation of pulses of electricity to process numbers. It was digital, meaning it processed data divided into discrete units. It was "general-purpose," meaning it could solve a variety of problems rather than being dedicated to do only one thing. And it could be programmed. That is, it could be supplied both with data and a sequence of actions to carry out on the data. It could compare numbers, and based on the results, it could determine what steps to take next.

ENIAC would be hailed as the first working electronic, digital computer. But even before ENIAC's construction was completed, its inventors and others recognized its limitations. Programming ENIAC was a laborious affair. This involved physically connecting wires on removable "plugboards" to establish the sequence of steps for any given problem. The improvement over this approach came to be known as the "stored program" concept. The sequence of steps would be entered into a computer's internal memory by any of a variety of inputs—metallic tape, punched cards, perforated paper tape, or even directly by keyboard. Programs could be more easily modified—and they could even be modified by the results of the calculations themselves.

The combination of these features—digital, general-purpose, electronic, and stored program—would ultimately gel as generally acknowledged elements of a "computer." While still at the university and even as ENIAC was under development, Eckert and Mauchly worked on the design of a pioneering stored-program computer, EDVAC, its name short for Electronic Discrete Variable Automatic Computer. But the EDVAC would not be completed by the time Eckert and Mauchly set off on their own, prompted by a dispute with the university over patent rights. The inventors wanted to develop their own computers for sale—faster, more advanced, more versatile, easier to use, and less expensive than ENIAC. They wanted these computers of the future to include the stored-program concept.

As Eckert and Mauchly went about creating the first commercial computing company in the United States, did they envision uses in journalism—and especially on election night? Or was it all just to be crunching numbers for the military, business, and science? When I was trying to answer that question, I learned that a collector in California, Jeremy Norman, had acquired a set of documents and artifacts that had belonged to Eckert. I reached out to Norman just in time to learn that he was auctioning off a collection dealing with the "origins of cyberspace," including the Eckert materials. The auction was to be held at Christie's in New York. I also learned that one can inspect, before an auction, the items to be sold. I made my way to Christie's and there, in a glass case, I spotted just the document to help me understand what Eckert and Mauchly saw as the future of computing. It was a typed, eight-page business plan for their proposed new enterprise in 1946. It would sell at the auction for $72,000.[49] The new company did not have a name yet— several were suggested—but the document did have this title: "Outline of Plans for Development of Electronic Computors."[50] The document was rich with futuristic visions. Fifteen ideas were spelled out in detail, plus a miscellaneous sixteenth category. The range was extraordinary: weather forecasting, automatic navigation, secret communications, television components, printing devices, high-speed knitting machines, equipment to monitor chemical reactions in real time, and more. Even new musical instruments were envisioned, with an explanation that while they might not seem related to mathematical computation, "electric organs can be developed using components and techniques which are used in electronic computing machines." The document did not foresee uses in journalism, politics, or elections. But it makes clear that the inventors were open to an extraordinary range of tasks. Some of these were not so far afield from the kind of information handling necessary on election night, such as the planning departments in large businesses or entities with lots of records. And the plan was open-ended, suggesting there might be new applications that future developments in computing "will bring to light." So while election-night forecasting was not listed, Mauchly and Eckert were certainly primed for unexpected, outside-the-box possibilities. Six years later, election night would present just that sort of opportunity to showcase their wares.

The business plan also made clear a willingness to take on Goliaths in the arena they were entering—the manufacture of machines for complex calculation, tabulation, and accounting. There were promises of dramatic advances over existing equipment—that is, improvements over machines that used punched cards for the storage and analysis of information. At the time—in the era before commercial computers—IBM was the leader in punched-card machines for information management. Applications ranged from work on the U.S. Census to the design of major weapons to the production of actuarial tables for insurance companies. As Eckert and Mauchly made contacts and interested a range of clients, they underestimated the time and cost involved in turning their ideas into workable machines. There is no small irony that following the articulation of their dreams in 1946, the realities of raising sufficient capital would see their small firm acquired in 1950 by another manufacturing giant—Remington Rand, an IBM rival.[51] Then in 1951 Eckert and Mauchly made a splash with a pioneering large-scale, stored-program commercial computer, UNIVAC, when it was officially turned over to the U.S. Census. The name "UNIVAC" stood for "Universal Automatic Computer," heralding the versatility envisioned in that 1946 draft business plan. And the Census was one of the potential customers envisioned in that document.

Remington Rand and IBM had been rivals for more than a generation before computers. Remington Rand was a more diverse corporation—selling products ranging from electric razors to typewriters to adding machines. Where the two businesses competed was in machines to help businesses manage information—keeping track of accounts, generating bills, issuing paychecks, and organizing inventory. Remington Rand had been ahead earlier in the century, but IBM came on strong and became the leader in that field by the end of World War II.[52] With UNIVAC, Remington Rand appeared to pull out in front in the computer business by beating IBM to market with a high-speed, all-electronic, stored-program behemoth. But that alone was not going to ensure business success for UNIVAC.

In the early 1950s, rivals in the nascent world of commercial computers did not have any guarantees—or even a consensus within their ranks—that there would be a large and inevitable customer base for their inventions. Pioneers were aware that the clientele—and potential uses—had to be manufactured right along with the devices. Ideas were exchanged both informally and at well-attended conferences with participants from across the country, including some who would come to play a role in election-night forecasting.[53] The customers who were envisioned in discussions of new computers were typically institutions—government agencies, military contractors, large businesses, and academic research centers. Decades would pass before the public itself was seen as a potential market for computers. It would be decades, too, before computers were modified enough in terms of size, price, and ease of use to make a market of individuals even thinkable. But in a pair of documents labeled "Company Confidential," John Mauchly laid out in the early 1950s a vision for the importance, nonetheless, of capturing the attention of the public at large. I came across these documents in boxes of Mauchly's papers archived at the University of Pennsylvania's Annenberg Rare Book and Manuscript Library.[54] One was drafted in 1951 and the other in July 1952. They help us understand why—when the idea surfaced for using the UNIVAC on national television for reporting on election returns—this idea would make perfect sense to Mauchly, despite the risks inherent in undertaking such a novel task live before an audience of millions.

In the 1951 document—titled "Are Computers Newsworthy?"—Mauchly started by taking note of a striking transformation.[55] Less than a decade earlier, he wrote, there had been skepticism about the prospect of developing an electronic computer. Next, there was disbelief that such a device could have commercial applications. Now, Mauchly reported, there were more than a dozen large electronic computers in operation. In addition, he wrote, there were "one hundred electronic computer projects in laboratories" and "hundreds of small electronic computers in commercial use," with "more than one million vacuum tubes operating in IBM units throughout the country." Here, he was clearly casting a wide net in his conception of a "computer." When the meaning of that term was not yet fixed, it could refer not just to UNIVAC-like devices that were rare in 1951, but also IBM's recently invented electronic calculating machines in the punched-card tradition. These still required wiring each program into the device. But Mauchly's point was that novelty could no longer be taken for granted. "In view of this rapid change in the last decade," he wrote, "computers are no longer front-page news." And yet, Mauchly suggested, "There is a kind of paradox here: although computers have become commonplace, they are still regarded with awe and wonder."

Computers were still an "abstraction" to most people, who, he said, had "no real understanding as to what they are good for and little appreciation of what they can really do." He underlined the next line, which was the wind up to his pitch: "Here is a real opportunity for a public relations program to step in and bring computers down to earth."

The trick in attracting public attention, Mauchly argued, was to show the value of computers for tasks that ordinary people cared about. He made a prediction: "It is the application of computers to problems affecting our daily life which will make news in the future—not the mere existence of a computer having fantastic abilities." But even within Remington Rand, he complained, few really understood what UNIVAC could do. As Mauchly saw it, by describing their own company's computer in "magical terms," these insiders were doing a disservice. As a result, he wrote, "Through a lack of education within the organization itself we are at present helping to foster the very same attitude of mystery and awe which is displayed by the general public toward devices of this sort."

Mauchly noted that at IBM, founder Thomas J. Watson Sr. had succeeded in continuing to get attention for the company's Selective Sequence Electronic Calculator—based on what the invention could accomplish, not on its massive size. The "SSEC," as it was known, was placed in service in 1948 and showcased behind a glass wall visible from the street in Manhattan. Flashing neon indicator lights drew crowds of pedestrians. By the time of Mauchly's "Are Computers Newsworthy?" document in 1951, the IBM device was already recognized as a technological dead-end.[56] It was an electronic machine that could run a program but a machine that also included older, slower electromechanical elements. The same was true for much smaller IBM electronic machines, including many Card-Programmed Electronic Calculators then in service. But Watson had dedicated the massive, glitzy SSEC machine to the use of science, and its value as a prestige builder and public relations bonanza was undeniable. IBM had the jump on Remington Rand in publicity. Even so, Mauchly saw a golden opportunity for Remington Rand with UNIVAC, which had beaten IBM to market with newer computer technology.[57] Mauchly argued that UNIVAC was more capable than any existing IBM equipment to attack the one sophisticated problem the inventor thought would be of greatest interest to the public: weather forecasting. For Mauchly these arguments were clearly being deployed to find an intersection of interests within his own company. He wanted Remington Rand to become fully engaged in a project close to his heart, one that he began researching in 1937 and that helped propel him into a career developing ever more powerful calculating and computing equipment. As he saw it, Remington Rand could become a fixture in the public imagination by doing something the public cared about. He also held out an alternate, more troubling prospect—that without undertaking this sort of work, Remington Rand stood to be upstaged again by IBM.

Mauchly continued to develop these themes in the second document, labeled, "Company Confidential," this one with a notation that it originally dated from July 19, 1952.[58] It was titled "A Scientific Research Bureau Is Needed." He articulated more forcefully the value of appealing to ordinary people who did not themselves comprise a market for computers. Mauchly was proposing that Remington Rand create a Scientific Research Bureau akin to a similar enterprise launched by IBM. In addition to weather forecasting, he proposed that such a center could undertake research on the application of computers to something else of widespread public concern—cancer. This could be done, he wrote, by developing "efficient methods for the coordination of scientific information." Like weather forecasting, the application of computers to information management had come to interest Mauchly personally. There is evidence the inventor was frustrated at the limitations of his role inside a large corporation.[59] So again, with the 1952 document pushing for a research bureau, Mauchly was looking to align his own scientific interests with the company's interest in prestige as a gateway to profits.[60] "We must aim our publicity at the public in general because our object is to expand the market until computers become as ordinary as telephone switchboards and bookkeeping machines," he wrote. "Everyone must know what they do, and take it for granted that certain types of jobs *should* be done by computers." The objective, as he framed it, was "to bring computers down to earth." How? This was his answer: "A succession of cases in which computers have been used to get valuable practical results." Awareness amplified by word of mouth would be key. "When an executive hears his friends talk about a UNIVAC, not as a piece of magic, but as a commonplace tool which everyone knows has done this or that important job," Mauchly explained, "he will think of the UNIVAC as a natural purchase—not as an experiment to be approached with utmost caution." Mauchly made no mention of using UNIVAC for election analysis. That idea would not surface until later in 1952. But three years after he wrote this document, Mauchly reprinted it in 1955. After the section on the benefits of appealing to the public, Mauchly added this parenthetical update: "UNIVAC has become a household word principally because of use on Election TV."

In between the July 1952 document and election night a few months later, Mauchly seized on another opportunity to publicize UNIVAC. The venue was a weekly prime-time science program on television. He used it to advance his agenda of demystifying the machine for a lay audience— albeit with a heavy dose of showmanship. In his datebook for August 11, 1952, Mauchly noted a call from Lynn Poole, host of *The Johns Hopkins Science Review*. The half-hour television program originated on Monday nights from WAAM in Baltimore, the home of Johns Hopkins University.[61] The program aired at the same time in New York, Washington DC, Philadelphia, Chicago, and several other cities, and on subsequent dates in yet more cities—about two dozen in all, on stations affiliated with the DuMont network.[62] For its shows in 1952, the *Science Review* would win one of the most coveted honors in broadcast journalism, a George Foster Peabody Award, topping an honorable mention two years earlier.[63]And it had won high praise from the *New York Times*.[64] Poole wanted to do a show about computers. Mauchly—who had earned his PhD from Johns Hopkins—was happy to oblige.[65] When the show was scheduled to air on October 27, Remington Rand circulated a city-by-city list of stations to its sales offices so they could show off the UNIVAC to business prospects, customers, and friends. "Make it a prestige builder for you," they were told.[66]

The show featuring Mauchly and the UNIVAC was titled, "Can Machines Think?" That title appeared on screen accompanied by dramatic, edgy music.[67] Host Lynn Poole appeared standing next to a goofy anthropomorphic robot as a prop, its head a boxy affair that seemed to be made of riveted plates. It had blinking light bulbs for eyes, slowly turning gears for ears, and cables coming out of its head. It was juggling a ball. When Poole threw a switch, the eyes went dark, the juggling stopped, and three themes that would dominate the broadcast were in play. One was the idea that computers were not forces unto themselves but were under human control. The second theme was the attempt, with various gadgets, to compare computer components to familiar mechanisms and activities. The third theme was an irresistible urge to engage in showmanship. In one of his "Company Confidential" documents, Mauchly had dismissed the trope of magic as an appropriate frame for the computer. But he seemed to share the magician's delight in moments of wonder—even, in a paradoxical way, by reducing the computer's amazing feats to iterations of familiar acts. Juggling—a consummate sort of wondrous performance—appears again in the show with a human juggler. Mauchly compared this to the way UNIVAC stored digital information—by the constant cycling of acoustic waves of energy through tanks of mercury. Mauchly also used specially constructed devices to demonstrate features such as the storage of information in a binary state—on or off, one or zero. There were examples of computer use that ranged from predicting the results of nuclear reactions to aggregating census data to calculating how much currency a company needed on pay day. The weather was mentioned, of course. And at the very end of the show, which had been prepared during the run-up to election night, Poole called attention to UNIVAC's upcoming task: "It's being used in elections to find out what the results are and prognosticate as the results of these elections come in by the hour in election campaigns."[68]

After the show first aired on October 27, a Remington Rand sales manager reported that it had generated "a considerable number of comments."[69] Poole received a letter of praise from the representative of a New York architectural firm who wanted to reach Mauchly to "get his opinion of floor load requirements or current requirements these machines might require in the 'Office of the Future.'"[70] The U.S. Census, the first UNIVAC customer, inquired about getting copies of the show.[71] *Variety*, an entertainment industry publication, ran a review.[72] It concluded that although Mauchly's attempts to explain the computer in simple terms were "overly technical and sketchy for lay viewers," the episode "got across the wonderful achievement which such scientific robots represent" and "underlined the importance of the human factor—the machine can only do what men direct it to do." The cooperation of the UNIVAC camp with the Johns Hopkins science program and with election-night planners at CBS was evidence of a belief among at least some at Remington Rand that in the fall of 1952, there was a competitive need to generate as much positive publicity as possible. In memos back and forth, Mauchly and Al Seares, a key marketing figure at Remington Rand, were frustrated that there was not more awareness of the need for publicity and the benefits of using a magazine circulated by Remington Rand in the business community.[73] In a memo aimed at getting the attention of the magazine's editorial staff, Seares wrote that the Eckert-Mauchly division, "with their limited staff and facilities, were doing more along this line than we have done since they became a part of Remington Rand."[74]

While IBM was behind in the race to get the first true electronic, stored-program computer to market, the company was already a key player in the evolution of advanced machinery for complex calculation. One of the precursors to IBM's move into commercial electronic computers was a device called the Automatic Sequence Controlled Calculator, also known as Mark I. It was gigantic—fifty-one feet long and eight feet high. IBM financed it, constructed it, and installed it at Harvard during World War II. Mark I was the idea of a Harvard graduate student, Howard H. Aiken. He would go on to become a professor there, head of the Harvard Computation Laboratory, and one of the biggest names in the early history of computing. Mark I was not electronic. It relied instead on electromechanical moving parts for its operation. And while it could carry out a program, those instructions could not be stored internally.[75] The Selective Sequence Electronic Calculator that IBM placed in service a few years later within view of crowds on 57th Street was more advanced than the Mark I. But it, too, did not represent the future of computing technology. Like the Mark I, the SSEC was a one-of-a-kind machine. On the other hand, IBM's bread-and-butter business was in machines that could be produced in quantity.

In the fall of 1952, IBM was working intensely to bring out its commercial electronic, stored-program machine—the Defense Calculator, also known as the 701. This was a computer, the company's first in the modern sense of the word. Unfortunately for IBM, the first of the IBM 701 models was not due to be completed and shipped for display at company headquarters in Manhattan until after the election, when it would take the place of the dismantled Selective Sequence Electronic Calculator.[76] Even so, being behind Remington Rand in getting the newest computer into public view did not mean IBM was behind in preparing the ground for a commercial computer industry. In fact, IBM was the leader in the type of information processing that relied on older technology—electromechanical punched-card equipment. After World War II, IBM pioneered and became the leader in the application of electronics to that technology. The company turned out a series of electronic calculators that could be set up to carry out a limited number of steps in sequence at speeds previously unheard-of for commercial machines. Thousands were eventually placed in service. Along the way IBM followed the lead of one of its customers, linking together an electronic calculator and other IBM equipment to carry out longer programs from punched cards and plugboards and make use of storage units that were "electromechanical." These clusters of equipment—marketed as Card-Programmed Electronic Calculators, or CPCS—were being produced by the hundreds in the early 1950s while customers waited for the arrival of more sophisticated devices—that is, computers.

The CPC was not a computer in the sense that word has come to mean, including the capacity for an internally stored program capable of modifying itself as it runs.[77] But it carried out computer-like functions. An IBM historian, Emerson W. Pugh, has argued that CPCS were critical to laying the groundwork for IBM's leadership in commercial computing. They supported IBM's customer base with equipment and experience in programming before the competition brought the UNIVAC to market—and then even afterward when only a handful of UNIVAC computers were in operation. Likening the evolution of computers to the sixteenth-century paradigm shift in theories about the cosmos, computer historian Paul Ceruzzi wrote that the CPC's "combination of program cards, plugboards, and interconnecting cables was like the epicycles of a late iteration of Ptolemaic cosmology, while the Copernican system was already gaining acceptance."[78] But while the CPC might have been a technological dead end, it was available, it was affordable, and, Ceruzzi wrote, "customers needing to solve difficult engineering problems . . . accepted it."

While IBM and Remington Rand were clear leaders in the emerging computer field, *Fortune* magazine reported that there was also a "battle of the robots" underway.[79] By *Fortune*'s count at the start of 1952, some ninety organizations were "working on some form of computer." These ranged from large-scale, general-purpose, electronic digital machines like the UNIVAC to special-purpose equipment designed for particular tasks such as handling airline reservations or magazine subscriptions. Laboratories were said to "hum and glitter with the look of another world." Notably there were small-scale computers being designed—and some were already built—by companies that made calculating machines and other office equipment. These companies were jumping into the fray in commercial computing. While giving up speed in return for reduced size, the small-scale computers, noted *Fortune*, "begin to foreshadow the true office robot."[80]

IBM was taking notice. In the company's top ranks, there was concern. In the late 1940s, word had made its way up through the chain of command about various engineering conferences around the United States where electronic computing projects were discussed.[81] Warnings were coming from customers, too, that the days of punched-card technology were numbered. Within IBM, electronics were not uniformly seen as the way forward. Thomas J. Watson Jr., son of the founder and then a high-ranking company executive, wrote in his autobiography about the "built-in resistance to exploring electronic computing."[82] The younger Watson himself admitted to not grasping at first the promise of electronics after having gotten a look at the World War II-era ENIAC. The unanticipated level of interest in IBM's first electronic calculators in the early post-war years helped him understand what might lie ahead. But even as IBM focused on bringing out its first true computer—big, powerful, and expensive—other companies were racing ahead in the arena of smaller and more affordable machines.

Engineering publications, conferences, and the *Fortune* article were not the only signs of this ferment. In May 1952 the Navy Mathematical Computing Advisory Panel convened a symposium at the Pentagon with a title reflecting the rising interest in smaller machines: "Commercially Available General-Purpose Electronic Digital Computers of Moderate Price."[83] By one account more than 250 people attended. The report's distribution list—which I came across in the archives of the National Museum of American History—had hundreds of names from government agencies, the military, universities, contractors, computing equipment manufacturers, and other corporations.[84] The report's preface was authored by Mina Rees, director of the Mathematical Sciences Division in the Office of Naval Research. She wrote this: "Until recently, all commercially available general purpose automatic digital computers were large and cost many hundreds of thousands of dollars. Within the past year, however, a number of manufacturers have developed smaller, more compact (usually slower) automatic computers for sale at less than one hundred thousand dollars."[85] She noted that these smaller computers made use of magnetic-drum storage—a means of saving and retrieving units of information from a metal cylinder. This advance also made computers cheaper to produce. "With this drastic reduction in the cost, it has become possible for agencies with modest budgets to consider acquiring such machines," she wrote. The symposium gave the manufacturers a chance to display their wares in Washington for potential buyers from government agencies. The report included copies of talks on seven small computers, along with diagrams and photographs. None of these small computers were the work of IBM or Remington Rand— but representatives of both companies were on the distribution list and may well have attended.

The free-for-all among firms vying for a place in the hoped-for small-computer market was not hard to miss in other ways, too. The September 1952 issue of *Scientific American* featured stories about computing. The New York-based Electronic Computer Corporation ran an ad announcing the Elecom 110—"A General Purpose Computer to meet all your Computing Needs"—for $62,500.[86] The Computer Research Corporation of California ran an ad announcing, "3 Important New Electronic Digital Computers," including a small general-purpose machine, the CADAC 102-A.[87] The computer division of Bendix Aviation Corporation ran an ad announcing the development of "Bendix Digital Computers."[88]

Inside IBM, various camps struggled over the best way forward in the face of threats that were clear by the fall of 1952.[89] On the one hand, the company would soon have on the market a computer to compete with the powerful UNIVAC for complex, high-speed computing jobs. But IBM was staring at a wave of competition for more standard business and scientific applications of interest to the sort of buyers who would not be willing to pay for high-end equipment. In the lower-cost market, IBM faced a new Remington Rand electronic calculator. And there was the threat of the newest wave—the relatively small, moderately priced stored-program computers using magnetic drum technology.

Internal debates over IBM's future engendered what historians of the company and its technology have termed a "chaotic period."[90] Some at IBM favored incremental enhancement of existing technology. Others favored abandonment of that traditional approach. But there was no doubt that action was needed. A memo from IBM's Future Demands Department is telling.[91] It described the fate that awaited IBM if the company did not move quickly. The memo was blunt. The older Card-Programmed Electronic Calculator, it said, "must be recognized as competitively obsolete, no longer able to maintain our position, and incapable of being improved sufficiently to reestablish our leadership."

That anxiety ramped up after IBM's chief competitor was featured on CBS television on election night in 1952. On November 12, eight days after the election, an IBM vice president called attention again to dire consequences if the company did bring a magnetic drum-based computer to market.[92] A few days after that, he prepared a list titled "Competitive Drum Computers."[93] It identified seven commercial machines and their manufacturers. These included a "Drum Computer" from Remington Rand, machines developed by Consolidated Engineering Corporation and Hogan Laboratories, and several computers from names well known for calculating machines and office equipment—Marchant, Underwood, National Cash Register, and Monroe. Among the seven computers listed was the Monroe Calculating Machine Company's new device, the Monrobot.

There is no mention in those November 1952 memos of the Monrobot's role on election night earlier that month. But during this period, the lack of consensus about a way forward was a problem that came before Thomas J. Watson Jr. By then he had succeeded his father as IBM's president. At a meeting on November 18, Watson voiced concern about competitive threats. A participant's notes reported "considerable discussion" of a magnetic drum machine that had been in the works at IBM for some time. Watson wanted to know "who or what" was holding up that project.[94] He wanted to move forward. IBM was referring to this computer as the "MDC," or Magnetic Drum Calculator. It had a target date fifteen months away. Watson breathed new life into the MDC.[95] It would hit the market in 1954 as the "650." Though not as sophisticated, powerful, or fast as IBM's other computers, the 650 would be compared to Ford's Model T—a mass-produced machine intended for basic business applications that would outsell all competing drum-based models and help move IBM into leadership of the market for commercial computers.[96]

All of that was in the uncertain future in the fall of 1952. The memos cited here do not reveal whether the Monrobot and the publicity surrounding its election-night role played a part in IBM's deliberations. The Monrobot certainly was not the most robust of the drum computers. But it was one of a class of machines—smaller, more affordable, and less complicated than the room-sized giants—that would play a key role as computer producers and consumers worked out, over time, what computers should be able to do, who should operate them, and how they should be used. The competition was not merely between companies in the emerging computer marketplace. There was also intense competition between ideas about computing. The Monrobot was based on a particular idea that would be seen in play on election night—small enough to be trucked to Rockefeller Center and installed at NBC's election-night headquarters. And it was accessible enough that NBC would tout the ease with which it could be mastered and operated.

That the Monroe Calculating Machine Company would help introduce Americans in 1952 to computers by playing a role in election-night reporting was not in any way destined to happen. In fact, fifteen years earlier, Monroe executives opted not to go down a path that would have gotten the company involved in the previously noted pre-computer project at Harvard. In 1937 Harvard's Howard Aiken had come up with the idea for a large-scale electromechanical machine that would carry out lengthy and complex calculations in an automatic sequence of steps. Aiken took the idea to George C. Chase, an inventor and Monroe's director of research. Chase, in turn, took the idea to the management at Monroe, hoping to enlist his company in Aiken's plan. But after mulling it over for several months, according to Aiken, Monroe's management decided at that point to take a pass. Aiken went to IBM instead, and IBM ultimately provided financial support and built Aiken's machine, the Harvard Mark

I.[97] Its home base upon completion, the Harvard Computation Laboratory, would become both a landmark in the history of computing and a place at which other pioneers would get their start.

In the late 1940s, the contours of a market for commercial computing were beginning to take shape. Aiken heard that Monroe had become interested in constructing a small computer. He passed the information on to a Harvard student, William H. Burkhart, who was then completing an undergraduate degree in mathematics. Burkhart worked in Aiken's computation lab, contributing to the theory and design of electronic computing and control circuits. Burkhart wrote to Monroe, expressing interest in working on the project mentioned by Aiken.[98] That 1949 letter survives and was provided to me by Burkhart's widow, Dorothy, when I visited her in California. Burkhart's own vision, made clear in that letter, was that a small computer such as one Monroe might be interested in building—he called it "a small digital calculator with provision for storage and sequencing"—was precisely what he would be producing himself if he had the resources.[99] Burkhart's vision was not the more common one of that period, in which machines filled entire rooms, worked at lightning speed, and required highly trained experts to operate them. In his letter to Monroe, he explained that he had a "well-founded suspicion that large-scale machines are inefficient when initial cost and total number of operation and maintenance personnel are considered." Burkhart got the job at Monroe. By the time of the 1952 presidential campaign a few years later, he had already applied for several patents for computer components and played a lead role in the design and development of the Monrobot computer featured on election night. He even ended up in a postelection edition of *Newsweek*, quoted as the Monrobot's "manager."[100] The magazine was a memento he saved for the rest of his life.

Burkhart was an unlikely person, in some ways, to have ended up where he did. Hailing from rural Honesdale in northeast Pennsylvania, he would recall decades later that he loved learning on his own about math and physics but did not care about grades. As a result, his high school record was not the best. His recollections, committed to writing in a series of biographical sketches he drafted before his death in 2000, suggest he was one of those boys who loved taking apart devices to see how they worked, including their circuitry. He sought out books to help him understand what he could not figure out on his own.[101] And he loved solving problems. He loved that, he would explain, the way a dog "loves to chase squirrels," adding, "I never got over that sickness." After graduating from high school in 1940, college was not in his plans—not immediately anyway. He went to work as a radio serviceman and then for Western Electric testing aircraft radio equipment and telecommunications systems. After the United States entered World War II, he found himself in the United States Army Signal Corps, studying electronics and electricity and waiting his turn to serve. But the trajectory of his life— and his future college prospects—would change when the Army sent him to Harvard with a group of soldiers who were tasked with studying engineering. After a semester the Army shipped him off to Europe. He moved from England to France to Germany setting up radio and telephone communications for the American forces. Following the war he applied to Harvard, he would say later, because he expected that his high school record would keep him from a college that cared about those grades. At Harvard, ironically, the matter of grades would be trumped, he wrote, by having "done very well" there when sent by the Army before his deployment to Europe.[102] He was admitted to study mathematics and would graduate in 1949.

Burkhart is not a standard figure in contemporary histories of early computing. But he began making his mark in two ways while still an undergraduate. The first of these was the construction of a machine combining electrical circuits and logical reasoning. From his earliest interest in what would come to be called computers, he had an idea that such devices could be small, accessible, and applied to more than numerical calculation.[103] During his sophomore year, Burkhart took a one-semester course in mathematical logic from the noted philosopher Willard V. Quine. Work in the course involved developing truth tables— basically, determining whether one or more statements are true or false based on a set of premises. Burkhart and a classmate, Theodore Kalin, had read a paper by another seminal figure, Claude Shannon, about a relationship between electrical switching circuits and mathematical or symbolic logic. In the spring of 1947, the two students set about building their device—from about $150 in materials—that would generate truth tables automatically from a set of conditions programmed into it by settings created with various types of switches.[104] The results were displayed as a pattern of lights, in which a glowing bulb was equivalent to "true." The machine was dubbed the Kalin-Burkhart Logical-Truth Calculator. It was small enough to fit under a bed—sixteen inches tall, thirty inches wide, and thirteen inches deep.[105] But it was robust—said to take less than a minute to determine the truth of one hundred "cases" based on a set of rules. It could solve problems in which there were up to a dozen different conditions. The Logical-Truth Calculator received some notoriety in that era, both as the first electrical machine to solve problems in logic and for its diminutive size. That notoriety included an entire chapter in a notable 1949 book, Edmund C. Berkeley's *Giant Brains, or Machines that Think*, one of the first works of its kind for a popular audience. The book's author was a 1930 Harvard alumnus who had returned to work in Aiken's computation laboratory during the war. Berkeley argued that although the diminutive Kalin-Burkhart machine was built at a tiny fraction of the cost of other "giant brains" described in the book—including ENIAC and the Harvard Mark I—one could "properly call this machine a mechanical brain because it transfers information automatically from one part to another of the machine, has automatic control of the sequence of operations, and does certain kinds of reasoning."[106] The device was demonstrated in June 1947 before several logicians and engineers. It was moved for a time to a life insurance company, where it was studied for its potential application in "drafting contracts and rules."[107] An impediment to its wide use, wrote Berkeley, was the inadequate appreciation of its potential applications. But, he concluded, here was "an electrical instrument for logical reasoning, and it seems likely that its applications will multiply."[108] In fact, Burkhart would later note, as would science writer Martin Gardner, that no practical application could be found for the Kalin-Burkhart device itself. But in a book first published in 1958 for laymen, *Logic Machines and Diagrams*, Gardner wrote that Kalin and Burkhart's invention was of "great historic interest, marking a major turning point in the development of logic machines."[109]

Burkhart's other contribution to early developments in computing was his work at Aiken's lab while still an undergraduate.[110] At the time, Aiken was overseeing the design and development of a new, large-scale digital computing device—the Mark III, the first of Aiken's machines to incorporate electronics.[111] Aiken set Burkhart to work designing electronic circuits. Burkhart later recalled applying his knowledge of symbolic logic for reduction of the number of vacuum tubes needed to carry out particular tasks.[112] Burkhart received a nod from Aiken in print when the enterprising student's work on "control-circuit theory" was included in a volume Harvard published in 1951.[113]

In his letter to the Monroe Calculating Machine Company in the summer of 1949, Burkhart wrote that "having now completed all but the final editing of the results of our research on design of calculator circuits, I feel no pressing obligation to remain at the Harvard Computation Laboratory and have turned my attention again to consideration of small-scale machine design."[114] He saw in Monroe the opportunity to do just that, writing that "in the event that construction of such a general purpose calculator at Monroe is still a possibility I should enjoy more than anything else working with such a project."

Monroe was headquartered in Orange, New Jersey, just outside Newark and about twelve miles from Manhattan. Burkhart found himself at a company with thousands of employees focused primarily on the design, manufacture, and sale of calculating machines and related equipment. The customers were businesses, government offices, educational institutions, and the military. The company's annual report covering 1952 dated the start of its "secret" work on computers to 1949, which was the year Burkhart arrived.[115] The company's report for 1949, published in early 1950, referenced work on an early Monrobot prototype as part of a discussion of the company's research initiatives: "What seemed most likely to be remembered about 1949's research was the important growth of its effort in electronics. Just where MONROBOT I (our study model) would lead nobody knew. But the dimly perceived possibilities were wondrous."[116]

Even as Monroe ventured into the world of computers, the base was expanding for its traditional calculating and business machine operations—deemed in the company report covering 1949 to be "less dramatic but more important to sales."[117] In a later report on its activities for 1951, Monroe boasted that the growing company had "made and sold more calculating machines than any competitor." It had manufactured more than 68,000 calculating, adding, and accounting machines.[118] In 1952, the year Monroe would go public with the results of its computer development efforts, the company started with 230 domestic branch offices and ended the year with 36 more. Monroe was also adding capacity to a plant in southern Virginia and a subsidiary in the Netherlands. Still, by the end of 1952, Monroe was also ready to increase its commitment to new technologies The company opened a new plant in Morris Plains, New Jersey, and moved its electronics operations there, including what it called the "Monrobot Laboratory."

A description of the work of the Monrobot Laboratory printed just a few months after the 1952 election provides a glimpse into the ferment then taking place nationwide within companies manufacturing an array of products—from office machines to television sets—where electronics were changing the way things worked.[119] Electronics were also changing the makeup of the workplace at that cutting edge. At the Monrobot Laboratory, the executive in charge, E. J. "Jay" Quinby, had a long resume. He had more than three decades of research experience, much of it with RCA Laboratories and then as a senior Navy officer during World War II.[120] He held patents related to radios, loudspeakers, phonograph records, and railway electric signals.[121] After concluding his Navy service in 1949, Quinby was brought into Monroe, he recalled in a memoir, to "establish the necessary research and development" to help the company move into computers.[122] In addition to Quinby, Monroe touted the work being done by its "inventors from the new world of electronics and electrical engineering."[123] The "key personnel" under Quinby were said to be "young men with an average age of thirty, progressive, imaginative men who are highly trained in the techniques of exploring the unknown, yet seasoned and practical men with a mature approach to their profession."[124] Over half had served in World War II. And they came from top schools—including three with master's degrees from Harvard. Richard LaManna, who would go on to rise through the company ranks, was a freshly minted engineering graduate from the University of Maryland when he arrived at Monroe in 1951. Dorothy Burkhart helped me track him down. He told me he had been excited back in the early 1950s about the prospect of being on the cutting edge. The work did not disappoint. "Everything we did," he said, "was new."[125] Dorothy Burkhart also helped me track down Irving Gardoff, who came to work at Monroe in 1952. All of those people who were designing and touting new computers, Gardoff told me, did not know for sure who the customers might turn out to be. And that, he said, was because the customers—the potential ones—did not know they were going to be customers.[126]

The Monrobot was not at all robust. But its other diminutive features—in size, price, and complexity—placed it among a category of early computers that attracted the attention of the Pentagon in 1952. The U.S. military was not only an important early customer of computers but an important player in the exchange of new ideas about computing. At the previously mentioned 1952 symposium organized by the Navy, the Monrobot—with the formal name of "MONROBOT III Electronic Calculator"—was one of the seven small computers that were featured.[127] The report submitted by Monroe for the symposium, under Quinby's name, featured a publicity photograph showing a young woman sitting at the computer's keyboard. And it included this claim: "The most important single feature of the MONROBOT is its simplicity. . . . Even a novice finds it possible to program problems after the first day's acquaintance with the input keyboard."[128] Another big selling point was the Monrobot's economy of space. The report noted that "only seven hundred vacuum tubes and two hundred diodes are employed throughout."[129] The Monrobot even looked like office furniture. The unit in which data was entered and programs were run was housed in a cabinet of the size and appearance of an office desk. This was connected by cable to the rest of the Monrobot's equipment, which could sit on top of an ordinary office desk. These peripheral components included a small keyboard for the entry of data and programs. There was a printer and a device for entering data and programs into the computer through holes punched in paper tape. The desk-sized computer unit included a magnetic drum on which data and instructions would be stored, along with the vacuum tubes and circuits for carrying out calculations. The Monrobot even had air conditioning—a mechanism for piping in cool air to counteract the heat generated by all those vacuum tubes.

The computer contained a special power source, too, that would allow it to start up gradually and avoid burning out its tubes, a hazard for computers and other electronic gear of that era. LaManna told me he could locate dead tubes by darkening the room to find the ones that were not lighting up.[130] The Monrobot could be programmed to do sequences of basic mathematical operations—addition, subtraction, multiplication, and division. It could compare numbers and, based on the result, select the next step to take in a program. It could undertake calculations on the results of previous calculations. And the program could be modified automatically based on the results of a particular step. A program could be set up to import data from punched tape and to print out results in text and numbers, including tables. Standard paper or special forms could be used. The Monrobot's magnetic drum memory could hold one hundred positive or negative numbers. Each number could be up to twenty decimal digits, with a decimal point fixed between the tenth and eleventh digits. The computer's memory could also hold the "operational orders" that comprised a program—listed in various Monroe documents as up to either one hundred or two hundred steps.[131]

Compared to other computers of the day, the Monrobot was slow. It could carry out 450 additions or subtractions per minute and 100 multiplications or divisions. On election night CBS correspondent Charles Collingwood would tell viewers that the UNIVAC could do 2,000 additions in a second, 500 multiplications, and 250 divisions.[132] The Monrobot was also slow compared to other small computers featured in that Navy symposium. Monroe made no secret of the Monrobot's rate of calculations but tried to put the best spin on that. The Monrobot's operating manual made a virtue of the computer's speed by comparing it favorably to pre-computing technology. With the Monrobot, said the manual, "computation is completely automatic and is carried out at a speed greatly exceeding that attainable by mechanical calculators."[133]

Company literature also wanted prospective clients to understand that the speed of a particular operation was not the only consideration related to time and efficiency. Ease of use was important, too. A brochure that appears to date from April 1952 described the Monrobot as a "general-purpose, sequence-controlled, digital computer" and noted that it had "been developed during the past three years to meet the increasing demand in many business, military, and research organizations for a compact, reasonably priced, and easily operated digital computer having wide numerical range and versatility of application."[134] Readers were reminded of the following: "The total operating time normally required to solve a problem by digital computation includes not only machine operating and printing time but also the time necessary for programming (or coding) the problem, scaling the problem, converting inputs to the number system used by the computer, and converting outputs back to the decimal system." The Monrobot's advantage, per its manufacturer, was that "these non-computational procedures have been either eliminated or greatly simplified." In addition, the fact that one could operate the Monrobot without a great deal of special expertise was also held up as an important factor in considering the time needed for computer use. "The programming of problems is straightforward and requires no special mathematical training," said the brochure. "Common sense and facility in handling elementary algebraic operations are the only prerequisites for a good programmer." It added, "No knowledge of the internal operation of the equipment is required."

Because of the Monrobot's relative simplicity and its ability to work from stored programs, Monroe positioned its new computer in two general ways. One was for problems that were not too complicated but involved repeated operations on large volumes of data. That was just the sort of thing needed in accounting, banking, and the actuarial work done at insurance companies. The other general category of use was for complex calculations in engineering, applied mathematics, and science. Some applications, said the brochure, were on problems where "the usefulness of electronic digital computers has already been firmly established." And other applications were on meeting challenges for which, as Monroe put it, "the potentialities of these computers are just beginning to be appreciated."[135]

Monroe's characterization of the market was not unlike that of other computer makers. But while computer boosters were eager to expand awareness of these "potentialities" in the early 1950s, there is no evidence before the second half of 1952 that they thought about the work of news organizations when envisioning future uses for these wondrous new machines. The dovetailing of the manufacturers' desire for attention with TV journalists' desire for accuracy, speed, and respect was not an intersection of interests in either camp's playbook before 1952. Election night would become the crucible for bringing them together.

4 | Project X versus Operation Monrobot

With the 1952 election just a few months away, television news executives had a problem. Despite their best intentions, efforts at reporting the election as a visual story in 1948 had fallen short—"fumbling rather badly," in fact, as the *New York Times* radio and television writer Jack Gould had put it.[1] And then there was that whole business of print and on-air journalists who were blinded in 1948 by preelection polls. They were embarrassed on election night by missing the trend in favor of the longshot and eventual winner, the incumbent, Pres. Harry Truman. Television's appeal and credibility as a news medium were on the line. Meanwhile, the idea of computers as commodities was alluring to companies that manufactured appliances and office machines. They were expanding into the computer space with models large and small, fast and slow, expensive and less so. All were eager for attention. They wanted to reach out beyond their initial deals with government agencies, the military, the insurance industry, universities, and big corporations.[2] The competition was fierce. In the months before the 1952 election, the paths of the computer people and TV news people would intersect. When they did, as a matter of circumstance rather than destiny, both sides saw an opportunity for mutual benefit. They worked together despite the risk of failure and embarrassment. Plans for collaboration developed quietly in the summer and quickened in the fall before going public with splashy announcements. Then the game was on—especially in the competition between CBS and NBC. For each, collaboration outside their domain of expertise and comfort—alliances with computer engineers, programmers, and mathematicians—would be the way forward in this grand gamble.

One axis of collaboration developed between CBS and makers of the giant UNIVAC computers. That chain of events can be pieced together from contemporary accounts and memoirs. The joint plan was most likely hatched in August or September of 1952. For CBS the idea that would forever change the way Americans experience election nights came not from the world of broadcasting but from an engineer. Arthur F. Draper, then in his early 40s, had worked for a pioneering manufacturer of radios. He had been a Navy aviator. And he had been in charge of engineering for an aviation company.[3] When that company was bought by Remington Rand, Draper became leader of a unit in Norwalk, Connecticut, that was focused on new products. His primary duty was to oversee the integration of another firm into Remington Rand—the Philadelphia-based Eckert-Mauchly Computer Corporation, named for the UNIVAC's two inventors.[4] Draper recounted in a 1953 paper about the election-night project that "the possibility of tackling this job was first discussed some six months before the election," which would date it to the spring of 1952.[5] He had no way of knowing then that he would be tested under fire on election night as the human face of the UNIVAC, having to explain live to a television audience of millions why things did not go as smoothly as planned.

But that was in the future. First, there was the question of whether the election-night task was feasible. Draper put that question to UNIVAC coinventor John Mauchly.[6] It became clear that outside help was needed.[7] Mauchly engaged an expert in statistics, Max A. Woodbury of the University of Pennsylvania, to work out the formulas.[8] When I traveled to Birmingham, Alabama, to meet Woodbury, he explained that he and Mauchly had gotten to know each other at a seminar led by a famous statistician, John W. Tukey.[9] In a postelection report, Woodbury gave October 7 as the date he was formally engaged. That was just four weeks shy of the election.[10]

Woodbury recalled that a Remington Rand publicist, Arch Hancock, had reached out to him at Mauchly's suggestion. The link to CBS was one step closer. Sig Mickelson, the news director at CBS, wrote in a memoir that the proposed collaboration with Remington Rand surfaced after the network's election-night plans were well along.[11] Paul Levitan, a senior member of the CBS election-planning staff, had gone to lunch with a Remington Rand publicist. As Mickelson recalled, Levitan "burst into my office with stars in his eyes. . . . His excitement was generated by an offer he had received to supplement our broadcasting of election returns by using a device that would enable us to predict the outcome of the election at an early hour, while polls were still open in many states." He was talking about UNIVAC. Levitan had been assured, said Mickelson, that the computer "could produce accurate projections, provided we could deliver the essential raw material to create a data base and a competent programmer could be found." Elmer W. Lower, who would later work at CBS before becoming president of ABC News, wrote of some conversations with Levitan about the origins of the CBS-UNIVAC plan.[12] In Lower's account, Levitan initially approached Remington Rand to secure hundreds of typewriters and calculators for election night. Levitan met with Hancock, described as "a veteran newspaper reporter-turned-public relations executive." "Before their conference was over," Lower wrote, "Levitan had a brand-new idea in his head and a $600,000 electronic toy in his pocket. . . . The new toy was UNIVAC I." Precisely when this encounter between Levitan and Hancock took place varies in the telling. Mickelson dated it to early August. Lower put it in the week after Labor Day. On election night CBS correspondent Charles Collingwood would report that twenty-five people had been working on the election-prediction project for six weeks—in other words, since late September.[13] While these and other accounts of the origins of the CBS-UNIVAC plan might not match in every detail, the overall picture is clear.[14] Initially, there was interest at Remington Rand. The brainstorming expanded beyond the realm of engineers to include a statistician, a publicist, and finally CBS news staff.

Mickelson saw this as a winner for CBS in three ways. The computer could be used for quick analysis. It could provide a competitive edge. And it could boost both ratings and prestige. "If the parts meshed properly and the program was properly written, we could in all probability announce the winner of the presidential race while our competitors were still floundering in a sea of unsorted data," Mickelson wrote later, adding, "The novelty value of using UNIVAC was certain to attract attention from both viewers and the print media."[15] He knew a computer could perform what he called "mathematical miracles." It could be promoted ahead of time, he said, and "might give us the additional top spin that we needed to build our ratings to a level that would permit us to fight it out on even ground with the (at the time) far larger NBC." He also recalled covering elections in Minnesota in the 1940s. Back then, in the pre-computer days, the analysis of past trends in key areas allowed him to foresee the outcome from early returns.[16]

CBS did not go public with the UNIVAC plans at first but did refer to them with an air of mystery. On September 25 the network issued a press release on its arrangements for election night. These were said to have begun taking shape in March. Walter Cronkite was named as "anchorman"—a relatively new term in broadcast journalism.[17] Key members of the "crack news team" were listed—Edward R. Murrow, Charles Collingwood, Douglas Edwards, Lowell Thomas, and others. Don Hewitt—who would go on to launch *60 Minutes*, one of the most successful television news programs—would be the director. Levitan would oversee "pick-ups" from cameras around the country. Fritz Littlejohn, the CBS television news managing editor, was to control assignments and the routing of incoming dispatches. And Mickelson, per the release, was to be in charge of "more than two hundred editorial, technical, and production personnel in the giant task of showing what happens as the nation's voters go to the polls." He boasted that the CBS team "constitutes the largest television task-force ever assembled to cover a one-day public event." The broadcast would originate from three large studios at Grand Central Terminal. There was mention of "new and improved visual aids—some of them still a trade secret." Staffers at CBS were getting ready with background information. There was a nod to the sponsor—Westinghouse Electric Corporation. And there was one other breathless hint of what was to come: "Mr. Mickelson said that details of a revolutionary method, involving the latest scientific principles, for informing the public of what is happening around the country as it happens—along with its possible significance—will be revealed just prior to Election Day."

That release did not elaborate. But CBS soon let the word out. On October 14 the network announced this: "CBS-TV to Use Giant Electronic 'Brain' [on] Election Night."[18] One benefit of this tool, together with the aforementioned "team of crack CBS-TV newsmen," was to be speed—"lightning-speed," in fact. This "latest and most versatile of the 'Giant Brains' that the new science of electronics has produced" was to help "give the viewing audience accurate foreknowledge of election results at an earlier hour than ever before possible." CBS pointed out that "the 'brain' does not think creatively, as yet." But it could do the work of four hundred clerks. At "about 18,000 times normal brain size," it was said to be able to do 2,000 additions in a single second, 500 multiplications, or 250 divisions. Returns were to be transmitted by various means to UNIVAC's home base in Philadelphia. Results of the computer's analysis were then to be transmitted back to CBS by means of a large screen mounted in the studio.

The CBS announcement provided details about the methodology: "For many weeks prior to November 4, a team of statisticians, mathematicians, researchers, and political analysts will have fed into UNIVAC's fabulous 'memory' the election results of each state in the 1944 and 1948 elections." This data would include the "total popular and electoral vote for each candidate in each state—all broken down to an hour-by-hour basis. The national popular vote for each candidate as it stood at each hour during those Election Days will also be fed into UNIVAC." The computer would have a base of comparative data: the voting history in eight states with separate figures for the metropolitan and nonmetropolitan vote. One could infer from the description that partial vote totals could detect trends consistent with or away from the past vote. Reports from the UNIVAC were to air at least once each hour.

The computer was also supposed to help CBS journalists by providing nationwide developments to help frame their own reports. But the plan had what would turn out to be a big flaw, one we can see in retrospect. That flaw was the flow of projections on election night in only one direction, from the UNIVAC team to CBS. There was no plan for the assessments of experienced CBS journalists to flow back the other way to provide the UNIVAC's keepers with a reality check on the computer's forecasts. This oversight would come back to plague the operation in real time. The problem stemmed from the way the risk of data errors had been envisioned. In the UNIVAC's "brain case," CBS explained, 3,500 vacuum tubes would perform the election-night math and another 2,000 tubes would keep tabs on them. The UNIVAC, per CBS, could not make an error without knowing about it. But what if there were to be a question of whether to trust the results? What if the computer program did just what one might hope for in a knockout demonstration of the UNIVAC's power by detecting a surprising deviation away from expectations? How would the computer team distinguish that sort of home run from an error? On that question the details made public in advance were silent. This now-clear oversight in planning by both Remington Rand and CBS would leave the UNIVAC team in Philadelphia on their own, struggling with whether to trust what turned out to be the computer's astonishing initial forecast.

The story of CBS plans to team up with the UNIVAC—dubbed the "Electronic Brain," the "Electronic Robot," and the "Machine with Memory"—was picked up by the Associated Press and the United Press, making its way around the country on October 15. In some places this was front-page news, in others just a brief item.[19] Both wire stories carried a Philadelphia dateline of October 14. The content suggests that Remington Rand put out its own information for the press. In Philadelphia papers the stories noted that the UNIVAC was a hometown product.[20] There was even a publicity photo. It appeared in at least one October 15 edition of the *Evening Bulletin* in Philadelphia. UNIVAC coinventor J. Presper Eckert and CBS's Walter Cronkite are seen conferring over a printout as a UNIVAC operator sits at the computer's console.[21] The Associated Press story described the UNIVAC with images its audience might grasp—the control unit was said to look "somewhat like the console for a pipe organ." The methodology was described in familiar terms as a comparison of the 1952 vote to past trends.[22] Touted as "the first use of one of the giant electronic computers on election returns," the UNIVAC's upcoming role was described as both an "adjunct" to the CBS coverage and "an experiment."[23] The coverage carried human-versus-machine overtones. While Remington Rand officials were quoted as stressing that the $600,000 computer was not psychic, it would be used to try to detect the winner from incomplete returns by making "comparisons on a scale and at a speed . . . impossible by conventional methods."

Not all journalists—some at CBS included—were ready to buy into that expectation. In a late-night broadcast over Washington-based WTOP and the CBS Network, veteran CBS newsman Eric Sevareid had reservations. He tacked these on to a news brief with this quip: "Whether the mechanical pundit will better its human betters remains to be seen."[24] Two days later Walter Cronkite displayed less than wholehearted confidence in the value of the UNIVAC plan when he was interviewed about arrangements for the November 4 broadcast.[25] The host of the interview on a CBS television affiliate in Cleveland, Dorothy Fuldheim, was herself a broadcasting pioneer.[26] Cronkite said the "basic formula" would be the same as before—a "straight report" of the returns. But, he added, there was also to be some gimmickry.[27] This would be the use of an "electronic brain," with Cronkite mistakenly referring to it as "the only one now functioning in the country." His description reflected awe for the "fantastic device," respect for the "careful" preparations by "scientists," and characterization of the gimmickry as "most interesting." But he concluded with this: "Actually we're not depending too much on this machine. It may turn out to be just a sideshow, we don't know, and then again it may turn out to be . . . very unique and of great value to some people."

Cronkite's ambiguous response and Sevareid's lack of enthusiasm for computer use on election night—when both would be called upon for their own reporting and analysis—were not universal reactions among the network's news staff. The October 14 press release from CBS noted that Charles Collingwood would have "the unusual assignment of working primarily with UNIVAC that night."[28] Collingwood took to the airwaves several times in advance of the election to talk about his assignment.[29] He did so enthusiastically.

"Project X!" The CBS plan to use UNIVAC now had a name. In his October 15 script for *Report to the West*, a CBS radio program, Collingwood described the CBS-UNIVAC plan at length.[30] He opened with a dramatic flourish and a description of the problem in need of solving. The solution was something he dubbed "Project X." "We've had a big secret around the CBS newsroom," he revealed, "but now it's out. On election night we're going to try something new." He set the scene: "You know what it's like as the results begin to come in—somebody starts rattling off a lot of figures," he explained. "You can't make any sense of it for hours, and even then some bulging brained commentator comes on to remark that it's all going to be different when the returns start coming in from the rural areas. You can sit up for hours before you get any clear idea of what's going on." The new approach was that Remington Rand was going to let CBS use the UNIVAC. He referred to it as "a prodigious monster of electronic thought." Collingwood would be assigned to consult with the UNIVAC and share the results with the audience. "I'm looking forward to it," he said, "because I've always believed that there's a mathematical basis to politics, and UNIVAC can do in his head in five seconds what it would take 50 or 60 mathematicians with slide rules and adding machines to do in a couple of hours." Collingwood used anthropomorphic imagery to help his audience get a sense of the machine: "In private life he is a retiring bureaucrat, providing the census bureau and other government branches with statistics." But on election night, said Collingwood, "he'll come into his glory." The methodology of comparison to past returns from specific areas was explained. The plan was to generate hourly predictions. The goals were not just clarity and understanding. "If it works," said Collingwood, "we should know earlier than ever before who the winner will be." In fact, as the UNIVAC is "crouched in his corner in Philadelphia, lights going on and off as he ponders the results," he said, it is "quite possible that UNIVAC will be the first one in the country to know who the next president will be."

Collingwood also sounded a theme he would repeat in the run-up to the election and right into election night. The "electronic marvel" had been programmed to detect errors when fed inaccurate data, such as a misspelled county name. "If it doesn't work," he asserted, "it won't be UNIVAC's fault." Without explicitly stating the comparison of journalist and machine, the UNIVAC was being credited with superior abilities in clarity, speed, and now accuracy. "I tell you it's a little uncanny," Collingwood said. "I'm a little scared of the thing. I don't know whether on election night UNIVAC is going to be working for me, or I'm going to be working for him."

The following week Collingwood again devoted his *Report to the West* script to the UNIVAC, which he had visited that day on a trip to Philadelphia. The man-and-machine trope was in play once more. Reminding the audience of the "mechanical brain" he described a week earlier, the self-effacing Collingwood said, "He and I are going to work together on election night—he's going to do the thinking; I am going to do the talking."[31] There were some things, he said, that "we're sort of keeping under our hat." But he gave a clue: the UNIVAC might be able to predict the vote in the West before the polls there closed. Collingwood returned to the theme of UNIVAC's infallibility—asserting that the computer "just *can't* make a mistake." But there were some caveats. UNIVAC is "a chap of absolute mechanical honesty" and "will admit that he might be wrong,"

Collingwood said. As "a gambler at heart," in Collingwood's humanizing words, the UNIVAC would report predictions along with the odds that they are correct. Beyond that, while the Remington Rand team possessed "a lot of faith not only in their mechanical brain, but in the method that's going to be used," he said, "even they admit that it may not work." There could be human error of some sort, in making assumptions, in data entry, or, he said, in "factors which we haven't taken account of." He made clear that the UNIVAC team—and he himself—had a lot riding on that not happening.

There was an unsettling awareness that public exposure on election night could cut both ways. A few days later in October, however, Collingwood made no mention of those concerns when he appeared on CBS television to promote the election-night broadcast, including footage of the UNIVAC in action. "The thing really works," he told the audience.[32] And he made good on Mickelson's earlier assessment that using the UNIVAC was promotable. Generating results "faster and more accurately than is humanly possible," the UNIVAC, Collingwood reiterated, could be the first to know the winner on election night. Whatever reservations some at CBS might have had, excitement was the public face of the computer plan. Right up to Election Day, newspaper ads proclaimed that "returns and predictions" would be made on the CBS network by the "new 'magic brain,' UNIVAC."[33] Local stations attached themselves to the same promise. In Baltimore an ad for WMAR-TV proclaimed, "A ROBOT COMPUTER WILL GIVE CBS THE FASTEST REPORTING IN HISTORY."[34]

As at CBS the precise origins of NBC's plan to deploy a computer on election night are not specified in available documents. Records do reveal that the arrangement between NBC and the Monroe Calculating Machine Company to use the Monrobot was worked out before CBS and Remington Rand went public on October 14 with the UNIVAC plan. As at CBS, NBC positioned the Monrobot in promotional materials as a novel and significant feature of the network's upcoming election-night performance.

Initial NBC plans for the 1952 conventions and election night were announced in the *New York Times* on New Year's Day.[35] The network would roll out an innovative new portable TV camera—dubbed the "walkie-talkie-lookie"—but no computer was mentioned. Philco, a manufacturer of radios, television sets, and home appliances, would pay $3.8 million to sponsor the NBC coverage. This presaged another sort of battle shaping up for the campaign season. Philco's rival, the Westinghouse Electric Corporation, had announced a few days earlier that it would be sponsoring the convention and election coverage on CBS. A third television manufacturer, Admiral, would be sponsoring ABC's coverage. "So rapidly has television grown that this year," said a Philco executive, "it is estimated that eighteen million homes will be equipped with television receivers by Election Day."[36]

Plans began ramping up in early August.[37] Reflecting a longstanding part of election-night culture nationwide among news organizations—consciousness of being on center stage—a memo between NBC executives began this way: "As you know, it has been the tradition of NBC to build an elaborate studio presentation which, while primarily for the service of the [NBC radio and television] networks, has also been used to invite important people to our studios to share in the excitement of an election night."

As the planning quickened, NBC crafted a three-page press release in September packed with details and superlatives.[38] The Monrobot was not mentioned. The headline and first sentence boasted of an "electronic brain," but context makes clear that this was not a reference to a computer. Rather, it was a term NBC applied to a custom-designed arrangement of equipment for aggregating and displaying election returns. The Monrobot was not mentioned, either, in an elaborate account of NBC's election-night innovations that appeared in the October issue of *Radio Age*—a publication of NBC's parent company, RCA.[39] A few weeks earlier, Charles H. Colledge, a manager of public affairs for NBC, had approached the National Cash Register Company requesting what was termed a "fast, visual means of presenting tallies to the television audience." The manufacturer's head of product development, Charles L. Keenoy, proposed using eight "super-sized cash register machines" with various functions. These included tabulating and displaying the presidential vote in each state, together with the percentage of the vote counted, plus the standings in congressional races. The design would allow television cameras to broadcast the numbers directly to viewers.

The Monrobot did show up in minutes of an NBC election-planning meeting on October 10 before news accounts about the CBS-UNIVAC plan.[40] "Electronic brain is being supplied by Monroe" and is "called

Monrobot," the minutes noted. Also noted was this: "Answers come out on tape and will have to be interpreted by PhD." The Monrobot was to be used for trends, while more ordinary office equipment from companies including Monroe would be involved in tabulating the votes and determining the percentage of election districts with completed vote counts.

Richard LaManna, then twenty-five, had been working on the development of the Monrobot at the time. He had come to Monroe after military service, where he was schooled in electronics, and after graduating in 1951 from the University of Maryland, where he studied electrical engineering. When asked decades later about the origins of the NBC-Monrobot plan, LaManna said he was not privy to just how the idea first surfaced. But he recalled coming to work one day at some point before the election—he has a memory of the weather being warm—and being told that he would be joining two others on a train ride from New Jersey into Manhattan. One was William Burkhart and the other was their boss, E. J. Quinby. LaManna recalled that their destination was Rockefeller Center at the offices of David Sarnoff, a titan in the broadcasting world and head of NBC's parent company, RCA. LaManna had the impression that Quinby knew Sarnoff from "way back when."[41] In fact, Quinby, like Sarnoff, had been a wireless telegraph operator back in the early years of that technology and had, like Sarnoff, worked for the American Marconi Company. In a memoir Quinby referred to Sarnoff as having been "one of our fellow seagoing radio telegraph operators."[42] Quinby went to work at RCA in 1922 in research and development, staying until World War II. And when Sarnoff's RCA acquired the Victor Talking Machine Company in Camden, New Jersey, Quinby was among those "shifted down to Camden," he wrote, "in the role of 'shock troops' to take over the old Victor establishment."[43] Whether—or how well—Quinby and Sarnoff knew each other is not discussed. And what role Sarnoff might have had to play, if any, in NBC's election-night arrangements is not clear from available records. David Sarnoff is not mentioned in those minutes of the NBC committee planning election coverage. But in the archives of the David Sarnoff Library in Princeton, New Jersey, there is a photograph of him at NBC studios on election night.[44]

LaManna remembered that when the three men from Monroe arrived at Rockefeller Center, he and Burkhart sat in a waiting room while Quinby went into Sarnoff's office for a meeting.[45] When Quinby emerged, LaManna was told that the Monrobot would play a role in NBC's election-night broadcasting. LaManna recalled expressing some concern. Work on the Monrobot, he told me, was still underway at the time. But the plan to use the Monrobot was set.

On October 14—the day CBS went public with the election-night role for UNIVAC—the fact that CBS and NBC were now locked in a competition over computers was highlighted in that day's NBC planning meeting. The minutes said this: "Discussed electronic brains—CBS's as compared to ours, with play-by-play description from C. H. Colledge, who stated that Monroe people claim the Monroe equipment is, without exception, the best and fastest available."[46] That such an exaggerated claim could be taken at face value is evidence, if nothing else, of how little computers and the distinctions between them had penetrated public consciousness. It is also apparent that the methodology to be used by the Monrobot had yet to be finalized. The minutes recorded this: "Mr. Colledge suggested the possibility of working out a system similar to that used in figuring standings of baseball teams during the last month of baseball season—when certain teams are eliminated from race (mathematically impossible for these teams to win) before final game is played." With just three weeks to go, it was also clear that how the Monrobot and the NBC news staff would interact had not been worked out until this meeting. That is when one of NBC's most experienced newsmen was tapped for the job and switched from a different assignment. The minutes noted the change: "Decided that one man should work closely with PhD; that this man should be good deal more than newsman and capable of analyzing every vote. MORGAN BEATTY selected—unanimously."

The Monrobot came up one more time in the minutes—reflecting, though not explicitly so, one major difference between the CBS and NBC plans. The giant, room-sized UNIVAC could not be transported from its home in Philadelphia. But the Monrobot was portable, which in 1952 just meant that it could be moved. Its main operating unit occupied a space about the size of an office desk and weighed about half a ton.[47] The October 14 minutes noted that the Monrobot—plus Monroe calculating machines to be used for other election-night duties—would be delivered to the NBC studios between 9:00 and 10:00 a.m. on the Saturday before the election.[48] At that point—and this would change later—a rehearsal was expected to begin that Saturday at 11:00 a.m., with others to be held on Sunday and Monday before the election on Tuesday.

The day after that meeting came news of what the competition had in mind. The CBS plan to use a computer appeared in newspapers around the country. NBC joined the battle of the "electronic brain" press releases with one of its own the next day. It was titled, "Meet Mr. Mike Monrobot, 'Electronic Brain,' Who Will Compute Election Count for NBC Radio and TV; Mechanical Wizard Can Tackle Many Problems at Once."[49] On election night, NBC's radio and television audience would, as the release promised, "meet Mike Monrobot, NBC's 'electronic brain,' for the first time." The announcement went on to tout—with more showmanship than accuracy—the machine's purported qualifications: "Mike is the fastest—not the biggest—electronic computer in the country. From his place in one corner of NBC's election night headquarters (studio 8-H, Radio City, New York), Mike will help predict and prove the outcome of presidential and state elections at the earliest possible hour." There it was, that traditional imperative for election-night journalism—speedy analysis. The computer was also seen as helping its journalistic counterparts in two ways: first, by keeping them "constantly informed on . . . trends" around the country, and second, by telling them "when a 'doubtful' state could be put in the 'sure' column . . . long before final vote counts are known." There was even a suggestion, though not articulated directly, that the computer might serve as a replacement for—or at least an equivalent to—some human functions. "In effect," the release claimed, "Mike will analyze national voting trends the way local newspapers and broadcasting analyze the trend of voting in their areas." Still, just as the NBC election-night managers had suggested in their internal memo two days earlier, a flesh-and-blood journalist would be a key part of the Monrobot presentation, per the release: "Morgan Beatty, noted news commentator, will be beside him to interpret the figures and the calculations to the viewing and listening audience."

At NBC, election-night planners must have known that the Monrobot might not be very exciting to look at when compared to the massive UNIVAC. The latter was not mentioned by name in the NBC release—nor was CBS—but the context suggests that the UNIVAC was on NBC's radar as a target to attack head on. Three strategies were evident to make the Monroe machine attractive to viewers. These involved developing a compensatory persona for "Mike" to go along with the human name. One strategy involved virtue, the second involved power, and the third involved sex appeal. The virtue was that "Mike's" diminutive size made "him" portable and innovative: "Mike looks like an office desk with an adding machine and an electric typewriter on top," the release explained. "Unlike earlier style computers that bulk so large that they can hardly be moved from the place where they were originally built, Mike will ride over from New Jersey and be installed in NBC election headquarters a few days before November 4." The Monrobot's small size, in other words, was touted as a virtue. The matter of that second strategy, power, was what viewers could not see underneath Mike's modest exterior. "Mike's makers, the Monroe Calculating Machine Company of Orange, New Jersey, describe him," the release went on, "as a 'general purpose, sequence-controlled, digital computer developed over the past three years.'" That description was likely to go over the heads of most journalists, along with the public. So the computer was recast in human terms, with a dose of humor: "Mike's real name is Monrobot and naturally he has a great head for figures. His electronic gray-matter perks so fast that Mike needs a cooling system to keep him from working up a sweat. He weighs one thousand pounds and won't lose an ounce despite constant effort all night long." And as for "all night long," there was that third strategy of sex appeal. In case viewers were not convinced that Mike provided exciting viewing, NBC appears to have adopted a stock element that shows up throughout this era in magazine and publicity photos for electronic equipment of all sorts: the girl.[50] The NBC trade release said this of "Mike": "He's fond of pretty girl secretaries, who can be readily trained to operate him, but on election night Mike will have a beautiful woman PhD for his companion. The learned doctor will establish the mathematical equations necessary to figure the trends of various election races and stuff this information into Mike's maw. A brief digestive whir and tap-tap-tap at six hundred figures a minute and out will come the answers typed automatically." The characterization continued: "Like any well-oiled brain, he makes no noise and needs only a bit of electricity for his nourishment, and perhaps a wee bit of affection from his operator."[51]

Here again was the "PhD"—and this frame is revealing in several ways. Emphasis on the "beautiful woman" who was also a "learned doctor" suggests that this, too, was another wonder—a surprise for a 1952 audience, perhaps, like the notion of a "brain" that is a machine. Having an attractive woman operating the computer might attract an audience.

The NBC release did get the attention of a genre of journalists who were emerging along with the new medium of television—newspaper columnists who wrote about television. One was Harriett Van Horne of the *New York World-Telegram and The Sun*. From the NBC release she picked up the quote about "pretty girl secretaries" and paraphrased this: "On Election night, Mike will have as his date a beautiful girl with—NBC swears—a PhD degree."[52]

In reality the "beautiful girl" was not a PhD. Her name did not appear in the release or newspaper column and would be mentioned just briefly on air on election night. She would be identified by name—Marilyn Mason—in an NBC release after the election that described her as a "photogenic PhD in mathematics" who "guided" the Monrobot.[53] But in a lighthearted account after the election, *Newsweek* would explain that the "beauteous brunette mathematician" had been given a "press agent's doctorate" and that she worked for Prudential Insurance Company, where her coworkers dubbed her "Marilyn Monrobot."[54] More than a half century later, I would learn about Marilyn Mason from her family. She had been young back then—just twenty-two years old—and had recently graduated from Pembroke, the women's college at Brown University in Providence, Rhode Island. She was gifted in mathematics and had gone to Pembroke on a scholarship. Prudential Insurance Company, based in Newark, New Jersey, had reached out to her—possibly even recruited her. By the time of the election, she had already been promoted at least once and was working in the fall of 1952 in the "methods" department, most likely on the application of business machines to the company's operations. Prudential was involved early in determining how to use computers for its work, and Mason was clearly part of that effort. Later in the fall, an after-action account at Prudential would indicate that the company had "loaned" Mason to Monroe for the Monrobot project at NBC. She not only learned how to operate the computer but would take part in rehearsals at NBC in the days before the election. She would also appear on NBC's *Today* show on Election Day in addition to the work on air that night. Monroe would pay her $300 for her work on the Monrobot effort at NBC—a tidy sum equivalent of more than $3,000 today.[55]

Women were not a common sight in the computing world at the time, even though some of the most notable pioneers had been women.[56] These included Grace Hopper, a pioneer in the development of programming and a key figure in the development of the UNIVAC. Extant records do not indicate why Marilyn Mason was chosen for the on-air work with the Monrobot at NBC. But given the cultural norms of the early 1950s— and the not-so-subtle tone of the press release—it is not hard to imagine that NBC and Monroe hoped she would stand out as a rarity in the role of expert—just as the network hoped the computer itself would attract attention. The irony is that in addition to her youthful looks, she was a talented mathematician—just not a PhD.

The NBC press release on October 16 hinted at the kind of work the Monrobot would do. The network claimed that "Mike's magnetic memory" held "hour-by-hour vote totals for every state and for every race—presidential, gubernatorial, and congressional—of the 1948 elections."[57] In late October NBC issued another release titled, "NBC Radio and TV Networks, with Staff of 250 Plus 'Electronic Brain' and Mobile Units, to Bring Election Returns to Nation; Top Commentators to Analyze Results."[58] Arrangements included a chartered airplane to transport film of Election Day. And the release quoted a network executive as saying, "The Monrobot, our electronic brain, is raring to go. He's stuffed full of information that will help him compare this year's presidential election with 1948. . . . In this all-electronic election we'll be out in front again with accurate and rapid reports."[59]

The publicity battle also featured on-air promotions and newspaper ads. In late October an NBC radio program provided a rundown of the election-night news staff and this teaser: "You need more than men to cover the myriad facts that can predict a trend."[60] What did that mean? "The fastest electronic brain will be computing the results, totaling, analyzing," NBC declared. "The job . . . will be done with lightning speed and accuracy by the Monrobot, a marvelous new electronic computer, especially designed by the Monroe Calculating Machine Company." And how would that be done? The account ended with an exaggerated claim about the Monrobot and some wishful thinking: "With this, the nation's fastest electronic computer at work, NBC will be consistently ahead with the all-important election trends." Meanwhile, an NBC newspaper ad boasted that "five hundred NBC experts, one thousand newsmen in NBC stations, and the Monrobot—America's fastest electronic brain—will bring election results, trends, and interpretations to you as quickly as the votes are counted."[61]

Monroe got in on the publicity battle, too. Here was a chance to tout other Monroe office equipment that would be used on election night—that is, calculating machines. These were the company's moneymakers. The ads addressed the imperative of speed—not by making comparisons between the Monrobot and other computers, but by proclaiming that the audience would see figures "digested in a twinkling by the unerring electronic brain of Monroe's mathematical marvel—the Monrobot and many other Monroe calculators."[62] Even companies with only a tangential connection to the computer-television alliance joined in the fray. A major utility company, Con Edison, ran ads featuring a staged photograph of NBC's Morgan Beatty, with vacuum tube in hand, leaning over the Monrobot with its top open, staring intently at the array of electronic components inside. What was Con Edison's connection? Sales of electricity stood to grow right along with an expanding market for television sets. The photo ran with a caption that touted the Monrobot as one of the country's fastest computers and noted this: "It's another reason for seeing the election on TV. And remember: 2 hours of TV viewing costs only 1¢ for electricity. Con Edison electricity is your biggest household bargain."[63]

Philco, which would be sponsoring the NBC broadcast, ran newspaper ads boasting of a first—in fact, the "WORLD'S FIRST," shouted in capital letters—and a "sensational innovation in news reporting": "ELECTION RETURNS ... BY ELECTRONIC TABULATOR."[64] Philco promised that "the electric brain that will bring you split-second vote tabulations and estimates." The ad did not mention Monroe or the Monrobot, and there is some ambiguity about just what equipment this ad was meant to describe. The anchor of NBC's election-night radio program, Merrill "Red" Mueller, would refer to results from the "Philco tabulator" when giving national and state-by-state returns. But Philco did not manufacture such a device, and the Monrobot was used for analysis rather than tabulation. Philco's logo would be ubiquitous in the NBC studio on election night, which was branded as "Philco Election Headquarters."

If IBM engaged in significant efforts to promote its own upcoming involvement in election-night news reporting, these have not left much of a trace. IBM is generally absent from accounts of election-night broadcasting plans that appeared in published wire-service dispatches, newspaper stories, the columns of television critics, and trade publications for journalism and broadcasting.[65] One exception was *New York Daily News* television writer Ben Gross, who mentioned the upcoming use at ABC of IBM equipment that he said would "aid in making lightning calculations."[66] But in other instances, IBM is not named even where there were references to ambiguously nicknamed devices to be used at ABC. The *Chicago Daily Tribune* television writer, for example, followed a mention of UNIVAC and Monrobot with a quip about "something frankly called the Monster over at ABC."[67] *Variety* reported that CBS and NBC would use "automatic electric 'brains'"—UNIVAC and Monrobot— but referred only to "a 'Robot Reporter' and a 'Trend Meter'" that ABC audiences would see, with "carbon copies" in New York, Chicago, and Los Angeles.[68] Typical accounts of "electronic brains" in election-night plans did not extend beyond UNIVAC on CBS and Monrobot on NBC.[69]

Nor was IBM's role promoted or even mentioned in newspaper ads in the way that the Monrobot and UNIVAC were. The ads for ABC touted reporters and commentators but made no mention of IBM.[70] *Philadelphia Inquirer* television writer Merrill Panitt published a column about the networks' publicity battle, including ABC's dismissive references to plans cooked up by its competitors. "Not to be outdone by the other networks' press releases on electronic brains," Panitt wrote, "ABC has issued a handout declaring that on election night, 'the trends, percentages, comparisons, analyses, and above all, the returns, will be reported over the ABC radio and TV networks by not one but forty of the fastest, most accurate brains known to human science.'"[71] Panitt continued in the tongue-in-cheek mode about those human brains: "After describing the brains as weighing approximately fifty-three ounces each and being powered by tiny and manifold electrical impulses, ABC confesses that they belong to such gentlemen as Walter Winchell, Drew Pearson, Elmer Davis, and other ABC staffers." Television writer Harriet Van Horne reported on the same ABC statement. She observed that ABC "sniffs grandly at the opposition's mechanical marvels."[72] Such sentiments mirrored this one noted in an earlier *Time* magazine item announcing the use of the Monrobot and UNIVAC and reporting that ABC was having none of it: "Says ABC's News Director John Madigan, professing a disdain for such electronic gimmicks: 'We'll report our results through Elmer Davis, John Daly, Walter Winchell, Drew Pearson—and about twenty other human brains.'"[73] In a memoir, television critic Ben Gross recounted the scene on election night 1952 at the Manhattan studios of the three networks.[74] At ABC, he wrote, "it was strictly business," with "no magical machines." He quoted John Daly as saying then that "the old-fashioned pencil and paper, plus political know-how, are still the best equipment of the political pundit." That sentiment is consistent with a letter Daly wrote four years later. In 1956, when ABC would use a computer, Daly quipped that to remain competitive on election night, "It would appear that I must concentrate on machinery and not reporting." He added contemptuously, "It's a hell of a way to do business."[75]

From available records it is unclear why IBM did not do more in the run-up to the 1952 election to call attention to itself, especially since ABC's election-night headquarters were just one of many venues where IBM would play a role in digesting returns. IBM boasted later in an in-house magazine that "batteries of IBM Electronic Calculators and high-speed IBM Accounting Machines" were used in various places.[76] There were installations of these pre-computer machines at ABC's Studio 1 in New York, site of the network's national broadcast, and in the city room of the *New York World-Telegram and The Sun*. That is where ABC's local station, WJZ-TV, would be broadcasting. The IBM service bureaus in more than twenty cities made equipment and staff available to wire services, newspapers, and government agencies for election-night work. The *Hartford Courant* and the Newspaper Printing Corporation, which handled joint business operations for the *Tulsa World* and *Tulsa Tribune*, secured help from IBM. Associated Press offices across the country were said to have lined up IBM support. So did the United Press. At Lockheed Aircraft in Burbank, California, the Mathematical Analysis Department was making its IBM installation available for NBC's reporting on affiliate stations in the West—Los Angeles, San Francisco, Denver, and Salt Lake City. Trends would be analyzed there to supplement the national broadcast originating from New York.[77]

Precisely what sort of IBM equipment was used at these venues was not made clear. The IBM account does say that the equipment at Lockheed Aircraft was a Card-Programmed Electronic Calculator, also known as a CPC. This was an arrangement of existing IBM machines serving in the late 1940s and early 1950s as a transitional technology to carry out computer-like work until IBM could get its first true stored-program commercial computers to market. A publication of the National Machine Accountants Association would later report that such Card-Programmed Electronic Calculators were used at ABC and at the *New York World-Telegram and The Sun*.[78] In describing the arrangement at both places, IBM reported that vote counts were recorded on punched cards and ingested by IBM accounting machines to produce periodic totals. Then IBM electronic calculators were used to compute percentages and compare returns from 1952 with previous elections.[79]

There must have been limited desire at IBM before and after the election to call much attention to the IBM technology to be employed. This electronic calculating equipment was already in wide use but could not compete for excitement with archrival Remington Rand's state-of-the-art UNIVAC. The first true commercial computer at IBM—the "701"—would not be rolled out until after the election. The use of IBM equipment on election night in 1952 has largely been out of sight in biographies, memoirs, and historical accounts of the company, its founders, and its machines.[80] Where the election is mentioned in such works, the references are to the use of the UNIVAC and the perception of IBM's leaders that Remington Rand had scored a public relations victory.[81]

At least two newspapers did tout IBM equipment as enhancing their own election-night plans. In a traditional "story of the story"—headlined, "The *Courant* Prepares for Operation Election"—the Hartford newspaper described an effort underway for weeks to collect data on previous voting.[82] To handle returns pouring in from across Connecticut, the *Courant* credited help from an IBM machine, described as "large mechanical-brains which by the push of a button can give an up-to-date mathematical picture of all election returns in the state in about two minutes." A photo—with the caption "MECHANCIAL BRAINS help, too"—shows a woman tending to a device that appears to be an IBM accounting machine.[83]

The *Courant* would not broadcast on election night. But it could expect that its ability to call the fate of Connecticut's electoral votes quickly would be reported by the Associated Press. Such a dispatch, in turn, might be reported to national radio and television audiences and attributed to the newspaper. The paper presciently predicted that the use of voting machines throughout Connecticut would likely enable the state to be the first with complete returns. "Because of that," the *Courant*'s preelection story reported, "the eyes of political leaders and political experts all over the country will be focused here as they look for trends."[84] There would be a chance for prestige in being on top of those trends, and the IBM equipment could help.[85]

The *New York World Telegram and The Sun* also called attention to its planned election-night use of what it called "super-speed IBM electronic calculators and accounting machines."[86] At first, IBM was absent from the newspaper's promotion of plans to collaborate with a local ABC affiliate.[87] But a subsequent story featured a breathless account, including photos, under the headline, "Lightning-Fast IBM Devices to Help Speed W-T&S Televised Vote Count."[88] There would be a card-punch machine for entering data, an electronic calculator, and an accounting machine to print out tables. Reports from these wondrous devices, it was said, would be handed off for analysis to the newspaper's "trained political observers and reporters." The IBM equipment would also help with comparisons to the 1948 vote. Newsroom activity in what was deemed the "election drama" was to be shared twice each hour with viewers watching the ABC television network.

One of the photos in that newspaper account—of a young woman tending to IBM equipment and smiling brightly at the camera—has the look of a promotional image that might have been provided by IBM. But in other ways large and small, IBM missed opportunities for advance publicity. One example was a *Los Angeles Times* account of television broadcasting that would be available to local election-night audiences. Writing of coverage originating out of NBC's new West Coast studios in Burbank, the *Times* wrote that "Lockheed's giant electronic computing machines will be used for lightning-fast calculations."[89] But there was no mention of the machines' maker, IBM. And on the same day that the *New York World-Telegram and The Sun* gave IBM a plug for its upcoming role in the city room, a separate column by television writer Harriet Van Horne mentioned the Monrobot and UNIVAC but made no mention of the IBM equipment to be used at ABC, reporting instead on that network's dismissal of its competitors' plans for electronic devices.[90]

Even at NBC and CBS, opinions about the networks' use of computers was not uniform. For example, while the NBC public-relations apparatus was positioning the Monrobot in laudatory tones, a column that ran on Election Day in the *Los Angeles Times* revealed more of a mixed reception among journalists who would be working on the NBC broadcast.[91] The writer, Bill Henry, was the 1952 version of a multimedia reporter. He had been a *Los Angeles Times* fixture for forty years—as a reporter, editor, foreign correspondent, and, since 1939, daily columnist.[92] For twenty-nine of those years, he had also been a radio reporter and commentator. When the political conventions rolled around in the summer of 1952, with the two major parties both gathering in Chicago, NBC chose Henry to play a pivotal role, including anchoring its television coverage.[93] He was comfortable broadcasting live. He had an easy manner and quick wit. On election night he would be at Rockefeller Center in New York anchoring the NBC television broadcast. In his Election Day column, he revealed what he knew of NBC's plans.[94] He referred to both the Monrobot and UNIVAC by a host of colorful monikers. "Computer" was not one of them. His more irreverent references—including "mechanical monster"—suggest he had not completely signed on to NBC's use of the Monrobot as an aid in the reporting process. But judging from his column, he understood perfectly well that grinding through a mass of numbers was not the Monrobot's only value to the network. After telling readers he was hopeful the election would terminate what he called "the disgraceful mudslinging that has characterized this campaign," Henry turned his attention to the business of reporting returns on television— that is, to the story of the story. He set up his column as a contrast of old and new. Those who had "lived long enough to be able to remember the preradio days when you eagerly awaited the shouts of the newsboys to buy an extra or waited for the wailing sound of the *Times*'s siren to cryptically tell you of the final outcome," he wrote, "you'll appreciate this TV election service all the more." Radio was cast as harking back to a simpler time, when results could be read over the air. Television brought new challenges, and election-night reporting called for innovations. The most "startling" of these, wrote Henry, "will be the official debut of the mechanical brain." In the keep of "some sort of human genius," he explained, the networks' "fearsome contraptions" were to figure results and spot trends faster than a human could.

Henry's column played the image of the machine off against NBC's venerated political commentator, H. V. Kaltenborn. Henry left no doubt that the notorious election-night gaffs of 1948 were still a fresh memory—not only at the network but among readers. And with the anthropomorphized "mechanical brain," there was a useful comparison, in Henry's tongue-in-cheek telling, by turning the image around. The machine, he wrote, was "to take the place of the human calculator, like H. V. Kaltenborn for instance, who gazed fixedly at figures, charts, and maps and kept right on insisting up to the last minute in 1948 that Harry Truman had been beaten and Tom Dewey had been elected." Henry went on to remind readers that "no less a personage" than Truman later mimicked Kaltenborn over the episode—adding to Kaltenborn's celebrity.[95] So now, wrote Henry, the "great minds of the television business" had come up with the plan to use the mechanical brain—"to do what Kaltenborn did, only it is supposed to guess right where Kaltenborn guessed wrong. And who knows?" Henry went on with the comparison, saying that while the NBC machine is named Monrobot, "the NBC boys think their machine should really be christened Nrobnetlak (Kaltenborn spelled backward) in honor of the dean of radio analysts."[96] Henry described the Monrobot methodology to his readers by giving an example of "Zilch County, California." Returns from election night in 1952 and data for the same county from 1948 would be fed into the machine. After that, he wrote, "the bright little collection of tubes and wires will whirr for a while and then come up with a prediction." But, Henry insisted, "the darn thing doesn't 'think'—as some people choose to believe—it merely calculates." After confessing that "most reporters can't add 2 and 2," he writes that the Monrobot and UNIVAC should be an improvement. Henry concluded with another mixed message. He was interested, to be sure, but ambiguously so: "Most of us who will be grappling with the election problem over at NBC, with the assistance of Monrobot, are viewing the activities of the mechanical monster with considerable interest." Henry noted that Morgan Beatty—who was familiar to radio and television audiences—would be "nursemaid or interpreter" for the Monrobot. Henry added that most who know Beatty "would bet on him against any calculating machine extant."

Henry's contemplation of a computer entering his world of journalism seems to have left him bemused as much as anything else—not accepting of it but not absolutely dismissive either. With humor as his approach, he had framed the computer both as a potential aid—for those journalists with no affinity for mathematics—and as a potential competitor. It was clear he would need to be convinced that a machine could outperform a star reporter. His column did not explicitly articulate why he was amused. But he implicitly raised and began to answer the question of what human journalists were good for: providing assessment, meaning, and context for whatever it was that the machine might churn out. Henry's amusement would be visible on election night—as would his return to this issue.

Henry's portrayal of the computer in his *Los Angeles Times* column meshed with what a number of print reporters and columnists who covered television wrote as they surveyed the networks' plans. Readers were told to expect a contest—not just between the candidates, networks, or types of media, but between humans and their mechanical devices. That meant addressing the question of whether computers would be doing the work of journalists. Associated Press writer Wayne Oliver began his story this way: "It will be men versus machines on radio and television election night to see who can pick out trends and forecast the winners most accurately on the basis of early returns."[97] He introduced the computers first—the UNIVAC and Monrobot—and then the "human contingent." Oliver explained that what he called "electronic robot brains" would compare early returns to the early results from prior elections. The machines do not think, he pointed out, "but can do only what they are told to do." As a result "their forecasts will be mathematically correct on the basis of the data they have been given and [the] way they've been instructed to use it," he wrote, and "they can be way off base if late returns develop unforeseen trends." He did not give the computers primacy, writing that "both CBS and NBC will have all the tried and proved methods in full operation, with UNIVAC and Monrobot merely in the role of helpers."

Larry Wolters, a television critic at the *Chicago Daily Tribune*, closely echoed the same themes, though with more dramatic embellishments: "It will be man vs. monsters (electronic) on television and radio on election night. The TV networks apparently are convinced that robots can pick out trends and foresee the winners more accurately than ordinary mortals."[98] In addition to telling his readers about the UNIVAC and Monrobot, Wolters wrote that there would be "something frankly called the Monster over at ABC," with no further clarification. Like Oliver, Wolters noted that "these robots will not think for the reporters, or for you." "Probably," he wrote, "they'll be just as fallible as the straw votes and polls of other years." A week later, on the day before the election, Wolters took one more run at the subject.[99] He suggested that network executives were promising something of a spectacle, "predicting that more people will stay up all night Tuesday night than on any night in American history." While as many as fifty million television viewers might have their eyes "glued on the one-eyed monster," he wrote, using a nickname for the television screen, they could expect to see the "electronic monsters all tuned up to spew forth trends, foresee winners, and count votes faster and more accurately than ordinary mortals."

Harriett Van Horne also employed the human-machine comparison in a preelection column but with a different spin.[100] She began with a nod to the historic nature of the use of computers on election night. "It would seem," she wrote, "that we've come quite a way since Ben Franklin first fetched in electricity from the skies on his little kite." She told her readers about the computers by contrasting them with the humans whom viewers would see on November 4. "Election night on television will demonstrate this progress with staggering eloquence," she wrote. "On both CBS and NBC," she explained, "the stars of the evening will not be the shirtsleeved commentators with overflowing ash trays, paper containers of coffee beside them, but electronic calculating machines with neither smoke nor drink. They just cogitate."

Not all who wrote about the upcoming employment of computers on election night felt compelled to work in any digs.[101] One such story appeared in the trade magazine *Editor & Publisher*. Taken verbatim from a CBS release, the magazine item described the UNIVAC and its planned use in wondrous terms and included just one original element, the headline: "Electronic 'Brain' Will Turn Election Reporter."[102]

While CBS was publicizing its plans in those wondrous terms, work behind the scenes at the Eckert-Mauchly plant in Philadelphia became increasingly intense. More and more people were drawn in to make sure that the UNIVAC would have a workable methodology for election night.[103] Reports, speeches, articles, and memoirs published later by the participants paint a picture of a pioneering attempt under deadline pressure to bring quantitative precision to the old election-night habit of reading meaning into early returns.

Not envisioned at first was just how challenging this would be. A theory was needed—informed by mathematics, politics, geography, and history. The theory would be an aid in extrapolating from early returns in one part of a state that might not be representative of the state as a whole. The theory would also help in extrapolating from some parts of the country when others had not yet begun to count votes. This theory would need to be expressed as a mathematical model. The model would need to be translated into a computer program. The program would need to make use of data gathered in advance about voting history if comparisons were to be made. There would need to be a means for gathering data in real time on election night, transmitting it to Philadelphia, coding it into machine-readable form, loading it onto reels of magnetic tape, and feeding that data into the computer—paying attention, all the while, to possibilities for errors. There would need to be a backup plan in case of a breakdown by the particular UNIVAC designated for the analysis, one of several then in various stages of completion and operation at the Philadelphia factory. And there would need to be a means of producing comprehensible output and transmitting it to CBS in New York for reports to the viewing audience.

Remington Rand's Arthur Draper, in a presentation prepared for an engineering association meeting after the election, wrote that the planning had begun with confidence: "We very blithely assumed that such a calculation was possible, and we were sure that UNIVAC would be able to handle anything that we could dream up."[104] But that confidence would be tested. "As time began to run out," he said, "we realized that the problem was getting bigger and bigger." So the next step, per Draper, was to call in Max Woodbury from the University of Pennsylvania to work with Herbert F. Mitchell Jr., who headed the UNIVAC Applications Department. The team discovered that they were going to have to invent their method from scratch. "There was not even a vague formula for prediction that could be applied, and our mathematical group with Dr. Woodbury set out to develop a theory and put this into practical mathematics," said Draper. "This was an exceedingly complicated job in almost a brand-new field." In their own report after the election, Woodbury and Mitchell were blunt: "Our first and most serious mistake was to underestimate the magnitude of the job."[105] When Woodbury was engaged in early October, the job was expected to take just a few days of working out a statistical model. But the job would mushroom—including using hand-operated calculating machines called comptometers—to work out the methods. Three weeks after he was brought in, Woodbury had a team of eight putting in sixty hours a week on that task. Woodbury, the report said, "investigated and was forced to discard for lack of sufficient data several promising approaches, and finally, eight days before election, completed his set of formulae." At the same time, another group was busy with programming. That job had grown from two part-time programmers to more than six working 90 to 120 hours in the final week. Two of the programmers singled out for special credit—Margery K. League and Hildegard Nidecker—were themselves pioneers whose work with Eckert and Mauchly on the UNIVAC predated the Remington Rand acquisition. The programmer in charge of the work, Stephen E. Wright, was a World War II veteran who had studied with Howard Aiken at the Harvard Computation Laboratory. When I had a chance to spend a day with him at his home in Pennsylvania, he recalled that he and others ended up essentially moving into the Eckert-Mauchly factory at the end. They slept on cots to be available in early morning hours to test out a program after another finished running.[106]

The final formulas are explained in several postelection documents. The most detailed of these is Woodbury and Mitchell's report. There is a list of more than three dozen equations, explanations of the variables, and a rationale for their approach. Data was gathered in advance for comparative purposes, including what was described as "detailed state data for 1944 and 1948, showing at hourly intervals the reported returns for each candidate and the percent of precincts reported."[107] The data was provided by CBS, as was "the number of precincts in each state and metropolitan county." The UNIVAC team had a copy of a political almanac put out by a leading pollster, Gallup, with historical election data. This was presumably the source of state-level data for presidential elections back to 1928, which was also used in the calculations. The goal was both to produce state-level predictions and to use these in generating an aggregate national prediction of three numbers: the likely electoral vote, popular vote, and total vote. Predictions would be reported with context—that is, the probability of being correct. For eight states where the political leanings of urban and rural areas tended to diverge, separate calculations were made for key metropolitan areas and for the balance of the state.[108] Except for the fact that a computer would be involved, the plan had a great deal in common with what journalists had been doing on election nights for decades.

The UNIVAC team had two basic approaches to generating predictions. One involved combining the expected vote from past elections with the vote coming in on November 4. Greater weight would be given to the cumulative vote as the night went on. The other approach was an answer to a thorny, evergreen election-night problem. That problem, which would spark controversy in later years, was how to generate national predictions at a point in the evening when many states had not begun counting votes or even finished voting. Sidney Alexander, who had recently been appointed by CBS as an economic advisor, was credited with devising a solution. Incoming data on election night from available states would be used to calculate any swing away from the expected vote, extrapolating from the trend in past elections. This would provide a numeric factor that could be applied to states that had not yet voted.

As good as the formulas might be and as clever as the programs might seem, there was awareness that the simplest data entry errors could compromise the entire methodology. In fact, with so many people involved in the data transfer process, Mitchell and Woodbury wrote, "it was a foregone conclusion that erroneous data would appear in our input."[109] A system was put in place so that vote counts coming in by teletype from CBS on election night to Philadelphia would be inspected and then entered in triplicate from keyboard operators onto magnetic tape. The three sets of returns were then compared to make sure they agreed. In addition, even where the three sets might agree, the data were screened for what was termed "reasonableness." These checks were meant to make sure that the total number of precincts with reported votes on election night did not exceed the actual number of precincts in an area. And the total number of votes per precinct had to be inside the expected limits based on past elections. Checks were also made to ensure that the incoming vote total from a particular area was not less than the vote for the same area reported earlier in the night.

While the UNIVAC team was focused on what the computer would do, the CBS team in New York was focused on how the UNIVAC would look. A week before the election, CBS issued a release with this new feature of the election-night set: "In one corner of the studio will be the New York unit of UNIVAC, the giant automatic computer that will make running analyses and trend predictions at instantaneous speeds periodically during the night."[110] Left out of this release was the fact that the UNIVAC actually doing all the work would be one hundred miles away in Philadelphia. What viewers would see in the New York studio would turn out to be a spare UNIVAC "supervisory control panel"—the component described as resembling "the console for a pipe organ."[111] The one in the studio was not hooked up to a computer. But on election night, the audience would see its banks of lights blinking on and off as if it were running a program, with newsman Charles Collingwood stationed in front. In an account written years later, Herman Lukoff, who had responsibility for the computer's physical functioning in Philadelphia on election night, gave this explanation of how that so-called "New York unit" came to be part of the broadcast. The control panel on the CBS set was to be "commandeered," as he put it, from one of the next UNIVACs being built. It would not actually do anything. "But," he said, "someone thought it would look better if the lights flashed on the panel rather than just having it sit there looking stupid." The solution? At the factory, he wrote, "the technicians quickly wired up a group of incandescent bulbs to Christmas tree light flashers, then off to CBS headquarters in New York went the supervisory control panel."[112] Though not explicitly stated as a goal in this account, the net effect was that now there would be not only analytical but visual competition between the computer-reporting efforts at NBC and CBS.

In a head-to-head matchup, UNIVAC would beat the Monrobot in almost every way. But there was one eminently visible exception: the Monrobot, at a fraction of the weight of the UNIVAC and about the dimensions of an office desk, could be moved. This was one of its features that NBC highlighted in advance publicity—the Monrobot would be installed right on the NBC election-night set in Rockefeller Center's Studio 8-H. Richard LaManna, the recent college graduate on the Monroe team, recalled that this plan, however, turned out to be fraught with difficulties before Election Day ever arrived.[113]

The Monrobot was designed so that its computation elements—tubes, circuits, magnetic drum memory, and other parts—fit inside a metal unit the shape of a desk. Many tubes and circuits were mounted underneath a surface that flipped up like a lid to expose components below. The Monrobot was still under development, said LaManna, so work on it had been done with that lid open. To truck it from New Jersey to Manhattan, the Monrobot did not need to be disassembled. But the top did need to be closed. The surface with the tubes had to be flipped down into a horizontal position. The design included a desktop made of glass to allow viewing the tubes through it. On top of the glass, it was also possible to place a real desktop, completing the office-furniture look that the Monrobot was intended to have.

When the Monrobot arrived at Rockefeller Center, it rode in an elevator to the studio and was powered up. The team from Monroe then discovered, the hard way, that there was a problem. When they had closed the Monrobot's lid for transport, small bits of metal solder fell into the interior of the computer and ended up damaging the magnetic drum. That was a component of some computers where programmed instructions and historical data would be stored. LaManna told me he spent hours bent over the Monrobot's frame, working with a small pick that had a fine point, like a dentist's tool, to remove bits of debris from the drum. He said the Monrobot's keepers were able to get the computer running again but without some of the functionality that was intended.

For the election-night broadcast, there would be no need to close the computer's lid again. A design that was intended to make the Monrobot fit unobtrusively into a business office was, ironically, not its strong suit for election-night showmanship. The computer would run with the lid open, intentionally, and with its components exposed and visible. "That's what they wanted," said LaManna. "They wanted the jazz. They didn't want it to look like a desk."

Just as there was a name for the UNIVAC plans at CBS—"Project X"—the Monroe project for NBC was dubbed "Operation Monrobot." The term appears in a letter from E. J. Tiffany Jr., vice president of a Manhattan advertising and public relations agency, to Marilyn Mason.[114] That letter dealing with her role in the broadcast does not make clear whether the PR firm had been retained by Monroe, NBC, or Prudential, where Mason worked. The letter is dated five days before the election and has a detailed schedule for what was to come. On Saturday, November 1, the Monrobot and a "number of mechanical calculators" were to be delivered to 30 Rockefeller Center. The next afternoon, a Sunday, there was to be a "full-scale rehearsal" for several hours in Studio 8-H. Another rehearsal was planned for that Monday. And Tuesday, November 4, was clearly going to be a long day for Marilyn Mason. She was due in Studio 8-H at 8:00 a.m. to appear with the Monrobot on the *Today* show with host Dave Garroway. The memo writer, Tiffany, expected two million viewers for that show between 7:00 and 10:00 a.m. The audience was to get three "tours" of Studio 8-H. During rehearsals in the two days before, he wrote, "Miss Mason will receive more specific instructions on what she is to say and do on the Garroway Show." The day after Tiffany's letter, Monroe's Jay Quinby circulated a final schedule. He identified Tiffany as "being in charge of this publicity effort" and added a new detail. In addition to the rehearsals before Election Day, there would be a "dress rehearsal" that day at 3:00 p.m. The crew was advised that the NBC election program would start at 8:00 p.m. on radio and 9:00 p.m. on television.[115] Election night could not be scripted, of course, but the preparation and promotional activities would not be without efforts to control the message about what audiences would see on Election Day.

Notwithstanding the pre-election difficulties with the Monrobot that LaManna recalled, he said the computer attracted attention in Studio 8-H during the days it was there. Celebrities would come by to have a look. "It was a curiosity," he said, "like . . . a freak in a sideshow."[116] Broadcast engineers at NBC who had some knowledge of electronics would come by, too, peppering him and his colleagues with questions. While LaManna's own role was to look after the physical operation of the Monrobot, he was not involved in developing the methodology to be used in analyzing the returns. Just what that was is not clear from records or the recollections of others. This methodology may have been intended to make comparisons of partial vote counts to the past. There are references in NBC publicity to data from 1948 having been stored in the computer's memory.[117] The approach may have also been less ambitious, designed to work more from the incoming vote and to make sure that in states with urban and outlying areas of different political complexions, both were taken into account.[118] But, said LaManna, with the computer operating in a somewhat diminished capacity, the backup plan included calculations that might be done by hand if necessary. The ace in the hole would be the political expertise of Morgan Beatty, the veteran NBC newsman who was assigned to aid in planning the election-night analysis and then to report on and provide context for the Monrobot's output on November 4.

Such expertise, however, was itself no guarantee of success for evaluating in real time the incoming vote in an election with its own unique set of circumstances. As had been the case for decades, election night was a chance for journalists to shine but also carried risks. And journalists were not the only ones at risk of having their reputations sullied by problematic prognostication. On election night, pollsters had their own reputations at stake—and their livelihoods, too. Awareness of that colored the way they presented their final polls. And that, in turn, would end up coloring election-night analyses by journalists and commentators as the vote came in.

By 1952 there was a well-established history of preelection polls coloring election-night reporting and coming back to haunt journalists and polltakers. Some of these events are legendary. One is the *Literary Digest* debacle of 1936 stemming from the magazine's large but unscientific straw poll. And then there were the embarrassments of 1948 shared by the new breed of scientific pollsters and the journalists whose reading of returns on election night was affected by preelection polls. Pollsters and social scientists labored to understand what went wrong in 1948 and restore a measure of credibility and public confidence in the survey process. Collaborative studies were undertaken, books were written, and individual analysts reevaluated their methods and assumptions. But even with that attention, one wildcard in the fall of 1952 was the number of preelection survey respondents who were not ready to indicate a preference. This prompted an open question about how pollsters should apportion that slice of the electorate. There were differences, too, in explaining what appeared to be a shift in voter sentiment away from the party of incumbent Harry Truman. Samuel Lubell, a public opinion analyst who studied voting data combined with door-to-door interviews, undertook a four-month "grass roots" tour.[119] He saw more than just independent voters at work in the political landscape's critical middle ground. He found what he said were "sizable defections" of Democrats. In his column for the Scripps-Howard newspapers eight days before the election, Lubell concluded that there were enough of these defections to swing the contest to Eisenhower. But his report was not completely confident. A "possible freak of the Electoral College," as he put it, could give Stevenson more electoral votes even if Eisenhower came out ahead in the popular vote. There was a plausible scenario by which Eisenhower could win in a landslide yielding what Lubell described as "an electoral alignment unlike any in modern times."

The final polls in newspapers on Election Day were Gallup's. The headlines, which would have been written by the copy desks at newspapers around the country, reflected the noncommittal nature of the poll, ranging from "Gallup Says Ike Has Edge" to "Stevenson May Hold Lead—Gallup," plus this one in between: "Gallup Poll Notes Possibility of 50–50 Popular Vote."[120] According to that iteration of the Associated Press story, which ran in Fayetteville, Arkansas, "The Gallup Poll . . . gives Gen. Dwight D. Eisenhower a slight lead, but says Gov. Adlai E. Stevenson was gaining so steadily he might be ahead by today . . . [and] even saw the possibility of a 50–50 split of the popular vote."[121] A large contingent of voters—13 percent—were said to be undecided. The Associated Press noted that on the day before the election, three other pollsters put Eisenhower ahead but not by enough to risk a prediction. A United Press story characterized the pollsters as seeing a "photo-finish."[122]

The Princeton Research Service reported on Election Day that its final poll, completed the Sunday before the election, gave Eisenhower

50.8 percent of the popular vote and Stevenson 48.8.[123] That polling operation had detected a late swing toward Eisenhower. But a lack of certainty reigned. The Princeton report noted that margins of error had "averaged slightly less than three percentage points since our operations began in 1947." That would seem to point, in this case, to a statistical dead heat. The report concluded ambiguously, "We never have failed to indicate a winner, and never have been wrong."

Unscientific straw polls of all sorts abounded, too. They were treated as curiosities. But they were also testimony, if nothing else, to an intense and longstanding interest in reading the signs of preelection political support as far back as 1824, when newspapers compared the number of toasts for candidates at Fourth of July gatherings.[124] In 1952 there was a "cigarette poll." The Louisville Tobacco Blending Corporation marketed cigarettes with competing presidential labels, one that said "I Like Ike"—precisely 26,731,740 were reported sold—and the other that said "Stevenson for President," coming in second at 23,531,600.[125] There was a nationwide barbershop poll. It favored Stevenson by a few points. There was a feed-sack poll among patrons of farm supply stores in the Midwest, favoring Eisenhower by a few points.[126] The Associated Press surveyed more than two thousand newspaper editors and political correspondents about voter sentiment.[127] *Editor & Publisher* magazine surveyed newspapers about their own editorial positions; two-thirds favored Eisenhower.[128] Of the rest, more had made no endorsement than had backed Stevenson. Not to be left out, bookies in Nevada found that their own predictions—in the form of betting odds—were reported as a news item by the Associated Press on Election Day. The odds favored Eisenhower, but Stevenson bets were said to be "pouring in."[129]

Ahead of the election, pollsters came in for a ribbing for what some editors and reporters viewed as timidity after 1948. "Straws in the Wind Hit Dead Center" was the tongue-in-cheek headline for an election-day editorial in the *Press-Telegram* of Long Beach, California. "If the actual returns amount to an eyelash decision, our Mr. Roper, Dr. Gallup, and Mr. Field of the California Poll can settle back and take a bow," it said. "But if the majority turns out to be fairly substantial either way, we would hate to have to answer the mail of any of these gentlemen or most of their rivals."[130] In South Carolina the *Florence Morning News* poked fun at the pollsters, too, but not before setting a serious tone for the day with an unusual and striking front page. Most of that page was left blank. Below the masthead, in the center of a sea of white, there was a single, seventeen-line item, one column in width, with a small headline that said, "BE SURE AND VOTE TODAY."[131] It began, "We have always reserved the front page of this paper for the most important news of the day, and there is no more importance to every citizen today than to go to the polls and cast his VOTE." On the bottom of page three there was a photograph just as goofy as the front-page presentation was serious. It showed the newspaper's acting editor, Jack O'Dowd, wearing a turban, his hands around an ersatz crystal ball (apparently a goldfish bowl), and his face eerily lit from below. "TELL ME, SWAMI," began the caption that identified O'Dowd as "a man of little faith in polls and none at all in forecasts," trying to "learn in advance how today's presidential election will turn out."[132]

Arthur Krock, the legendary Washington bureau chief of the *New York Times*, weighed in with a column about pollsters. He took to task the "professional vote-statisticians, who fear they can never again sell their wares if they go wrong again, as in 1948."[133] They were "hiding behind bomb-shelters," Krock declared, and were "not taking even the smallest of chances this year." Krock was not going out on a limb, either, though he did note that his colleague David Lawrence was "courageously" willing to make a prediction without reservation—for Eisenhower. Meanwhile, the *Times*'s own ambitious reporting concluded on the day before the election with the last of seven surveys carried out by its correspondents nationwide. The *Times* deemed the presidential contest too close to call.[134]

If some reporters and commentators at the networks were less than thrilled about the inherent risk in employing a machine that might outperform them, those organizing the broadcasts put human-computer interaction at center stage. The arrangements between CBS and Remington Rand, for example, called for Collingwood to interview the UNIVAC—or at least to make a show of interviewing the UNIVAC by asking it questions directly. While this would be an election-night novelty, it was not an entirely new concept at the network. The year before, in December 1951, CBS newsman Edward R. Murrow showcased the Whirlwind computer at the Massachusetts Institute of Technology on his new *See*

It Now program. The Whirlwind had generated headlines for carrying out twenty thousand operations per second. That was fast enough to operate where "real time" processing was necessary, as in air traffic control.[135] A few days later, when the Whirlwind debuted for a television audience, Murrow opened the segment with a note of wonder. "These are the days," he said, "of mechanical and electronic marvels."[136] But there was also a hint of ambivalence. "With considerable trepidation," he said, "we undertake to interview this new machine." While effecting a tone of spontaneity, the show was clearly well scripted. One of two small television monitors on Murrow's New York set brought viewers to the famous university, where the message "HELLO MR. MURROW" flashed in points of light on the video screen of an oscilloscope. This, in fact, was one of the innovative features of the Whirlwind—the capacity to display output graphically on a screen.[137] Jay Forrester, director of the university's digital computer lab, gave a tour and then asked Murrow, "Would you like to try to use the machine?" Murrow deferred to Adm. Calvin M. Bolster, the head of naval research, who was brought in on another screen. Bolster offered up a question for Whirlwind about the fuel consumption and speed of an eleven-thousand-pound Viking rocket. The computer set to work. Its oscilloscope displayed a pair of bar graphs representing changes in fuel use and speed while a sequence of dots on the screen traced out a parabolic rocket trajectory. Forrester narrated. The admiral approved. But Murrow played the Luddite: "I'm just a middleman here," he said with a chuckle. "I didn't understand the question, and I don't understand the answer." He had a question of his own: If he had sold Manhattan for twenty-four dollars in 1626—referencing an oft-repeated tale—would that have been a good investment? Forrester was ready for this question. Viewers watched two members of the staff demonstrate entering the data on punched tape and loading it into the machine. The Whirlwind typed out an answer. At 6 percent interest per year, the investment would have generated a return of more than $4 billion. Murrow approved. Setting up the Whirlwind's final trick, Forrester said there was "another kind of mathematical problem that some of the boys have worked out in their spare time in a less serious vein for a Sunday afternoon." One of the most complicated pieces of machinery of its day then belted out a flat-toned version of "Jingle Bells."

Even then, in 1951, this sort of mix—of the technical and the frivolous, showmanship in the midst of a serious endeavor, and human-computer interaction—was already a trope in the nascent computer world. It was part of what we could call a culture of demonstration. An earlier landmark event in this culture of demonstration had taken place in 1946. The occasion was a public debut of the Electronic Numerical Integrator and Computer, or ENIAC, as it was called. It was conceived of during World War II and built in secret for the military at the University of Pennsylvania. After the war ended and the machine was operational, reporters were invited to see ENIAC in action. Lights that were part of ENIAC's regular operations were enhanced for the affair to make them stand out. Because ENIAC's work was classified, including calculations for nuclear weapons development, special programs were crafted for the demonstration. The *New York Times* hailed ENIAC on the front page. Its blinking lights were featured in a Movietone newsreel.[138]

What the election-night computing plans in 1952 had in common with these earlier wondrous displays was a consciousness among inventors, engineers, and marketers of the advantages of showmanship.[139] But there was a big difference this time. Unlike demonstrations that could be worked out in every detail ahead of time, there would be no way to do that on election night. The data would be live, and the computers would be processing in real time. The journalists and the technologists would be performing a high-wire act of sorts. There could be no canned results to serve as a net. So, the publicity that had been invited for the computers and the networks could cut both ways. On the one hand, the computer makers reached out to potential customers to watch the broadcasts. This was a chance for Remington Rand and Monroe to show their wares.[140] But on the other hand, there was a prescient observation a few days before the election in a review published in *Variety* about UNIVAC coinventor Mauchly's performance on the *Johns Hopkins Science Review*: "As regards its use in deciphering voting trends on Election Night," *Variety* noted, "the value of UNIVAC will depend on the interpretations the newsmen make on what factors UNIVAC is to measure. Unless the significant polling places are watched, one shrewd politico and a man with an abacus could scoop the electronic marvel."[141] And that was not even taking into account the possibility of error or malfunction.

The UNIVAC camp had made efforts to hedge their bets. With several UNIVAC computers in various stages of completion, a backup plan was to use one of those if the computer designated for election-night work malfunctioned. They also had systems in place to detect problems with the quality of data being fed to the computer. The broadcasters hedged their bets, too, primarily by continuing to use traditional means of reporting on returns. Collingwood made efforts to prepare his audience. In his *Report to the West* scripts before the election—and again early on election night—he said that if there were a mistake, it would be the fault of humans, not the machine. But in one of those reports ahead of the election, his remarks also show he was not free of concern. "When I left Philadelphia today," he said, "I asked the scientist in charge of UNIVAC what he would do if UNIVAC turned out to be dead wrong. 'Well,' he said slowly, 'on November fifth there's a United Fruit boat leaving for an obscure part of South America. If UNIVAC is wrong, that's where I'll be.'"[142] Collingwood added, "Me too."

A great deal of thought had gone into the mechanics and methods for data processing and analysis on election night. The application of new computer technology offered the chance to serve election night's traditional tandem imperatives—journalism on the one hand, with a premium on speedy and accurate analysis, and showmanship on the other hand, with a premium on attracting an audience and enhancing prestige. But there would be no adoption of this innovation without a willingness to gamble. The players were not blind to the risks and made efforts in advance to contain them. In the end, however, there was no guarantee that every contingency could be foreseen. Despite all the preparation, Collingwood noted in his script, "We're all keeping our fingers crossed here at CBS and at Remington Rand."[143]

Stirred Up by the Roughest Campaign of Modern Times

The morning papers greeting Americans on November 4, 1952, carried front-page headlines about violence at home and abroad. In Ohio the State Highway Patrol had fired on rioting prison inmates. The National Guard had moved in with fixed bayonets, machine guns at the ready.[1] In the central Korean Peninsula, a fierce battle for control of hilltops and ridges had devolved into hand-to-hand combat, signaling a deadly stalemate between Allied and Chinese Communist troops.[2] But the biggest headlines were reserved for the American elections. Wire stories carried reports on final preelection polls in the race for the White House. Analysis by the pollsters was clearly colored by caution over lingering embarrassment from their faulty predictions in 1948. Eisenhower was deemed to be ahead. But Stevenson was said to be gaining enough ground that a victory for the Illinois Democrat could be possible.[3] Also at stake was the Democrats' hold on both the House and Senate. Contentious races and ballot questions faced voters at the state, county, and local levels. Across the nation a record-setting turnout was predicted.[4]

Once the polls opened, reporters in communities with afternoon papers scurried to tell the story. "Early Vote Is Record" blared a headline in Bismarck, North Dakota.[5] "Valparaiso Early Vote Heavy" appeared in bold type across the front page of the *Vidette Messenger* in Indiana.[6] The heavy vote was not just a scattered local phenomenon. The United Press reported "massive" turnout across the country.[7] Voters were said to have been "stirred up by the roughest campaign of modern times." Nationwide, fifty-five to sixty million Americans were expected to vote. That would be a record, exceeding the 1940 turnout of just under fifty million as World War II raged in Europe.[8] Heavy voting led the United Press to predict that the outcome would not be known until the next day.[9] The Associated Press detailed one scenario in which the winner might not be known for weeks.[10] The national vote would have to be so close that it hung on California, and the California vote would have to be close, too. An unusual law in that state delayed the unsealing of absentee ballots until later in November. But that turn of events was deemed unlikely.

Election night would also provide a contrast between, on the one hand, the wondrous place of computers in efforts to draw an audience, and on the other hand, the actual place allotted to computers in live broadcasts on election night. This can only be seen after reviewing broadcasts in their entirety, obtained and scrutinized for the first time here. These include complete broadcast footage from the CBS and NBC television networks, along with the first several hours of NBC radio plus transcripts of brief segments on CBS radio. Taken together these reveal something important about the UNIVAC at CBS and the Monrobot at NBC. They were deployed not as the main source of forecasts but as one way among many ways of making sense of returns coming in. NBC and CBS were giving the computers a shot at fame, but the networks were not setting up an all-or-nothing gamble on them.

Official counts from state election authorities would not be completed and certified until well after election night. That left to news organizations—as it always had—the job of informing the public about the outcome as it took shape. In the hours, days, and years after that election night, a commonly told story about the UNIVAC's role would involve the claim of an early prediction that was held back from CBS and its viewers. As that story goes, the computer had been able to detect quickly what humans could not: a sweeping victory for Eisenhower. That was the version of UNIVAC's exploits that circulated with an eye to enhancing the behemoth's reputation in the new marketplace for computers. A review of the broadcasts provides a chance to explore this claim and to place the computer forecasts in the context of other efforts to detect trends that night. In national broadcasts we will come to see in the next two chapters that these varied ways of knowing included straight news reports, commentary, and context provided by journalists. There were on-air analyses by pollsters. The observations and declarations of pundits, partisans, and campaign officials were reported, too. When local newspapers declared a victor in the presidential race in their own states, those reports were circulated by wire services and then read on air. Later that night, broadcasts carried speeches of the candidates themselves, including the loser's concession.

At the same time, both CBS and NBC evidenced a certain tension that has long had a way of showing itself on election nights. On the one hand, returns are evaluated for clues about the outcome. But there must also be caution about reaching premature conclusions. Reputations are at stake on both sides of this continuum running between detection and restraint, between speed and certainty. As election night played out in 1952, the performance of the computers and their keepers stood to be judged against the other players who were assessing returns. The networks themselves stood to be judged by their decisions to adapt these novelties to traditional election-night tasks. Shortly before the election, *Business Week* ran an article about those facing a "big test" on election night. There were the pollsters, of course, who were hoping to make out better than they had in 1948. And there were broadcasters experimenting with what the headline referred to as "Robot Brains."[11] "So politicians won't be the only ones," said the magazine, "who cross their fingers Tuesday night." The audacious idea of looking at politics through the art and science of crunching numbers would be on trial.

On Election Day the networks continued to promote their plans for that night with newspaper ads. These played up, by name, the reporters and commentators who would have been known to radio and television audiences. In New York an ad for ABC's WJZ radio and WJZ-TV carried in large, bold letters the names of Walter Winchell, John Daly, Drew Pearson, and others.[12] Ads for the NBC and CBS broadcasts featured thumbnail photos of their star reporters and commentators—and included a mention of the technological marvels the networks planned to deploy. A CBS ad urged readers to "see your vote count . . . through the eyes of television's foremost reporters." Among the photos was one of Charles Collingwood, accompanied by text indicating he would be assigned to provide "returns and predictions as made by [the] new 'magic brain,' UNIVAC."[13] An NBC ad occupied the entire back page of the *New York Times*. It reminded readers of the network's television and radio ratings victories during the political conventions. The ad had photos of a dozen broadcast journalists together with their assignments. There were descriptions, too, of other resources that would be brought to bear. These included the Monrobot, with exaggerated claims about its speed: "Beginning at 8:00 on Radio and 9:00 on Television, 500 NBC experts, 1,000 newsmen in NBC's stations, and the Monrobot—America's fastest electronic brain—will bring election results, trends, and interpretation to you as quickly as the votes are counted."[14] A smaller version of the same ad—without the images or names of the reporters but including the Monrobot—appeared elsewhere, including the *Washington Post*.[15] These ads continued to promote the "magic" and "electronic" brains as integral to competition between the networks.

I found NBC's "Master Broadcast Reports"—logs and scripts of its programs—at the Library of Congress, where they are kept on microfilm. These documents and records kept by Marilyn Mason, the young woman who would be tending to the Monrobot on air, reveal that during Election Day, the diminutive computer was part of the network's attempt to generate excitement.[16] The Monrobot was featured on at least three daytime programs. The *Today* show was one, then in its first year as a pioneering blend of news briefs, feature stories, and conversation. Host Dave Garroway played up the Monrobot during his morning broadcast while telling viewers what to expect on election night. "Today we're going to take you on a tour of NBC's complex election center in Studio 8-H," he promised. "In about forty-five minutes, we're going to have the first public showing of the center's electronic brain . . . Mike Monrobot . . . a machine that not only computes the results but analyzes what they mean."[17] NBC's Morgan Beatty led the tour of Studio 8-H and appeared on camera in front of the Monrobot. A publication of the Monroe Calculating Machine Company—*Keynote*, a monthly in-house magazine—reported later that Marilyn Mason, identified as an "expert mathematician," was shown with the company's computer during two segments of the *Today* show that morning.[18]

In the afternoon viewers of *The Kate Smith Hour* on NBC were introduced to the network's election plans by the variety show's announcer, Ted Collins.[19] Stationed at NBC's election headquarters, he said, were "news printers, telephones, lights, cameras, special sets, and miraculous machines that seem like something out of Buck Rogers." The latter was a reference to a fictional character from futuristic space adventures well-known to Americans through comic strips, radio, film, and television. The viewers were promised they would "hear and see a good deal more about these machines." During another segment from Studio 8-H, Collins elaborated on the network's plans. "NBC is certainly prepared to do this job as quickly, as accurately, and as graphically as possible," he boasted. "All in all something like 250 people—not to mention any number of machines from the simple, old-fashioned pencil to the most complex mechanical brain, and other interesting devices, will be devoted to keeping you informed on who's winning."

Still later in the day, after two children's programs—*Howdy Doody* and *Rootie Kazootie*—plus several other shows and the news, the Monrobot got one last promotional outing on NBC at 7:00 p.m. This took place during a show called *Advancing Human Frontiers*, designed to acquaint viewers with the latest scientific research.[20] The script shows host Ed Herlihy telling the audience, "The big thing we want to talk about in the second half of the program is the tabulation of records in our NBC studios here, using the new electronic brain machine." Howard Fleming Jr., a Monrobot engineer, explained how the computer worked. He answered questions about "automatic sequence control," the storage of results, and "uses in business."[21]

CBS, too, was not shy about touting its election-night lineup, human and otherwise. During a break in afternoon programming on CBS television, an announcer named some of the journalists, all well-known to Americans, who would be providing "trends and reports." They were Edward R. Murrow, Douglas Edwards, Don Hollenbeck, Charles Collingwood, and Lowell Thomas. He noted that they would "be assisted by UNIVAC, the electronic brain that works faster than human beings can think."[22]

Breathless accounts of methods for gathering, aggregating, analyzing, and disseminating the vote counts continued a long election-related tradition of journalism about journalism. Newspapers reported with gusto on their arrangements for what promised to be a busy and high-stakes evening. In Wisconsin the *Oshkosh Daily Northwestern* boasted of reporters standing by at polling places, "ready to rush the final returns to the newspaper offices."[23] In New York readers of the *Oneonta Star* were asked not to call because "all telephone lines and personnel will be busy compiling results."[24] Technology of various sorts figured into the newspapers' accounts. One small-town paper boasted about the installation of "special telephones . . . to speed returns."[25] Precinct-level election officials were asked to phone in promptly with their tabulations. A paper in Middleboro, Kentucky, described the "special reporting facilities" it had arranged jointly with a local radio station.[26] These included "a direct wire" in the courthouse for local and county returns, plus an "extraordinary wire system" for state and national returns.

Not to be denied its share of glory, Western Union reminded the nation that the telegraph system was still an important link in the reporting of election news. It was more than a century since the telegraph had taken its place in the roster of election-night players. But this mature technological system still had the capacity to generate wide-eyed stories.[27] One item reported that "some 35 million words of election news have been carried by telegraph wires," making this the "wordiest election campaign in the nation's history."[28] Much of that had come from reporters riding on the candidates' campaign trains. Western Union placed special representatives on these trains to handle the daily crush of copy coming from eighty to one hundred reporters traveling with Eisenhower and one hundred traveling with Stevenson.[29] A twenty-four-thousand-mile network just for the "flash handling of news stories" was a key element of Western Union's system. Human actors in that system were portrayed as equally important. "Work on a campaign train is a day and night assignment permitting little sleep," readers were told. "One Stevenson trip was called 'Operation No Sleep.' Western Union press men are used to a quick switch from train to plane, and a motorcade trip in a cold, driving rain over muddy, backcountry roads adds to the challenge of getting the press file through under any conditions."

The Election Day "story of the story" in 1952 often took special note of television. Though not entirely new, TV was still novel. Wonder was attached to the new coast-to-coast arrangements for transmitting video in real time. Television would be knitting the nation together as an audience after the voting had knitted people together through their common democratic act at polling places. The United Press reported on this with dramatic flourish in a story that appeared in newspapers around the country, sometimes on the front page: "Across America, a hush will fall. There are 19,000,000 television sets now, according to a research firm, compared with 700,000 in 1948."[30] Even larger than the television audience, the size of the potential radio audience was staggering, with some "44,000,000 radio homes." This wire story even marveled at the global audience: "Around the world, newspapers will be held for extra editions. Radios will be tuned to returns. Bulletin boards will light up. . . . Ships at sea will get the news. Transcontinental airplanes will pipe the returns to passengers in flight via loudspeaker systems." In far-flung places where people had radios, it was reported that "the Voice of America, pouring out news in 46 languages to countries outside and behind the Iron Curtain, will address itself to a potential radio audience of 300,000,000 outside the North American continent."[31]

Then there was the technology that millions of Americans would be seeing for the first time. The computers got attention in national wire stories, local news, on-air promotions, print ads, and the columns of writers covering television. Accounts on Election Day employed monikers like those used in the weeks leading up to the vote. There was the by-now familiar "electronic brain," as well as "mental marvel," "electronic prophet," "robot computer," "electronic crystal ball," "mechanical brain," and just "the 'brain.'"[32]

Cultural icons were to be a feature of election-night broadcasting in some venues. The ABC affiliate in Hollywood, KECA, was going to have a "celebrity room."[33] Another Southern California station was inviting the public to come to an "election night 'jamboree'" at a local theater.[34] The bill included Lawrence Welk, a favorite of older Americans for his orchestra's fare of polkas, waltzes, and other conservative, easy-listening music.[35] In some places the competition for attention featured names familiar to political news junkies. There were local reporters known for their savvy coverage of politics. There were network television and radio reporters and commentators whose names, voices, and faces were widely recognized. There were pollsters—Roper, Gallup, Lubell. There were even leading scholars. In New York City WNYC had lined up two of them—sociologist Robert K. Merton, a professor at Columbia University, and political scientist Harold Lasswell, a professor at Yale University—to analyze election-night trends.[36]

For those watching or listening at home, some newspapers provided readers with the means to become their own experts. They could be active participants in tabulating and analyzing vote counts delivered on radio and television. Papers around the country ran blank tally sheets on Election Day. They also published "guessers" guides to help viewers become "experts." The demystification of special expertise and its replacement with do-it-yourself templates of various sorts was certainly not an unknown phenomenon in the early 1950s, nor was it limited to politics. A "paint-by-numbers" craze attracted adults who had no artistic training but did have newfound leisure time. Hobby kits for assembling model trains, planes, and cars from injection-molded plastic parts sold briskly. *Betty Crocker's Picture Cook Book*, with illustrated, step-by-step instructions, had sold its first million copies within months of publication in late 1950.[37] Even homes could be built from a best-selling how-to guide. But the invitation to be part of the election-night forecasting excitement also had a long tradition, as we have seen.

The do-it-yourself scorecards published on Election Day came in a variety of forms. Some took up half a page or more—a significant amount of space hinting at the belief of editors that readers would find this service useful. A scorecard from the Associated Press announced at the top, "You Can Keep Your Own Record of Returns."[38] It had the number of electoral votes and the number of precincts or other voting units in each state. There was space to list returns at four separate times during the night. The columns for Eisenhower and Stevenson were marked by their parties' icons—the elephant and the donkey. In Syracuse the *Post-Standard* and station WSYR ran a scorecard that was even more elaborate, with detailed data from the 1948 presidential vote, including state-by-state pluralities and percentages. There were spaces to record election-night figures for races of local interest along with historical data. The newspaper also ran a brief guide, "How to Assess Returns." The *New York Times* published an elaborate "guide and tally sheet."[39] It listed, for each state, the number of electoral votes and the top vote-getter in 1948. There was a historical note or trend-spotting hint for each state, too. The note for Texas, for example, said, "Normally Democratic. Gov. Shivers, Democrat, endorsed Eisenhower after Stevenson backed U.S. ownership of offshore oil lands."

Beyond just following along, how could viewers get an edge in the prediction game? In a widely printed story, the Associated Press described two approaches.[40] One involved watching states with "hefty" electoral votes. The other boiled down to this: "History is likely to repeat itself." One could focus on what the story called "compass pointer" states with a history of picking winners. Some papers suggested that their local vote would signal the national outcome. The *Lima News* in Ohio ran a front-page story that began, "Political experts from thruout America will be watching election returns from Limaland Tuesday night for an early indication of a nationwide trend."[41] The story went on to note, "It was the farm vote in half a dozen northwestern Ohio counties which was credited by many expert observers with providing the Democratic gains which finally swung Ohio into the Truman column four years ago."

In Wisconsin the Associated Press took a more whimsical approach, mixing facts and figures with the wink of an eye. Running in the *Oshkosh Daily Northwestern* under the headline, "Handy Guide in Wisconsin Vote Watching," a lengthy article acknowledged the special place in American culture of election-night forecasting: "Vote-watching comes in for its quadrennial one-night stand as the nation's most popular parlor pastime."[42] The story went on to offer "a handy guide by which you may become your own expert and be just as confused as anyone over what's happening before the decisive totals emerge from the adding machines." The counties that gave the biggest boost to Truman were listed and then this: "If you could detect a shift in sentiment in these counties . . . you might make a quick reputation among your friends." Readers had the chance, the story asserted, to "emerge as a minor prophet."

One of the most elaborate tally guides came from NBC sponsor Philco. It was a thirty-two-page booklet I found on eBay—a source not to be overlooked! There were even some penciled-in tallies from whomever had used it in 1952.[43] National magazines also got in on helping readers become experts. *Collier's* enlisted two CBS veterans, Robert Trout and Paul W. White.[44] After enjoying "a good dinner and early movie" on November 4, they wrote, interested readers were invited to "sharpen a handful of pencils, sit down by your radio or television set, spread open this issue of *Collier's*, and settle down for some practice in the more or less fine art of keeping score." Western states had the best track record, they noted. But those states would be reporting late, so Missouri was best to watch, a bellwether state since 1900. There were some good bellwether counties, too—Coos and Stafford in New Hampshire, for example, and Vanderburgh in Indiana. Readers were cautioned about a technology gap. States with larger cities, which trended Democratic, had voting machines and would more rapidly compile returns. An elaborate, data-rich chart came with the story. Trout and White also wrote of "an ultra-modern 'mechanical brain'" to be used on at least one network. Their election-night preview finished this way: "Nothing better spotlights the scientific advances of our age than the simple fact that a machine very likely will be the first to know the identity of the thirty-third man to be President of the United States."

The *Collier's* article asserted that "elections are basically stories told in numbers," deemed to be a radio sort of thing. Television's proper domain was deemed to be "pictures instead of words and figures," a task demanding "a large share of imagination and enterprise." Trout and White predicted that television would make more use than radio had of "street scenes like Times Square." Just as vote-watchers had little choice other than to turn to the past to make sense of the present, the turn to Times Square on election night was surely an American reflex in 1952. In Traverse City, Michigan, in Valparaiso, Indiana, and in Hayward, California, wire editors chose for their readers a telling United Press summary of the way election returns would be broadcast to millions.[45] There was mention of technological wonders, including the "electronic brains." There was also a paragraph or two on a unique device installed for election night in Times Square—dubbed the "new electric election indicator"—to attract and serve the expected crowds there.

Indeed, on election night in 1952, the *New York Times* was not leaving anything to chance when it came to Times Square. The paper might have a reputation as serious and elite, but it also had showmanship in its genes. And showmanship might be more important than ever in attracting and holding an election-night crowd. In the era of radio and then television, NBC had made efforts to compete with Times Square by erecting election-night displays outside Rockefeller Plaza. *New York Times* reporter Meyer Berger had been among those chronicling a change in the character and size of the Times Square crowds.[46] The wartime gathering on election night in 1944 was massive—said to number between 250,000 to 500,000— but was not as boisterous as in earlier elections. After that the energy and size of the crowds were not what New Yorkers had come to expect in elections for city, state, or national office.[47] At first police officials were baffled.[48] Reporters sensed apathy. Later, broadcasting came to be seen as a factor.[49] And there was no small irony in the fact that broadcasters, looking to add color to their reports, turned to Times Square. In 1948 Berger noted that radio commentators set up camp to relay bulletins as they appeared on the *Times* display.[50] Television cameras were there to bring the Times Square scene into American living rooms. In the same 1948 story, Berger declared flatly that "Times Square saw the death of a tradition yesterday."[51] Thousands did show up, but they were not packed shoulder to shoulder as in the past. One could even find bare spots on the pavement. Again in 1949 and 1950, Meyer penned obituaries for the massive Times Square gatherings of past generations.[52]

Still, the *New York Times* wasn't ready in 1952 to give up on the storied physical landscape of election nights past. Management arranged for an overlapping set of technological wonders—some dating back to the nineteenth century, some decades old, and some brand new—to attract attention, display the vote count, and call the election when the time was right. These nonprint media were hyped in advance on the pages of the *Times*. The oldest was the traditional searchlight that would signal the outcome—when the newsroom was ready to do so—by a prearranged code published in the paper.[53] The so-called "zipper" that circled the Times Tower with headline versions of the news in electric lights was, by 1952, a mature technology—a generation after it debuted on election night in 1928. But it was still capable of generating excitement. The newest in this mix of glitzy technological offerings by the *New York Times* was an eighty-five-foot high "electric election indicator" running up the north wall of the Times Tower, described as the culmination of months of painstaking work.[54] It was to measure, like a giant thermometer, the rising count of electoral votes for each candidate until one of them reached 266, the threshold for victory. It would, predicted the *Times*, "tell the dramatic story of the election in the simplest terms." A second sign, just below the zipper, would provide periodic reports on a state-by-state basis, one state at a time.[55]

The *Times* arranged to employ still other technologies to get the word out far beyond Times Square. Every half hour, updates would go by teletype from the newsroom to thirty campus radio stations.[56] The newspaper's own radio station, WQXR, set up a twenty-person news operation in the *Times* city room. Announcers would broadcast returns from there, and Washington bureau reporter William Lawrence would provide analysis. Listeners would hear live reports from Democratic and Republican headquarters. The *Times* station also arranged to position an announcer high up in the Paramount Theater marquee to report on the scene below in Times Square. In addition to being carried on its own station, reports of the *Times* "election service" would go out on twenty-one other stations from Boston to Washington.[57]

Times Square has been studied as a venue where all sorts of cultural values have intersected—spectacle, commerce, amusement, and religion among them. The very notion of a national audience for popular culture had roots there predating the rise of Hollywood and broadcasting.[58] Certainly, democracy, technology, and journalism could be added to that list of intersecting interests most salient in Times Square on election nights.[59] In 1952 just blocks away from that storied location, in spectacles originating from state-of-the-art television studios, the Monrobot and the UNIVAC were the latest in a tradition of election-night attention-getters. How perfect that they surfaced in a city famous for election-night confections of news, technology, and spectacle—and in a nation wholly attuned for generations to election-night exuberance and wizardry.

The rich array of election-night choices for Americans by 1952 was testimony, if nothing else, to a well-established desire to know the outcome of the day's voting without undo delay and without waiting for an official tally. Around the country newspaper editors certainly understood that their readers would not want to wait for the next day's paper. So it would be a night for returns to be delivered in a wide variety of venues featuring an alliance of news and entertainment—from movie theaters to parties thrown by newspapers. Interests would overlap, with furniture and appliance stores seizing on the election as an opportunity to draw in customers. A range of technologies would be used. Competing arms of the news business—radio, television, newspapers, and wire services—would also find ways to collaborate. Interactivity would be featured, whether an invitation to watch a newsroom at work or the publication of scorecards that audiences could fill in. And there would be ample reporting about the reporting. The diverse ways that returns would be gathered, analyzed, and disseminated were themselves the subject of news stories. In 1952 the wondrous technologies that would be employed to carry out those tasks were part of the story, just as they had been for more than a century.[60] In short the salient features of election night reporting that had been developing for generations continued to be part of the election-night scene. It was wild.

This profound public appetite for election returns—and a long history of satisfying it with a marriage of news, entertainment, and technology—formed an important part of the landscape in which the "electronic brains" would make their election-night appearances. This continuity helps us understand why—despite the costs, difficulties, and risks—computers operating live found a receptive venue for their insertion in American culture through election-night reporting.

While CBS was confidently promoting its electronic brain, the situation behind the scenes was hectic. At Remington Rand's Eckert-Mauchly plant on Ridge Avenue in Philadelphia, members of the UNIVAC team were busy checking out programs developed on a tight schedule.[61] Detailed plans for "Project 'Election Return'" also specified who could be in the plant and how they would be identified.[62] There would be green-striped passes for visitors, white passes for employees working on the project, and red-striped passes for other employees. Since several UNIVAC computers were operating or being completed, individuals working on those, such as employees of the U.S. Census, were to be given special passes, too. Anyone who might appear on camera had to sign a release. The memo offered this advice about appearance: "All persons likely to be in the critical area should be freshly groomed (shaven, haircuts, etc.) and *not* wear white shirts or blouses as white does not televise well." A team from CBS would be sent to operate a remote telecast from the plant. The memo mentions "CBS engineers and technicians," and of course there would be camera operators. There is no indication in the memo that CBS would be sending a correspondent—and none would appear from Philadelphia during the telecast. The task of interacting on-air with the UNIVAC's keepers would fall to correspondent Charles Collingwood, who was in the CBS election headquarters at Grand Central Terminal in New York and had a phone line to the Philadelphia plant.[63] Teletype lines had been readied to transmit incoming returns from CBS to the Eckert-Mauchly group.

At NBC's headquarters at Rockefeller Center, rehearsals were held before Election Day and again that afternoon, and the "Operation Monrobot" team from the Monroe Calculating Machine Company was preparing their computer for its debut.[64] Meanwhile, invited celebrities and other guests of NBC—more than a thousand of them—were gathering at Rockefeller Center to watch the broadcasters at work.[65] The guests' experience had been anticipated down to fine details. Arrangements were made for food and drink.[66] Staffers designated as "guidettes" were in place. Records from NBC include an undated script—two pages, single-spaced—that had been assembled for the guidettes. They were to memorize whatever facts they would need to repeat in showing guests around the studio.[67] The script included names of the news staff and their responsibilities. Among these was Morgan Beatty, who had been assigned to "interpret the findings of the Monrobot electronic brain to both radio and TV audiences." The Monrobot was also mentioned a second time in the guidette script: "Directly to your left you see the Monrobot, the electronic brain, used to compute important trends as ballot counts pour into the headquarters from 48 states." Monroe was to provide pamphlets describing the machine. Once the tour of the set was over, guests would be urged to take a seat in the Studio 8-H balcony to follow the action.

Broadcasting on WNBC, NBC's radio station in New York, Ed Herlihy described the scene for listeners at home in an early-evening preview.[68] "I speak to you tonight from Election Headquarters in Studio 8-H, which right now is just beginning to get up to speed for our complete returns of the election returns to you," he told listeners. "8-H is now full of electricians and mechanics and television people, all trying to get the last things together, the last wires in place, just so that everything will be in apple-pie order for the correct reporting." He gave the massive studio's dimensions. "We think it's the largest in the world," he said. It was 78 feet wide by 132 feet long, and it was packed. He described what would take place and who was there to work for the news-consuming audience. In the center was a platform for commentators. Behind them were what he referred to as tabulating machines. On one side there were "communications facilities which will bring in points from all over the country at an instant's notice." And there were the journalists themselves: "Editors, news writers, reporters, all flocking around, ready to take their place and do their job for you."

After a discussion with several newspaper editors, who would be helping to analyze the local and regional voting, Herlihy was joined by two celebrities, Jinx Falkenburg McCrary and Faye Emerson, who were part of the NBC radio team for the election. Herlihy expanded on the story-of-the-story theme, noting that this was his fifth election for NBC. The first had been in 1936; the setting had been modest. "When I look at this vast spectacle of 8-H tonight," he said, "I'm just completely amazed."

The promotions were done. The hour had arrived to answer the question *Business Week* had posed a few days earlier: whether computers "have any real place in the Election Night hurlyburly at radio-TV studios."[69] So much was at stake for the innovators. Nothing could be easily predicted about how the prediction business would work out. Anxiety reigned.

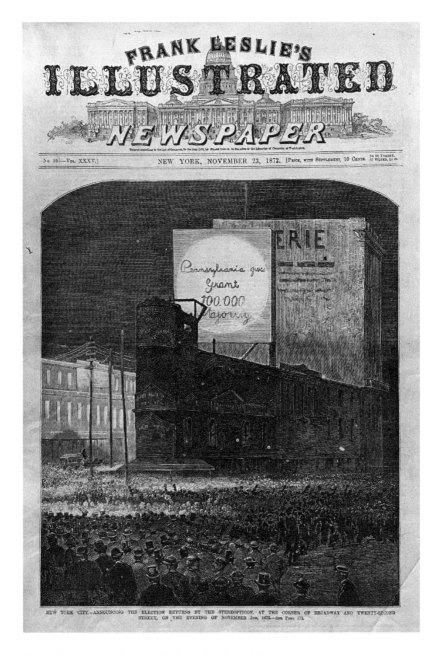

Fig. 1. Street scene in New York on election night, 1872, as crowds watch returns projected by stereopticon—or "magic lantern." *Frank Leslie's Illustrated Newspaper*, November 23, 1872, 1.

EXPERTS COMPUTING THE RETURNS.

The Crowd That Turned Out in Times Square Last Night to Watch the Election Returns

Fig. 2. (*opposite top*) Outside help was recruited on election night in 1890 to compile returns for the *New York Herald*. In this "story of the story," the newspaper boasted of having the best "expert accountants" in the city. "How the Herald Gets Election Returns," *New York Herald*, November 9, 1890, 16.

Fig. 3. For decades Times Square was a gathering place for massive crowds to get the latest returns on election night. The crowd here is captured looking up at the Times Tower. The *New York Times* had rolled out the "zipper" on election night twelve years earlier, featuring breaking news in lights that circled the building. "400,000 in Times Sq. in a Genial Mood," *New York Times*, November 6, 1940, 3.

Fig. 4. (*above*) In advance of the 1952 election, the UNIVAC was featured in a newspaper photo of CBS anchor Walter Cronkite learning about the computer from coinventor J. Presper Eckert Jr. and operator Harold Sweeney in Philadelphia. Too big to move for the broadcast, the UNIVAC would generate predictions from there on election night. "Network 'Drafts' UNIVAC for Election Coverage," *Philadelphia Evening Bulletin*, October 15, 1952.

Fig. 5. *Johns Hopkins Science Review*, an award-winning program on the DuMont Television Network, featured an episode titled "Can Machines Think?" as a way of introducing computers to Americans in advance of the 1952 election. The segment was hosted by Lynn Poole, seen here with a mock-up of a juggling robot. "Can Machines Think?" *Johns Hopkins Science Review*, October 27, 1952, Johns Hopkins Television Programs, 1948–60, Special Collections, JHU-EL.

Fig. 6. UNIVAC coinventor John Mauchly explains how the UNIVAC operates, including the use of this reel of magnetic tape for data storage, during an episode of the *Johns Hopkins Science Review*. "Can Machines Think?" *Johns Hopkins Science Review*, October 27, 1952, Johns Hopkins Television Programs, 1948–60, Special Collections, JHU-EL.

What to Look For on Election Night

Two experts offer a simple guide for interpreting the tabulations that will pour from your radio and TV sets. Don't let early returns fool you. There's a way to spot trends yourself

By ROBERT TROUT and PAUL W. WHITE

IF YOU live on the Atlantic seaboard, the first satisfactory meal you'll have on election night is a good dinner and an early movie. But if you invest your interest in the election night returns on radio and television, over the internet, sharpen a handful of pencils, sit down by your radio or television set, and settle down with the Colliers, and settle down for some prolonged hours of fun and the art of keeping score.

True, the radio and television networks more than earn their keep if returns about seven o'clock. Eastern standard time, usually empty of specific information.

For the men, the broadcasters have something to talk about. Every Scotsman up to a dozen states in New England and a few Midwestern states will have begun to report their poll results. But since these returns are very small P.M., Eastern time, they are not much help in early evening trend-spotting. Indeed, by midnight, Eastern standard time election night has really just begun. Governor Dewey's in New Mexico and last until an hour later than Truman's been wrong in the polls before. There are three dozen states which haven't been wrong in the last 10 Presidential elections. Nevada, Montana and California. Idaho has been wrong since 1901, when it voted in favor of William Jennings Bryan.

Always on Winning Side

Two have a perfect record of picks national elections have been able to focus on Presidential elections and the other way around.

In the close election of 1948, Truman had a hard in Missouri with only 4 per cent of the votes in, and about once was threatened. So the Show-Me State line really been the Dixie Division, the Missouri mule is a way to keep your glasses on in the East.

It is also worth while to focus on the close. Counties like Coos and Strafford, in New Hampshire and Vanderburgh, Indiana (Colliers, November 18), have been good to study in nearly every Presidential election since. In the days before the century, Strafford County distinguished itself even in the primary election January 7, as March 7, once again over Senator Taft on the Republican side, and Senator Kefauver over the Democratic. Since the President later withdrew as a candidate and backed Governor Stevenson, the Granite State primary portion of the Granite State figures won't be much help...

State-by-State . . . Hour-by-Hour

THE accompanying chart is designed for the millions who will be scoring their returns at home—and these can be listed in the columns alongside our figures as they come in from Republican and Democratic headquarters...

Close battle or landslide, most prominent politicians have their own private betting reels with which to determine the chances of the candidates. James A. Farley, former chairman of the Democratic National Committee, used to figure in it at our broadcasting studio every election night. He would keep a sharp eye out and as the Dewey strength among the farmers had by no means lost. When the returns were conclusive from Syracuse and Rochester, early Wednesday morning. At that point he would go on the air and give a remarkably accurate forecast of the national vote.

Farley, you'll remember, was the only prominent forecaster in 1936 that Governor Alfred M. Landon of Kansas would carry only two states—Maine and Vermont.

Why Our Pollster Was Late

Even the professional experts, when job requires them to keep their fingers on the nation's political pulse, sometimes are reluctant to commit themselves. One of the newer agencies are able to turn in a remarkably fast and complete picture through the aspect of their labors is that no matter how rapidly the election figures, the radio and television networks regularly "scoop" the election returns.

Nevertheless, the election figures are obviously able to leave completely the studies used to be Socialist Norman Thomas and to hope to have the ability to call the turn early in the evening. And he was accurate as a prophet. In his forecast invariably was accompanied by his qualifying election. Thomas' analysis always tries to complete its count. Indeed, in 1940 by our network, which conducted its survey in every state.

But that's not the real secret. Radio and television, plus newspaper, syndicate and wire service, always try to carry the latest complete election returns at every hour from every state. This fast accumulated material is for pulling winners will still be in

the "victorious candidate—wound up with less than a 2 per cent edge over his Democratic foe.

The numbers of the article were Republican or Democratic of the news broadcasts will decide as soon as the conclude who finally carried each state in the Presidency... never lost it. The "Sepoia-through" columns is for the blue states in which

Collier's for November 8, 1952

1952 OUTLOOK STATE	Elect. Votes	1948 RESULTS — HOUR-AT-HOME RETURNS BY PERCENTAGES							
		9 PM	10 PM	11 PM	12 MID	1 AM	2 AM	3 AM	4 AM
PROBABLE DEMOCRATIC									
ALABAMA	11	10	14	22	—	41	44	44	44
ARIZONA	4	—	1	—	5	31	22	34	55
ARKANSAS	8	—	4	12	27	29	33	36	38
GEORGIA	12	14	21	39	37	38	38	38	38
KENTUCKY	10	—	2	35	48	62	67	69	70
LOUISIANA	10	—	1	7	13	18	24	25	28
MASSACHUSETTS	16	—	1	12	25	31	41	47	47
MISSISSIPPI	8	1	7	25	33	41	46	47	47
MISSOURI	13	7	32	30	45	59	64	66	66
MONTANA	4	—	4	4	43	47	47	47	47
NEVADA	3	5	8	—	43	69	82	82	41
NEW MEXICO	4	12	33	40	57	65	81	81	30
NORTH CAROLINA	14	1	23	48	72	75	80	81	81
OKLAHOMA	8	—	3	22	48	72	73	92	92
RHODE ISLAND	4	1	14	34	90	100	100	100	100
SOUTH CAROLINA	8	6	62	72	75	75	73	75	75
TENNESSEE	11	62	38	64	82	82	88	92	92
PROBABLE REPUBLICAN									
COLORADO	6	3	3	1	4	8	11	22	35
DELAWARE	3	3	17	21	33	38	43	63	71
INDIANA	13	5	11	18	33	38	46	46	46
IOWA	10	—	8	1	12	31	46	46	64
KANSAS	8	12	13	12	12	18	22	29	50
MAINE	5	5	16	34	79	89	89	89	89
NEBRASKA	6	—	1	6	10	22	47	47	68
NEW HAMPSHIRE	4	3	17	22	32	67	77	77	86
NORTH DAKOTA	4	—	3	3	7	7	7	24	33
OHIO	25	11	25	30	39	41	51	68	72
OREGON	6	—	—	11	11	26	37	43	43
SOUTH DAKOTA	4	3	7	7	24	24	44	52	52
VERMONT	3	11	51	62	90	90	100	100	92
IN DOUBT									
CALIFORNIA	32	—	5	18	19	23	49	38	38
CONNECTICUT	8	31	51	63	80	91	99	100	100
FLORIDA	10	—	10	41	50	63	63	63	63
IDAHO	4	—	—	15	15	32	62	70	79
ILLINOIS	27	4	10	31	31	48	54	57	72
MARYLAND	9	25	29	48	64	74	82	93	93
MICHIGAN	20	—	2	6	17	22	22	37	36
MINNESOTA	11	—	5	11	13	19	19	19	28
NEW JERSEY	16	2	13	56	70	84	87	99	99
NEW YORK	45	—	5	25	7	90	99	94	99
PENNSYLVANIA	32	5	24	38	59	71	87	94	97
TEXAS	24	11	35	55	61	82	88	88	88
UTAH	4	—	—	1	—	21	32	65	65
VIRGINIA	12	60	67	77	77	91	92	94	94
WASHINGTON	9	—	—	8	—	8	11	30	30
WEST VIRGINIA	8	12	22	36	51	51	62	63	63
WISCONSIN	12	2	33	50	50	73	73	45	45
WYOMING	3	—	1	—	1	41	66	70	76

KEY TO COLOR PANELS
DEMOCRAT
REPUBLICAN
STATES' RIGHTS

Fig. 7. (*opposite*) *Collier's* magazine published a guide for do-it-yourself prognosticators to use on election night in 1952, complete with a discussion of states to watch and a chart with comparative data from 1948. "What to Look for on Election Night," *Colliers*, November 8, 1952, 22–23.

Fig. 8. Walter Cronkite anchors his first presidential election broadcast for CBS on the night of November 4, 1952, from a massive studio above Grand Central Terminal in Manhattan. "Election Coverage," CBS Television Network, November 4, 1952, CBS and the Paley Center for Media.

Fig. 9. Charles Collingwood reports in the CBS election-night studio in New York in front of the console of a UNIVAC computer, tricked out with blinking lights. "Election Coverage," CBS Television Network, November 4, 1952, CBS and the Paley Center for Media.

Fig. 10. (*top*) A remote camera in Philadelphia brings the CBS audience a view of the UNIVAC team at work as the computer's first on-air projection is announced at about 10:30 p.m. "Election Coverage," CBS Television Network, November 4, 1952, CBS and the Paley Center for Media.

Fig. 11. CBS newscaster Eric Sevareid (right) quips to anchor Walter Cronkite, "I'm delighted that UNIVAC, our machine competitor, was wrong for a while and we were consistently right with a human voice, or we'd all be victims of technological unemployment pretty soon." "Election Coverage," CBS Television Network, November 4, 1952, CBS and the Paley Center for Media.

Fig. 12. (*opposite top*) Late on election night 1952, Remington Rand's Arthur Draper issues an on-air mea culpa for the troubles with UNIVAC projections, explaining that they were actually human troubles. "Election Coverage," CBS Television Network, November 4, 1952, CBS and the Paley Center for Media.

Fig. 13. Bill Henry, a *Los Angeles Times* columnist, anchored the election-night television program for NBC in 1952 and introduced the first Monrobot segment with a slightly amused look. A few days earlier, he had referred to computers in his column as "fearsome contraptions." "Presidential Election Coverage," NBC News, November 4, 1952, NBC Universal.

Fig. 14. (*above*) NBC newscaster Morgan Beatty sits in front of the Monrobot computer with the top opened so that the audience can see the lights from its vacuum tubes. Marilyn Mason enters commands via a keyboard and retrieves printouts of projections. "Presidential Election Coverage," NBC News, November 4, 1952, NBC Universal.

Fig. 15. Good weather was deemed to be a factor in the record turnout of Election Day 1952. NBC came up with a way of showing this by passing a handheld transparency with an image of a shining sun between the camera and a map of the United States. An image of an umbrella was used to show where it rained. "Presidential Election Coverage," NBC News, November 4, 1952, NBC Universal.

Fig. 16. At the end of the election-night broadcast on NBC, Morgan Beatty joined Bill Henry at the anchor desk to offer insights on Dwight Eisenhower's landslide victory, with 442 electoral votes to Stevenson's 89. Beatty referred to the Monrobot computer as "our new star." "Presidential Election Coverage," NBC News, November 5, 1952, NBC Universal.

Monrobot Flashes E

The most widespread publicity Monroe has ever had centered around the appearance of our electronics computer, Monrobot, and our conventional calculators on NBC's telecast of returns on election night. In addition to the evening appearance, the Monroe performance included:

(1) Miss Marilyn Mason with the Monrobot on the Garroway show twice Tuesday morning; (2) introduction of the Monrobot on the Kate Smith show Tuesday afternoon; (3) an interview on "Advancing Human Frontiers" program when Howard Fleming, Jr., project engineer responsible for the computer's physical structure, explained its operation.

The Monrobot was mentioned in *Time, Business Week* and *Newsweek*, and in hundreds of newspapers throughout the country, and was featured in NBC's and Philco's pre-election and on-the-air advertising.

Marilyn Mason, expert mathematician who knows what goes on inside the electronic "brain," told Monrobot what to do.

Director E. J. Quinby, Electronics Supervisor Bill Burkhart, Engr. Howard Fleming, Jr. check Monrobot's innards.

Fig. 17. In its magazine, *Keynote*, the Monrobot's manufacturer devoted a two-page spread to the computer's role in the NBC broadcast and the people involved, including Marilyn Mason. She was twenty-two years old. *Keynote*, Monroe Calculating Machine Company, November 1952, 10, Monroe Systems for Business.

Director E. J. Quinby, Electronics Supervisor Bill Burkhart, Engr. Howard Fleming, Jr. check Monrobot's innards.

Fig. 18. With the Monrobot on the NBC set are E. J. Quinby (left), director of
the Monrobot project, Bill Burkhart (center), one of the Monrobot inventors,
and Howard Fleming Jr., a Monrobot engineer. *Keynote*, Monroe Calculating
Machine Company, November 1952, 10, Monroe Systems for Business.

NBC commentator interviews two Monrobots, Marilyn and mechanical

Fig. 19. A photo of Morgan Beatty and Marilyn Mason with the Monrobot appeared in a lighthearted *Newsweek* review of the election-night debut of computers on television. An NBC press release had described Mason as a "photogenic PhD in mathematics." *Newsweek* quipped that the "beauteous brunette mathematician" has been granted a "press agent's doctorate" and reported that she worked at Prudential Insurance, where colleagues were now calling her "Marilyn Monrobot." *Newsweek*, November 17, 1952, 63.

6 | This Is Not a Joke or a Trick

The excitement was palpable as CBS launched its television coverage at 8:00 p.m. on November 4 from a studio above Grand Central Terminal.[1] A camera positioned above the action panned across one side of the studio to zoom in on the main anchor desk where Walter Cronkite was at center stage. Dozens of men and women could be seen carrying out their assigned tasks, members of the election-night staff: reporters, producers, assistants, camera operators, secretaries, messengers, and more. Some were standing off to one side of the anchor desk. Some were milling about or moving purposefully to confer with each other, even passing in front of the camera. Others, equipped with telephones or headsets, were packed side-by-side at desks loaded with stacks of paper. There were typewriters, adding machines, and the click-clacking teletype machines bringing fresh dispatches. Bulky television cameras on moving platforms were attached to cables that snaked across the floor. The UNIVAC computer's election-night role would not be formally introduced until about twenty minutes into the broadcast. But audiences did get a glimpse of a strange-looking device resembling an organ console. This was a spare UNIVAC "supervisory control panel," placed there for effect and tricked out with blinking lights. The massive UNIVAC doing the actual work of forecasting was at its home on the factory floor in Philadelphia where it was built.

On either side of Cronkite at the anchor desk were two assistants. One was a young man in a jacket and tie, who appeared to be carefully checking a set of papers on the desk. The other was a woman in a dark dress with a pen or pencil in one hand and a cigarette in the other. She examined some papers. Then as Cronkite was introducing the program, she picked up one of the telephone receivers on the desk and put it to her ear. She would be giving Cronkite cues throughout the broadcast. The audience at home was in on the excitement of more than just the election. Cameras and microphones immersed them in the newsroom at work: its sights and its sounds, muted conversations, the periodic distant tinkle of bells—perhaps from teletype machines—and at one point even a hammer. Broadcasters have had more than seven decades since then to work out the fine points of election night on television. But in 1952 it was all so new. They were inventing production values in real time. Much had been planned and scripted of course. But this was live. Anything was possible.

There were many unknowns about what might happen, and when. Cronkite did not have a lot to go on by way of experience in anchoring election-night broadcasts on television. This was his first. And yet beneath his calm exterior, there were years of deep and intense experience in journalism. He had reported for newspapers. He had been a wire-service correspondent in Europe and North Africa during World War II. He had risked his life to fly with the Army Air Forces on bombing runs and covered some of the most intense battles on the ground. He was later stationed in Moscow. He transitioned to radio and soon to television. He was still just thirty-six years old. In fact, this was his birthday. Now if all went well, he stood to make his mark as an anchorman—a new concept in this new medium for news—on the biggest news day of the year. He would have been within his rights to wonder whether the UNIVAC would be a help or a hindrance as he took the helm. After all, he had been equivocal in an interview a couple of weeks earlier—in awe of the revolutionary new device but also not entirely convinced that it would add to the broadcast. The unknowns on election night were not just about who would win. Much more was at stake.

This story as you will read in this chapter—from our exploration of the seven-hour CBS broadcast—was not told before completion of the research that led to this book. And telling this part of the story in detail almost did not happen. Historians can only tell reliable stories about the past if they have access to primary source materials—in this case, recordings. These lay hidden, though not by intent. It just happened. The event itself—the pioneering use of UNIVAC on election night—was not a secret. Like a story told around the campfire, again and again, year after year, the outlines were repeated from time to time, the edges getting duller and errors creeping in. There were snippets that appeared in some autobiographies over the years, or, more often, in second- and third-hand accounts that repeated the same basic themes. The stories went like this. In 1952 a computer was first used on an election night to forecast the outcome from early returns. The computer got it right but was greeted with skepticism. Machine outsmarts man. And so forth. The rest is history, as that version of the story goes. Voila, computers become part of the election-night scene on television forever after.

Now we get to take a more detailed and nuanced look at what really happened. But in addition to tidying up the historical record, you might ask, who cares? Good question. Here is why this matters. When we lack a full picture, it is easy to fill in the gaps by making assumptions. It is easy to lose sight of the way disruptive innovations are not only embraced but also resisted. It is easy to miss what it takes for innovations to get the critical mass of support necessary to be adopted. This inaugural use of computers in news and on election night was a contest, not a slam dunk. And the competition was multidimensional—a cluster of competitions between networks, between types of news media, between individual journalists, between computers, and, ultimately, between ideas about what journalism is and what it could be. If we pay attention, we can find clues here about what it takes for an innovation to be tried, to take hold, and to spread. We can even find surprising clues about how to avoid—in the future—the sort of deeply disturbing events that followed election night in 2020.

It is worth pausing to look at that "almost did not happen" part of telling this story. The discovery of these recordings took place over several years, with a string of discouraging developments before I finally found all the segments of the full broadcast. I also learned an important lesson about historical research—to cycle back around for a second or third look at repositories that did not seem at first to be promising. One of the most important reasons for doing this is that archives may have new acquisitions, freshly digitized holdings, or enhanced catalogs, databases, and indexes called "finding aids" for exploring their collections.

My experiences in obtaining the complete seven-hour CBS television broadcast succeeded, in stages, when I realized that I needed to push past the initial appearance that much of the broadcast had disappeared.

The CBS News Archives was able to locate the first thirty minutes in its holdings. A few additional minutes turned up at the Computer History Museum in California. One terrific find was a thirty-minute compendium, including several key UNIVAC segments. This turned up in the archives of entries for the Peabody Awards in Georgia. Transcripts of some segments involving the UNIVAC were filed among the papers of CBS correspondent Charles Collingwood at the Wisconsin Historical Society. It seemed that would be all. But then well along in my research, I requested from the Computer History Museum a copy of a 1951 episode of the CBS *See It Now* program in which host Edward R. Murrow did a segment about the Whirlwind computer. Much to my surprise, I found several extra undocumented minutes tacked on at the end of the video. From the content, I knew these must be part of the 1952 CBS election-night broadcast. There was footage, albeit brief, that I had not seen anywhere else. Now I thought there must be more. I redoubled my efforts and ended up on the website of the Paley Center for Media. Named for William S. Paley, who built CBS into a broadcasting empire starting in the 1920s, the Paley Center is one of the leading repositories of old CBS broadcasts. The center's online database had listings for lots of episodes of election-night programs for many years, but none identified as the broadcasts from 1952. I decided to search the database for any election-night segment with no year listed and no specific detail that would rule it out as part of the 1952 broadcast. My search returned fifteen segments. A curator determined that eight of these were not from 1952. The remaining seven were a mystery. The Paley Center staff agreed to have a look. The seven segments were, indeed, from election night 1952—from 9:00 p.m. to about 3:00 a.m. the next morning. There was also an edited compendium of segments at the end of the final reel. Between the Paley Center footage and the half hour from the CBS News Archives, I had almost the entire broadcast. But I was still missing almost thirty minutes between 8:30 and 9:00 p.m. Months went by before I struck on a way to find the missing segment. I had noticed that several of the segments I already knew about had sequential catalog numbers in the Paley database. I went back into the database, this time searching for entries with catalog numbers similar to the ones for segments I had. Up popped a record for "ELECTION COVERAGE PT.01 (TV)." It had not turned up in the database searches I had done in the past. Again, the Paley Center staff agreed to screen that video. Bingo. It was the full first hour of the broadcast, including the previously missing material between 8:30 and 9:00 p.m. Sometimes doing historical research involves luck— and maybe a bit of desperation—plus the good will of knowledgeable archivists and curators. Let's have a look.

Minutes into the CBS broadcast on November 4, Cronkite set the stage with the first news of the evening. This was not about the direction of the vote but about the volume. Cronkite reported "a record turnout apparently throughout the United States." He explained that there had been long lines at polling places, with estimates that the vote could reach as high as sixty million. That would far outstrip the previous record of under fifty million in 1940.

At the outset of the broadcast, Eisenhower and Stevenson had slightly more than a half million votes between them. Eisenhower was ahead. Running tallies were displayed under photos of the candidates. Electoral vote standings were listed in another display. Eisenhower was ahead there, too. Polls had closed in thirty states and would close in another dozen by 9:00 p.m. As vote counts trickled in from nearly half the states, Cronkite reminded viewers that these were only scattered returns.

That reminder was the start of a tension in Cronkite's own presentation. The urge to read meaning into early returns is always powerful. But the anchor also felt compelled to issue repeated notes of caution about the limited information. We could suppose any number of reasons for this evergreen tension in election-night reporting, which can be fraught with risk. On the one hand, there is the solid journalistic practice of sticking with what is known. But there is also the imperative on a public stage to hold on to an audience with the lure of an uncertain outcome. And then there was the specter of 1948. The networks would be constantly checking on a steady flow of reports from the wire services. A telling memo on the issue of speed versus accuracy was drafted several weeks before the election. The memo, found in the Associated Press Corporate Archives in New York, was circulated to Associated Press bureaus around the country in connection with advance planning for election night. It was written by Alan J. Gould, executive editor of the wire service. "With the experience of the 1948 upset in mind, all of us must guard against any prejudging of the outcome," Gould urged. "Roll out the returns as quickly as they can be tabulated. Give them proper backgrounding and they will tell their own story."[2] The same memo made clear, however, that even when the Associated Press was not willing to declare a race over, there was news in the forecasts of other news organizations. Associated Press bureaus were advised to contact "leading newspapers" to get forecasts on election night. Gould noted that it would be "particularly newsworthy . . . when a paper supporting one candidate concedes its state (or the nation) to the other candidate." Some papers might be "so well known that it is news when they make a definite statement that any candidate will carry their state—even one they are supporting." In a sense, Gould wanted to have it both ways: reporting the forecasts of others was apparently okay even before, as he put it, those at the wire service "feel justified in 'electing' anybody on our own." On election night, wire service dispatches would be relayed to the broadcast audiences by networks not yet comfortable making their own forecasts.

About two minutes into the CBS broadcast, Cronkite began a rundown of state returns in alphabetical order.[3] Despite Cronkite's tendency to be cautious, there were surprises. These seemed to be going in just one direction—Eisenhower's—as Cronkite's roll call came to states deemed key to Republican reversal of the 1948 election or states where any swing away from a toss-up would be significant. One of the latter was Connecticut. Cronkite reported that Eisenhower had "jumped into an early lead in [that] pendulum state," with 13 percent of the vote in. States among the so-called "Solid South," a traditionally Democratic stronghold, were also of special interest. In Florida, where Cronkite said the Republicans had hoped to crack the Solid South, Eisenhower was off to an early lead. Cronkite cautioned though that Florida's early returns came mostly from "southern resort counties" where Republican strength was expected. Kentucky was noteworthy. It was typically considered a border state between the South and the band of states from the Northeast to the Midwest. Cronkite reported a "surprising lead for the Republican Party so far" in Kentucky, though he noted it had come from urban areas that tended to vote Republican. Maryland, also a border state, was described as "another one of the bellwether pendulum states the Republicans are hoping to crack." With 5 percent of the Maryland vote counted, Stevenson was ahead, but just barely. "The early returns," said Cronkite, "are mostly from Baltimore, which should be heavily Democratic, according to past performances, but so far the Democratic lead there is very narrow indeed." In Ohio Eisenhower was ahead by more than two to one. The total vote count there was small, but its source was presented as significant: "Partly from the city of Cleveland in Cuyahoga County, and that may be an indication there that the Democrats are in some trouble." Stevenson would need a big win there to carry Ohio. Cronkite appeared to attach the most significance to returns from South Carolina. This, he said, was one of the southern states that the Republicans hoped to crack. "With nearly a fourth of the vote counted in South Carolina," he reported, "the first real trend seems to be indicated from any of the forty-eight states." He deemed Republicans there to be "running ahead by a rather sizable majority." In Tennessee Stevenson was ahead but just barely, with almost a fourth of the vote counted, and it was coming from a heavily populated area in western Tennessee that Democrats needed. In another southern state, Virginia, Cronkite reported that Eisenhower was off to an early lead. But again Cronkite urged caution. "This might have been expected," he said, since the early vote was from "the Arlington County and Alexandria areas outside of Washington DC, where Republicans were expected to gain their largest strength."

In recapping, Cronkite came back to South Carolina, which he described as "the big surprise so far." He explained that the state's governor, a Democrat, had endorsed the Republican candidate. Cronkite ventured a modest assessment: "It looks as if General Eisenhower at this moment may be cracking the Solid South, in South Carolina at least." A few minutes later, just after 8:15 p.m., Cronkite ended a review of the national vote count by returning to South Carolina. He termed it "the only really startling surprise in the returns." And then a minute later, after noting again that polls had closed in thirty states and would soon close in a dozen more, he offered this remark, with no elaboration: "Looks as if we're going to get an early trend tonight, and it may not be very long before we see definitely which way the wind is blowing." In essence this was a hint of a forecast, even if Cronkite was not saying that outright. So, before the UNIVAC was introduced, there were already telltale signs of the outcome for those watching closely.

There was also some color thrown in. Viewers learned that Eisenhower was following the returns in his residence at Columbia University, where he was president. Stevenson was said to have waited in line for thirty minutes to cast his vote in Chicago. Cronkite also talked about several big states in which Republicans hoped to have some success—including New York, Pennsylvania, Illinois, and possibly California. In only one of these was there any trend to report—Stevenson's home state, Illinois, where he was ahead because of early returns from traditionally Democratic Cook County. Here Cronkite made use of the kind of historical data that had been employed for generations to assess early returns. "The previous Cook County margin for the Democrats has been around 54, 55, sometimes up to nearly 60 percent," he said. Stevenson was running well ahead of the historical figures from that county, said Cronkite, leaving the governor "in fairly good shape in his own home state."

As the first twenty minutes of the broadcast came to an end, it was the UNIVAC's turn on air. Betraying no observable disconnect between his own cautious approach and the computer's bold task, Cronkite set up the segment this way: "And now for perhaps a prediction on how this voting is going, what the vote that is in so far means, let's turn to that miracle of the modern age, the electronic brain, UNIVAC, and Charles Collingwood." The camera panned slowly from the anchor desk to the veteran CBS newsman, who was seated on one side of the studio. A large microphone was attached to a harness looped over his neck and shoulders. Behind him was the blinking UNIVAC console.

Collingwood's first task was to introduce the forecasting challenge, the equipment, and the methodology—and to do that in terms his audience could understand. Collingwood's demeanor was relaxed and folksy. His approach was to humanize the machine. "This is the face of a UNIVAC," he began. "A UNIVAC is a fabulous electronic machine, which we have borrowed to help us predict this election from the basis of the early returns as they come in. UNIVAC is going to try to predict the winner for us just as early as we can possibly get the returns in." He continued with the anthropomorphic approach, as he would throughout the night: "UNIVAC lives down in Philadelphia. He's one of a family of electronic brains made by the Eckert-Mauchly Division of Remington Rand, and in a little while we'll go down there and take a look at it." Without calling the computer console a prop, he was distinguishing between the "face" of the computer and the computer itself. Collingwood wanted to make clear to the audience that this was not magic, not some sleight of hand, not just a gimmick. So, he ventured slowly and deliberately into the domain of election-night mathematics. It was a nod to transparency. "Let me tell you a little bit about the theory of this," he began. "This is not a joke or a trick. It's an experiment. We think it's going to work. We don't know. We hope it'll work." In a sense he was inviting his audience into the drama of this bold experiment. Would the UNIVAC do its intended job? Collingwood had positioned the computer as something that might tell viewers what they most wanted to know—the election's outcome. But he had also hedged his bets by avoiding any outright claims. He had invested the arrangement with seriousness of purpose. And he had been direct about the risk that things might not work out as planned.

Collingwood described how much effort had gone into the planning: "For the last six weeks or so, some twenty-five mathematicians, statisticians, and researchers, including some of the country's best mathematical brains, have been working on the problem, which we've given to this electronic brain to try to solve for us tonight." The theory behind their work, however, was "pretty simple," he explained. "It is that if you knew all about previous elections, if you knew how the votes came in and so forth, then, as the votes come in in this election, you ought to be able to compare them with what happened in the past and judge what the result will be tonight." While that would take hundreds of people doing calculations by hand, said Collingwood, the UNIVAC could complete hundreds and even thousands of calculations per second. The goal was to get a prediction from UNIVAC based on what he termed "statistical principles." But in case trouble cropped up, Collingwood was absolving the machine in advance. "Now as I say, if it does give a wrong answer, if it does make a mistake, it won't be the machine which does it," he asserted. "It will be some fault of ours, some assumption that we made, something we didn't foresee in giving it the figures." This echoed a theme Collingwood had sounded before the election. As things turned out, this alert to viewers would foreshadow some of the night's difficult events.

What the audience saw next was a scene that came in from Philadelphia via a CBS camera positioned at the Eckert-Mauchly plant. Collingwood narrated as he gave a remote tour of the UNIVAC installation. He described various components in familiar language. He made analogies to familiar objects. And he spoke as if he were addressing questions directly to the machine. In an account of the CBS-UNIVAC plan written decades later, Sig Mickelson, who in 1952 was the director of television news and public affairs at CBS, provided a glimpse into the likely thinking behind Collingwood's approach. First, according to Mickelson, the correspondent tasked with the UNIVAC assignment would need to "have a sympathetic attitude toward the experiment."[4] There had also been, according to Mickelson's account, a conscious consideration of minimizing the risks of failure and humiliation. Options had been weighed. "We could take it seriously and offer election projections as serious news reports," Mickelson recalled. "If we did so, we would run the risk of being ridiculed for preferring the output of a machine to that of the human mind." But ridicule was not the most terrible fate he could imagine. "Even worse," he wrote, "if the machine had balked or its output was patently in error, we could be subjected to unmerciful criticism." His catastrophic thinking did not stop there. "We could go a step further and make it the centerpiece of our coverage," he continued. "That would greatly increase the risk and make us a laughingstock if for any reason it failed." As he weighed the pros and cons, not taking UNIVAC-as-forecaster seriously was also potentially perilous: "We could slough it off as a gimmick and risk the loss of any benefit it might deliver." Mickelson wrote that a decision was made to "humanize it, to treat it gently and semi-humorously but at the same time give full attention to the data it would produce." In addition to minimizing the risks, wrote Mickelson, this approach had another potential benefit. It would "appease an audience that we speculated might not yet be ready for overly rich doses of high technology." In Collingwood, as Mickelson saw it, the network had a correspondent who could use "a soft touch without degrading the results," and Collingwood's "obvious warm relationship with the machine would help deliver the mood we were seeking."

As Collingwood gave his remote tour, he pointed out the control panel— looking like the one in the studio—where he said the operator "pushes those keys and punches the buttons and tells it what to do."[5] There were reels of magnetic tape, which he referred to as "those round things [that] look kind of like candy mints." There was the "brain of UNIVAC" against a wall, he explained, with "all those tubes and things" and some "spiny things, which are mercury tanks." These, he told the audience, were UNIVAC's memory. They could store millions of digits or characters. Playing off a cliché about keen memory, Collingwood said of the UNIVAC, "He's got a brain that would put to shame the whole race of elephants." Next to the console was a device that looked like a typewriter. Mixing the anthropomorphic and the familiar, with a bit of magic-show lingo creeping into his narrative, Collingwood explained what that device was all about. "That's the way UNIVAC talks," he said, but he did not mean "talking" as in sound. "When he wants to say something, the keys move with no hands touching them, and UNIVAC says his piece," Collingwood explained. "That's the way he communicates to us, through that typewriter there. And it's on that typewriter which moves without any human agency that we hope UNIVAC will give us his predictions."

Now, it seemed to be the computer's chance to perform. Collingwood gave a cue. He asked, "Can you say something UNIVAC? Have you got anything to say to the television audience?" But the typewriter just sat there doing nothing at first. Collingwood ad-libbed, "You're a very impolite machine, I must say. But he's an awfully rapid calculator." Then there was a bit of activity, a few characters were typed, and then the typing stopped. "There he goes," said Collingwood. "What's he saying?" When the words did not seem to form a message, Collingwood ad-libbed again: "I think he's saying hi, anyway."

Things were not going as planned. The veteran broadcaster took the hiccup in stride, continuing with his discussion of the UNIVAC's features. When the camera returned to the New York studio and focused in on Collingwood again, he tried to get back on script. He addressed the audience: "I got so interested in telling you about UNIVAC, I forgot to ask him what his prediction is." Then he spoke as if he were addressing a question to the machine: "UNIVAC, can you tell us what your prediction is now on the basis of the returns that we've had so far? Have you got a prediction for us, UNIVAC?" Collingwood turned toward the console and seemed to glance up briefly. Out of view was a large monitor that had been installed to convey UNIVAC's output to the television audience. The camera stayed focused on Collingwood, who seemed to be waiting for a response. Again, nothing happened. Once more Collingwood ad-libbed. "I don't know—I think that UNIVAC is probably an honest machine, a good deal more honest than a lot of commentators who are working," he said, letting out a brief, slightly nervous chuckle, "and he doesn't think he's got enough to tell us anything about yet, but we'll be back with him later in the evening."

With that, Collingwood turned the broadcast back over to Cronkite. The segment had lasted five and a half minutes. Cronkite simply moved on to the next order of business, with no comment, no reference to what had just transpired, and no effort to cover for the less-than-stellar launch of UNIVAC's election-night debut. In fact, another hour would go by before Collingwood had a second turn on camera to ask UNIVAC for a prediction. In the meantime Cronkite returned to results that continued to come in. Eisenhower was still leading. There was a report from CBS veteran Douglas Edwards on several Senate races. Cronkite then reiterated "the rather startling results so far" in South Carolina. Noting a "rather heavy Republican majority building up in Connecticut," he added a new detail. In Danbury, which he explained was "a normally pendulum area" that leaned Democratic in the past, Eisenhower was running ahead. Still, Cronkite was not willing to draw sweeping conclusions about a half hour into the broadcast. He steered clear of explicitly connecting the dots from bits and pieces of evidence in the South, the border states, the Midwest, and New England, which together might have suggested that Stevenson was in trouble.

Just after 8:30 p.m. it was time for a segment—some eight minutes in length—not about the election but about the CBS arrangements for reporting on the election. There it was again, the story of the story. Cronkite turned the floor over to veteran broadcaster Lowell Thomas, who was standing in front of the anchor desk. "I'm not actually thinking about the returns at this hour," Thomas said. "I am more interested in what is going on around me here in this house of television." He continued: "It seems to me that television has certainly come into its own this year. At the previous election night four years ago, why, it was a case of television portraying radio. But this time everything seems to be specially designed just for television." Speaking directly to the audience, Thomas said, "If those of you who are looking in will come along with me for a moment or two, I'd like to take you on a tour of this establishment." He walked around, pointing out visible features of the studio and directing the cameramen to show these to the audience. He called attention to various individuals, from the managing editor to the switchboard operator. He described the flow of news coming in by telephone and on fourteen teletype machines from "the great press associations and from every other source under the sun." He pointed out a large display along one wall with state-by-state vote tallies in the presidential contest. He pointed out the "computers," a term he used to refer to a group of men at a desk with ordinary calculating machines. There was a cadre of uniformed young men—all wearing double-breasted jackets and bowties—whose job was to take the numbers from those human "computers" and post tallies on the presidential board. There were displays for congressional, senatorial, and gubernatorial races. A large map showed states leaning one way or the other in the presidential contest. States shown in black were for Stevenson and states in black-and-white stripes were for Eisenhower. Color television broadcasting was still something in the future. Thomas came to the display for presidential totals. This showed Eisenhower with 655,000 votes, an 89,000-vote lead. But Thomas also sounded a note of caution, saying, "It is so early that that may not mean a thing." One change from the past, Thomas indicated, was that less space was set aside in the studio for guests. The layout had been designed with the television audience in mind. "Practically all wives have been left at home," he said, "for the first time." At one point in his tour, Thomas pointed out Betty Furness, the celebrity actress-turned-pitchwoman. She mugged for the camera. She was working her way around the studio taking photographs. She would appear in commercials later in the program hawking a variety of Westinghouse products and appliances, praising their convenience, aesthetics, technical superiority, and novelty. These ranged from light bulbs to television sets to a clothes dryer that bleated out the musical notes to the ditty "How Dry I Am" when its work was done.[6]

Absent from Thomas's tour was the UNIVAC. But it was there as an unseen foil in something Thomas did say. When introducing what he called the "super duper engineer" in charge of the layout of studio gear, Thomas said this: "From now on [he] is to be known as the mechanical brain."[7] And when introducing Sig Mickelson as the other "genius" responsible for the night's arrangements, Thomas quipped, "From now on he will probably also be known as the brain, but not the mechanical brain."

At about 8:40 p.m., the first reported predictions came not from UNIVAC or members of the CBS news staff but from two political partisans. Republican National Committee chairman Arthur Summerfield was cited by Cronkite as saying, "It looks like a Republican landslide to him." Cronkite reported that former governor of Minnesota Harold Stassen, who was shown among the small audience at the CBS studio, had concluded that Eisenhower would be elected by the largest popular vote ever. Stassen, then president of the University of Pennsylvania, had himself been an unsuccessful candidate several times for the Republican presidential nomination.[8]

As Cronkite continued to report significant state results, he asserted shortly before 8:45 p.m. that "on the basis of these early returns, it does appear that General Eisenhower has gone into an early lead in most areas including the critical areas."[9] The one exception was said to be Illinois, where Stevenson was still ahead in his home state. More state results came in favoring Eisenhower, including Oklahoma. Shortly before 9:00 p.m., Cronkite announced, "We have a report from the *Hartford Courant* predicting that General Eisenhower is going to win the pendulum state of Connecticut this year." Cronkite would repeat this prediction several times without endorsing it. He even commented ambiguously on it a few minutes after 9:00 p.m. "No state has been decided as yet with the very possible exception of Connecticut," he said, but then added, "We couldn't say that. The *Hartford Courant* only is the source for that."[10] Not until about 9:45 p.m. did Cronkite report that Eisenhower was apparently going to "ring up a sizeable victory in Connecticut, where the Democrats had high hopes." And it was not until about 10:20 p.m. that the anchor reported flatly that Eisenhower had won that state by precisely 127,878 votes based on "complete returns."[11] This was about two hours and forty minutes after the *Hartford Courant*'s prediction had first been circulated by the Associated Press, which was before the CBS broadcast had even begun.[12]

Among the notable news early in the CBS broadcast's second hour was surprising Republican strength in two areas that favored Democrats in the past.[13] One was Marion County, Indiana, which includes Indianapolis.

The other was Tarrant County around Fort Worth, Texas. But there was an odd report, given the direction of the night's events. Shortly before 9:30 p.m., Cronkite reported on the national figures, which continued to show Eisenhower well ahead. But then he showed the electoral vote standings. Eisenhower was ahead in more states, but Stevenson had more electoral votes. This could have been jarring to any members of the audience who had been tuned in for a while, but Cronkite reported these figures without comment. A few minutes later he repeated the same count, again without explanation. It was not until fifteen minutes had elapsed, just after 9:30 p.m., that Cronkite reported a new set of electoral vote standings with Eisenhower clearly ahead. The Republican led in states with 279 electoral votes, more than the 266 needed for victory. Still, Cronkite continued his conservative approach. "These are scattered returns," he cautioned. "No state is complete." Viewers were not let in on just what it took for CBS to list a presidential candidate as "leading" in a particular state and what it might take to have that designation switched to "sure."

Shortly before 9:30 p.m., Cronkite set up the second UNIVAC segment this way: "And now to find out perhaps what this all means, at least in the electronic age, let's turn to that electronic miracle, the electronic brain, UNIVAC, with a report from Charles Collingwood." But there would be no report from the computer just yet. Collingwood ad-libbed again when the camera turned to him. "UNIVAC, our fabulous mathematical brain, is down in Philadelphia mulling over the returns that we've sent him so far," he said, continuing the anthropomorphic frame. "He's sitting there in his corner, humming away." Collingwood was clearly not yet willing—at least on air—to cast blame on the UNIVAC or the team of experts tending to it. "A few minutes ago," said Collingwood, "I asked him what his prediction was, and he sent me back a very caustic answer, for a machine. He said that if we continue to be so late in sending him the results, it's going to take him a few minutes to find out just what the prediction is going to be." Collingwood continued, "So he's not ready yet with his prediction, but we're going to go to him in just a little while." Instead, Collingwood was ready with a human-interest feature—in the "story of the story" vein. He had a guest. Harold Arlin had been a pioneering broadcaster for Westinghouse on KDKA in Pittsburgh in 1920—thirty-two years earlier—at the dawn of commercial radio. In Collingwood's folksy way, he set up a brief chat with Arlin this way: "Well you know, I got to thinking, what with UNIVAC and this studio here with all of its mechanical gadgets and its hundreds of people milling around trying to bring you the election returns, that television has never done such an elaborate piece of work as this. And I got to thinking about the days before television and radio." Arlin was still with Westinghouse. He and Collingwood reminisced about that earlier era and changes since then.

A few minutes after UNIVAC was a no-show, correspondent Edward R. Murrow got a turn to weigh in with analysis. He was well known to Americans since his daring radio reports from Europe during World War II on CBS. Murrow began with what sounded like a nuanced dig at prognosticators—both animate and inanimate. He had just a hint of mirth in his face. "As Walter Cronkite just suggested," Murrow began, "it may be possible for men or machines to draw some sweeping conclusions from the returns so far, but I am not able to do it." Yet, Murrow did read great meaning into the returns from a few areas. "The most surprising thing undoubtedly to date has been Connecticut," Murrow asserted with confidence. "I say surprising because the Republicans did not reckon to win it by more than about forty or fifty thousand. With only a few scattered returns still to come, they have an advantage of about 110,000 in Connecticut, which certainly registers as a landslide." For comparison, Murrow added this: "They carried it in 1948 by only fourteen thousand." After pointing out that Connecticut was also sending two Republican senators to Washington, he did some extrapolation. "The interesting point of speculation there is that a great many of the voters in Connecticut, particularly in the industrial areas, have the same interests, the same concern, as a great number of the voters in the state of New York, a crucial state, of course," Murrow said. "One thing one notices in looking about over the scattered returns so far, and that is a very considerable number of communities and precincts that are switching from the Democratic to the Republican column." Murrow also had news about the vote count. A new tally showed Stevenson leading in the partial count from Massachusetts. But Murrow concluded with a telling detail. The first Massachusetts city with a complete vote count was Brockton, a place Murrow described as a Democratic stronghold known for the manufacture of shoes. There, he said, Eisenhower had claimed nineteen thousand votes to Stevenson's thirteen thousand.

One more notable CBS broadcast journalist would have a chance to weigh in just before 10:00 p.m. He was Eric Sevareid, who had been one of Murrow's wartime colleagues reporting on radio for CBS from Europe, as had Collingwood. Sevareid was seated next to Cronkite at the anchor desk. "Well," said Sevareid, "it's still going, I think, the way it started to go at the very beginning." He said he had detected "an Eisenhower trend from the start," and added, "I've seen nothing really substantial to change that."[14] Sevareid's approach was traditional: looking for comparison to past trends. He noted that Stevenson was running "well behind" where fellow Democrat Truman had run in the same places to win in 1948. Meanwhile in the Republican column, Eisenhower was now "far ahead" of where Thomas Dewey had been in 1948. Some detail was offered. "Where the Republicans were strong four years ago, as in Maine, for example, they are far stronger," Sevareid explained. "And where the Democrats were very strong, in a good many industrial cities, such as those in New Jersey and places like Lynn, Massachusetts, and so on, the Democrats are far too weak." Sevareid was not making a prediction, but the chances of a Democratic turnaround were now hard to imagine without some sort of major surprise.

Just after Sevareid concluded, Cronkite addressed the audience: "So far, as you have noted, a slight trend has begun to develop and some of our people think the trend may be indicative of the final result." It was now the beginning of the broadcast's third hour, around 10:00 p.m. While no one at CBS had come right out and said so—and while Cronkite was characterizing the trend as slight—the direction was unmistakable. A great many indicators were pointing toward not just an Eisenhower victory but one with surprising strength in many places. The UNIVAC was yet to be heard from—at least on air. But various other players had been heard from: members of the CBS news team reporting vote counts, political reporters weighing in with their analyses, at least one newspaper declaring a state result, and political party figures declaring the presidential contest a landslide. On CBS radio, the public opinion analyst Samuel Lubell had weighed in at 8:35 p.m. with a key development. He mentioned having referred earlier to five indicators useful for detecting a landslide. Based on what he termed "special telephone calls," he was ready to predict that Eisenhower would "crack the South."[15] Before making that prediction, Lubell had posed a question to Robert Trout, anchor of the CBS radio broadcast. "First of all," said Lubell, "I want to find out, has UNIVAC reported yet?" "No," replied Trout, adding in an effort at humor, "It hasn't conceded yet either." "Well then," said Lubell, "I'm ahead of UNIVAC."

In fact, the UNIVAC and team of experts in Philadelphia had yet to weigh in with an on-air prediction, even by 10:00 p.m. But that did not mean there was no prediction from the computer. By then the computer had foreseen a landslide. But that was behind the scenes and was not aired at the time. In fact, the existence of that prediction would not be revealed on air until after midnight.[16] Shortly after 10:00 p.m. viewers watching NBC would have seen the Monrobot get its first turn on air, followed by a segment on radio.[17] At CBS Cronkite was engaged in another state-by-state rundown showing more developments in Eisenhower's favor. Then, there was a brief switch to the Commodore Hotel in New York, where Eisenhower had come not to claim victory but to greet his wildly enthusiastic followers. Meanwhile, Cronkite reported that an aide to Stevenson had said the following soon after 10:00 p.m.: "The news is not good, and it looks pretty grim."[18] Cronkite noted that Stevenson's campaign manager, Wilson Wyatt, speaking "a little later . . . said it's far too early to definitely say what the final result of the election will be." Even Wyatt's remarks were indicative of the Stevenson campaign's defensive position at a time when the Eisenhower camp was jubilant. This was yet another way of reading the signs. And there were more. Several minutes before 10:30 p.m., Cronkite was reporting on two newspapers that had called their states for Eisenhower—the *Baltimore Sun* in Maryland and the *Boston Post* in Massachusetts. Eisenhower was well ahead in New York, held leads in pivotal southern states, had a clear majority in the popular vote, and commanded a striking lead in the electoral vote standings. So, where was the UNIVAC?

Finally, just before 10:30 p.m., Cronkite was preparing to switch to Collingwood for a third try at a computer-generated forecast. "Now let's find out how our electronic brain is getting along on the prediction of the trend tonight," said Cronkite. "We turn for that story to Charlie Collingwood." Things were still not going as planned. Collingwood was clearly disappointed, but he was not giving up. "Well, as a great believer in the machine, I hesitate to say that we're having a little bit of trouble . . . with UNIVAC," Collingwood confessed. "It seems that he's rebelling against the human element." Continuing in the humanizing vein, Collingwood explained, "We've fed him some figures which were a little out of line of the sort of thing that he'd been expecting, and so UNIVAC came up and said he just wouldn't work under these conditions." "However," Collingwood continued, "the people who operate him are so loyal to him that they say that it wasn't his fault at all, that it was their fault and our fault for giving him the returns in the wrong order."

In subsequent decades, as computers became more common in American life, it would not be uncommon for government officials and others to blame various sorts of problems on a "computer error"—whether real or just cover for human incompetence. But here in the infancy of the computer as a commercial product, no such excuse was forthcoming from the UNIVAC camp. Too much was at stake to deflect blame that way. Collingwood did have some state results that he said had come from UNIVAC. He read the first few in alphabetical order. They contained no surprises, and Collingwood seemed to be trying to buy time. The camera switched briefly to Philadelphia and then back to New York. Collingwood continued to speak. Then from off camera, someone tapped him on the arm to get his attention, cuing him perhaps that something was about to happen. "Have we got anything through there yet coming up on the teleprinter?" Collingwood asked, referring to the large video monitor, unseen by the audience, installed in the studio to display typed output from the UNIVAC in Philadelphia. Again, Collingwood made a comment about the UNIVAC "humming away in his corner." Then, the camera once more switched to the activity at the Eckert-Mauchly plant. Several individuals could be seen. They were focused intensely on tasks at various parts of the computer—including the console and the printer—as if they were trying to get the computer to respond. Collingwood was trying to get someone to speak with him. "Have we got a return down there?" he asked. "Can anyone down there hear me? Tell me whether we've got a national figure yet from UNIVAC? Draper?" Arthur Draper, a Remington Rand executive, replied, "Yes, here." Collingwood asked him, "Have you got a national prediction from UNIVAC?" "Yes," Draper answered. "UNIVAC's finally come through." Collingwood asked for the prediction. Draper, who was heard but not seen, obliged, as the commotion around the UNIVAC console continued: "We've got Stevenson, twenty states, Eisenhower twenty-eight states. That adds up to an electoral vote for Stevenson of 217, for Eisenhower 314. The prediction on this basis is 24,456,000 and some for Stevenson, 27,445,000 for Eisenhower."

That was it. After two and a half hours and three segments, here was a prediction from UNIVAC that, at best, did not leave the audience with anything more than they could already see for themselves at that point—a comfortable victory for Eisenhower, in general terms. And the total vote predicted, at just under fifty-two million, was well below the expected turnout that Cronkite had reported. Collingwood thanked Draper and then offered only a one-line comment: "In other words it looks as though Eisenhower is going to get it as far as UNIVAC is concerned. Now back to Walter Cronkite."

Cronkite barely acknowledged the report, saying only this: "And that's the prediction from UNIVAC, the electronic brain." He then moved on from the computer prediction segment to look at what he termed the "actual totals." This was followed by a report that another newspaper, the *Boston Herald*, with one-sixth of the Massachusetts vote counted, had predicted Eisenhower would take that state. For its part, CBS showed Eisenhower's electoral vote tally having reached three hundred in states where he was deemed to be "leading." At about 10:40 p.m. the first state would be moved to the "sure" column. It was Virginia. About fifteen minutes after the UNIVAC prediction, Cronkite returned not to Collingwood but to an announcement with a bit more detail about a new UNIVAC prediction: the odds of an Eisenhower victory. "Incidentally you know our UNIVAC machine, our electronic brain, has predicted that on the basis of present returns, General Eisenhower has a three-to-one chance—its figures—to win this election," Cronkite reported. "He would win with over three hundred electoral votes—according to UNIVAC's prediction—the presidency in this year of 1952." This was the first instance in the broadcast that a UNIVAC prediction was simply integrated into Cronkite's report as a straight news item. It was in the mix now with various other reports and statements—from political partisans, newspapers, and the network's own commentators—about the meaning of the vote. But this did not mean that Cronkite had now irreversibly accepted the computer's prognostications as a worthy addition to the broadcast. Any idea of doing so would be sabotaged by a bizarre report that was soon to emerge from the UNIVAC camp.

First, however, the subject of predictions in general—and their pitfalls—came up in a conversation between Cronkite and Robert Trout, anchor for the CBS radio broadcast that night. Trout had joined Cronkite at the television anchor's desk. Shortly after Cronkite reported that a second state had been added to the "sure" column—plus word of "deep gloom" at Stevenson headquarters—Cronkite introduced Trout as someone who might have covered more election nights than any other CBS reporter.[19] It was nearly 11:00 p.m. Trout made a cautious assessment: "It's been awfully dangerous to make predictions, but it certainly looks as if it is a landslide in the making." Just as Murrow and Sevareid had done before him, Trout spoke of all the communities around the country that seemed to be switching from Democrat to Republican since the last election. He also spoke of all the places that had been Republican in 1948 and were leaning even more strongly in that direction now. Still, he had come armed with examples of states that had flip-flopped late on election night and into the next morning in 1948. "We'd better not be prophets so early, don't you think?" he cautioned. Cronkite referred to Trout's words nearly twenty minutes later—just after 11:15 p.m.—when noting that Eisenhower would win by a landslide if he held on to the states where he was ahead. Cronkite added a caveat. He was not "making any predictions," he said. "That's simply the way the vote looks at this time."

All signs pointed with increasing strength in Eisenhower's favor. But then just around 11:30 p.m., UNIVAC was about to stumble badly—as if complete isolation from other election-night news had set in at the Philadelphia plant. Cronkite turned the floor over to Collingwood. "Well UNIVAC is rolling now," Collingwood said with great enthusiasm. "UNIVAC is chewing up figures as fast as we can give them to him and turning out results. It's down there, in its corner there, all the tubes working, so let's go down to Philadelphia and take a look at UNIVAC as it works on the election problem that we've been giving it." As the camera view seen by audiences switched to Philadelphia, Collingwood repeated the previous prediction—Eisenhower with a margin of 314 to 217 electoral votes with odds he gave as four-to-one. He noted that the UNIVAC had 2,000 vacuum tubes assigned to "watching" some 3,500 other tubes "to make sure that it won't make a mistake." Cued that a prediction was ready, Collingwood asked that the camera be switched back to the studio. He pointed at the screen mounted above him on which the computer's output would be shown magnified enough to be legible to the audience. He read the prediction out as it scrolled up on the screen, and someone out of view could be heard to say, "Aw, come on!"—as in disbelief—at what appeared. It was this: twenty-four states each for Stevenson and Eisenhower, with Stevenson to get more popular votes—twenty-six million to twenty-five million—but with Eisenhower edging out Stevenson in electoral votes, 270 to 261. And even at that, the odds were slim—given as an eight-to-seven probability that Eisenhower would win. At a point in the evening, when each fresh dispatch brought mounting evidence of a powerful victory for Eisenhower, here was UNIVAC essentially declaring the race a toss-up. "That's even!" Collingwood said, astonished, as he first began reading out the prediction to the television audience and came to the twenty-four-to-twenty-four state count. But when Collingwood was done, and without missing a beat, he injected some humor. "If you ask me, UNIVAC is beginning to act like a pollster," he quipped. "Anyway, this is what UNIVAC says, Walter, so now back to Walter Cronkite." Collingwood was grinning at that point. And Cronkite appeared bemused, too. He ad-libbed, extending the man-versus-machine comparison that Collingwood had introduced. "Charlie, very interesting indeed on that UNIVAC prediction," he said. "We who are only human and have to operate with flesh and blood instead of with electronic gadgets still think this thing looks like it's pretty much on the Eisenhower side at the moment. We'll be back to you a little later to see how you're getting along with that machinery over there though."

A few days later, *New York Times* critic Jack Gould would say that UNIVAC's on-air troubles during the evening led several CBS stars—Cronkite, Murrow, and Sevareid—to give the computer a "rough ride."[20] But back in the studio, Collingwood soldiered on. He took a turn at the microphone for CBS radio listeners, where he tried to put the best face on the computer's odd prediction, judging from a brief portion of the broadcast captured in a transcript found among Collingwood's papers.[21] Collingwood was introduced by a member of the CBS radio news staff as having been "out consulting with one of the mechanical marvels of the age, that CBS radio specialty, the peculiar device known as UNIVAC." Collingwood recounted UNIVAC's election-night chronology to that point, starting with "a little trouble at first" due not to any failings of "one of the mechanical marvels of the age," but "because we gave it some figures, which it didn't like." "And you know," Collingwood continued, "the human element's very important in this." He then told of the UNIVAC's first on-air prediction of an Eisenhower win with twenty-eight states, followed about an hour later—a few minutes before Collingwood appeared on radio—by the prediction of the thin Eisenhower victory just seen by television viewers. "I merely quote this to you as UNIVAC's prediction," said Collingwood, who proceeded to talk about a UNIVAC prediction for Connecticut that came out at the same time as the computer's first national prediction. In Collingwood's telling this Connecticut prediction was remarkable because with "only" 60 percent of that state's vote in, UNIVAC had forecast an Eisenhower win there by 128,000, just 2,000 less than the final tally. "You can't do much better than that," he said. Not mentioned was the fact that the *Hartford Courant* had called Connecticut as a landslide for Eisenhower nearly three hours before the first UNIVAC prediction.[22]

Meanwhile, a few minutes after the televised report of UNIVAC's prediction of a toss-up, Cronkite cued Murrow again for his take on the election-night developments. Murrow spoke with gravity, at a steady clip, glancing in turn at his notes, the camera, and what appeared to be a stopwatch that he picked up and held in the palm of one hand. "I think it is now reasonably certain that this election is over," he began. "Traditionally, the Democratic strength comes from the big cities, and they have failed to deliver in this election."[23] He cited several of these—Chicago, Boston, Kansas City—where Stevenson's lead was too thin to overcome Republican strength outside the cities. He also introduced yet one more way of assessing the returns on election night—a concession by New York's top state Democratic official that Eisenhower was the victor there. He concluded his analysis, seventy-nine seconds in duration, as he had begun: "It seems clear on the basis of the big city reports, and on the general trend, that General Eisenhower has won the election."

But as the camera switched back to the anchor desk, Cronkite again exhibited the caution that had marked his reporting from the start. He read out numbers showing Eisenhower ahead by a million votes but also noted that the total vote count so far was under twenty million out of fifty-five to sixty million expected. "So you see," Cronkite remarked, "that prediction of UNIVAC a moment ago that perhaps this will come out with twenty-four states for each of the gentlemen and Governor Stevenson with a little higher popular vote—General Eisenhower just a four-vote or five-vote margin on the electoral side—well, with all the votes yet to be counted, of course it's still conceivable." There soon followed an announcement that UNIVAC had issued a new prediction more in line with Murrow's declaration. Shortly after 11:45 p.m. Cronkite interrupted a report on the latest vote count to read out the latest computer analysis, handed to him on a slip of paper by one of his assistants. "And now UNIVAC—UNIVAC, our electronic brain—which a moment ago, still thought there was a seven-to-eight chance for Governor Stevenson, says that the chances are one-hundred-to-one in favor of General Eisenhower," said Cronkite. "I might note that UNIVAC is running a few moments behind Ed Murrow, however. Ed Murrow, some fifteen or twenty minutes ago, said he thought it was in the bag for General Eisenhower."[24]

A few minutes later, Collingwood, smoking a cigarette, appeared seated next to Cronkite at the anchor desk. After reporting that Eisenhower had "forged into a lead" in Stevenson's home state of Illinois, Cronkite explained Collingwood's presence: "Charlie Collingwood has a report from that electronic predictor, Mr. UNIVAC." "Well, Walter," Collingwood began, "Mr. UNIVAC suffered a momentary aberration." Collingwood was referring to the previous prediction of a tight race before what was now a striking reversal: Eisenhower was predicted to amass overwhelming wins in the popular vote, at twenty-nine million to twenty-three million, and the electoral vote, at 424 to 107.

Cronkite offered no commentary then. But the CBS veteran Eric Sevareid did so a few minutes later, just before midnight. At the end of the fourth hour of broadcasting, it was Sevareid's turn at analysis. He began by calling attention to UNIVAC's troubles and extending the man-versus-machine—or journalist-versus-machine—theme. "Well," said Sevareid, "since our time is short, Walter, I will only say that I'm delighted that

UNIVAC, our machine competitor, was wrong for a while, and we were consistently right with a human voice, or we'd all be victims of technological unemployment pretty soon." Cronkite chuckled and replied, "I'm beginning to wonder, as I do every election night and every campaign, if there isn't a marginal point though where it'd be nice if machines *took* over."

At about twenty minutes after midnight, with Eisenhower continuing to extend his lead—including returns in Missouri, the home state of the incumbent Democratic president—Sevareid and Murrow took a turn in front of the camera together for several minutes of analysis. Murrow spoke of the failure of the big cities and labor unions to deliver for Stevenson. Sevareid spoke about a national mood that may have trumped any issues, though he also said that the Korean War, inflation, and corruption had been key. He spoke, too, of the importance of the individuals in the race: "The most popular single figure in the country against a man who was utterly unknown three months ago."

Then it was back to Collingwood for what would turn out to be the final UNIVAC appearance, just before 12:30 a.m., though the broadcast still had more than two hours to run. Cronkite set up the three-and-a-half-minute segment with a quip. This foreshadowed remarks made after election night by others who were probing, through humor, the place of computers in the mental landscape of journalism and in the culture at large. "Now let's go over to UNIVAC, the electronic brain, which some time ago predicted this victory for General Eisenhower," said Cronkite. "Everyone else seems to be predicting the victory now for General Eisenhower, so perhaps—it is suggested— UNIVAC and Charlie Collingwood can tell us who's going to win the World Series—next year." Collingwood picked up where he had left off about forty-five minutes earlier, talking about what he termed UNIVAC's "momentary aberration" with Eisenhower having only eight-to-seven odds of victory. Continuing with his approach of investing the machine with human—or at least animate—characteristics, Collingwood said of UNIVAC, "He shook himself, all 5,500 electronic tubes of him, and came up a few minutes later with a prediction that the odds were beyond counting." Then Collingwood, suggesting that the whole episode had been personally unsettling, gave the UNIVAC camp a chance to dig its way out. "Now I've got a lot of faith in this machine, and I was sadly shaken by this aberration that it had," said Collingwood. "So let's go down to Philadelphia and see whether we can get an explanation of what happened to UNIVAC from Mr. Arthur Draper, who is the head of the New Products Division of Remington Rand's Laboratory for Advanced Research. Art, what happened there when we came out with that funny prediction?" From the CBS camera in Philadelphia, the audience saw Draper seated by the UNIVAC console. He had a headset on and held a microphone. He had a pleasant smile on his face as he prepared to launch into an explanation—certainly not a pleasant moment for him. The story that would be told for decades afterward about UNIVAC's election-night debut would come to hinge on what Draper said next. Of more immediate relevance, certainly, was the near term and whether the election-night difficulties could be cast into a useful narrative for Remington Rand's still nascent commercial computer business. Draper would not just be seen on television. His words were also broadcast on CBS radio and would be recounted—on air and in print—the next day.[25]

"Well, we had a lot of troubles tonight," Draper began, speaking slowly and calmly.[26] "Strangely enough they were all human and not the machine." Speaking of a prediction that the audience never saw, Draper said, "When UNIVAC made its first prediction with only three million votes in, it gave five states for Stevenson, forty-three for Eisenhower, 93 electoral votes for Stevenson, 438 for Eisenhower. We just plain didn't believe it." Draper and others would say after election night that a number of factors, including the expectation of a close race, had prompted the initial disbelief that first greeted this prediction. But on election night he offered no details to the viewing audience—no details about when this prediction appeared, about why it was not believed, or about who, exactly, comprised the "we" who did not believe it. He simply moved on, attempting to explain to Collingwood and the audience how, from that point of disbelief, the prediction process morphed into generating something the audience did see. He used language that might have made sense to someone steeped in the forecasting methodology but must have been challenging for most of the audience to follow: "So we asked UNIVAC to forget a lot of the trend information that we had put into it, assuming that that was wrong. So UNIVAC worked on a smaller margin of knowledge. This won't give a wrong answer, but it'll throw the odds to the extent that you saw." Draper did not elaborate. He wrapped up by reiterating his message—the one that would end up at the core of the UNIVAC narrative thereafter. This was less about what the audience saw and more about what, in Draper's account, had happened out of view. "As more votes came in," he explained, "the odds came back, and it was obviously evident that we should have had nerve enough to believe the machine in the first place. It was right, we were wrong. Next year we'll believe it." Collingwood jumped in: "You mean four years from now, Art?" Draper replied, "Well, yes."

Collingwood had the floor again in New York. Here was just the sort of scenario he had foreshadowed four hours earlier—a mistake—and Draper had taken the fall. "Well," said Collingwood, "I think that was very handsome of Mr. Draper and the people down there to take the blame for UNIVAC's error. It just goes to show that you can't outsmart the machine." But as Collingwood extended the segment briefly to talk about one of the UNIVAC's state predictions, the computer's on-air troubles were not quite over. An hour earlier Cronkite had reported that three Massachusetts newspapers had called that state for Eisenhower, who had a significant lead that strengthened over the next hour.[27] So, Collingwood was struck by what UNIVAC was forecasting for Massachusetts now in the early morning hours of November 5: "One interesting thing is that UNIVAC still shows that Massachusetts will probably go for Stevenson. We may see whether that works out right or whether UNIVAC changes its mind."[28] He concluded the computer's election-night performance with one final iteration of the human-versus-machine trope. "At the moment, then," said Collingwood, "UNIVAC predicts, as everyone else is predicting now, that Eisenhower is way ahead in a big sweep. UNIVAC says he'll carry all but eight states. So that's the way it stands now with our electronic brain back in working order and agreeing with all the human brains." He carried the trope to the end as he tossed the broadcast back to the anchor: "Now to another human brain, Walter Cronkite." "Thank you, Charlie Collingwood," Cronkite replied, picking up the cue. "I suspect that's the nicest thing that has been said about me tonight and the nicest likely to be said. I also like that report of Mr. Draper in Philadelphia, proving that humans shouldn't tamper with the thinking of electronic machines. Very nice, indeed." Cronkite made no mention of the Massachusetts prediction that was as odd, under the circumstances, as UNIVAC's brief late-night national prediction of a tight race. But just a few minutes later, Cronkite would join those Massachusetts newspapers in describing that state as "definitely in the Republican column" for the first time in twenty-eight years. A subsequent Remington Rand report would reveal what the Philadelphia team did not know at the time, despite the systems in place to screen returns and detect problems. The vote counts given to UNIVAC for Massachusetts had been in error throughout the entire night.[29]

With those words of Draper in the early morning of November 5, 1952—"We should have had nerve enough to believe the machine in the first place"—a legend was born. That is the "man-bites-dog" sort of story that journalists like and makes everyone else chuckle. And it is the cartoon-like version of events retold every four years like some campfire tradition. The machine had outsmarted its human keepers— its creators!—and they had a hard time believing it. The legend is based not on what audiences could see for themselves. Rather, it is based on what they did not see, the drama playing out behind the scenes on the factory floor in Philadelphia. This was the drama the audience only learned about with Draper's account after midnight along with similar accounts—in postmortem reports, speeches, and articles—that Draper and others provided, starting immediately after the election.

There is one other key part of the durable legend as it gelled over time into a standard, incomplete, and sometimes inaccurate narrative. This has to do with the purported timing of that first UNIVAC forecast, the one that foresaw a landslide coming and was not shared with the audience. Over time, postelection accounts—complete with artifacts— have generally settled on 8:30 p.m. as the point when the UNIVAC called the election for Eisenhower behind the scenes. This was said to be too early for ordinary mortals—journalists and commentators—to detect the same thing. As we will see, that frame is problematic. And that lack of clarity, in turn, raises one more mystery. If—as we shall see—there were journalists detecting a strong Eisenhower trend in early returns, why was the UNIVAC team unwilling to embrace the idea that the computer had it right in its first, withheld prediction of a landslide? We will get to that question, too, in a moment. It will tell us a lot about whether CBS saw the computer as integrated into its roster of trusted prognosticators. And it will tell us whether the UNIVAC team was seen by CBS news executives as a thing apart, relegated, literally, to a distant outpost and not brought into any brainstorming about mounting evidence that the outcome would not be at all close, rather than the expected tight race. Spoiler alert—the computer, its team, and their analysis did end up as a thing apart. And that contributed to UNIVAC's so-called "rough ride" in its first election-night outing. One more question. If the computer was framed as something apart, what kind of lessons can we draw as we reexamine the legend that built up about this episode? What does it tell us about the impact of the way innovations—so important in election-night history—are perceived by innovators and their collaborators?

So, back to the first of these questions—a crucial one—about just when UNIVAC spit out that first forecast behind the scenes with uncanny accuracy. And to reiterate, this is important in making sense of the legend surrounding UNIVAC's use in 1952 and what that tells us about innovation. What is clear from all available accounts is that at some point well before the first on-air prediction from UNIVAC—the one seen by viewers at around 10:30 p.m.—the computer had processed early returns and generated at least one prediction that was met with disbelief by the UNIVAC team and was not aired.[30] This behind-the-scenes forecast was said to be based on about 3.4 million votes counted at that point. It predicted a massive victory by Eisenhower—by 438 to 93 in electoral votes, by forty-three to five in states won, and by a popular vote of about thirty-three million to about nineteen million. One more thing—the UNIVAC at that point was not hedging its bets. The computer gave itself overwhelming odds of being correct—odds of at least one-hundred-to-one. Several documents that have been described as copies of the actual UNIVAC printout of this prediction start with these two lines:

IT'S AWFULLY EARLY, BUT I'LL GO OUT ON A LIMB.
UNIVAC PREDICTS—with 3,398,745 votes in—[31]

What comes next in some of these versions are odds in favor of an Eisenhower victory listed as "100 to 1" and in others listed as "00 to 1." The latter—"00 to 1"—was said to result from programmers not accounting for odds of a correct prediction so large that three digits would be needed to express them.[32] Some of these copies have a handwritten notation at the top—"8:30 p.m."—though the handwriting varies on different versions. What they all have in common is that they lack a computer-generated timestamp. This turns out to be important. And this gap to date in the historical record raises questions about what to make of a version of events that has persisted for more than seventy years.

What is not certain—though critical to discussion of the computer's touted election-night advantage—is just when this early prediction of a landslide was generated. Because of the fast-moving nature of any election night—and this one in particular—knowing the time of UNIVAC's early prediction would be helpful. But while the most commonly cited time given for the first prediction was 8:30 p.m.—including the time cited in a subsequent account by Draper—there are also accounts that give the time as 9:15 p.m., including one written by Arch Hancock, the Remington Rand publicist.[33] In fact, one of the most curious discrepancies turns up in a report prepared after the election and authored by two participants. One was Max Woodbury, the University of Pennsylvania statistics expert working with the UNIVAC team, and the other was Herbert F. Mitchell Jr., head of the UNIVAC Applications Department. My tour of several archives has turned up two versions of this report that are virtually identical except for one detail—the time of the first prediction. It is given as 8:30 p.m. in one version and 9:15 p.m. in the other.[34] Again, why does it matter? Because the story that has formed around these events is that the computer did what no human could. But did it? Timing is essential to answering that question—and to testing the legend against the evidence. Bear with me as we sort this out. Along the way we will encounter the high-stakes drama—or, in fact, trauma—felt by the UNIVAC team as things were moving at breakneck speed. And we will see that the computer's own keepers did not believe what it was telling them—a conclusion they would sorely regret.

One possible clue to the time of the first, unaired UNIVAC prediction of a landslide is the vote count on which it was said to have been based. That figure is typically given as 3.4 million, similar to a round figure of 3 million votes mentioned by Draper during his mea culpa for the CBS audience.[35] But all available evidence suggests that there were not 3 million or 3.4 million votes available to analyze until well after 8:30 p.m. And even that does not take into consideration the lead time needed to ready the data for analysis nor the several minutes needed to run the computer program.[36] By all accounts the vote tallies being used by the UNIVAC team in Philadelphia were coming via teletype from the CBS election headquarters in New York.[37] CBS was relying primarily on wire service reports for vote counts, which were being posted on displays in the studio and being passed on to Cronkite, who, in turn, updated viewers frequently. Cronkite opened the broadcast at 8:00 p.m. with a total combined vote under six hundred thousand. At about 8:30 p.m., just after the segment in which Collingwood introduced the UNIVAC, the total vote count was about 1.2 million—nowhere close to the 3.4 million that has long been thought to be the basis of an 8:30 p.m. prediction from UNIVAC.[38] Even at 9:00 p.m., the total vote noted at CBS had only reached 2.4 million. The tally shown to CBS viewers first topped 3 million a few minutes before 9:15 p.m. and stood at 4.1 million by about 9:20 p.m.[39] These figures are also consistent with an early edition of the *Baltimore Sun* reporting that at 9:00 p.m. the national vote total for Eisenhower and Stevenson combined stood at about 3.4 million.[40] Just to complicate the picture further, the International News Service generated a dispatch that ran in the *Hartford Courant* the day after the election reporting that UNIVAC's forecast of an Eisenhower win with 314 electoral votes—the one the television audience saw at about 10:30 p.m., not 8:30 p.m.—was based on 3,398,745 votes. That is the precise figure later claimed to be the basis of the never-aired 8:30 p.m. prediction.[41]

Another important feature of Draper's early-morning confession was the reaction of his team in Philadelphia to the initial UNIVAC prediction of a landslide. Their reaction was disbelief. A few more details about that disbelief turned up in subsequent accounts. In a postelection report, Woodbury and Mitchell wrote of what happened when that landslide prediction appeared on UNIVAC's printer. It clearly clashed with pollsters' preelection forecasts of a close race. "There was a hurried consultation among the top Remington Rand people present and Dr. Woodbury," the report revealed. "Could this prediction be correct? In view of the obvious state of fatigue of all of us who had programmed the job and the lack of time to test the entire procedure on prior election data, it was decided that it would be too risky to release this prediction."[42] Herman Lukoff, the engineer in charge of keeping UNIVAC in working order, gave a similar account in his memoir. "Our election officials, Herb Mitchell, Max Woodbury, Art Draper, and Phil Vincent looked on in disbelief," he wrote. "The officials put their heads together and said 'We can't let this go out. The risk is too great.'"[43] Vincent's own account, in a speech a few years later, included this observation: "Unfortunately some of us had more confidence in the Gallup Poll prediction than in the UNIVAC extrapolation, and decided that the machine could not possibly be right."[44]

After the election Draper would identify several factors responsible for the failure to believe that the UNIVAC had nailed it. The race was expected to be close. Based on a small fraction of all votes cast, the prediction gave Eisenhower a number of southern states with barely any returns. And at the time of the first prediction, returns had not yet come in from many other states. Draper said that under those circumstances, "It was beyond comprehension that the machine could predict with such a degree of certainty that the odds would be greater than 100 to1."[45] In other words how could UNIVAC be absolutely sure that its prediction was correct?

Following the original stunned reaction, the next reaction, according to those involved, was to look for programming errors. Finding none, the step after that was to water down the part of the program that had detected a wide swing away from previous voting history. This trend was applied to areas with votes that had not yet come in. As the evening wore on, according to these accounts, the mounting raw vote swung the prediction back to one-hundred-to-one odds of an Eisenhower victory.[46] Not clear is exactly how all of this translated into the UNIVAC predictions seen and heard during the evening on CBS. Contributing to this lack of clarity is that several accounts of behind-the-scenes activity are at variance both with each other and with what can be seen in the broadcast itself.[47]

Another intriguing part of the behind-the-scenes story is this: Did the UNIVAC team in Philadelphia make a unilateral decision to withhold the first prediction of a landslide from CBS? Or were members of the CBS staff in New York aware of that prediction and involved in a decision not to air it? Accounts by members of the UNIVAC team in

Philadelphia contain no suggestion that CBS was informed of that first prediction.[48] In an account published in 1972, CBS's Mickelson wrote that the initial projection of a landslide was not released to "the impatient CBS news executives who were not aware at that time that one run had been made."[49] Consistent with this is another account he published in 1989, in which he describes the decision to withhold the first prediction as having been made in Philadelphia.[50] Neither Collingwood nor Cronkite gave any suggestion on air that they had known in real time of the first UNIVAC prediction of a landslide. Their on-air demeanor—including both Collingwood's surprise and then frustration at not getting a prediction until 10:30 p.m.—is consistent with not knowing about the early forecast of a landslide. And had they known of that prediction, they might have even proposed airing it once evidence of a strong Eisenhower victory began to mount. In his script for a radio broadcast the next day, Collingwood places the responsibility for suppressing the first UNIVAC prediction with the "miserable statisticians who were handling him."[51]

Another question we posed is worth addressing at this point—whether journalists and others taking part in election-night reporting would have greeted the early landslide prediction as preposterous. Or, to ask this another way, were there signs available, to those looking closely at the details of early returns, that an Eisenhower sweep was developing? In the CBS newsroom, certainly, there was a range of comfort levels with reading an outcome into the early returns and sharing any such conclusions on air. Collingwood himself wrote in a radio script the day after the election that the desire of journalists not to repeat the errors of 1948 left them underestimating Eisenhower's strength. "Reporters can cover football games, fires, every variety of human experience," Collingwood said, "but put them on an election and you can't get them to believe their eyes and ears."

Yet, in a number of places, reporters and analysts were taking note of surprising early developments favoring Eisenhower. And they were doing so before any UNIVAC-generated forecast, whether that might have been at 8:30, 9:15, or 10:30 p.m. Soon after the CBS television broadcast began at 8:00 p.m., Cronkite called out such data points in South Carolina, Connecticut, Florida, Baltimore, Cleveland, and elsewhere—all before his first introduction of the UNIVAC. The *Hartford Courant* reported even earlier, at 7:40 p.m., that Eisenhower had carried the much-watched state of Connecticut.[52] Douglas Cornell of the Associated Press Washington bureau wrote after the election that "the outcome was obvious almost from the start," and that "by 8 p.m. we were writing that Ike had crashed into the lead and was running strongly."[53] In the first few minutes of the radio network coverage that began on NBC at 8:00 p.m., correspondents in the field were filing dispatches of surprising Eisenhower strength in various states by looking at complete returns from particular cities and towns and how they compared to 1948.[54] At the *New York Times*, experienced reporters were working their contacts around the country to get a read on the early voting.[55] One checked with the managing editor of the *Miami Herald* and was told by 8:30 p.m. that Eisenhower would take Florida. After word came at 9:05 p.m. that Eisenhower was ahead by two thousand votes in industrial Rome, New York, another veteran *New York Times* reporter remarked to one of the editors, "Looks like it's all over." And in a postelection recap, *Time* magazine would report that by 9:00 p.m., with less than 5 percent of the vote counted, "almost every indicator was beginning to point Ike's way."[56] In addition, Arthur Summerfield, the Republican National Committee chairman, was making pronouncements at about 8:00 p.m. that a "landslide" seemed to be developing. Before 9:00 p.m. Summerfield had escalated his imagery, with CBS reporting that he had claimed victory and deemed Eisenhower to be "rolling on like a tidal wave."[57] Summerfield was a partisan, to be sure, but his remarks were reported nonetheless by CBS, and his assertion certainly introduced the notion of a landslide early on into the evening's discourse.

Perhaps the most interesting aspect of the UNIVAC camp's reluctance to believe the early forecast, then, is what this might tell us about how they and CBS envisioned the computer's role. It was clearly to be a thing apart. The computer would be included in the broadcast, to be sure, but its use would not be integrated with the other means by which journalists on election night try to make sense of returns. There was a CBS camera crew in Philadelphia but no correspondent. A curious memo from Remington Rand to a business prospect—Prudential Insurance—asserted before the election that Collingwood would be in Philadelphia with the UNIVAC on election night.[58] But that is not how it turned out. And as

Collingwood had noted colorfully in his on-air reporting, the computer, in Philadelphia, was "sitting there in his corner."[59] The experts in programming, statistics, and engineering had anticipated a great many sources of error and built in a variety of means by which to detect them. But there was a glaring omission visible only now in retrospect. Those experts did not anticipate a scenario in which the computer would generate a correct prediction so surprising that it would not be believed. Their implicit approach on election night was to compare the prediction to expectation—based on preelection polls—rather than comparing the prediction to other fresh data points. These would have been easily obtained by listening to the radio or watching television or brainstorming with experienced reporters and political observers. Draper and his colleagues hunted, instead, for errors in their statistical model and their program.[60] No clear evidence has emerged that the election-night plan included a means for the UNIVAC team to discuss predictions with the CBS staff before airing them. There was no apparent scenario for both groups together to assess both the validity of the computer-generated predictions and the validity of trends detected by other means. The computer and its team were a thing apart.

The UNIVAC had been added to the election-night formula to attract viewers and generate headlines and, just maybe, provide an edge in forecasting the outcome. But it was not well integrated into the journalism of election night. At CBS this even had a physical dimension, with the computer operating in another city. At NBC, where the Monrobot had been used to attract viewers, there would also be a lack of integration on election night. This would be manifested, in part, by not incorporating the Monrobot into the NBC television and radio broadcasts until well into the evening, just after 10:00 p.m. as we shall see. Even so, in one of the details that would be absent until now from the historical record, the relatively tiny Monrobot actually beat its giant competitor with an on-air forecast that audiences would see. With that piece of the story missing until now, a UNIVAC-only version of the election-night debut of computers has had profound staying power.

After nearly seven hours on air, CBS wrapped up its election-night program with no reference to the UNIVAC but with brief remarks from Lowell Thomas, Ed Murrow, and Eric Sevareid—a summing up, as Cronkite called it.[61] What had happened in the election, an Eisenhower landslide, was known and agreed upon by all the various sources of analysis—journalists, commentators, pollsters, political party officials, wire services, newspaper editors, computer, and, finally, Stevenson's concession and Eisenhower's acceptance of victory. The remarks that ended the evening for CBS took on the question of what led to that outcome and questions about what could and could not be known about those causes. There were digs at those who would deign to be able to know what the voters had been thinking and to predict what voters might do. The resistance here was not explicitly to technology—UNIVAC was not mentioned—but to the notion that people could be reduced to simple numbers, and that by whatever means, their intentions and motives could be known with certainty. And yet, these journalists, among the best known and most respected broadcasters of the day, tried as best they could to offer their own understanding of what it was the voters had done and what the vote meant.

Lowell Thomas kicked off that final segment with a dig at the pollsters: "One interesting sidelight on all this victory of General Eisenhower is the way the eminent gentlemen who conducted the polls were fooled. Don't you think so? I wonder if they were just too scared this time."[62] He went on to share some anecdotes about meeting or encountering Eisenhower—in France during World War II, in a New York restaurant, and even in Thomas's own home. The point of these stories was to communicate the personal traits that transcended Eisenhower's initial lack of political know-how and accounted in a large measure for his eventual success. "Don't you believe that that personal warmth played a great part in winning this tremendous political victory?" said Thomas. "I do." Murrow was up next. Speaking in measured tones, looking alternately at his notes and the camera, he was still striving for eloquence at the end of a long and hectic night. "Walter," he said, "it seems to me that this was the end of an era in American politics, a great exclamation point in our national history—because tonight, after twenty long years, the traditional concessions of defeat came not from Republicans, but from Democrats." Then he raised a question about what could be known in advance, or even after the fact, about the voters. "To me the most impressive thing about tonight is again the demonstration that the people of this country are sovereign, that they are unpredictable, and that somehow in a fashion that is as mysterious to pollsters as it is to reporters, the great normal majority in this country made up its mind as to the man it wanted to lead it," said Murrow. "And I believe as of now, no man can say what produced this result or indeed what consequences may flow from it." Even so, Murrow was willing to speculate. "The figures indicate," said Murrow, "that Eisenhower did not win with the indispensable aid of Senator Taft or the farmers or labor or the South. . . . He owes his victory to no man and to no segment of our society." Murrow talked for almost four minutes. Then he leaned back, as if drained, and in a fluid motion brought an unlit cigarette to his lips, reached into his pocket for a match, and lit up. Cronkite made a few remarks about the challenge Republicans would face after playing defense for so long. Then it was Sevareid's turn. He offered a cogent analysis of the political challenges Eisenhower would face—including the implications of a landslide victory. "I think this places upon him personally a magnified degree of responsibility in the presidency such as few presidents have exercised," Sevareid argued. And again the mystery of deciphering the voter was on the table. "I think that one of the things the vote shows," he said, "is that the independent voters, so called, have been very much misinterpreted, misunderstood." How was one to make sense of this group who were thought to have been important to the election's outcome? He thought Ohio Sen. Robert Taft, a leader in the Republican Party, had it right: those were people who did not normally participate in the political process, and organization was more important than argument in getting them to the polls. "A great name, a great figure," said Sevareid, "will bring them out more than any kind of persuasion."

Beneath the surface of the presidential horse race on center stage that night, deep questions had been lurking. What could be known? How could it be known? And what answers—or methods for getting answers—could be trusted? On cbs the broadcast featuring a computer would not resolve those questions. But the computer now had a seat at that table, at least, in tackling journalistic imperatives. The need for timeliness. The need for accuracy. And the need to use both what is visible and what is not so easily visible in making sense of the world.

7 | The Mechanical Genius

In an election-night legend that would persist for decades, the uncanny behind-the-scenes accuracy of the UNIVAC computer was triumphant, and the Monrobot was typically forgotten, ignored, or downplayed. The irony, clear now from the complete CBS and NBC broadcast footage, however, is that the diminutive Monrobot—representing a very different vision for computing—made its first on-air forecast before the mighty UNIVAC did. The David-versus-Goliath frame might have been an enduring story line. But that is not the one that took hold. It would also be a mistake to assume that the Monrobot's debut was an unmitigated triumph. It was not. And yet with that debut, no matter how the computers performed, this episode allows us to see something else. An innovation that eventually becomes successful—in this case the computer as an aid to journalism and election-night forecasting—does not always perform spectacularly in its first outing, no matter how well the advance planning goes. That is worth remembering if we are tempted to dismiss other innovations that come along in our own time because there is some stumbling at the outset. Sometimes the new thing may have value at first just for being new, rather than for its contribution to achieving the task at hand. That might not come until later.

As night fell on November 4 in Manhattan, NBC's massive Studio 8-H in Rockefeller Center—like the CBS studio a few blocks away at Grand Central Terminal—was buzzing with activity. Reporters, commentators, and producers were taking their places. Cameras and microphones were readied, with cables snaking across the floor. A horde of special guests and celebrities had been shown around by NBC "guidettes" and were milling about off to the side or moving to the balcony. The team from Monroe had been in place for hours, getting ready for the Monrobot's debut before an audience of millions. It was all exciting—and, for so many reasons, it was nerve-racking, too.

NBC began its election-night coverage at 8:00 p.m. on radio. The network's television coverage would not start for another hour, which was also an hour later than CBS television. The delay at NBC allowed a popular variety show, the *Buick Circus Hour*, to run in its usual time slot.[1] Themes paramount in the CBS election-night broadcast could also be seen at play in NBC's coverage from the outset. NBC highlighted the night's drama and claimed a place at center stage. The Monrobot would have a role in touting the special nature of the NBC effort, even if the computer itself would not be heard from for more than two hours on radio or for more than one hour after the television cameras were switched on. As with the UNIVAC at CBS, the Monrobot would be an ambiguous player in the NBC coverage—described in wondrous terms at the outset but then not quickly or tightly integrated into the evening's agenda for delivering news.[2]

At NBC, the wonder of radio's nationwide audience, the wonder of the election's mass action, and the "story of the story" were combined as the network positioned itself at the heart of the night's events—along with Philco, the company sponsoring NBC's radio and television broadcasts. "From all over the nation," announcer Bob Murphy told the radio audience, "your votes are coming in—votes from free Americans in a free election."[3] Together, NBC and Philco were presenting the results "in the public interest," said Murphy. The audience could hardly have missed the sponsor's self-interest, too, as Murphy listed Philco's products: radios, television sets, phonographs, refrigerators, freezers, electric ranges, and air conditioners. These were not just appliances notable for their special or innovative features. Throughout the evening they would be touted as technological wonders. The radio audience would hear repeatedly about the Philco television set with a unique "golden grid tuner."

The anchor for NBC's radio broadcast, Merrill "Red" Mueller, was introduced in heroic terms. He was a distinguished reporter. His career included covering World War II in North Africa, Europe, and Asia, and other key stories since. As this story began, Mueller noted that there were not yet any meaningful trends. He promised a state-by-state rundown of returns at the top of each hour, and he invited the audience to take part in analyzing them: "So get your pencils ready," he urged, "have your charts at hand, and sit back and enjoy the 1952 election with the greatest NBC radio staff ever assembled for political coverage."

H. V. Kaltenborn was introduced as the "dean of American news analysts." His initial remarks gave the appearance that he might not have learned from the drubbing he received in 1948 after letting expectations of a Dewey victory interfere with his ability to see the developing Truman win. "Everyone agrees that the popular vote will be close, and the early returns suggest that that will be the case," he told his radio audience now in 1952. "That will make it all the more difficult to determine the electoral vote."

Next, it was time for another member of the NBC radio news staff, George Hicks, to extend the "story of the story" with a description of Studio 8-H. There was the raised table with six microphones for radio broadcasters. There were four sets for television commentators to report on various contests. Hicks noted that this was the first time NBC had combined radio and television operations in this way. There was machinery. Tabulating and adding machines were operated by several dozen people. Teletype machines were bringing news, as he put it, "from every hamlet in the country." And there was one more device. "Over our shoulder against one wall is the Monrobot," Hicks said. "This is a huge machine." Perhaps it looked huge to Hicks when compared to hand-operated calculators, but the Monrobot was notable in the world of computing for its small size. Hicks continued his description of the computer with what it would do. "It will add, subtract, give odds, multiply," he explained. "All you do is feed in the new figure and out on a square card comes the printed result you want." The studio also had arrangements to monitor other broadcasts to see how NBC was doing in comparison.

As NBC switched to correspondents around the country, listeners could hear about vote counts, which, when compared to historical patterns, did point in Eisenhower's direction. Noting that Connecticut might show the way to a broader trend, Mueller introduced a reporter from local affiliate WTIC in Hartford. There, it was said, "General Eisenhower is scoring a smashing victory in Connecticut on the basis of unofficial but substantial returns." Upside surprises were reported for Eisenhower in several cities, including coastal Bridgeport. In 1948 Truman, the Democrat, had taken that industrial city by seven thousand votes. Now in 1952 Eisenhower, the Republican, carried Bridgeport. This was just the sort of difference from past trends that journalists had looked for in early returns since the mid-1800s. In Boston the complete vote from several small towns was dissected to show a similar pattern. In Boxford, for example, a community north of Boston, the Republican candidate had won handily in 1948. Now, the margin in Eisenhower's favor was even more overwhelming.

Even this far into the era of network radio, the switches back and forth to correspondents in cities far from New York were treated as wondrous. Mueller introduced a report from the West Coast this way: "Now it's time to go really jumping across the country—out across the wide Missouri, over the Continental Divide, and through the Sierras, to California."[4] Mueller set up the next report in a similar fashion. "And now it's time to keep up with the speed of electronics, having jumped back from Hollywood to New York, three thousand miles we go halfway back across the country again," he said excitedly. "For another report from the Midwest, we switch to St. Louis and station KSD."

Less than an hour into the radio broadcast, at about 8:50 p.m., Kaltenborn was given a second turn at the microphone for his analysis. He was still cautious. But comments from the Republican National Committee chairman about a developing landslide gave Kaltenborn an opening to talk about signs in Eisenhower's favor. There was a "glimmering" of a landslide, he conceded, but "not yet bright sunshine."[5] Deemed especially interesting was South Carolina, with Eisenhower leading in a traditionally Democratic state where the Democratic governor had endorsed him. But Kaltenborn's efforts to parse the vote in particular areas hit a wall when he talked about Eisenhower's steady lead in the national popular vote. That lead might mean a landslide if it continued, Kaltenborn suggested. But he voiced a note of caution: "Since we don't know exactly from what states and what areas in each state these votes come, the vote is too small out of the expected total of fifty-five to sixty million to be definitely indicative." For now caution seemed to be his motto.

At 9:00 p.m., with the NBC radio broadcast underway for an hour, NBC launched its television coverage from the same headquarters, Studio 8-H in Rockefeller Center.[6] Newscaster John Cameron Swayze, who would be covering the presidential contest throughout the night, opened by explaining an oddly shaped map behind him. It displayed states proportioned in size according to their number of electoral votes. In the new medium of television, Swayze was already well-known to viewers through a fifteen-minute nightly newscast that drew its name from the cigarette brand of its sponsor—the *Camel News Caravan*. After a discussion of various regions of the country and their voting history, Swayze launched right into returns from what he termed eight "key" states. In six of these, there were surprises favoring Eisenhower—Connecticut, Florida, Ohio, South Carolina, Virginia, and Maryland, the latter said to have gone with the winner in all but one presidential election since 1888. Swayze attributed Stevenson's lead in the Illinois governor's home state to the city vote. Swayze deemed Stevenson's lead in Tennessee to be no surprise.

With television the network now had the ability to present the "story of the story" in a visual way. The program's producers did this by allowing viewers to see the studio arrangements. During much of the program, the shots would be mostly close-ups. There were fewer of the CBS-style sweeping views of the studio and its infrastructure of cameras, cables, lights, and support staff. But after Swayze the NBC television broadcast was more grandly introduced by an unseen newscaster, Kenneth Banghart. He described what the audience was seeing as a camera slowly panned around the studio. Banghart boasted that the network had assembled a team with the "hardest-headed political observers." While the Monrobot was not immediately mentioned by name, it was among the novelties that the announcer used to tout special features of the broadcast. "Our experts," said the announcer, "will be aided for the first time by amazing new machines, scientific brains rallied by NBC television to bring you the most accurate picture with split-second timing."

The first thing seen by the television audience in Banghart's tour was the audience *in* the studio. Men in coats and ties and women in evening wear milled about in a roped-off area to one side. With them were a number of young men and women in uniforms, presumably the NBC ushers, or "guidettes." The camera picked up a long desk on a raised platform where at least ten individuals, the radio staff, were already in their second hour of broadcasting. Other NBC staff tended a bank of teletype machines, where wire-service dispatches were bringing election news and returns. There were individuals seated at desks with calculating machines. The audience could see camera operators and members of the crew operating microphone booms. Four small sets could be seen—each with a desk and prominently observable Philco signs, a nod to the broadcast sponsor. One set was for the anchor and the others featured the Electoral College vote, the House of Representatives results, and the Senate standings, along with a display for governors' races. Banks of special National Cash Register machines had been assembled for showing state-by-state results to the television audience. And then, said Banghart, continuing with his excited tone, "Let's come around to the fabulous electronic indicator—Mike Monrobot, we call it—stuffed with information to compare speedily the figures with those of 1948, to show the trends. Morgan Beatty is there, ready to report those trends." The audience could see, behind Beatty, the desk-sized computer, with its top flipped up vertically as a backdrop, showing some of its electronic components underneath. In front of Beatty and facing him across another desk was a young woman tending to the computer's keypad for input and the automatic typewriter for its output, both of which sat on the desktop. This was Marilyn Mason, but she was not named at that point. The tour was completed as the camera circled back to the studio audience. Banghart promised that returns would be brought to television viewers as fast as the "battery of computing machines can work."

Finally, Banghart came back around to Bill Henry, the anchor. Henry was the 1950s version of a multimedia journalist who had penned an election-day column in the *Los Angeles Times* talking about the Monrobot, comparing it to Kaltenborn, and poking some fun at both.[7] Henry began his first segment with a report on the weather, including transparent cartoon-like drawings of a smiling sun and an umbrella that said "RAIN" being passed over various parts of a map of the United States by an unseen hand.[8] The rest of the first half-hour included a state-by-state rundown by Swayze. All the latest surprises were in Eisenhower's favor among states with at least 4 or 5 percent of their votes counted: Kentucky, Ohio, Oklahoma, and Rhode Island.

At about 9:35 p.m. it was Kaltenborn's turn to join in at the anchor desk for his first television appearance of the night. He was now ready to shed the cautious approach he had taken earlier on radio. Introduced by Bill Henry as a "veteran expert" and an "old friend," Kaltenborn launched right in. "Well if you want me to make a prediction," he said, "I predict that Eisenhower is going to be elected."[9] The overriding reason for his call was this observation: "Eisenhower is ahead in every doubtful state from which we have sufficient reports to indicate any kind of a trend." He went on to talk about a few states and the South, where he said Eisenhower's strength was especially important. At the end of his turn in front of the camera, he came back to the point with which he had started. "One might be safe in saying," he reiterated, "that it looks quite definitely like General Eisenhower at this hour."

The Monrobot would get its first turn before the television audience a half hour later, at about 10:05 p.m.[10] The small computer would not get quite the "rough ride" that the UNIVAC was said to have gotten from some of the CBS news staff. But there did seem to be a slightly amused look on Henry's face when he cued the first Monrobot segment. "One of the more interesting features of our election coverage here," he said, "is the mechanical brain, the Monrobot, which is being watched now by our man Beatty, who is riding herd on it. And Morgan is ready to explain it, so now to Morgan Beatty."

The camera switched to Beatty, with the Monrobot behind him. With its top flipped open, the audience could see some of its hundreds of vacuum tubes. Operating the computer was Marilyn Mason, who sat behind a second desk facing Beatty. On top of that desk were the Monrobot's controls and printer, connected by unseen wires to the computer. Without missing a beat, Beatty launched right in after Henry's cue, with an excited—if not completely clear—report. "And the Monrobot, the electronic brain, has raced far ahead of the election returns at this moment," he said, "and they have tabulated five million votes and combined them with millions of digits that have run through these electronic tubes here and have calculated the odds at this point of the election returns, and they show General Eisenhower is favored to win six to five on an isolated basis." The meaning of "isolated basis" was not explained, and viewers who were not familiar with betting odds might have been uncertain about the meaning of "six to five." From the context it was not a reflection of the margin of Eisenhower's lead but rather the degree of certainly—slim—that the prediction of a win was correct. Referring to a recent bulletin in which a Stevenson aide had said the news looked "grim" for the Democratic contender, Beatty boasted, "That was confirmed a half hour ago by the electronic brain." But as would be the case with the UNIVAC later in the evening at CBS, the NBC audience would have to take the word of someone associated with the computer project—Beatty in this case—that the computer had been a genius behind the scenes. No records have surfaced to explain why no analysis was reported from the Monrobot until after 10:00 p.m. One possibility—given the degree of advanced planning for the NBC broadcast—is that the Monrobot was simply not scripted to be part of the television or radio program until the second hour, when there might have been an expectation in advance that the contest could still be close. Or, given Richard LaManna's account of the Monrobot's preelection troubles, with bits of solder falling onto the computer's magnetic drum memory, perhaps there was some behind-the-scenes intrigue over the computer's operation.[11] Or, perhaps the computer was simply seen more as a promotional tool than one that might yield valuable insights. We do not know, in part, because unlike those promoting the UNIVAC, there does not appear to have been as much of a postelection publicity campaign to tell the Monrobot story.

Beatty did not introduce the machine the way Collingwood had introduced the UNIVAC on CBS with a discussion of the election-night forecasting challenge, the methodology, and the computer. Instead, the well-known NBC broadcaster's presentation may have baffled at least some viewers, from the betting-type odds to his sometimes rapid-fire delivery. It was all just so new—serving as the intermediary between a computer and the audience. Beatty was deeply experienced as a print, wire service, and broadcast journalist. He had been a wartime correspondent and distinguished himself in covering some of the biggest stories of the twentieth century.[12] But this was something else again. Beatty did present comparative data—such as the odds at the same time of the evening in 1948 that had favored Truman five-to-four.[13] But he did not explain what to make of that sea change in connection with the "six-to-five" odds for Eisenhower. His enthusiasm led him to return several times to the Monrobot's powers of detection, though even here the details in his report could be hard to follow. For example, he said the odds favoring Stevenson were six-to-four in Illinois, but that the "brain has raced far ahead of that" by taking the "downstate" vote into consideration and thus favoring Eisenhower one-and-a-quarter-to-one. What he apparently meant was what he said next. He was not suggesting that the current odds favored Stevenson but that they showed Eisenhower ahead in the predictive odds "despite the fact that Governor Stevenson is far ahead"—apparently referring just to Illinois. At one point Beatty asked Mason for fresh information on Connecticut. She pulled a sheet of paper out of the printer and handed it to him. He used that information to return to the point he had made at the outset. Referring to the dark assessment given by a Stevenson aide, Beatty said that "the suspicions of the governor of Illinois that things look pretty grim were confirmed well over—well ahead of the governor himself—by the electronic brain."

Notably, in comparing machine to human, the humans Beatty chose as foils were Stevenson and his aides—not for being wrong but for being slow. And in making machine-versus-human comparisons, he avoided skewering the pollsters for predicting a close race. He also steered clear of critiquing some of his journalistic colleagues for their cautious approach to positing a likely outcome based on early returns. He was not, in other words, positioning the Monrobot as an improvement over either the journalist or the pollster.

The Monrobot segment lasted two minutes. Next on camera was Swayze. He made no reference to the Monrobot or to Beatty's report and repeated the same news with which Beatty had begun—about the Stevenson aide describing the situation as grim. Beatty and the Monrobot would not come back before the television audience until after midnight. Nor would the computer or its output be discussed before then, with one exception. That was a quip by Henry when adding up presidential votes in his head. "That's just a rough guess," he said. "I haven't got that Monrobot at my fingertips here."

Minutes after concluding the first Monrobot segment, Beatty did make his way over to the radio desk—apparently accompanied by Marilyn Mason—for a turn with the listening audience.[14] Radio anchor Red Mueller set up the segment with a human-versus-machine motif, speaking of the "two brains" that just sat down with the radio staff. "One," said Mueller, "belongs to a very famous Washington correspondent of ours,

Mr. Morgan Beatty, and the other one belongs to a mechanical genius that he's operating over here in the corner of the room." Mueller then asked Beatty for "the report from the dual brain."

Beatty picked right up with the same theme. "I've got a lot of respect for this mechanical genius over there," he said. Then in a bit of self-deprecation, he added, "Marilyn, I don't think you need my brain anymore at all." Beatty gave the radio audience a report much like the one he had given on television, including a claim that "our mechanical brain was exactly one hour ahead" of the Stevenson aide "in figuring that things looked pretty grim." Beatty came back to the same notion of the machine being ahead of the Stevenson camp when he talked about the Chicago vote count and the national returns. "This machine," he said, "was a little smarter than the governor of Illinois." Beatty spoke of the Monrobot as being so fast that it could "figure the odds while the race is being run." In a quest, perhaps, to find new ways of describing the odds, Beatty came up with one set of curious terms, an apparent reference to a female figure with proportions larger at the bottom than the top. "I would like to point out a solid state," he said, "one that's got a nice, good, round-sized vote, this is a luscious pear-shaped vote we've got here, and it's very indicative of the situation in the East." Luscious? Perhaps this was a reference to the fruit, or maybe to female anatomy. He went on to identify the state and give a few numbers, this time adding some clarity to the terms he was using. "With nearly half the vote counted in the state of Connecticut," he said, "odds in favor of Eisenhower [are] five-to-three, meaning there are eight chances there, and Eisenhower has five out of those eight in his hands already."

And that was it. Beatty turned the radio microphone back to Mueller. In an attempt at humor, Mueller offered up an image suggesting that he may have found Beatty's assignment hard to take seriously. "We'll excuse you to get back and fan those tubes," said Mueller. "Don't let that blow out over there, boy."

In addition to computer analysis, the various ways of divining the direction and meaning of the vote that had been seen on CBS television were also in play at NBC. In between accounts of Senate, House, and gubernatorial races, the NBC coverage of the presidential contest skipped around among a wide range of voices: reports by NBC staff in the studio, reports by correspondents in other cities, dispatches of newspapers, comments of those seen as keen observers of politics or public opinion, statements of national party figures, and concessions of state party chairmen. Those who appeared live on NBC broadcasts were generally introduced in a deferential manner by the two anchors, Henry on television and Mueller on radio. One of the most notable differences among the various commentators who appeared live on NBC was their comfort level at various points in the evening in saying something definitive about the outcome based on a largely common set of available facts. The ghost of election-night 1948 still haunted some of them.

Pollster Elmo Roper had appeared on the radio broadcast at about 9:35 p.m., when Mueller introduced him as a "real expert."[15] Roper was introduced on television about an hour later as someone who could "really explain" the situation as more votes came in.[16] In both segments Roper chose to lay out a scenario by which Eisenhower, who had an increasingly solid lead in the national returns, could win the popular vote but still lose the electoral vote. He made clear that he was not deeming this probable but possible. And in his television segment, he went on to mention not just the surprising Stevenson weakness in parts of the South but also developments in Pennsylvania that could break in Stevenson's favor.

H. V. Kaltenborn got another chance just after 11:00 p.m. to offer up his analysis before the Monrobot's return to the air. He reminded viewers of the very definite prediction they had already heard from him of an Eisenhower victory, which was made at about 9:35 p.m.[17] He went further this time, saying that Eisenhower was about to score one of the most convincing Electoral College wins in American history. Henry wrapped up the segment by commending Kaltenborn for the veteran broadcaster's early call, even while making it clear that this was Kaltenborn's assessment, not the network's. "Well, H. V.," said Henry, "I'm glad to have that analysis of the situation from you because this certainly is a very crucial moment now in the night's returns, and I think that we got in first with our—with your—uh, suggestion that Eisenhower was very vitally in the lead." Henry continued, as Cronkite had done on CBS, to waiver between what was apparent—mounting evidence in favor of Eisenhower—and an apparent need to make clear that the counting was not done and the outcome was not certain. A few minutes after the Kaltenborn segment, and after a report reiterating the concession of New York to Eisenhower by the state Democratic Party chairman, Swayze was back. He poked fun at "political observers" who had been unwilling to make definitive statements about the likely outcome before the election. It looked like they had been "fooled," Henry added, joining in on the dig. But Henry would go on then, and later, to note that results were definite only for a few states. Just before midnight Henry pointed out that "there's no such thing as a forfeit in politics," with nothing definite until a state's final vote count.[18] He also painted a scenario by which the tide could turn in Stevenson's favor with a few key states—including California, Pennsylvania, and Illinois—even though Eisenhower would win easily if he claimed all the states in which he was then leading.

Just before the Monrobot's second appearance, one more category of election-night analyst appeared, a partisan. That was James Farley, a Coca-Cola executive who was also a former national and New York Democratic Party chief and had served as postmaster general under Pres. Franklin Roosevelt.[19] Farley said he was sorry to have to admit the apparent Democratic defeat. "That was evident to me," he said, "from the early returns."[20]

Then it was time for Beatty and the Monrobot again. At about 12:10 a.m. Henry once more had a mirthful look on his face as he gave a cue for the segment: "And now, let's go across the hall to the 'brain' and to Morgan Beatty." Though there was little mystery left about who would win, Beatty's enthusiasm had not waned. His segment lasted nearly six minutes. He repeatedly praised the computer's performance, starting with his opening: "And over here at Monrobot, the electronic brain, we've been ahead of these trends all evening long." He recited in rapid fire the changing odds projected by the Monrobot during the evening—six-to-five, nine-to-seven, five-to-four, and now three-to-one. He compared Truman's victorious odds at midnight in 1948 to the much more favorable Eisenhower standings at midnight in 1952, even though the gap in the popular vote was similar. He took a shot at explaining the methodology being used. Pointing his pencil over his shoulder where some of the Monrobot's electronic components could be seen, he said, "You know we run the popular vote in through these electronic tubes in comparison with mathematical formulas based on the last election and the expected vote, and the result is that trends are established." He added, by way of explanation, "We're not predicting anything on the mechanical robot." Beatty discussed some state votes. In connection with one, he suggested that "the electronic brain here has picked up something that everyone else seems to be missing." It was the odds favoring an Eisenhower win in Tennessee—which Beatty confirmed by asking Mason to check them for him. In fact, his own network had been reporting for well over an hour that Eisenhower had a surprising lead in Tennessee, and Roper, the pollster, had remarked on that development even earlier.

Beatty signed off. Henry, smiling, thanked him "for that very enlightening information on the situation." Then, without any commentary on the content of Beatty's report, Henry called Elmo Roper in again as "the noted expert on these things." Even this late in the evening, while conceding that an Eisenhower victory was looking likely, Roper cautioned that "there are still some big question marks." It was soon Kaltenborn's turn once more, at about 12:35 a.m. Again, he reminded viewers of his televised prediction for Eisenhower, the one made at about 9:35 p.m. And again Henry remarked on Kaltenborn's call, this time saying that it was "mighty fine" that Kaltenborn had been "the first one to state the situation."[21]

Within an hour—just after 1:00 a.m.—Henry was about to cue Beatty at the Monrobot set one more time. But Henry noted first that those who had been predicting a landslide seemed to have been correct. New York had clearly sided with Eisenhower, and the California Democratic Party chairman had conceded his state as well.[22]

The Monrobot was up for its third and final appearance on NBC television about a half hour after CBS had retired UNIVAC for the night. Beatty might have been forgiven for losing his enthusiasm by then, but he did not. Again he brought out the machine-versus-human theme. He did it not by claiming that the Monrobot had been ahead of the journalists and commentators but by zeroing in on what might have been a safer target: the politicians who had been in the election-night mix for analysis and prognostication. Perhaps as a follow-up to the report of concession by the California Democrats, Beatty opened with this: "Very interesting that our electronic brain has stayed ahead of the politicians all night, and we're very proud of it." Again, he cited the history of the night's odds and said that Marilyn Mason was calculating the latest national odds.

He continued to talk about several states while he waited—including an ambiguous remark that Eisenhower was favored one-to-one in Pennsylvania and in Montana, too. He returned to ask Mason whether she had finished calculating the odds. As she began to answer, Beatty cut her off and said, "I think we're getting them now." Someone he addressed as "Rex" handed him a sheet of paper from outside the camera's view. Reading that sheet Beatty said the odds had now risen from three-to-one up to ten-to-one, and then laughing and tossing that sheet of paper off to the side, he added, "You'd just as well make it one-hundred-to-one." If the Monrobot was having trouble, Beatty betrayed no hint of that. But he may have left the audience wondering why the final round of odds he cited had come to him not from Mason but from someone off camera.

Once more Henry was in command back at the anchor desk. This time he did make a comment about the computer but not a complimentary one. "One of the things that I don't think that that brain can tell us," he said, "is what accounts for some of these things that have happened."[23] Here was pushback from an important journalist to the narrative of the computer as "brain." The computer might be a tool for calculation, but from Henry's perch, it seemed, the computer was not a tool for explanation. That was the domain of humans. Henry seemed to have been holding himself up as one of those who could deliver the kind of sense-making that the computer could not. Perhaps in response to Beatty's report that Eisenhower was favored to win in Arizona, Henry talked about how remarkable it was to see that state go Republican. He characterized the recently-elected Republican governor as a "ball of fire"—a former "radio man" and "alumnus of this particular business"—who had been successful in running the state.

A short while later, there was one more important election-night voice to weigh in: the *New York Times*. Henry told his audience a few minutes after 1:00 a.m. that the *Times* would be announcing Eisenhower's election in the next edition. "They are ready," said Henry. "They're not going to wait for anybody to concede." His remarks suggest that in 1952, no matter what reporters and pundits and even computers might say, the fact that an important newspaper was going to call a race before the losing candidate had conceded was still news for an election-night broadcast audience.

As NBC was wrapping up for the night, Beatty got one more turn before the cameras. This time he joined Henry at the anchor desk. Like a dog on a bone, Henry was himself not ready to concede the relevance of the Monrobot to the broadcast. One could hear it in his tones and his words, including, again, an image giving primacy to humans unaided by electronic brains. Beatty, on the other hand, was not giving up his boost-crism. Beatty chuckled as Henry opened the segment this way: "We've had quite a time this evening, and one of the interesting features of what we've been doing tonight has been the work of Morgan Beatty with the Monrobot, the wonderful electronic thinker," said Henry, "and we want to prove to you that it is possible for Mr. Beatty to speak, think, and act without having an electronic tube in one ear. And Morgan, tell us what you think of this election."[24] Without missing a beat, Beatty delayed his own analysis to heap praise on the computer, "Well I think Mike Monrobot, our new star, performed beautifully." Beatty went on to reference a way of breaking down the voting public—by gender. There is no evidence that this figured into the Monrobot's algorithm. Maybe Beatty was channeling a combination of preelection polls and NBC's preelection humanizing of the computer as being fond of pretty secretaries. Still, this gave Beatty an opening to make a point about an electorate in which women had reached numbers in equity with men. "Seems to me the most important thing about Mike was that he was right because for once, he gets the women," said Beatty. "Now I think we've got a very important element there." He continued to explain what he meant by that. "It's quite obvious that a high proportion of these voters were going to be women this time, and they weren't voting according to past party loyalties because they didn't need to have any," he asserted. "And if you assume that 50 or more percent were women, you assume that they didn't like the idea about withholding and inflation, all at the same time, and also assume the Korean—interest they had in the Korean issue—and when we put that factor into Mike Monrobot over there, he gets the women." He also referenced something he had said four and a half hours earlier when he had gotten his first turn on camera with the computer: that forty-five minutes before word had come from Stevenson's camp that things looked grim for the Democratic candidate, the computer had come to the same conclusion. What Beatty did not say at this early morning hour was that this feat of prognostication was not aired right away and was only announced at a point in the broadcast when both the stream of returns and one of Stevenson's own aides were hinting strongly at the governor's defeat.

At 3:00 a.m. the NBC national television broadcast from New York ended as it had begun, with the "story of the story" yet again. The camera pulled back and panned the room—now, as Henry put it, "This rather deserted scene before you, just a few people left." Henry noted by name some correspondents and news managers who were part of the network's coverage of the campaign and elections. He thanked the companies that had brought their expertise and equipment to bear on election night, including the Monroe Calculating Machine Company, National Cash Register, and the Victor Adding Machine Company. "The excitement is now over," he said. "But those of us who have had a part in it are not going to forget it for a long time."

Besides getting things right and being first with the news, news organizations had other imperatives on election night. One of these, as we have seen, was positioning themselves at the center of attention. The rise of television marked the demise of another traditional venue for election news—the streets around newspaper buildings as election-night gathering spots. They were part of the print world's version of center stage. What newspapers had to say certainly remained important in 1952. Witness Henry's reporting just after 1:00 a.m. that the *New York Times* was putting out its next edition with headlines of an Eisenhower victory even though Stevenson had not yet conceded. Nowhere was the demise of newspapers as historic election-night gathering places truer than New York. Times Square had survived in that role well into the era of radio broadcasting. It had even seen crowds that numbered in the hundreds of thousands as late as the wartime election in 1944.[25] But after the war, Meyer Berger, a chronicler of city life for the *New York Times*, began writing postelection stories taking note of both the diminishing crowds and speculation that radio and television were to blame.[26] Still, in 1952 the *Times* itself had not given up on drawing a crowd to Times Square. Elaborate new displays to track returns had been commissioned to accompany the traditional searchlight and the "zipper" that spelled out headlines in a band of lights ringing the building, itself an election-night innovation from 1928.[27]

The displays in Times Square were orchestrated from the *Times* newsroom, where decisions were also made in advance of election night about the timing of press runs. Management opted not to rush early editions to print until there was definitive news. The managing editor, Turner Catledge, concluded that with television and radio providing reports through the night, "We can afford to hold back until we have a fairly complete picture."[28] The first *Times* editions hit the presses at 10:52 p.m., an hour later than usual, with a headline that Eisenhower was in a strong lead. Then at 12:40 a.m., the *Times* was ready to declare the race over in multimedia fashion and with precise timing. A bulletin was to be read over the *Times's* radio station, wQXR, which had set up shop at a broadcast desk in the *Times* newsroom. Orders were given for a searchlight atop the Times Tower to signal Eisenhower's victory by a prearranged code that had been shared with readers, a beacon shining steadily to the north. Orders were also given for the "zipper" to carry the news around the building in lighted letters. A thermometer-like display that extended several stories high on one side of the tower would shoot to the top on the column that tracked Eisenhower's electoral vote tally, flashing word of his win. The top management at the *Times* was eager to see both the Times Square displays and the crowd's reaction. Publisher Arthur Hays Sulzberger and Maj. Gen. Julius Ochs Adler, vice president and general manager, along with some of their aides, walked into Times Square just before 12:40 a.m. The scene was captured in *Times Talk*, an in-house publication of the *New York Times*. "Mr. Sulzberger found himself standing beside an excited watcher—a stranger—whose eyes were glued to the board and to the running golden letters above it," the story recounted. "The publisher quietly told the man, 'I'll bet that Eisenhower thermometer will shoot right to the top at 12:40.' The man snorted without taking his stare from the board." When 12:40 arrived, "All the signs and the turret beacon broke out in sudden concord," the story continued. "The little man's head slowly looked in wide-eyed disbelief at the quiet prophet beside him. Mr. Sulzberger smiled and turned back to the office."

But what the *Times Talk* piece did not capture was the thin crowd itself. This can be seen in newsreel outtakes I found at the National Archives.[29] The crowd was so thin that there was enough room for vehicles to easily pass through Times Square. The scene was also captured by Meyer Berger, who authored his final obituary for Times Square as a gathering spot for crowds seeking election-night news.[30] No more than ten thousand were in the square between 9:00 and 10:00 p.m., and fewer than twenty-five thousand were estimated to have been there at any time, including patrons of the nearby theaters around Broadway. Police suggested that television and radio were the only plausible explanations. "A tradition was dead," Berger concluded, "with only a few thousand pall-bearers to see it peacefully interred." In an editorial the *New York Herald Tribune* concurred and pinned the blame on television.[31] The venues for election-night news were shifting, and the technologies that would be employed both to generate and transmit that news were changing. But there had been continuity, too. That continuity was the deployment of innovations to help attract an election-night crowd, whether the sort of physical crowd that gathered at places such as Times Square or the virtual crowd of millions watching and listening at home.

When the counting was done, Eisenhower had, indeed, won by a wide margin. Stevenson carried only nine states, all in the southern part of the nation. Even there Eisenhower had eroded the traditional Democratic base. He took Florida, Kentucky, Virginia, Texas, and Oklahoma. Eisenhower won Missouri, too—the home state of the sitting Democratic president. It was also the state that *Collier's* magazine had declared—in its preelection vote-watching guide—as the best state to watch, having sided with the victor in every election after 1900.[32] Stevenson could not even carry his own state of Illinois, losing nearly as badly there as he did nationwide.[33] Eisenhower's national margin of victory was more than 10 percentage points. More than sixty-one million votes had been cast—exceeding expectations—and Eisenhower had claimed about thirty-four million of them. In the Electoral College, Eisenhower's victory was a blowout: 442 to 89.

Eisenhower ran ahead of his own party. Massachusetts was a case in point. He carried the state even though his national campaign chairman, Henry Cabot Lodge Jr., lost a bid there for reelection to the Senate, defeated by a young Democratic congressman and future president, John F. Kennedy. Still, it had been a remarkable night for the Republicans. They recaptured the White House after losing it a generation earlier to

Franklin Delano Roosevelt. They picked up enough seats in the House and Senate to become the new majority party in each chamber. They also won five new governorships, extending the lead they had established two years earlier.[34]

While the night's big news was a power shift in politics, only with the benefit of hindsight can we now see that the broadcasts carrying this news to Americans had also served as another sort of sentinel event. They showcased two technologies—television and computers—that would arguably come to define public and private life far more over the subsequent decades than the outcome of the day's political contests. Television had extended its reach from coast to coast for the first time in the live coverage of a presidential election. Television would go on within a few years to reach nearly all homes and become a dominant American news medium. And millions of Americans had gotten their first glimpse of computers in action. These new machines had played a role—however uneven—in the kind of prognostication previously delegated exclusively to humans, foreshadowing the devices' increasing integration into the most fundamental aspects of daily life.

But in real time, the historic nature of that night's deployment of "electronic brains"—both in the general context of American life and the specific context of election-night reporting—was not clear to those at the center of events. In fact, for at least some of the key players, what prevailed when they reflected on this innovative use of computers was a sense of unease. After his nationally televised mea culpa, Remington Rand's Arthur Draper would go on to describe this as one of the worst nights of his life.[35] Charles "Joe" Colledge, the NBC news executive whose duties had included arranging for the Monrobot to have a place in the Studio 8-H broadcast, did not feel triumphant either. Reuven Frank, then a young staffer and future head of NBC television news, recalled Colledge saying he left the studio that night wondering whether his career was in jeopardy after facing withering criticism of the program from the NBC "brass."[36]

Despite later accounts portraying election night 1952 as a landmark in an unstoppable trajectory of computers, the place of computing in election-night broadcasting—let alone in journalism—seemed unclear. It remained to be seen, as *Business Week* had written before the election, whether computers would be acclaimed as appropriate tools for the "Election Night hurlyburly."[37] Just as important as what happened on election night would be the stories about what happened. These would take on a life of their own. They would drive collective memory of the debut of computing in real time on the newest public stage in American life—television.

8 | The Trouble with Machines Is People

The story of election night 1952 has, over time, become one in which a computer—and in almost all accounts this is Remington Rand's UNIVAC alone—scores a publicity coup by getting the outcome right, being smarter than its human keepers, and being seen in action by an audience of millions. That story has some problematic features. For one thing if Americans were more acquainted with "electronic brains" by the morning after the election than they were before Election Day, the CBS broadcast featuring UNIVAC was just part of that exposure. The NBC broadcast featuring the Monrobot scored higher election-night ratings than CBS.[1] The Monrobot was also featured on radio, which was still the dominant broadcast medium. The Monrobot was presented to NBC viewers during at least three daytime programs on Election Day, including the *Today* show. And it was featured in other publicity in print and on air. The standard UNIVAC-CBS story also misses the wide range of responses to the use of "electronic brains" on election night. This, in turn, contributes to the impression that a single event, an election-night debut, changed the course of computing history, popularizing the computer and fixing a place for it in election-night forecasting forever after. The record suggests a more complicated story. And that story calls for a more nuanced understanding of what happens when innovations appear. Change is not as direct a process as the standard story would suggest. The available evidence also suggests that what kept the UNIVAC story going was not just what people saw on election night in 1952. Rather, momentum came from after-the-fact efforts to keep the story alive. There was also inherent appeal in a version of election-night events with a strong "wow" factor—machine outsmarts human. This episode did open the door to considering computers as tools with a place in journalism generally and election-night forecasting in particular. This episode also engendered a widening circle of interested parties. The 1954 elections would see the use of another new computer to help call an election for a newspaper, the *Detroit Times*, working with the computing lab at nearby Wayne University. In advance of the 1956 election, IBM engaged in an aggressive push to secure a place on the election-night stage as part of its fight for leadership in the rapidly developing commercial computer industry.

Still, the events of election night in 1952 did not close the door to naysayers—or to active resistance. The process of coming to terms with computers for even a limited use in journalism—election-night analysis—would by no means be an automatic response. The framing of computers in a human-versus-machine way would continue to have appeal both in their deployment for election-night forecasting and in critiques of their use. Even as the twenty-first century arrived, decades later, the election-night marriage between journalism and computing continued to have famously shaky episodes.

In the rearview mirror, we can see election night 1952 as a sentinel event, one that featured bold experiments and a willingness to take risks before a live audience of millions. Here was an attempt to quantify in a new and more precise way the real-time analysis that journalists had been practicing on election nights for a century. And here were computers emerging from behind the closed doors of the military, academia, and the government. Behind those closed doors, computers had been put to work on such tasks as the calculation of missile trajectories, the solution of problems in thermodynamics, and the preparation of census tables. Now, they were doing something that ordinary people cared very much about. One could arguably date the dawn of the computer age to this event just as well as any other. But for at least some of those in the middle of this event, the use of computers on election night did not have a triumphant aftertaste.

For public consumption NBC issued a postelection press release with a glowing account of the Monrobot's performance. In the studio audience, NBC boasted, "Notables in the arts, science, and industry watched the Monrobot, widely heralded 'electronic brain,' predict General Eisenhower's election on the basis of incomplete returns three hours before Stevenson conceded defeat."[2] NBC also boasted of drawing more election-night viewers than the competition in the ten cities surveyed by the Trendex ratings service.[3] But the conclusion of Joe Colledge at NBC that the network brass were unhappy with the broadcast was echoed a few days later in a behind-the-scenes memo between network executives Davidson Taylor and Joseph McConnell. Though pleased by the ratings, Davidson wrote, "I agree that our coverage did not live up to our own expectations."[4] As for the Monrobot and its assigned correspondent, Morgan Beatty, Davidson wrote, "Beatty was commanding and informed as usual, but I think maybe we could have used him to better advantage away from the baleful influence of our mechanical brain, the monrobot." Taylor, whose own tasks on election night included keeping an eye on the competition, was not impressed with the computer experience at CBS, either. "We weren't the only ones who had troubles," he wrote. "The CBS UNIVAC was a real embarrassment. They kept asking the machine questions, and it wouldn't give any answers."

In the wake of the 1952 experience, the trajectory of computers as potential tools for election-night journalism was not one of automatic adoption at NBC. For the midterm elections in 1954, in fact, NBC would retreat from computer use altogether. In a preelection press release, news director William R. McAndrew described an election-night plan that would focus heavily on correspondents reporting from around the country. "A good local reporter," he explained, "is better than the best out-of-town statistician or mechanical device."[5] Following the 1954 election, NBC issued a press release making the same assertion and extending the journalist-versus-machine comparison: "Prognostication and trend-following was left to Joseph F. McCaffrey, a veteran Capitol Hill observer who was informally billed as 'NBC's improvement on election computers.'"[6] In the grand tradition of rolling out innovations on election night, however, the absence of a computer in 1954 did not leave the network without an "NBC-developed TV wonder" to boast about. It was a "four-way split screen 'editorial conference,' enabling reporters in four key cities across the nation to compare results and trends while appearing simultaneously on viewers' sets." The NBC release added this breathless detail about the split screen's election-night debut: "The technical men worked at top speed to present the new effect, and finally perfected it two hours before air time."

The Monroe Calculating Machine Company, meanwhile, would celebrate its 1952 election-night appearance on the national stage with a two-page spread in *Keynote*, a magazine for its employees.[7] The NBC broadcast was deemed "the most widespread publicity Monroe has ever had." The election-night role, with photographs, would also appear in a Monroe brochure in 1953 to solicit contracts from the military and other customers for electronics and engineering products.[8] But there is not much evidence of concerted efforts by the company to keep the story of the Monrobot's election-night debut alive in the public's mind.[9] No Monrobot would again be part of an election-night broadcast on network television. The line of computers did go through several iterations over the next decade and a half. A Monrobot III—this was the model used on election night—went to an Air Force research facility in Massachusetts.[10] A subsequent model, Monrobot V, was built to be carted over rough terrain—vacuum tubes and all—to aid the Army in mapping.[11] In the late 1950s, Monroe became part of Litton Industries, a defense contractor, and continued to manufacture computers.[12] One of these, the Monrobot Mark XI, captured the attention of the *New Yorker* in a 1960 "Talk of the Town" piece. It began this way: "More news from the spooky world of automation!"[13] As with the features touted by NBC in 1952, the *New Yorker* noted the latest Monrobot's surprising size. At just 375 pounds, it was deemed in 1960 to be "completely portable." Also notable was that Monrobot's equally diminutive price for the times— $24,500. The Monrobot line of computers faded out in the 1960s.[14] Monroe itself—after being bought and sold several times, adding and removing other product lines, and changing names to Monroe Systems for Business—continued to be focused, as it was when the company was originally founded in 1912, on the sale of desktop calculators.[15]

As for the 1952 election-night experience at CBS, that network did not pull away from computing. CBS would use a UNIVAC again for the 1954 midterm elections and the next presidential election in 1956. That experience also drew the attention of the *New Yorker* in a piece titled simply, "Brain."[16] Unlike the Monrobot, UNIVAC would have a long and storied history—with continuing publicity of its election-night role in 1952. Unisys, the eventual successor company to Remington Rand, remained in the business of providing computer-related products and services to customers worldwide.[17]

But at CBS in 1952, the immediate reaction to the pioneering debut of a computer on election night was well short of ecstatic. In a four-page postelection press release that went on at length with details and superlatives about the network's television broadcast, a single line was reserved for the computer use: "UNIVAC, the electronic 'brain,' as early as 10:30 p.m. predicted the sweeping victory of the Republican standard bearer."[18] At Remington Rand's Eckert-Mauchly Division, UNIVAC engineer Herman Lukoff would write later that some officials were "kicking themselves" after the election for not having aired the initial early prediction—a landslide—that was withheld from CBS.[19]

Sig Mickelson, the CBS news and public affairs director, was more upbeat and wrote a letter of thanks to a manager on the UNIVAC team.[20] Mickelson explained that he had waited ten days to send the letter to get a sense of the public's response. "I can assure you now that the reaction is almost without exception very favorable," Mickelson wrote. "While UNIVAC had its troubles at one point, the public was very tolerant of the error and quite appreciative of the quick correction." After consulting with a member of the CBS research staff and a publicist for Remington Rand, Mickelson said of the computer, "I think it is our unanimous feeling that we were completely right in using it and that UNIVAC can be enormously important in anticipating election trends in the future." Some at CBS apparently felt good enough about the UNIVAC performance to seek a Peabody Award for 1952.[21] The CBS entry was a tightly edited thirty-minute version of the election-night broadcast featuring the computer—but not all its problems—and playing up the human analysis as well.

The night after the election, Charles Collingwood crafted a self-deprecating script for a weekly radio broadcast.[22] He poked fun at himself and other journalists for missing signs of an Eisenhower victory for fear of repeating the mistakes of 1948. His remarks about the UNIVAC prefigured mixed responses to the computer from outside observers. He called attention to the UNIVAC's difficulties. He reported that the machine's early prediction was off by just four electoral votes but had not been believed by its keepers, who then tinkered with the data and made the computer "look silly," in his words. He referred to the UNIVAC as "my machine" and "him." Collingwood said he had believed in the UNIVAC and was proven right. His conclusion: "It just goes to show that the trouble with machines is people."[23] At the same time, Collingwood scored the election's unexpected outcome as a "victory for the ordinary man" over the "soulless political scientists" who would "treat him like a cipher."[24]

Beyond those involved in the broadcasts, a range of others weighed in with postmortems—journalists, columnists, talk-show hosts, and on-air celebrities. Their takes on the computers ranged from praise to dismissal. One standard response was humor—whether it was laughing with or laughing at those involved. In fact, the UNIVAC soon became a foil for comedic routines. There was not, early on, a single or uniform narrative thread. But there were common elements.

In postelection stories that appeared in the popular press and trade publications, network television broadcasts in general came in for high marks.[25] Where distinctions were made, CBS was seen by several critics as having had the best coverage overall.[26] As for election-night computing, some accounts evidenced wide-eyed wonder. In the genre, perhaps, of "man bites dog," some observers were enthralled by the idea of a machine outsmarting its human keepers. Here was evidence that a wonderful new technology had arrived. In Philadelphia—where the UNIVAC was invented—a radio station began its day-after broadcast this way: "At 8:30 last night, a weird robot capable of juggling page-long equations with amazing dexterity and even operating alphabetically, passed along word that the chances were one-hundred-to-one that Eisenhower would win! Its name is UNIVAC."[27] The story included an interview with a UNIVAC spokesperson, who explained the decision not to go with the computer's initial prediction by saying, "Well, we lost our nerve!" The piece ended the way it began, praising UNIVAC's "complete ease" and "uncanny accuracy," adding, "When you think about it, the whole thing is almost frightening!" A newspaper column by British-American journalist Alistair Cooke ran under the headline "'UNIVAC' Forecast the Landslide."[28] Cooke reported that on election night, the computer had been "a couple of hours ahead of everything that walks and talks." A talk-show host on the Rural Radio Network in upstate New York referred to the UNIVAC in amazement as a "kind of a look into the future."[29]

A reviewer in the entertainment industry publication *Variety* was not impressed. NBC and CBS per the review, had gone to "extraordinary and expensive lengths to 'gimmick up' the Ike-Adlai ballot coverage, with robot-like calculators occupying a prominent place on the TV rostrums."[30] The value of using the computers was deemed "dubious at best." The issue was not that these devices performed poorly but that they could not deliver meaningful analysis. While they looked "expensive and awesome," *Variety's* review argued, the machines did not know or understand "what the voter felt in his heart or what disturbed his mind." That was deemed a job for the likes of Edward R. Murrow, H. V. Kaltenborn, Bill Henry, Lowell Thomas, John Daly, Walter Winchell, and others. The computers—also mentioned by name—became foils in the service of lavish praise for flesh-and-blood journalists. The message, in short, was spelled out in the lead: "If anything, TV's unprecedented coverage of last Tuesday's . . . election returns demonstrated that the machine will never take the place of the human." Not all reviewers in the human-versus-machine mode put the blame for election-night problems on the computers themselves. Ahead of the election, television columnist Harriet Van Horne had poked fun at newsroom humans, referring to the computers as "stars of the evening," who "neither smoke nor drink," comparing them to "the shirt-sleeved commentators with overflowing ash trays, paper containers of coffee beside them."[31] After the election she called attention to UNIVAC's troubles on CBS, writing that it "broke down before ten o'clock." But she added, "Statisticians operating the machine said it was not UNIVAC's fault: somebody fed him the wrong kind of figures."[32]

On their New York-based radio talk show during the morning after the election, popular hosts Dick Kollmar and Dorothy Kilgallen skewered the computers as unfit for election-night work. Kollmar said of Remington Rand, "I would hate to be a member of that company this morning if I'd had anything to do with the UNIVAC."[33] Television writers for the *New York Times*, the *Washington Post*, and the *Philadelphia Inquirer* turned out equally dismissive accounts. At the *Times* Jack Gould, who heaped praise on the CBS coverage in general, wrote of UNIVAC and the Monrobot that "Tuesday also saw the first use on Election Night of the supposedly super-duper electronic brains, which can think in terms of a couple of quintillion mathematical problems at one time."[34] Gould then added a series of tongue-in-cheek digs. "The C.B.S. pride was called 'Univac,' which at the critical moment refused to work with anything like the efficiency of the human being," he wrote. "This mishap caused the C.B.S. stars, Walter Cronkite, Ed Murrow, and Eric Sevareid, to give 'Univac' a rough ride for the rest of the evening in a most amusing sidelight to the C.B.S. coverage." His take on UNIVAC's election-night competition was no more sympathetic: "At a late hour, N.B.C. still was taking its electronic brain, 'Mon-Robot,' pretty seriously." By contrast Gould praised the "old journalistic technique" used by William H. Lawrence, a political correspondent for the *New York Times*, to report several scoops over the *Times* radio station, WQXR. "When votes came in from doubtful states," Gould wrote, "he called newspaper men in different cities who could interpret what a relatively few ballots in key areas would indicate by way of statewide trends." In the *Washington Post*, television writer C. E. Butterfield hit the networks, too. While computers might be good at solving complicated mathematical problems, the Monrobot and UNIVAC were still in what he called "the kindergarten stage as far as TV returns are concerned."[35] And at the *Philadelphia Inquirer*, television writer Merrill Panitt's snickering review opened this way: "Say, those electronic brains NBC and CBS had for their election result telecasts were really impressive, weren't they? Made you feel kind of—if you'll excuse the expression—humble. Amazing the way the gadgets accepted questions, flickered their tubes for a few seconds and, bingo! Wrong answer."[36] Computers, in Panitt's telling, were just the wrong tool to use on election night. "How can anyone," he asked, "determine precisely what basic information to give a machine before putting to it the question of how an election will come out?" The headline captured the sentiment of the column: "Electronic Brains Prove They Need Smart Men."

One theme among reviews that did not consider the "electronic brains" a success was to assign the blame for UNIVAC's misadventures to its human keepers. In some cases CBS and Remington Rand were targeted together. In others a distinction was made between the two, with CBS cast as something of a victim. In the *New York Daily News*, television critic Ben Gross recounted the "about-face" in predictions attributed to the UNIVAC. Gross did so with a touch of misogyny that gave him two digs in one, beginning this way: "UNIVAC Like a Woman."[37] He dismissed the machine as consistent as "you-know-what," by which he made clear he was referring to "gals." He also made clear there was some postelection finger-pointing. "The boys around CBS are taking a lot of ribbing and they admit the laugh's on them," Gross wrote. "But one thing they emphasize: These predictions did not come from the mouths of their commentators, but from the mouth of UNIVAC." Another reviewer described the UNIVAC as responsible for "the real laugh of the evening" by predicting a close outcome when a sweep was obvious.[38] The turn of events, he wrote, both "irked" and "embarrassed" Collinwood.

Even when CBS, Remington Rand, or UNIVAC came in for bruising treatment, there was a tendency to make a distinction between the machine's operation—deemed to have worked as programmed—and the operation of its human operators. The latter were portrayed as the source of UNIVAC's troubles. These stories seem to have absorbed in some way—sometimes directly, sometimes indirectly—explanations offered by the CBS and Remington Rand camps. The Associated Press quickly turned out a story about Arthur Draper's early morning mea culpa from Philadelphia in front of the CBS audience. This story ran in the 6:00 a.m. edition of the *Baltimore Sun* under the headline, "Electric Brain's Aberration Is All Its Masters' Fault."[39] A broadcast trade publication reported that CBS had won kudos for timely reporting of returns but had what the writer called "a less happy experience in the use of the UNIVAC 'brain' as a prophet."[40] Unidentified "spokesmen" were said to have laid the blame with "outside statisticians employed to operate UNIVAC." A column in the *Chicago Daily Tribune* included a two-paragraph item headed "Man vs. Machine."[41] It reported that the "somewhat inglorious behavior of those highly publicized election night electronic marvels" was said to have been the fault of "the people charged with presenting the problems in solvable fashion." For that, a share of the blame also went to the effects of "overcautious pollsters" in the run-up to the election.

Electronics magazine also panned the performance of computers. Lumping together the UNIVAC on CBS, the Monrobot on NBC, and what it referred to as the "IBM Calculator" on ABC, the magazine reported, "In the opinion of many viewers and listeners, the results were considerably less spectacular than they were led to expect by advance publicity."[42] The article added, "Technically speaking, the calculators did what they were expected to do, but difficulty arose in selecting appropriate past election data for setting up the problems and interpreting results." Featuring advance publicity photos of the UNIVAC and Monrobot in operation, the caption took note of a contest between the two: "UNIVAC (left) and Monrobot (right) also ran on November 4 in race to predict outcome of election on basis of preliminary returns and past elections." The two-deck headline read, "Computers Sweat Out Election Results; Nonpartisan electronic machines vie with human experts to predict outcome."

In between kudos and outright dismissal, there was a middle ground of attempts at humor. A tongue-in-cheek *Washington Post* editorial, titled "Unhappy UNIVAC," began this way: "Well, it now seems that Professor UNIVAC, the celebrated mechanical brain, damn well knew what he was talking about. . . . The trouble was that none of those stupid humans, including his inventors, would believe him."[43] The piece went on to speculate about whether the computer's feelings were hurt and whether it might be "sensitive to a degree quite beyond the power of our coarse and callous species even to imagine." In the *San Francisco Chronicle*, a columnist tossed around the idea of just running UNIVAC for president.[44] At least twice on the morning after the election, newscasters at a Los Angeles radio station recited the events of Arthur Draper's difficult night. One referred to it as "a lack of faith that turned into a serio-comic battle of the machine against man in which the machine finally triumphed and the man turned up with a collective red face unparalleled in election history."[45] The UNIVAC was described as "the mechanical monster which will apparently treat you right if you treat it right, and if you only trust it." The other account advised the audience, "Take a firm grip, you humans, we have evidence this morning that the day of the flesh and blood brain may be waning."[46]

On-air celebrities also got in on the comedic postmortems. On his program the day after the election, celebrity Arthur Godfrey aimed for laughs with this tongue-in-cheek account of the UNIVAC's first prediction, as captured in a transcript made for Remington Rand.[47] He set up his gag this way: "It's supposed to be an amazing electronic device that would, at an instant's notice, before any human being could possibly detect a trend, it would predict which way the voting was going." He continued, "So what happened? So first of all it wouldn't work at all. I understand they fed the very first returns into the thing, and you know what came out? The winner of the fourth race at Hialeah." Two days later

Godfrey brought up the subject again, this time saying he owed UNIVAC an apology after learning that it had been "uncannily accurate."[48] Still reaching for a laugh, he told someone else on the program, "You could be replaced by six vacuum tubes and a roll of wire."

Comedian Ernie Kovacs latched on to UNIVAC the morning after the election and was still milking it the next month. On his television program on November 5, he reported that "J. Burlington Gearshift"—the character of an oddball inventor played by Kovacs himself—would be on the next day with a "brain machine that will confound the nation." It was to be called the "Koviac."[49] When the Koviac did appear the next day, it was described this way by a transcription service hired by Remington Rand: "A burlesque model of an electronic computing machine" on which "various levers, control knobs and electric light bulbs were arranged in ludicrous fashion on the top and sides."[50] In an outing on December 1, the Koviac mockup had "a slit marked 'For Used Razor Blades,'" along with "two small marks with 'His' and 'Hers' written under them." On the side there was "an opening marked 'Out.'"[51] And in the center was a switch Kovacs used to turn the machine on and off. Special effects included sounds of a motor, thuds, and a bell. Although the Koviac never seemed to function as expected, the Kovacs character named "Gearshift" said he wanted to treat it right. The device "is almost human in its likes and dislikes," he said, "and I find that, much as throwing a fish to the seals, a shot of beer or two to the Koviac rewards this little machine." Thus nourished the Koviac exhaled in apparent satisfaction.

The most enduring record of responses to computer use on election night was left in newspapers and a smattering of available broadcast transcripts. But some letters and telegrams from ordinary viewers have also survived, including those in files of the late Walter Cronkite at an archive in Texas.[52] They reveal a sense of novelty at watching news on television, excitement at being brought so close to the action in a newsroom, and awe at seeing broadcast journalists handle the election-night chaos with the calm of officers in battle.[53] Letter and telegram writers deemed the performance of Cronkite and others to have been "excellent," "magnificent," "marvelous," "terrific," and "a whale of a job," among other terms of praise.[54] It was not lost on viewers that all of this was taking place in an atmosphere of competition. Some letters refer to checking out the various networks' offerings and settling on CBS. One enclosed Jack Gould's column, and another referred to it: "I agree with Jack Gould's opinion in the *New York Times*: CBS (and Cronkite!) won by a landslide."[55] Typical of this enthusiasm was a letter written by a couple from Closter, New Jersey.[56] They did not get the name of Cronkite's network right—praising his "really great N.B.C."—but his "expert" handling of the night's events, they wrote, "made our spines tingle." The letter expressed the "hope we will long remember these historic hours, which you all brought to us in our homes." Not all letters, however, were positive. For one writer from Jacksonville, Florida, the notion of watching news on television—which she did at a friend's house—was not a happy one. "The way your announcers put on was the most nerve-wracking thing," she wrote, explaining that they "couldn't say the simplest things without stuttering."[57] She concluded, "I do not ever want no damn TV set, and I don't care much for my radio. The printed words in newspapers and magazines do not stutter or stammer."

Many of the letters praising the broadcast did not mention the UNIVAC but two that did are instructive. One, from the president of a floor covering company in Chicago, adopted an anthropomorphic tone: "I am certainly glad that UNIVAC recovered from its workout and is in good shape today."[58] The other letter provides evidence that in the ephemeral circumstances of a television broadcast, it was easier to remember that a computer had been used than to remember whether the computer had been right or wrong. The owner of a furniture store in Keokuk, Iowa, wanted Cronkite to settle a wager.[59] "When your Remington Rand Uni-Vac, or mechanical brain, went off the beam and gave a report of 100-to-1 odds about midway through the evening, who did it report had the odds in his favor, as that is the argument we are engaged in," the writer asked. "One says the odds favored Stevenson and the other Eisenhower. Your written reply stating the man favored by the 100-to-1 odds will be greatly appreciated by return mail."

One letter suggests that calling elections from limited and skewed early returns could prompt complaints of bias. A viewer in Brooklyn, favorably disposed to Cronkite before election night, wrote two days later that she was "bitterly disappointed and annoyed by your election coverage."[60] She concluded that Cronkite was "an Eisenhower man."

"You deprecated every lead the Democrats had during the evening," she wrote, "and in certain instances where the margin of lead was much greater in some states for the Democrats than it was in other states for the Republicans, you made statements like, 'The Democratic margin is too narrow to hold' and 'The Republican margin is a sure sign of victory.'"

At an archive in Laramie, Wyoming, the papers of NBC's Morgan Beatty contain eighty-nine items in a folder of correspondence with listeners or viewers for November 1952. Only two of these dealt with the election-night coverage.[61] One was a letter from an old schoolmate who noted having seen the broadcast and praised Beatty for a "swell job."[62] A man in St. Louis wanted information about Monroe's "mechanical brain." The letter itself does not survive but a response to the letter does. In Beatty's absence—he was on vacation in the latter part of November—his secretary wrote to inform the writer that she was forwarding his letter to the Monroe Calculating Machine Company.[63]

As for Edward R. Murrow, his papers are available on microfilm. Among them is a relevant letter from one of Murrow's old acquaintances, Ed Beattie.[64] The two had known each other in London during World War II when Murrow was famously reporting for CBS radio on the German bombing of that city, and Beattie was reporting for the United Press.[65] Charles Collingwood, referenced in the letter, had also been a United Press reporter early in the war before becoming one of the "Murrow Boys" at CBS in London.[66] Writing to Murrow two days after the election, Beattie adopted the same tone of humorous ambiguity seen in various accounts of the broadcasts. "Dear Professor," he began, "Having followed with some fascination the difficulties experienced by one Charles (Toujours L'amour) Collingwood with his friend UNIVAC two evenings ago, not to speak of certain admissions of tampering with the latter's cerebration, I feel it is opportune to suggest that in the future, UNIVAC be left to its own devices and that, precautionarily, it be equipped with a gadget which will promptly spot any tampering and illuminate a small sign saying 'TILT.'"[67] The letter writer also called attention to the varying comfort levels that broadcasters showed in calling the election for Eisenhower: "Bill Henry was still playing it close to his chest a couple of hours after you and Eric [Sevareid] had labeled the trend for what it obviously was."

Though certainly just a fraction of the correspondence sent to broadcasters after November 4, these letters, taken as a whole, do not contradict the conclusion that election night was less than an immediate and unequivocal shot in the arm for computers—the UNIVAC in particular. That idea would take more time to gel. A version of that story—in which the night's comedy of errors starred fallible humans rather than a fallible machine—may have gotten a shot in the arm from Remington Rand's publicity apparatus. A week after the election, an editorial appeared in a Florida newspaper, the *Jacksonville Journal*, under the headline, "A Machine Makes a Monkey Out of Man."[68] The UNIVAC was seen as such a remarkable device that it was described in terms of both wonder and terror, including a description of election night as "the dawn of a horrendous new day." Working with both greater speed and accuracy than humans, the "world-famed . . . electronic brain" was said to have "made monkeys out of the political prophets and the statistical experts." This narrative was old news by November 11, so why was it being recycled? The editorial gives a clue: "The full story of the UNIVAC's fruitless efforts to convince its human operators that General Eisenhower would win by a landslide—a prediction that was overruled by human experts—has been disclosed by its makers, Remington Rand."

Additional stories and references appeared around the same time. Two days after the *Jacksonville Journal* editorial, comedian Ernie Kovacs featured another "Koviac" segment. He indicated that UNIVAC, which he felt compelled to lampoon, had been "brought again to the light and publicized" and "seems to have caught on with the public fancy."[69] Two days after that, on November 15, an article depicting UNIVAC as "America's newest conversation piece" appeared in the *Christian Science Monitor*.[70] It was written from Washington by Mary Hornaday, a respected veteran journalist.[71] Her article described the UNIVAC as "an uncanny electronic brain that burst upon most of our horizons on election night when the Columbia Broadcasting System featured it in its TV coverage."[72] There was little ambiguity in Hornaday's piece. She was in the camp of UNIVAC admirers. She described Remington Rand's "harrowing election night experience" as one in which the computer's human keepers lost their nerve. "A lot of people," she wrote, "seemed to get the impression that UNIVAC wasn't much good, when actually the mistakes were all human." Her account detailed UNIVAC's impressive price tag, its dimensions, its

memory, and its speed, for which, she wrote, "the human is no match."
Hornaday also described UNIVAC's "potentialities," as she called them,
from tracking freight cars to solving complex mathematical problems.
The latter, she wrote, included "matrix algebra" and "elliptic partial dif-
ferential equations." Those references were certainly lost on almost all
readers. But the terms sounded impressive, nonetheless. And it is not a
stretch to surmise that Remington Rand was the source of such details.

Partisans from the Remington Rand camp were busy with other efforts
to spread the word. Arch Hancock, a company publicist, authored an
article for the December issue of *Systems Magazine*, a Remington Rand
publication that circulated in the business community.[73] Hancock held
up the UNIVAC's behind-the-scenes election-night prowess as evidence
that a new era had dawned. This new era made obsolete the previously
dominant technology in information management: high-speed punched
card equipment. Remington Rand's Arthur Draper also expanded on his
own election-night apology and his revelation about the UNIVAC's early
prediction of landslide. In a presentation to a meeting of the American
Institute of Electrical Engineers, he kept up the portrayal of humans,
not the machine, as fallible.[74] "There have been five major occasions of
extreme importance where we have doubted that the UNIVAC was correct," said Draper. "In every single one of these occasions it has come out
that UNIVAC was right and we poor humans were wrong." He concluded
with what he said was the moral of the story: "Don't THINK, let UNIVAC
Do It For You!" This last line, in all likelihood, was meant not only to
tout the UNIVAC but to taunt Remington Rand's chief rival, IBM. It was
probably understood by his audience as a dig. The single word "THINK"
was an IBM motto as well as the name of an IBM magazine.[75] The statistics professor who devised UNIVAC's prediction algorithm in 1952 and
was associated with the UNIVAC in subsequent elections, Max Woodbury, recalled in a 2004 interview that Hancock also involved him over
time in efforts to spread the word about what the computer could do.[76]

The story taking hold was irresistible, the sort of tale that journalists
refer to as "man bites dog." The 1952 version was that UNIVAC had made
an accurate forecast but that the computer's keepers did not believe it.
The machine was right and the humans were wrong, a trope relevant at
a time when computers were being called "electronic brains" and when

comparisons to human capabilities were part of the landscape. On that point one of the letters that UNIVAC coinventor John Mauchly received after the election came from Warren Wightman, who had helped produce the preelection episode of *The Johns Hopkins Science Review* involving Mauchly.[77] "We watched CBS on election night," wrote Wightman, "and were all very much interested and considerably amused when it was announced that somebody somewhere along the line had lost his nerve and refused to believe the 'brain.'" But maybe that was not so bad, Wightman explained: "Seems to me that it makes a good story, if not better, for publicity purposes, the way it turned out."

Four years later Phillip S. Vincent, who had been part of the 1952 election-night effort at the UNIVAC facility, gave a talk about that experience to the Stamford Engineering Society in Connecticut.[78] While it had been a difficult night, he saw later what could not be seen at the time. In retrospect there was an enormous benefit in the decision not to release that first prediction early in the evening. "Although we can take no credit for it, our reactions were one of the very fortunate occurrences in Remington Rand history," Vincent explained. "If we had released the first prediction, a few lines would have appeared in the next day's papers under some such heading as 'Ain't science peachy!,' but our very evident human frailties coupled with Art Draper's public confession . . . gave the whole performance a human-interest slant and resulted in making UNIVAC almost a household word."[79]

In the end, perhaps, what also made this a good story was that it could be deployed, like the computers on election night, in the service of many agendas, and that a variety of meanings could be attached to it. Over time the Monrobot largely disappeared from accounts of election night 1952 and the UNIVAC-only story became standard. This was true even for experts involved in the nascent computer industry, who would have been aware that two very different computers had been in play on that night. One of these experts was Edmund Berkeley, an early advocate both for computer use in the insurance industry and for public knowledge about computers.[80] He knew William Burkhart from the Monrobot camp. Berkeley had featured a Burkhart invention in a 1949 book on computing machines for a general audience, *Giant Brains, or Machines that Think*. In January 1953 Berkeley had also featured both the Monrobot and the UNIVAC in "Automatic Computers on Election Night," an article he coauthored.[81] The article appeared in an early computer journal he had started, *The Computing Machinery Field*, later renamed *Computers and Automation*.[82] But just three years later, when he coauthored a 1956 follow-up book to *Giant Brains*, the Monrobot had disappeared from Berkeley's account of election night 1952.[83] Though the new book mentioned that computers "including a UNIVAC" were tasked with election-night predictions for television audiences in 1952 and 1954, the telling in detail of the 1952 story was a UNIVAC-only tale. Berkeley and his coauthor used the UNIVAC story to illustrate a section of the book on then-current and future uses of computers in areas other than business and the military. "It seems evident," they concluded, "that automatic computer commentary on elections will henceforth be a regular feature of election nights." True enough, even if not a done deal, as was the case with NBC's retreat from computers for one more election cycle, the midterms in 1954. But others were lining up to take their chances.

9 | A Hazard of Being Discredited in the Public's Mind

The decision at NBC to back out of using a computer on election night in 1954 created an opening for IBM. The giant data processing company was known for tabulating equipment that digested input on punched cards, serving government and business for decades. But IBM was slower than Remington Rand to market a computer that would compete with the UNIVAC. For IBM executives, seeing an archrival in the limelight on election night in 1952 had to sting. Files from the IBM corporate archives show a response: internal memos were circulated and meetings were held. At issue was whether—and how—to get in on election night for the next presidential contest in 1956. Advocates within IBM imagined the company in a starring role on television. They thought IBM could capture public attention and take on Remington Rand in a head-to-head battle for supremacy in the expanding market for commercial computers. Potential customers included major corporations, government agencies, the military, and universities. But within IBM there was also an aversion to risk. The lessons of 1952 were clear. If an IBM computer were to spit out a surprising projection that would only be confirmed later as correct, how would the computer's keepers decide whether to trust it in real time? And what if they trusted a forecast that turned out to be wrong? One executive laid out the dilemma in a 1955 memo: "Were we to predict on NBC, and UNIVAC predict on CBS, a battle of giant brains conceivably might be built up by some energetic publicity man, with a hazard of being discredited in the public's mind, if our predictions were not completely accurate."[1] During behind-the-scenes exchanges of ideas and research, a lead surfaced that gave IBM officials some comfort. This was not the decidedly mixed experience of CBS or NBC in 1952. Rather, it was a pioneering foray into election-night forecasting by a newspaper in 1954.[2] In an award-winning project, the *Detroit Times* used early returns in Michigan to forecast results in the state's elections. That project has heretofore been missing from intersecting histories of computing, journalism, and politics. It was the result of an unlikely collaboration between the newspaper and a new computation laboratory at Wayne University in Detroit. I say "unlikely" not because the lab was not up to the task. It was. Rather, this collaboration might never have happened because the lab's pioneering director was caught up in controversy two years earlier, in 1952. His secret past surfaced that year in a nationwide "red scare." As a young man in the 1930s, he had been convicted in Finland as a Communist spy. He made headlines in 1952 when his past was outed by none other than Whittaker Chambers, one of the most notorious names in the history of American red scares. Chambers was a journalist who had also once been a Soviet spy.

In addition to the entry of IBM, the *Detroit Times*, and the Wayne computation lab into the election-night mix in the mid-1950s, other changes were taking place—albeit not at blinding speed. Though ABC would get into the forecasting action in 1956, it was only with a gimmicky "man versus machine" competition. Meanwhile, notable critics writing reviews of television for newspapers would remain slow to embrace the idea that computers were a value-added proposition in newsrooms on election night. What we see in the rearview mirror—computers becoming fixtures on election night—becomes far more nuanced the closer we get going back in time.

The story of the *Detroit Times*'s pioneering election-night efforts in 1954 did not survive long. Within six years the newspaper itself would be gone.[3] But in 1954 the *Detroit Times* was part of a robust news environment in a city with several newspapers and broadcast news outlets. The newspaper's place in the history of election-night forecasting helps flesh out the themes we have encountered. While some journalists were dismissive of the new technology, others saw opportunity. And in the early years of computing in journalism, collaboration between journalists and outside technologists was crucial.

The Wayne computation laboratory was headed by Arvid W. Jacobson. Until the early 1950s, Jacobson's dark past remained buried while he became a leader in establishing computer science as an area of study in higher education. After leaving school at thirteen to work, Jacobson lost several fingers in a farm accident when he was eighteen.[4] With the compensation he received, he resumed his education, graduated from college, and began teaching high school mathematics in a Detroit suburb.[5] He also joined the Communist Party.[6] In the early 1930s, he was dispatched by party superiors to Finland. There he was arrested on espionage charges and convicted. He spent nearly three years in prison before American officials helped secure his release.[7] Once back in the United States, he went on about his life and continued his education. He ended up on the mathematics faculty at Wayne, where his past was not initially known.[8] He discussed that past privately and voluntarily with the university leadership when his name appeared in a 1950 book, *Seeds of Treason*, and in related newspaper articles.[9] No connection had been made publicly then between his past and present. No one put the pieces together at first that Arvid Jacobson from the Finland story was the Arvid Jacobson at Wayne. Records in the Wayne archives show that the university's leaders decided to keep Jacobson's past a secret and supported him in efforts to build up the computation laboratory.[10] But with the 1952 publication of *Witness*, a bestselling memoir by Whittaker Chambers, the name "Arvid Jacobson" was again in print as an American Communist from the 1930s.[11] Chambers did not make the connection to the Arvid Jacobson at Wayne, either, but that connection did emerge.[12] When the story became public, the administrators at Wayne continued to stand with Jacobson. So did members of Detroit's business and industrial community, a surprising stance in those red-scare years. They had gotten to know Jacobson through cooperative efforts to support the laboratory and have it conduct research to benefit local enterprises.[13] The 1952 crisis passed, and Jacobson continued his work in the lab, in the classroom, and in the community. He secured an experimental computer from the Burroughs Corporation. It was named UDEC, for Unitized Digital Electronic Computer.[14] In the summer of 1954, Jacobson was instrumental in organizing a national conference at Wayne on training individuals to work in the fast-growing computer field.[15] Speakers and attendees came from around the country and included two luminaries we have already encountered—Harvard's Howard Aiken and UNIVAC coinventor John Mauchly.[16]

A logbook from Jacobson's laboratory from 1953 to 1955 survives in the Wayne archives. It shows that a variety of groups sought assistance.[17] Among them were the Ford Motor Company, U.S. Rubber, Detroit Edison, the Detroit Health Department, and, from his own campus, the economics department. Item forty-five on that list is identified as "Election Problem" from the *Detroit Times*. The first entry for this project was dated October 19, 1954.[18] It noted that Jacobson and others from the lab had talked with *Times* reporter Lou Arkles about election predictions. There was already a sample of Detroit precincts selected. More were to be chosen from elsewhere in Michigan. The prediction method was to be worked out by Jacobson and the lab's Saul Rosen, who would also become a notable figure in the early history of computing.[19]

The work of processing historic data for comparison began on October 22 and was not completed until 4:00 p.m. on Election Day. Time ran out to continue checking for errors.[20] The *Detroit Times* was an afternoon paper. It reported in late editions on the day after the election that a predawn "extra" had rolled off the presses with a forecast that seemed "fantastic" in a nationally watched U.S. Senate race. In that predawn edition, Democrat Patrick V. McNamara, who was then behind, was predicted to emerge the victor with a margin of precisely 42,380 votes over his opponent, Republican incumbent Homer S. Ferguson.[21] That prediction would prove correct, and the margin of victory would be off by just a few hundred votes. The newspaper celebrated its journalistic victory with a front-page story. This was the lead: "The Detroit Times scored a major 'first' yesterday when it successfully utilized the $200,000 computer, UDEC, as a practical tool for newspaper election coverage." The article connected the dots for readers: "Previously such computers had been used in making broad predictions on radio and TV early on election nights, but no newspaper had adopted them for serious election coverage because the results were not considered reliable." The story also mentioned that CBS's Edward R. Murrow had announced during election night, "with a lifted eyebrow," that although Ferguson was ahead in the vote count, the *Detroit Times* was predicting a win by McNamara with a margin of forty-two thousand votes. What a coup for the newspaper! It was also a coup for the Wayne lab and for Burroughs, which had provided financial support for the effort. The lab's Saul Rosen spread the word to scholars in a journal of the Industrial Mathematics Society, which was based at Wayne.[22] The article included pages of formulas, a description of the way the state was divided into regions, the role of historical data from one thousand precincts, and the use of four hundred of these for the final prediction at 1:00 a.m. With 10 percent of the vote in at that early morning hour and McNamara far behind in the Senate race, the program predicted a McNamara win with 51.08 percent of the vote—within a whisper of the final figure of 50.92. The early prediction for the governor's race was even closer at 55.78 percent—just .02 percent above the final figure. Rosen concluded his account by noting that the method was "quite elementary" and could have other applications in business.

In recognition of the unusual project, the *Detroit Times* later received an Associated Press award in Michigan for best coverage of a breaking news story.[23] Even before winning that accolade, however, the newspaper's election-night computing effort was singled out for recognition in publications including *Time* magazine and a newspaper trade publication, *Editor & Publisher*. Echoing what the *Detroit Times* had proclaimed, *Editor & Publisher* reported that this was, "so far as is known, the first time that such a device has been utilized by a major newspaper as a practical instrument for election coverage."[24] *Time* magazine compared the Detroit effort favorably to CBS's 1954 election-night experience with UNIVAC, noting that the latter had been plagued for a time by data errors.[25] The same issue of *Time* also noted that the *New York Times* had to recall about eighty thousand early-edition newspapers out of concerns, as more returns came in, that its declaration of victory for Averell Harriman in the New York governor's race was premature.[26]

On election night in 1956, the *Detroit Times* teamed up directly with the Burroughs Corporation. Burroughs provided a new commercial computer, the E-101. It was set up in the *Times* newsroom—where its use was heavily promoted in advance. Predictions were broadcast live to Detroit-area viewers on election night and celebrated later through stories in the newspaper and in a Burroughs publication.[27] The disappearance of the story of the *Detroit Times* as an early adopter of computers for election-night journalism may be due, in part, to the disappearance of the newspaper itself. But in its efforts of 1954 and 1956, the *Detroit Times* had extended the pattern of election night as a venue for the collaboration of journalists and technologists. The paper had also demonstrated the ability of the computer to fulfill multiple roles—from analysis to promotion to after-the-fact bragging rights. And IBM would later take notice.

The *Hartford Courant*, the *New York World-Telegram and The Sun*, and the Associated Press Washington bureau had all mentioned back in 1952 that their election-night efforts had gotten a boost from IBM equipment. But IBM itself appears to have generated little publicity beyond an article in an in-house publication to celebrate its election-night role.[28] One likely explanation for this tepid response is that the IBM equipment was not the latest technology. In 1954, though IBM had brought some of its more modern computers to market, they did not play a role in national broadcasting for the midterm election. But soon afterward, key IBM executives became convinced that their new machines should be in on the election-night action in a big way in 1956. Records of behind-the-scenes deliberations at IBM show how seeking a place at center stage on election night could reach the highest levels of a major corporation. These records reveal something else in common with the run-up to 1952. The technology provider—in this case IBM—sought out an alliance with a news organization, ultimately NBC, by framing the 1956 election night as an event in which their agendas would intersect. Memos and reports of meetings at IBM also suggest an awareness of the risks.

Conversations came to include key executives with responsibilities related to the company's media relations, image, sales, customer relations, technology, and management. In late November 1954, within days of a meeting on possibilities for an IBM role on election night in 1956, an IBM executive vice president was receiving memos and then reporting to company president Thomas J. Watson Jr.[29] Though IBM would eventually collaborate with NBC, that arrangement was not envisioned at the outset. One memo involving key IBM executives is telling.[30] It discussed a proposal to use an innovative IBM monitor, called the "740" cathode ray tube, to visually compare the 1956 vote to data from 1952. That device had been the subject of a wondrous account days earlier in the *Wall Street Journal* for doing something we take for granted now— the graphical display of a computer's calculations.[31] Where would IBM get the live data and historical figures? One idea was to collaborate with the Associated Press. The memo added, "Of course, the facilities of one of the principal television networks would also have to be made available." As the idea of IBM involvement on election night began to take shape, it was conceived of—at least at IBM—as an event in which IBM would play a starring role.

The working group at IBM soon came across what had been done by the Wayne computation lab for the *Detroit Times*. A memo that circulated among IBM officials referred to this project as "the job that Burroughs UDEC did for the Michigan elections"—a reference to the computer manufacturer and the model used. One IBM manager concluded that, so far, "This is the most sensible approach . . . for the contribution of computers to election returns."[32] Cuthbert C. Hurd, a leading figure in IBM's move into the computer field, also reached out to Sig Mickelson at CBS to learn about the network's forecasting in 1952.[33] After hearing about the behind-the-scenes drama involving the "wide discrepancy" between early UNIVAC-generated results and preelection polls, Hurd was alert to the risks. He sounded a cautious note in a memo to an IBM executive in advertising and promotion.[34] "I want to point out the very large extent to which the whole forecasting procedure depends on individual judgment," wrote Hurd.[35] This ranged from the selection of counties for extrapolation to decisions about the mathematical models to be used. "Finally, and most importantly," wrote Hurd, "if you obtain a result which is a startling one, as in 1952, do you then trust your formulas or do you change your formulas in midstream as Dr. Woodbury did?" Only if IBM were willing to spend heavily and hire top statisticians, Hurd argued, could the company jump into election-night forecasting. Writing in February 1955, more than twenty months ahead of the election, Hurd declared, "It is already late to start."

Hurd's caution generated more discussion. One memo suggested that IBM solicit the names of potential consultants from John Tukey at Princeton, a major figure in statistics, and Solomon Kullback, the head of research and development at the National Security Agency.[36] More questions surfaced. Should IBM engage in forecasting or focus instead on reporting the vote count? Going in either direction posed some peril— from the potential for a ho-hum result to a faulty prediction that would harm IBM's reputation.[37] As the conversations continued, IBM's director of information summed up the situation.[38] He talked about the difficulty of making overtures to "the TV people." There was also clearly disagreement at IBM about what the company's involvement on election night might look like. Given the need to code the data and enter it onto punch cards, there were doubts whether "a stunt" using a display via cathode ray tube would produce results faster than "a person with a crayon can mark the same results on a board." The same official noted that the Associated Press was not wild about providing information directly to IBM. Yet, his memo does suggest that he saw no choice for IBM but to continue seeking involvement in election-night broadcasting. To drive home the point, he relayed a conversation with Charles Collingwood. "It seems to me we have to do some stunt that may be a calculated risk," the IBM official concluded. "I was talking with Charles Collingwood at CBS-TV Sunday. . . . He felt, and I agree, that even the last UNIVAC stunt, despite its kidding press, was worthwhile and had generally favorable results."

The IBM working group considered contacting top pollsters and reached out to Woodbury, too. They even considered developing "a continuing program of election coverage, which might involve support of a fellowship, for example, for a long-term investigation."[39] By the fall of 1955, more than a year ahead of the election, IBM was in talks with J. Davidson Taylor, NBC's vice president in charge of public affairs. And so it was that IBM finally found its partner. In late October 1956, the arrangements were touted in a pair of breathless NBC press releases. These were passed up the chain of command at IBM to Thomas J. Watson Jr., who by then was the company's CEO as well as its president.[40] A memo to Watson, dated six days before the election, indicated that the public relations advantage would extend to more than election night, with an "all-out advanced promotion" by NBC: "Spot announcements showing our equipment will be appearing frequently, and we will participate in two or three of their regular programs between now and election night."[41] In addition to the NBC broadcast from New York on election night, according to the memo, NBC would also be switching to local stations around the country once every half hour. IBM branch offices would work with sixteen of those stations. For ten stations in nine cities, IBM's model 650 computers would be used. In San Francisco a more powerful IBM 705 computer would be used. And in five cities, IBM would provide help using what was referred to as "conventional punched card equipment."

The NBC-IBM plan for the national broadcast included trend analysis without any mention of "forecasting" or "prediction." But the centerpiece turned out to be an elaborate arrangement to report the vote. An NBC press release touted this as "a major innovation in collecting and transmitting election returns," a "unique transcontinental electronic system that will enable the network to report returns faster than ever before."[42] In October NBC issued releases hailing the "electronic computing wizardry" that would be critical to election-night coverage.[43] A second technology partner in this system was the Teleregister Corporation, which would provide a fifty-foot-long bank of tally boards to display IBM's vote counts. Davidson Taylor, NBC's vice president in charge of public affairs, deemed four goals to be paramount: "Speed, completeness, accuracy, and analysis."[44] Unspoken were other values for the journalist-technologist alliance: that is, showmanship and bragging rights for technological wonders. An NBC release boasted of advances over "traditional manually based collection and transmittal of returns."[45] An elaborate array of equipment was to be installed in Studio 8-H at Rockefeller Center. Out of view would be the guts of the system. Hundreds of people would be deployed along with a nationwide network of computing equipment and telecommunications facilities. These would aggregate returns from the Associated Press at the state level and speed them to New York. The data was to be used both in updating tally boards and reporting on trends. Analysis was also to be done at IBM's Manhattan headquarters. Taking part in the operation there for NBC would be a veteran political analyst, Joseph C. Harsch, and a pollster, George Gallup. One NBC release reported that the computer to be used there was a giant "electronic brain" known as the "705."[46]

In fact, NBC was sending out mixed messages. On the one hand, newspaper ads promoted the network's coverage using "a new IBM electronic system that analyzes returns and automatically spots trends."[47] A two-page ad in *Life* magazine went further. It spoke of an "ingenious all-electronic system" to speed results and "specially adapted IBM equipment" that "eliminates all chance of human error." And it touted the use of "the miraculous IBM electronic brain to analyze the data and project the ultimate direction of the election."[48] Plus this: "NBC will be first to bring you all developing trends, and first to announce the final winners." A preelection item in a trade publication, *Broadcasting Telecasting*, lumped all three major networks together in using "electronic accessories" to "predict the outcome of the balloting." But at least two newspaper columns, one before and one after the election, suggest that NBC had made a point of distinguishing its analysis from the process of predicting winners from early returns. Two days before the election, the *New York Times* reported that there would be a "battle" between "electronic 'brains,'" but it would only involve ABC and CBS.[49] In contrast, NBC was said to be "a bit conservative," deciding to "forego the battle of the electronic forecasters" and focus instead on its new system to speed up the vote count. No mention was made of the use of IBM computers to aid in analysis. After the election a *New York Daily News* columnist wrote that "NBC snubbed what it termed 'guess work' and, instead, chose to employ IBM and Teleregister machines for speed and accuracy . . . content to allow the actual votes unfold the battle of the ballot."[50]

Despite the mixed messages, there was a shift over the space of two years. In 1954 NBC's publicity machine cast humans—and specifically reporters—as superior to mechanical devices and statisticians. Now in 1956 the same publicity machine hoped to assure the public that "all computations will be done electronically to eliminate all chance of human error."[51] And there was this: "Each item of IBM and Teleregister equipment will have a vital functional role in the operation; none will be used merely as set dressing."[52] The election-night coverage was, as it had been in 1952 and 1954, under the supervision of William R. McAndrew, director of news. But machines were now billed as not only "vital" but serious. Perhaps the references to "human error" and "set dressing" were inside jokes or digs aimed at CBS, given that network's past use of a faux UNIVAC on the election-night set in New York and the troubles blamed on humans who caused the real UNIVAC based in Philadelphia to go astray. But in any event, at NBC the acceptance of computers and collaboration with technologists as both having a place in journalism had taken a step forward—at least in election-night journalism. By comparison an independent television station in Newark, New Jersey, made a point of announcing before the 1956 election that its coverage "would not involve any electronic wizardry."[53] A spokesman for the station, Channel

13, was quoted as saying, "The only machines used on this program will be a news ticker and possibly a slide rule for late returns."

Meanwhile, at ABC computers were added to the election-night mix using the familiar frame of "man versus machine." But for some at ABC, the attitude toward computers was not an enthusiastic embrace. This is apparent in the papers of John Daly, ABC's well-known and award-winning newscaster, who held the lengthy title of "Vice President in Charge of News, Special Events, Sports, and Public Affairs."[54] In September 1956 Daly wrote to a former colleague from ABC in New York, referencing the election-night arrangements of competing networks with computers. He noted with disdain that he would have to move in the same direction.[55] There was no small irony, then, in the way Associated Press television writer Charles Mercer referred to Daly in a preelection rundown on the various networks' computer plans: "On ABC-TV we have Elecom 125 developed by the Underwood Corporation, with John Daly at the controls, which will make its own forecasts of the outcome approximately every half hour."[56]

In a pair of ABC press releases, Daly announced the network's debut of the Elecom computer on election night.[57] Daly also turned up at the Elecom's home base in Manhattan. He was there for a preview arranged, according to Underwood, for business writers, newspaper reporters, and what were referred to as "television personalities."[58] A few day later, *Nation* magazine's preelection issue revealed this: "John Daly at ABC will pit human brains against Elecom."[59] Daly himself spelled out the arrangement in an account after the election in an Underwood publication.[60] The account suggests that if he were feeling compelled to join the computer age for the imperatives of election-night showmanship, he was going to remain grounded in what was familiar. Computer use at ABC was cast as an experiment rather than an abrupt transition to something new. "Since scientists tell us we are entering the age of automation with machines increasingly taking over tasks formerly done by humans," Daly was quoted as saying, "our approach to the election coverage this year was inspired by a natural curiosity to find out . . . just what role electronic automation can play in predicting election results of the future." He set up a contest, one he himself framed as "Man versus Machine," to determine "whether man, creator of the machine, could beat the machine at its own game." The "Man Unit" was to be headed by pollster Louis Harris, working with a team from *Collier's* magazine. They would use historical data from fifty-four voting areas selected based on demographics and other characteristics. The Harris team would have access by phone to more than one hundred correspondents around the country. In New York another twenty-five people were to help Harris compile the results. On the Elecom team would be Louis Bean, author of a book on predicting election outcomes.[61] The audience at home was invited to join in, too. Ahead of the election, *Collier's* ran an elaborate guide to the fifty-four voting areas—their characteristics, location, voting history, and a place to write in the 1956 returns—along with an article by Harris titled, "Be Your Own 'Armchair Expert'—A TV Game for Election Night."[62] The contest notwithstanding, Daly also made clear that the "Man versus Machine" arrangement was itself just a supplement to ABC's traditional election-night routine. "Our principal tool," he was quoted as saying, "was still the team of some 300 newsmen, technicians, and clerks."[63] In the end Underwood conceded after the election "the fact that Eisenhower's decisive margin of victory became so apparent so soon lessened the challenge between the Elecom and the *Collier's* unit." Still, Underwood insisted, there remained "plenty of visual excitement . . . created by the seemingly all-knowing" Elecom. Even in 1956, the third election featuring computers, what still mattered was their tendency to serve intersecting agendas and have multiple meanings—from tool to prop. And, as Daly and ABC had arranged it, computing could be tried out and observed in action by collaboration with the technology's providers—but without dismissing or replacing traditional means to the same ends.

There had been no preordained trajectory for computers to enter journalism on election night in 1952. Neither did that episode guarantee a future for computers in journalism. There was also no immediate acceptance of computers as appropriate for journalism in general—or election night in particular—among writers who covered television news both as journalism and as performance. That would take years. Even then, as the technology and its application changed over time, the marriage of journalism and computing could not be taken for granted as a done deal. And the "man versus machine" approach to evaluating the worthiness of computers in journalism would live on long after 1952.

Several days after the 1954 midterm voting, when CBS was the only network with a computer on election night, *New York Times* television critic Jack Gould weighed in. His column ran under the dismissive headline, "Election Projection: A Great Click-Clack in the Back of the Sacred UNIVAC."[64] Gould delivered a pointed critique that gathered steam as it went along. "Television's coverage of the election returns on Tuesday night was probably not too bad in light of the general confusion arising from the close contests and unforeseen late shifts in tabulation," he began. "If some of the broadcasters got caught with their statistical projection showing, so did most of the assorted experts, both mortal and electronic." Gould reviewed the various networks' arrangements, dishing out compliments but also attaching a note of dismissal to each. The four-way screen on NBC was "intriguing," he wrote, but it "did not add too much in terms of straight news coverage." Tally boards at CBS were deemed elaborate, but the studio operation sometimes lacked coordination. Arrangements at ABC did not rate a description, except to say that they "had the considerable advantage of simplicity." Gould's most scathing comments were reserved for a computer not clever enough to know that it could still not count on its human keepers to supply it with correct data. "There isn't much doubt that Tuesday night will best be remembered for woefully wrong guesses of UNIVAC, the electronic brain, in predicting over C.B.S. a sweeping Democratic landslide," Gould wrote. "As UNIVAC's valet, Charles Collingwood, explained on the air, the electronic brain can only solve those problems presented to it: the gadget doesn't choose the problems in the first place. UNIVAC's mistake, it seems, was simply to trust the human race on election night."

Time magazine's take on the computer's role was no more generous.[65] *Time* declared, "Probably the outstanding TV casualty of the night was UNIVAC." After first predicting a Democratic return to majorities in both the House and Senate with large margins, *Time* noted, UNIVAC reversed course late in the evening and left Collingwood facing a prediction of a Republican majority in the House. The memory of 1952 was still fresh. *Time* quoted Collingwood as saying this: "We didn't know what to do. Should we change the machine? After all, last time the experts were wrong. I decided to stick with the machine." The mistaken assignment of a House majority to the Republicans was attributed to a transcription error by a teletype operator. The mistaken prediction of the size of the Democratic majority was attributed by Collingwood to a model giving too much weight to outsized Democratic margins in two states that were early to report. As in 1952 Collingwood's take on the situation—and on the computer—was defensive, but with a bit of irony. "After all," he was quoted as saying, "UNIVAC is only human—that is, it can only make predictions based on the material that humans feed into it."

On election night in 1956, the *New Yorker*'s Philip Hamburger, writing as the peripatetic "Our Man Stanley," visited a UNIVAC installation at Remington Rand's Manhattan headquarters. He chronicled the scene in a wry account.[66] Hamburger's response was, at best, ambiguous. Humor was his medium. He captured the hubbub this way: "Room a madhouse. Close to a hundred human brains, attached to bodies, occupied room, some bending over teletype machines, others poring over stacks of papers at desks, others standing before restaurant-refrigerator-type machines with glass fronts and whirring disks inside. Control boards everywhere—red, green, amber. Terrifying." Hamburger met with Max Woodbury, who had moved on to the Mathematics Department at New York University's college of engineering. Woodbury was described to readers as a "tall, tense brain." The professor explained the use of past data and told Hamburger the machine "brain" was working "like a dream." Hamburger also met with UNIVAC coinventor John Mauchly, described as a "quiet-looking man." The writer captured Woodbury's manifest pleasure, at first, that the computer's work was turning out to be "perfectly splendid." The UNIVAC had spit out a forecast of an Eisenhower victory with such confidence that odds of one-hundred-to-one were attached to it. But then there was trouble. The computer said Tennessee was going Democratic. Woodbury thought that must be wrong. He was validated when a courier arrived with a United Press dispatch saying that Tennessee was, in fact, going Republican. Then a courier arrived with some more disconcerting news. The machine, said Mauchly, had "become persnickety about accepting some data." There was debate between Mauchly and Woodbury about the human and machine roles, with Hamburger relaying the dialogue. "'Error lights,' said Dr. Woodbury," and then, "'Easy to blame the machinery,' said Dr. Mauchly. 'Could be human failure.'" Then another problem. "She's goofed on the Senate," said Woodbury. And that is where Hamburger left things, with one last dig: "Drs. Woodbury and Mauchly joined technicians at control board. I went home and listened to returns on radio. Eisenhower by landslide." At the *New York Times*, Jack Gould also wrote dismissively of computer use in reviewing the various networks' election-night broadcasts in 1956: "All three chains employed their own versions of electronic computers, which brilliantly confirmed the obvious."[67]

The critics notwithstanding, computers did become fixtures on election night, and the computer makers continued to see the exposure as valuable. In an ad after the 1960 election, IBM made this clear by posing a question: "Who won the computer battle last night?"[68] IBM's answer —telling readers, "You did"—was perhaps predictable. But then IBM also made clear the stakes for itself: "Election reporting is a dramatic way to demonstrate the reliability of modern computer systems under conditions of stress and urgency." That might be, but the writers who covered broadcasting were still not all ready to concede that this was either good journalism or good television. *Variety*, for example, generally heaped praise on television for the unexpected "Alfred Hitchcock touch" in covering the seesawing on election night in 1960 between Democrat John F. Kennedy and Republican Richard M. Nixon.[69] But the use of computers by the networks—referred to as "nets" and "webs"—was panned outright. "The electronic brains used by the three nets again raised a serious question as to their value," *Variety* argued. "At best, they confused televiewers, and made the webs look a little silly. They should, in fact, be good source material for comedians."

Finally, after the 1962 midterm elections, Gould proclaimed in the *New York Times* the marriage of computing and election-night broadcasting to be solid. The headline read, "TV: Election Coverage; Electronic Computers Prove Value in Forecasting Results—C.B.S. Excels."[70] The technology that Gould saw as a questionable part of the process a decade earlier now got top billing. "Electronic computers," he wrote, "clearly have taken over the drama of reporting returns and introduced a new sophistication in quick forecasting of results." Gould was also willing to part with a dismissive postelection tradition. "Computing machines have been the target of almost as many jokes as mothers-in-law," he wrote, "but on Tuesday evening there was no gainsaying their influence. Their projections of probable winners on the basis of limited returns proved almost uncannily accurate." Gould drew a larger lesson, too, about the value of computers going forward—for analysts and for the viewing public. "Political analysts always have been more impressed by the results in pivotal districts than in early total returns," he wrote. "The computing industry now has placed an incredibly fast tool at their disposal, and television has been the means of acquainting the mass public with the procedure." One can read Gould's take on the election-night reporting as a sort of bookend—acceptance of computers, with their use evolving in sophistication over a single decade. He would go on to make a similar pronouncement a year and a half later. Ahead of the 1964 California primary, he declared, "The incredible computing machines have led the revolution in election reporting."[71]

Acceptance was still far from universal, complete, or permanent. After the 1962 election night that saw Gould tip his hat to computer analysis, another significant television critic of that era, Lawrence Laurent of the *Washington Post*, was full of concerns.[72] "Election Night, 1962," he wrote, "just about did away with men and replaced them with machines."[73] Humans, it seemed, even had to put up with working conditions that the machines required. "Chilled CBS reporters," he observed, "had to shiver while a cool, optimum, temperature was maintained for computers." Laurent's critique was that somewhere in the ascendancy of computer analysis on election night, serious questions had become manifest about turf that was once the purview of journalists unaided by technology. "An electronic brain is surely an awesome instrument and certainly civilization has to depend on them for solutions to complex problems," he wrote. "However, TV newsmen have been intimidated, and it is just about time to take the devices out of the newsrooms and return them to space laboratories." Among his concerns was this: "For reporting, there remains that nagging doubt that some human being might have given the machine a bad diet of statistics or that a computer, in surpassing human capacity, may have taken on some of the doubts that are the beginning of true wisdom." His prescription? "What I am suggesting is that the reporters return to the one trade for which they are fitted: Accurate details, given with calm assurance and without the mania for beating the opposition—by three-tenths of one second—to a forecast of a winner."

Even Jack Gould's admiration for election-night computer use in

1962 and 1964 did not mean he was beyond criticizing the way they were employed. Just as radio broadcasters earlier in the century had wrestled with the best way to avoid overwhelming listeners with returns, Gould argued in 1966 that the new ability to provide very detailed analysis with great speed should be tempered with the need for clarity.[74] "The computers need to be kept in their place," he wrote, "lest a torrent of information merely clog the channels of communication." What was wanted, Gould insisted, was more "careful reflective commentary that gives shape and perspective to the meaning of the electorate's will." Two years later, in his final column about election-night television, Gould echoed similar sentiments and some old themes.[75] Computers were still inviting the evergreen comparison of cold machine versus human journalist. Computers also seemed to invite another sort of contest. On one side was an alliance of computers and pollsters. On the other side were voters who could not be reduced to predictable patterns of thinking and acting. "The era of automation could not cope with the tightest presidential race in years," Gould concluded. "Old-fashioned vote counting became an overnight vogue as the human beings took over from the machines."

Just as the permanent campaign became a feature of twentieth-century politics, the networks developed a permanent apparatus for election coverage, with long-term planning before each new political cycle.[76] And the cycles of innovations, problems, new innovations, and new problems continued, too. One of the most significant innovations was so-called "exit polling" of voters on Election Day after they cast their ballots.[77] Seen as an addition to both preelection surveys and computer-aided methods of comparing early returns to historical data, exit polling eventually became both a wondrous and then essential boon to election-night reporting and forecasting right into the twenty-first century. But exit polling also became a periodic source of controversy. Some of the unresolved troubles would play no small part in the chaos that followed the 2020 election.

In 1967 CBS gave exit polling a try in Kentucky's election for governor. The approach was developed under Warren Mitofsky, who became known as "the father of exit polling," and it was used live on that election night in the network's coverage. Deemed a success in that outing, exit polling was next used by CBS in 1968 for six primaries and then twenty-one states in the November election, according to Mitofsky and associate Murray Edelman. Other networks followed suit. In addition to getting a handle on outcomes, exit polling also provided insight into why voters made the choices they did. There were triumphant successes. There were agonizing snafus. And there were controversies. One of the earliest of these came in 1980 when NBC called the election for Republican Ronald Reagan. The network was correct. But NBC made that call hours before polls closed on the West Coast, and Democratic incumbent Jimmy Carter conceded while votes were still being cast. There were debates about whether the early call affected voter turnout. Congress held hearings. The networks promised to do better. But in 1984 NBC made a call before polls closed in the West—for a Reagan victory over Walter Mondale—and so did CBS and ABC. Congress jumped in again, passing a resolution asking the networks to hold off on calling races until the voting was done. More hearings were held. The election-night forecasting business was no longer just about competition between the networks. There were turbulent political waters to navigate, too.

The networks continued to see exit polling as useful in the competition that news organizations had been waging with each other on election nights for more than a century. But exit polling was expensive. It required boots on the ground—teams of people to wait outside polling places to conduct interviews—and then other teams to import and analyze the data by computer. The answer? Collaboration. Major news organizations formed a series of alliances to share the cost of exit polling. Despite the competition, collaboration on election night was not new. Three networks and two wire services had formed a consortium starting in 1964 to address another election-night problem—the cost of aggregating the vote tallies nationwide. This consortium was called the News Election Service—NES—and it was the first in an alphabet soup of election-night alliances of various sorts in subsequent decades. Each of the participating organizations—NBC, CBS, ABC, the Associated Press, and United Press International—used the data to do their own analyses. They also made their own decisions on when to "call" races. The first collaboration on exit polls came in 1990. It had another acronym—VRS—for Voter Research and Surveys, and it included the three major networks plus CNN. New issues prompted the creation of yet another three-letter entity in 1993 when NES and VRS were combined to become VNS, which stood for Voter

News Service. The Associated Press was included. Fox News joined in for the 1996 election. So there it was again, as had been the story on election nights for a long stretch of American history to that point: cycles of problems and solutions, crises and innovations, rinse and repeat.

And the election-night dramas were far from finished.

Especially notable was 2000. The outcome hinged on Florida. Election-night forecasting featured seesawing projections of who had won Florida and the presidency. The outcome would ultimately be decided five weeks later as the result of a Supreme Court ruling. A study commissioned by CNN afterward did not mince words: "On Election Day 2000, television news organizations staged a collective drag race on the crowded highway of democracy, recklessly endangering the electoral process, the political life of the country, and their own credibility."[78] A bipartisan review of the 2000 election problems chaired by two former presidents—Jimmy Carter and Gerald Ford—even tried to dissuade Americans from participating in exit polls.[79]

But exit polling and election-night forecasting continued. They continued to serve up more cycles of trouble and innovation, too. And there were new additions of the alphabet soup of collaborations. In 2003, for example, VNS came to an end, and its members formed another three-letter entity, NEP, the National Election Pool.[80] Around the same time, there was also growing concern about changes in the ways Americans were casting their ballots. More and more were voting ahead of Election Day, either by absentee ballot or in arrangements that varied from state to state for early voting. The result was a new set of challenges for exit polling. These would eventually help set the stage for cataclysmic events on and after election night 2020.

Long after 1952 some journalists also remained nostalgic for the days when the insights of veteran political reporters trumped computer analysis. On the contentious election night of 2000, NBC's Washington bureau chief, Tim Russert, tried to help the audience comprehend the stakes in the evolving and uncertain electoral vote count.[81] He jotted down the key contested states on the back of a legal pad and held it up to the camera. As more results came in, he crossed some states out and added others and revised his arithmetic, exploring possible and likely outcomes. As the evening wore on and the pad became messier, an NBC producer sent out for a pair of handheld dry-erase boards and markers for Russert to use. At one point, when asked a question by NBC *Nightly News* anchor Tom Brokaw about how the Republican candidate might win without Pennsylvania, Russert replied, "Tom, forget all the high-tech computers. Take out your slate and your pen, and it's the good old days are back." Later in the evening, again speaking with Brokaw, Russert advocated grouping states that were too close to call and looking at their past performance: "It's better than the computers tonight, Tom. Trust me."[82] Still later, several hours after midnight, Brokaw was recounting the embarrassing performance of various television networks, including NBC, when calling the pivotal state of Florida. Russert's reply was this: "If you'd just stayed with these simple boards, you wouldn't have those problems with those highfalutin computers, Tom."[83] Russert's down-to-earth, low-tech approach would itself become a subject for news stories. A year after Russert's death in 2008, his colleague Keith Olbermann referenced the episode in an on-air tribute: "As the technology increased and overwhelmed the news, he alone had the presence of mind to throw on the brakes and reduce the chaos of that election night to terms and means that were unmistakably clear."[84]

Decades after computer-based methodologies first appeared, election nights offered an increasingly rich buffet of data points to seasoned commentators and journalists, but the hoped-for abatement of risk over issues of timeliness and accuracy was still not a settled affair.

And unthinkable challenges lay ahead.

In 2002 Mitofsky and Edelman coauthored an article titled "Election Night Estimation" and addressed the question of why networks go through the expense and trouble involved in that task.[85] "The transfer of power in a democracy is probably the most important news event of the year," they wrote. "We take this transfer of power for granted in this country, but we should not. If you want a feeling for its importance all one wants to do is follow the news of any emerging democracy when control of government switches hands."

No one could have imagined back then, in 2002, what would happen on an election night in the not-too-distant future that threw the norms of more than two centuries out the window.

10 | Truly the Question of Our Time

On November 8, 2016, Donald J. Trump's victory in the presidential contest stunned pollsters. And it stunned journalists who had come to rely on those pollsters. In that way, election night proved once again its ability to be about more than just the candidates. Plenty of soul searching followed. There were mea culpas. There were vows to do better at both polling and reporting. There was plenty of interest, as in the run-up to election night in 1952, to find new ways of fulfilling that most elusive of human desires—the ability to see what's ahead.

But then came the election of 2020.

That year's chapter in the saga of election-night forecasting was not written by innovation, but by something that neither fact nor reason were ready for. It boiled down to this—a candidate whose strategy was that if he did not win, he just needed to convince tens of millions of Americans that he did win. And he needed to get a critical mass in Congress and politicians at the state level to join in the charade.[1] This fraud—which fueled a violent insurrection by Trump devotees on January 6, 2021—failed to overturn the election.[2] A majority of Republicans in Congress—147 of them—also tried to keep the House and Senate from certifying the election of Joe Biden, citing the same bogus claims.[3] They failed, too. But damage to the place of election night in American culture was immense. As cries of "Stop the Steal" resonated among the most ardent Trump supporters, a majority of rank-and-file Republicans went along with their claim—absent any credible evidence—that Biden's election was illegitimate.[4] Here was a dark vision of how a vocal political minority could, with the right constellation of sympathetic officeholders, threaten a mature democracy.

For adherents of the Trump-orchestrated conspiracy theory, exhibit A was the turning of the tide on election night. Rising totals had moved away from an early Trump lead. One factor was the delay in counting mail ballots in places where they tended to skew away from the GOP. Slow reporting from some urban Democratic strongholds also played a role. There was nothing nefarious about the shifting count. In fact, the pattern was well-known from previous elections as the "red mirage." Strong Republican leads in the early tabulation of votes cast on Election Day could fade as the counting wore on. But millions of Trump supporters did not care about that history, despite news reporting ahead of time raising just such a possibility. These Trump fans wanted to roll back the clock to the point where their candidate was ahead and stop the count there—defying nearly two centuries of understanding that being ahead before the count is complete does not mean victory. Whacky conspiracy theories contributed to a "Stop the Steal" frenzy. There were claims that Italian satellites changed digital vote counts, that a long-dead Venezuelan strongman had somehow laid the groundwork for voting-machine chicanery, and that ballots needed to be inspected for microscopic bamboo fibers to determine whether they had come from China. Not all Trump voters bought into claims that the election was stolen. But surveys show that a majority did—even long afterward.[5] Or maybe just the steady barrage of claims from high-profile partisans and talking heads had the intended effect, fostering doubt.[6] Although internal documents unearthed in a lawsuit against Fox News showed behind-the-scenes disbelief about Trump's claims of victory and fraud, the cable channel's evening stars fed the flames on air to hold on to their Trump-loving audience and protect Fox's stock value.[7] Sarah Longwell, a conservative political strategist and online publisher, hosted focus groups to try to understand, as she put it, "why Trump 2020 voters hold so strongly to the Big Lie."[8] "For many of Trump's voters," she wrote in the *Atlantic*, "the belief that the election was stolen is not a fully formed thought. It's more of an attitude, or a tribal pose. They know something nefarious occurred but can't easily explain how or why."

There were dozens of challenges in court.[9] There were recounts and audits. None of this produced credible evidence of a rigged election. Claims were debunked in meticulous postmortem studies by journalists and scholars, plus a seventy-two-page report by eight veteran Republicans—senators, judges, and lawyers.[10] But that did not stop legislatures and governors in states with Republican majorities from acting on baseless claims to create new forms of voter suppression.[11] Cries of a stolen election became a core element of the GOP at the local, state, and national level.[12] And Trump remained defiant. More than two years after losing, he called for throwing out the bedrock foundations of American democracy to get back in the White House, posting this message on social media: "A Massive Fraud of this type and magnitude allows for the termination of all rules, regulations, and articles, even those found in the Constitution."[13] Trump also doubled down on demonizing journalists. At a rally in Texas in 2022, he suggested that a reporter or editor who refused to reveal a confidential source should be thrown in jail to become what he called "the bride of another prisoner."[14] That is, Trump would subject the journalist to the prospect of being raped in order to force a confession. The crowd approved.

It was hard to see how the damage might be reversed. Even in a landslide, the specter of 2020 will hang heavy. A concession from the losing candidate will always mean more now than the proforma act it was before. So, as we await the next round of election-night innovations, the challenge is more chilling than just shortening the time needed to project winners. In 1952 an innovation we have explored in this book—adding computers to the election-night mix—was driven by that question of how quickly the outcome could be forecast. In fact, the whole history of election night until 2020 was about how quickly we could tell who won. Now, it will be about how quickly millions on the losing side may accept the results. In a flash, election night has become not what it always was, but something dark, to be anticipated with dread. This chapter asks what can be done and explores an approach I will describe shortly.

The fallout from 2020 cannot be divorced from many layers of context. Among Americans as a whole, confidence in the news media has declined steadily in recent decades, with deep partisan divides in the way Americans feel about sources of news.[15] Some of this damage to the status of journalism has been self-inflicted. At the same time, a stunning array of actors with self-serving motives have sought to drive a wedge between Americans and fact-based news reporting—or just facts in general. These actors range from politicians and corporate lobbyists to foreign adversaries and so-called "conflict entrepreneurs," who profit from the chaos they fuel. A foundational tenet of American democracy is that a free press is essential. If Americans are able to govern themselves effectively, access to trustworthy information is critical.[16] That includes information they need to make decisions about voting—and to satisfy themselves that no one tinkered with their vote. As we have seen, Americans in the past were full of wonder at the process that would bind them together as a nation and bring them together to pick their leaders. In 1864 the *New York Herald* breathlessly spoke of surging crowds awaiting the latest election returns with this assessment: "A similar scene cannot perhaps be witnessed in any other country than democratic America."[17] In 1884 the poet Walt Whitman wrote of the immense power of "America's choosing day," dwarfing all the physical wonders of a vast continent.[18] And in opening NBC's election-night program on radio in 1952, the announcer marveled at a virtual spectacle playing out in countless cities and towns. "From all over the nation," he intoned, "your votes are coming in—votes from free Americans in a free election."[19]

That sort of wonder—election after election—came crashing down in the hours, days, and weeks after the polls closed in 2020. There was no clear path out of the wreckage. But giving up on democracy is not acceptable. Could there be future tools that would counter the type of chicanery and confusion we witnessed? It is hard to imagine now what could overcome such a willingness to abandon fact and reason. I would argue that the answer goes beyond looking for better data, better statistical models, and better algorithms on election night. So, what is to be done?

This final chapter is what might be called a "thought experiment." It seeks to tackle that very question: What is to be done? My intent is not to offer specific answers. Rather, I wish to propose a framework for approaching this question. Some of the ideas I explore here may strike you as unworkable or misguided or odd. I am okay with that. But I do hope you will bear with me for a few more pages. And I would like to throw one other critical issue into the mix. In a recent email exchange, I posed a question to Margaret Sullivan, a former top newspaper editor and one of the sharpest observers of the state of journalism today. I asked her how trust in the news media can be restored among those Americans who are inclined to engage in magical thinking rather than follow what she has termed the "reality-based" press. "That," she replied, "is truly the question of our time."[20] Beyond those who preferred to think of the election as stolen without any reliable evidence, we must also consider the long decline in the amount of trust many Americans have in the news media. That trend predates Trump. Here are some sobering numbers. Back in 1972 a majority of Americans said they had a "great deal" or a "fair amount" of trust in the mass media to report the news "fully, accurately, and fairly."[21] That number was 68 percent. By 2022 it had dropped in half, to 34 percent. Among Republicans that level of confidence in the news media stood at just 14 percent. And among independents the number was not much more reassuring at 27 percent. Democrats felt better about the news media, with 70 percent saying they had a "great deal" or "fair amount" of trust. But a deeper dive into the data proved concerning. Among younger Democrats—aged eighteen to thirty-four—barely half trusted the news media. When the numbers were parsed to ask about having the highest level of confidence—a "great deal" of trust—only 18 percent of Democrats said they did and just 2 percent of Republicans.

I bring to this issue a deep concern for the future of journalism. I was a journalist for a quarter century. For more than two decades since then, I have been teaching future journalists. I am committed to the idea that preserving and enhancing American democracy is not negotiable and that strengthening journalism must be part of that endeavor.

So, I want to raise here a question about whether two things can and should be linked: the future of credible election-night reporting and the future of trust in the news media. That is, while there have been thoughtful studies, proposals, and programs for dealing with this issue of trust, we have seen in this book that one particular venue for news reporting—election night—can be a showcase for innovation. Sometimes, the way forward in solving a problem is not with a widely implemented approach at first, but with a single, high-profile endeavor to get broad attention for a new way of doing things. In 1952 the computer world's innovators understood that. If they could do just one thing well—jump into the election-night mix with their hardware and their algorithms and their problem-solving frame of mind—then they might make a convincing case to the public that computers had something to offer the world.

By teaming with these innovators in a highwire act, news executives at CBS and NBC also saw an opportunity. They might show what television news could do after a lackluster visual performance on election night in 1948 and a crisis of credibility over that night's flawed forecasts. The use of computers in 1952 was risky and did not work quite as well as envisioned. But it got attention.

I suggest here four lessons from 1952 that could be applied in making election night a showcase for enhancing trust in journalism. The news media today should, as the networks did in 1952, think outside the box of conventional journalistic practice. The news media should look to other disciplines for novel approaches, just as NBC and CBS did when they considered what the new world of computing had to offer. The news media should understand the value of collaborating in previously unimaginable ways, just as the networks did in partnering with engineers, statisticians, and programmers in 1952. And the news media should understand the importance of transparency in explaining innovative approaches to audiences, just as broadcasters did when they described what was going on behind the scenes and under the hood to generate the computers' election-night forecasts more than seven decades ago. We cannot wait to find out whether the fever of 2020's revolt against facts will burn itself out or whether journalism's deepening crisis of trust will resolve on its own. If these issues are not addressed in an effective way, the idea of journalism as a bulwark against enemies of democracy is in doubt. Innovating on election night by taking cues from the past might show the way forward.

To go back to something I suggested earlier, why aren't better algorithms the answer? Don't get me wrong. I cannot imagine an election night without the fine-grained detail and historical knowledge provided by veterans like Steve Kornacki on MSNBC and John King on CNN, along with their giant touch-screen graphics. Constant enhancement of reporting models on election night has been and will continue to be important to the audiences of news outlets that undertake those improvements. But we must think hard about other audiences—such as the ones that have fueled the "Stop the Steal" movement. We are safe in concluding that their main sources of political news are not the *New York Times*, NPR, the major broadcast networks, CNN, or MSNBC.[22] The ranks of what would later become known as "election deniers" were much more likely on election night in 2020 to turn to Fox News. And as Chris Stirewalt learned the hard way, getting it right on Fox ahead of all those other news organizations—which he did with the help of a new system for calling elections and explaining the results—was not a great career move. In fact, his team's correct call that Trump had lost Arizona unleashed a firestorm of angry protest from Fox viewers, Republican politicians, and the soon-to-be former president. Stirewalt went on air to explain the call, but the die was cast for him. Here is how he put it: "I got canned."[23]

How did that happen? As Americans increasingly chose to vote before Election Day and exit polling became more problematic, Fox pulled out of the exit-polling collaborative used by other networks and news organizations. Instead, Fox turned to yet another election-night innovation. Called VoteCast, it was developed over several years and debuted for the 2018 midterm elections.[24] It was used for the first time in a presidential election in 2020.[25] VoteCast came out of a collaboration between the Associated Press and an organization known by the acronym NORC— the National Opinion Research Center—at the University of Chicago. In the run-up to the 2020 election, the AP-NORC team surveyed more than 130,000 registered voters, gathering data from every state. Stirewalt credits the use of VoteCast for Fox's ability to make the first call on the outcome in Arizona. In nontechnical terms, they nailed it. But rather than accepting the reality that Trump had lost Arizona—a key to his loss of the election—the Fox fan base chose instead to attack the messenger. Stirewalt reflected on that in a book he published after his departure. "The rage directed at me was so intense because so many Fox viewers had grown accustomed to the casual exaggeration and relentless happy talk from opinion shows from morning till midnight," Stirewalt wrote. "Had viewers been given a more accurate understanding of the race over time, Trump's loss would have been seen as a likely outcome."[26]

In other words the antidote to potential election-night chaos in the future must be set in motion well before the next election. To get election night right, it is not first and foremost about making the right call. It is about the journalism done ahead of time. And it is not about what news organizations report to their respective audiences on the political leanings of people in, say, Mohave County, Arizona, or Catoosa County,

Georgia. What matters is the understanding that people "out there" have about the rest of the country. Ultimately, it is not about who gets the most accurate forecast first. It is about whether the outcome will make sense to people whose candidate loses.

But how can that be done? For people who think an election had to be rigged because of the outcome, what could change in the news they consume on a regular basis that would make those doubts less likely? The question is not how to get everyone to agree, but how to get more people to understand that the outcome of an election is reasonable— and that it is a reasonably accurate picture of how a majority would vote. Clearly, this is not a simple question. There are profound challenges.

Let's consider some of these challenges, starting with what are called "news deserts." These are black holes in the information cosmos. Between 2005 and 2022, the United States lost 2,500 newspapers.[27] That was one-fourth of all newspapers, according to Penny Abernathy, a veteran journalist who studies news deserts. The rise of new digital alternatives did not come close to replacing what was lost. The biggest effects have been felt in local news. Abernathy wrote this in a 2022 study: "More than a fifth of the nation's citizens live in news deserts—with very limited access to local news—or in communities at risk of becoming news deserts." That is seventy million Americans. Here are the details: more than 200 counties lacked a newspaper, and another 1,630 counties had only a single news source for communities spread across a large area. Other studies have found deficits in news serving diverse audiences. A feared "digital divide" that might leave minority communities behind because of a lack of access to technology did not develop as expected. Something else happened. A study published in 2014 even before the latest contraction in local journalism surveyed the two largest minority groups—African Americans and Hispanics. "These Americans," in the words of the study, "do not believe that the growth of the web and mobile media has fulfilled the promise of more coverage, and more accurate coverage, of underserved ethnic communities."[28]

Research has linked the decline in local journalism—including less coverage of local government and schools—to a decline in engagement with local politics and elections.[29] And we would be justified in thinking that without reputable local news organizations, there might be limited local pushback against the misinformation that could fill such a void. Efforts are underway in some communities, at least, to strengthen local journalism by having news organizations collaborate to focus on meaningful local issues. An initiative known as the Solutions Journalism Network works to foster local journalism that focuses not just on revealing problems but on identifying solutions. This reporting is made possible with partnerships, with expertise needed for in-depth coverage, and with other assistance.[30] Philanthropists and nonprofit foundations have directed funding at other projects to shore up local journalism. Some donors have joined collective enterprises such as the American Journalism Project.[31] In the fall of 2023, some of the same donors were part of a new twenty-two-member coalition with plans to devote more than $500 million over five years to strengthen local newsrooms.[32] That initiative, named "Press Forward," is headed by the MacArthur Foundation and includes the Knight Foundation, which has long been focused on supporting news organizations and journalism schools. Others are focusing their resources on particular endeavors, such as the Local News Network based at the University of Maryland's Philip Merrill College of Journalism.[33] As its first reporting project, students under the guidance of Jerry Zremski, a faculty member and award-winning journalist, developed a voting guide for local school board elections across Maryland in 2022. It was shared by many news organizations without the resources to do the same time-consuming reporting themselves. The project was also published as an interactive database by Capital News Service, based at the school.[34] This is certainly a model that could be replicated.

In the run-up to the 2022 midterm elections, broadcast journalist Ali Velshi used his weekend program on MSNBC to air group interviews with voters across the political spectrum, giving them—and his viewers—a chance to see and hear each other.[35] That is another sort of model. But it also raises a challenge. Velshi has given his own audience a much-needed window into the thinking of people whose views they may not share. How could that be scaled up? What about people living in news deserts, including those who do not watch MSNBC, which has a much higher following among liberals than conservatives?[36] And who could organize and fund such a thing? Large foundations, perhaps? There are some in the journalism space. What about a collaborative effort led by news organizations nationwide? That could happen—an all-hands-on-deck effort—only if the news industry were to understand as a whole that rising distrust and expanding black holes threaten them all because democracy itself is threatened. The history of American journalism is not without precedents for collaboration. We could look all the way back to early history of what became the Associated Press and nineteenth-century efforts to share the expense of news delivered by telegraph. Even sharing of the cost of exit polls stands as an example of collaboration. And maybe there are sources of information hiding in plain sight that journalism could access in collaborative ways more effectively. Tom Rosenstiel talked with me about this and has written about it. He is a journalism leader, a respected voice on the future of news, and was the chief architect and author of an important project on news media values that we will come to shortly.[37] He advocates rethinking news as "collaborative intelligence."[38] He sees the pillars of this collaborative intelligence as harnessing computing power, serving communities, and leveraging those communities for information, all at the same time. "At their best," he writes, "connected citizens bring more perspectives, more views, and more collective experience to our understanding of the world than journalists could ever have achieved from their individual rolodexes." One result could be what he calls "a nuanced understanding of the public mind." In this approach, professional journalists bring the access and skills to ask tough questions of those in power. As he puts it, the professional journalists can also "triangulate the intelligence of the computer data and the networked community." They are skilled at storytelling, too, and they can employ what he called "a discipline of verification and an ethos of openminded inquiry that is different from those actors in media and society, including most citizens, focused on argument and persuasion."

The need for high-quality journalism is so important now given high levels of misunderstanding that even well-meaning people may have about each other in ways that matter in elections. Researchers have found that stereotypes figure heavily in Americans' perceptions of party makeup—even within their own parties. For example, in one survey, respondents said they believed 32 percent of Democrats were LGBT, compared to the actual number, which is about 6 percent. Respondents thought 38 percent of Republicans had annual incomes of more than $250,000, but only about 2 percent do.[39] The prevalence of these stereotypes was even greater in the answers that Democrats and Republicans gave about each other. Researchers also tested the power of corrective facts. "When provided information about the out-party's actual composition," they found, "partisans come to see its supporters as less extreme and feel less socially distant from them." Corrective information is just the sort of thing that local media might provide. While Democrats and Republicans are divided in the national news media they follow, both sides say local television is one of their main sources of news about politics and government.[40] Where there is no reality-based news media to counter stereotypes as the news landscape shrinks, partisans may more easily be swayed by messages fostering contempt for people they do not know.

That gets us to the issue of those who are spreading falsehoods on purpose. We will return to that. But even without these provocateurs, there are calls for new ways that journalists might report on complex situations in which people tend to misunderstand each other. One of these approaches comes from Amanda Ripley, a journalist and author who urges "complicating the narratives." In an article by that name, she asked, "What if journalists covered controversial issues differently—based on how humans actually behave when they are polarized and suspicious?"[41] She went on to take a deeper dive in a book titled *High Conflict: Why We Get Trapped and How to Get Out*. One of the big takeaways from that book is the importance of getting at the "understory," which she defines as "the thing the conflict is really about, underneath the usual talking points."[42] Mónica Guzmán is another journalist who turned her attention to exploring the role of curiosity in getting beneath division. She wrote a book about what she turned up in her research, titled, *I Never Thought of It That Way: How to Have Fearlessly Curious Conversations in Dangerously Divided Times*.[43] An endeavor called Trusting News, formed by the collaboration of two leading journalism think tanks, has engaged in what is described as "a continual cycle of research, learning, and sharing."[44] They put the goal this way: "We learn how people decide what news to trust and turn that knowledge into actionable strategies for journalists."

There are still more challenges to consider if we are to address this matter of restoring trust and how that might intersect with election-night forecasting. One of these challenges has to do with values. As someone who has spent his entire adult life in and around journalism—practicing it, teaching it, and studying its history—I had assumed that the values informing my approach to journalism were widely shared. I could not have been more wrong, according to the results of a groundbreaking study published in 2021 by the Media Insight Project. This is a joint endeavor involving a think tank called the American Press Institute, the Associated Press, and the previously mentioned NORC at the University of Chicago.[45] One striking conclusion of the 2021 study stood out to me: "The trust crisis may be better understood through people's moral values than their politics." The study built on work previously done by social psychologist Jonathan Haidt and published in the book, *The Righteous Mind: Why Good People Are Divided by Politics and Religion*.[46] Haidt pioneered something called "moral foundations theory." In a nutshell it posits that "different people instinctively respond more strongly to certain moral values than others—such values as care, fairness, loyalty, authority, and purity."[47] The authors of the Media Insight Project study determined that there were five core values at work in journalism. One was described as "the importance of spotlighting problems in society as a way to solve them." Another was the "notion that more facts are likely to get us closer to the truth." The study found that only 11 percent of Americans supported all five of these journalism values. And only one of the five values—that one about the importance of facts—had the support of a majority of Americans.

The Media Insight Project findings led me revisit a poll that caught my eye a few years earlier, while Trump was in the White House. Respondents were asked if the president should be able to shut down news organizations engaged in what was termed "bad behavior."[48] About one quarter said yes—including more than four in ten Republicans. Nearly half of the Republicans also deemed the news media to be "the enemy of the people," a Trump rallying cry. These are clearly not my values. But the upshot of the Media Insight Project study is not hopeless. Far from it. Here is a conclusion based on some of the study's experiments: "There are ways journalists can broaden story choices and framing to reach and be relevant to more of the public, skeptical and trusting alike."[49] In 2017, while Margaret Sullivan was a media critic at the *Washing-*

ton Post, she spent six weeks working remotely from a small town in western New York State and took time to listen to residents talk about their news habits. Here is some of what she concluded: "We need to heed complaints about the blending of news and opinion. . . . We need to focus more intently—and more engagingly—on subjects that matter most to ordinary people's lives. . . . Perhaps most important, we need to be much more transparent."[50]

All of this would require efforts well ahead of any future election night to be effective. And we have not even gotten to the hard stuff yet.

There is a category of seemingly insurmountable challenges that social scientists call "wicked problems." This does not mean they are "wicked" as in "evil." These problems are so complex, with so many unknowns, that solutions are hard to imagine. Tackling them means bringing together a variety of disciplines. Certainly, journalists looking to confront the issue of trust and how that plays out on election night are not likely to be able to solve the hardest of these "wicked problems" on their own.

One such problem is belief in conspiracy theories despite an absence of reliable evidence. On election night, could people in this camp come around to what the evidence does show if that evidence conflicts with their conspiracy mindset? Some conspiracy believers have their individual and group identity wrapped up in these fictions. They cherry-pick facts in a way that fits their beliefs. This is hard to shake. If an attachment to misinformation is tied up with grievance, that is hard to shake, too. James Kimmel Jr. is a lecturer in psychiatry in the Yale School of Medicine and explores the effects of grievance on the brain. He has written that "your brain on grievance looks a lot like your brain on drugs."[51] What does that have to do with the way people may gravitate to silos of information that intensify skewed perceptions of the world? Mónica Guzmán offers this explanation based on brain chemistry: "Dopamine is a neurotransmitter that plays a part in how we feel pleasure, reward, and motivation. . . . In our digital silos, with their endless streams of information . . . dopamine hits are always a tap or click away."[52] It is not a stretch to see, then, how social media platforms have become a haven for so-called "conflict entre-preneurs" of all sorts who nurture grievance for gain.[53]

It may be no wonder that the actions of conflict entrepreneurs in recent decades have corresponded with Americans' declining confidence in major institutions—not just the news media, but also Congress, the criminal justice system, schools, and more.[54] In 2016 the Oxford English Dictionary designated the term "post-truth" as its "word of the year."[55] Playing a leading role in devaluing facts and undermining trust in fact-based institutions are what two historians of science have termed "merchants of doubt."[56] In a 2010 book, Naomi Oreskes and Erik M. Conway detailed the creation of a durable template for creating doubt. It started with a tobacco industry campaign—not to convince the public that their product was safe, but to create uncertainty around claims that tobacco was unsafe. That template has been in constant use since then to muddy debate about causes of environmental destruction and climate change. It has also been adopted for all sorts of other uses. "Stop the Steal" was just one more campaign to confuse the public, planned out well before election night. In 2022 a congressional committee presented evidence that Trump privately admitted losing but publicly insisted he had won as part of a strategy to convince his followers that he was the victim of massive fraud. Days before the election, Trump adviser Steve Bannon was caught on tape saying that Trump's strategy would be to take advantage of the expected "red mirage" to sow doubt. "He's gonna declare victory," Bannon said. "But that doesn't mean he's a winner. He's just gonna say he's a winner."[57]

High on any list of conflict entrepreneurs are foreign actors who seek to interfere with the central events of American democracy—elections—by sowing confusion. One of the most notable, a Russian oligarch and mercenary leader, bragged openly about doing just that. In a taunt one day before the 2022 midterm elections, he said, "We interfered, are interfering, and will interfere."[58] Conflict entrepreneurs and agents of doubt are especially adept at taking advantage of what have been called "data voids." These are corners of cyberspace where specific sorts of online searches—using wording connected to conspiracy theories, for example—may not encounter corrective information as readily as they encounter misinformation. Such data voids, say researchers Michael Golebiewski and Danah Boyd, "can be exploited by those with ideological, economic, or political agendas."[59] Even individuals who pride themselves on doing their own fact-checking research online may inadvertently find themselves getting results that only serve to confirm their biases.[60]

One of the most challenging of wicked problems is how to walk back decades of manufactured doubt and the willingness of so many to buy in. Low-quality journalism of the "he said, she said" type may only serve to exacerbate this problem. And some of the media catering to Trump followers did not even bother with the counterpoint part of that point-counterpoint formula. In *Weapons of Mass Delusion*, which looks at the way fraudulent claims about the election metastasized, author Robert Draper writes this about the postelection suspicions of tens of millions of conservatives: "That their beloved Donald J. Trump might somehow be a historically unpopular president—one whose Gallup approval ratings never topped 49 percent at any point during his four-year term—was a reality from which right-wing media and self-segregation had thoroughly buffered them."[61]

A detailed study of misinformation in the 2020 campaign concluded that to undo these destructive trends going forward, a "whole-of-society response" is needed.[62] That would include government, the media, social media platforms, technology companies, community leaders, universities, public interest organizations, religious groups, and more.[63] I suspect that a "whole-of-society" approach is also needed to reverse the decline in the public's trust of the news media enough to avoid a recurrence of what happened on election night in 2020. Beyond roles for news and information professionals, there could be a place for public figures of various sorts, whether national or local. It is not hard to imagine a campaign of public service announcements by celebrities, athletes, religious leaders, and others. Anne Applebaum, an author who writes about threats to democracy, has made a related point about the televised congressional hearings into the assault on the Capitol. She argued that the hearings were an exercise in the "construction of trust" by relying on witnesses who had once been part of the Trump administration.[64] There is also certainly a place for research by experts in a variety of fields outside journalism. Neuroscience is one. A 2018 study, for example, found that people with an inflated sense of their understanding of politics have an increased likelihood of believing in conspiracy theories.[65] Yet, there was also a ray of hope. "Our findings might suggest," said one of the researchers, "that showing people the limitations of their understanding can lead to more informed, evidence-based opinions and beliefs."[66] Tom Rosenstiel and Margaret Sullivan have each argued for understanding what makes people receptive to truth, especially those who may be open to reason even if they are skeptical.[67]

No single news organization acting alone can meet the challenges I have discussed here. All who care about the future of democracy need to be on a war footing—trying things, engaging lots of people, seeing what sticks. For nearly two centuries, election nights have been a place of innovation and problem solving. Linking the future of election nights now to efforts aimed at the future of trust in journalism is a big ask. But what else are we to do? If we cannot solve this decline of trust and its implications for democracy's main event—the drama that plays out on election night—how can we address other things that matter, from climate change and social justice to an economy that works for everyone?

It is hard to imagine how strange it was in 1952 for television news to turn to computers and engineers to help meet the imperatives of election night. In early 1776 a writer named Thomas Paine was trying to convince his fellow colonists of another strange idea—the need to separate themselves from England. He published a pamphlet titled *Common Sense*. Paine urged the colonists not to reject his ideas out of hand. The opening paragraph had this memorable line: "Time makes more converts than reason." If what I have written here seems strange, too, and far afield from the problem of election-night forecasting, let me offer one last argument. When it comes to trust in journalism and new approaches to the stories we call news, election nights matter.

Notes

1. FEARSOME CONTRAPTIONS

1. "Election Coverage," part 1, CBS Television, November 4, 1952, PCM.
2. "Election Coverage," part 2, CBS Television, November 4, 1952, PCM.
3. Lukoff, *From Dits to Bits*, 128.
4. Behind-the-scenes accounts are dealt with more fully in later chapters and come from a variety of sources: internal reports by UNIVAC's maker, Remington Rand; interviews with participants; memoirs; and other archival sources.
5. "Buick Circus Hour," advertisement, *New York Times*, November 4, 1952, 36.
6. "Presidential Election Coverage," part 1, NBC Television, November 4, 1952, NBC-NA.
7. Richard LaManna, in discussion with the author, December 14–15, 2004.
8. "Election Night: Test for Polls and Robot Brains," *Business Week*, November 1, 1952, 30.
9. "Election Coverage," parts 2, 5, and 8, CBS Television, November 4–5, 1952, PCM.
10. "New Device to Be Used to Give Public Election Returns," transcript of broadcast hosted by Dorothy Fuldheim at 6:30 p.m. over WEWS-TV, Cleveland, October 16, 1952, prepared by Radio Reports, for Remington Rand, box 6, folder 8, Charles Collingwood Papers, WHS.
11. Bill Henry, "By the Way with Bill Henry," *Los Angeles Times*, November 4, 1952, part 2, 1.
12. Attributed to ABC News Director John Madigan, "Univac & Monrobot," 52. Similar sentiments appear in an ABC release cited by Merrill Panitt, "Networks' Full Resources Tuned for Election Night," *Philadelphia Inquirer*, November 2, 1952, 23, 28.
13. "Godfrey Explains Secret of UNIVAC," transcript prepared for Remington Rand, WCBS, New York, November 5, 1952, box 6, folder 8, Charles Collingwood Papers, WHS; "Koviac May Outdo Union," transcript prepared for

Remington Rand by Radio Reports, wcbs-tv, New York, November 6, 1952, box 6, folder 8, Charles Collingwood Papers, whs.

14. "Election Coverage," part 5, cbs Television, November 4–5, 1952, pcm.

15. "Election Coverage," parts 1–8, cbs Television, November 4–5, 1952, pcm.

16. Gray, "univac i."

17. nbc, "Meet Mr. Mike Monrobot, 'Electronic Brain,'" press release, October 16, 1952, nbc Trade Releases, lab.

18. Details here about the races and electorate are from the following sources: "Facts about the Electorate: How the Potential Voters Divide," *New York Times*, November 1, 1952, e6; and Leo Egan, "Good Weather Due; Each Side Claims Victory but Poll-Takers See Close Fight Likely," *New York Times*, November 4, 1952, 1, 21.

19. Sources for the third-party candidates include Alvin Shuster, "Minor Parties Run 12 for Presidency," *New York Times*, November 3, 1952, 21; "It's a Free Country," 13–15; Associated Press, "Many Candidates Seek Election as U.S. President," *Arizona Daily Sun* (Flagstaff), November 4, 1952, 1, 8; "Irked by Ike? Against Adlai?" *Wall Street Journal*, November 3, 1952, 1; Dwight D. Eisenhower Presidential Library and Museum, "The 1952 Presidential Campaign," archived by the Internet Archive Wayback Machine at https://web.archive.org/web/20070613035346/http://www.eisenhower.archives.gov/Quick_links/1952_campaign/1952_campaign_fact_sheet.html; H. Allen Anderson, "Hamblen, Carl Stuart," *Handbook of Texas Online*, Texas State Historical Association, https://www.tshaonline.org/handbook/entries/hamblen-carl-stuart; "Progressives Ratify Convict for President," *Chicago Daily Tribune*, July 6, 1952, 2; "Hallinan Choice of Labor Party," *New York Times*, August 29, 1952, 10; "Election Coverage," part 2, nbc Radio, Script and Recording Library, nbc Records, November 4, 1952, whs; Johns, "Presidential Candidates," 156–59.

20. "Election Coverage," part 2, nbc Radio, nbc Records, November 4, 1952, whs.

21. Details about the races and electorate are from sources including the following: "Facts about the Electorate"; Egan, "Good Weather Due," 21. Wire stories like these would have been seen around the country: Associated Press, "Elections at a Glance," *Brainerd Daily Dispatch* (mn), November 4, 1952, 1; Associated Press, "Victory by Eisenhower Could Mean First Divided Congress Since 1916," *Sun* (Baltimore md), November 4, 1952, 4.

22. Egan, "Good Weather Due"; Associated Press, "Victory by Eisenhower."

23. United Press, "Voting at 18 Fails; Loyalty Oaths Adopted," *Washington Post*, November 6, 1952, 3.

24. United Press, "Mississippi Set All-Time Record in Election Votes," *Delta Democrat-Times* (Greenville ms), November 11, 1952; "Voting at 18 Fails,"

3; "Hidden Meanings," *Delta Democrat-Times* (Greenville MS), October 26, 1952.

25. "Voting at 18 Fails," 3.

26. Barnouw, *A History of Broadcasting*, 2:298.

27. Jill Lepore, "Project X," Spring 2020, in *The Last Archive: Who Killed Truth*, podcast, https://www.thelastarchive.com/season-1/episode-5 -project-x.

28. Arthur Edson, "55 Million Voters Due to Cast Ballots Today; No Favorite Picked between Adlai, Ike," *Florence Morning News* (SC), November 4, 1952, 3.

29. "Newsmen Find Covering Dixie No Rose Bed," *New York Amsterdam News*, October 18, 1951, 1.

30. Bogart, *The Age of Television*, 10.

31. Collingwood, "Report to the West," CBS, October 15, 1952, WHS.

32. "Univac & Monrobot," 52.

33. Described in chapter 9.

34. "Billy Graham Uses Text of St. Paul's 3 Words," *Albuquerque Journal*, November 4, 1952, 11; "'Greatest Election' Billy Graham Topic," *Albuquerque Journal*, November 5, 1952, 12; Knoll, "Evangelist Billy Graham," 58.

35. "Dance Tuesday, November 4," advertisement, *Oneonta Star* (NY), November 4, 1952, 11.

36. "National Horse Show," advertisement, *New York Times*, November 4, 1952, 32.

37. "Lincoln," *Northwest Arkansas Times* (Fayetteville), November 4, 1952, 7; Women's Basketball Hall of Fame, "Hazel Walker," https://wbhof.com /famers/hazel-walker/; Grundy and Shackelford, *Shattering the Glass*, 103–7.

38. "Marlow Theater," advertisement, *Helena Independent Record* (MT), November 4, 1952, 10; Bosley Crowther, "The Screen in Review; DeMille," *New York Times*, January 11, 1952, 11.

39. "Theatres in Pitch for Election Nite," 2.

40. "Time," advertisement, *Oshkosh Daily Northwestern* (WI), November 4, 1952, 17.

41. "Extra! Republicans–Democrats," advertisement, *Oshkosh Daily Northwestern* (WI), November 4, 1952, 17; "Don't Bother to Knock," *New York Times*, n.d.

42. "Paramount," advertisement, *Oakland Tribune* (CA), November 4, 1952, D24.

43. "Enjoy Your Favorite Italian and American Foods," advertisement, *Fitchburg Sentinel* (MA), November 4, 1952, 2.

44. "Jorges," advertisement, *Greeley Tribune* (CO), November 4, 1952, 8.

45. "Maddux & Van Sandt," advertisement, *Modesto Bee* (CA), November 4, 1952, 11.

46. "Ride C & O and Get Up-to-the-Minute Election Returns," advertisement, *New York Times*, November 3, 1952, 47.

47. "KJRL-Journal to Provide Returns on Election," *Idaho State Journal* (Pocatello), November 4, 1952, 1.

48. "Daily News to Provide Election Returns Tonight," *Newport Daily News* (RI), November 4, 1952, 1.

49. "Radio Stations to Broadcast from SUN Office," *Arizona Daily Sun* (Flagstaff), November 4, 1952, 1.

50. "Press, Radio to Collect Vote Total," *Oxnard Press-Courier* (CA), November 4, 1952, 1.

51. For example, "Call 3-1610 for Returns," *Lima News* (OH), November 4, 1952, 1.

52. For example, Charles L. Hurst, "Here's Local Breakdown on When, Where to Vote," *Florence Morning News* (SC), November 4, 1952, 3, 5.

53. Dayan and Katz, *Media Events*, 272, note 17.

54. Charles E. Egan, "Straw Polls Help Market Research," *New York Times*, November 8, 1936, F9.

55. Buchanan and Zerenga, *County Chairmen*, iii.

56. Buchanan and Zerenga, *County Chairmen*, 1.

57. Gallup, "We Won't Be Red-Faced This Time!" 64–65, 97–99.

58. Associated Press, "Stevenson May Hold Lead—Gallup," *Brainerd Daily Dispatch* (MN), November 4, 1952, 1; Associated Press, "Gallup Says Ike Has Edge," *Bismarck Tribune* (ND), November 4, 1952, 1; Associated Press, "Gallup Poll Notes Possibility of 50–50 Popular Vote," *Northwest Arkansas Times* (Fayetteville), November 4, 1952, 2.

59. See, for example, United Press, "Samplers of Public Opinion See Photo-Finish for U.S. White House," *Panama City News* (FL), November 4, 1952, 2.

60. "Presidential Election Coverage," part 1, NBC Television, November 4, 1952, NBC-NA.

2. SOMETHING UNUSUAL

1. Keyssar, *The Right to Vote*, 29, 34–35, 51, 340–54, 363–67, 399–403.

2. Whittier, "The Poor Voter on Election Day," 93–94.

3. Brewin, *Celebrating Democracy*, 77–83, 123–28; Brewin, "The History and Meaning," 153–69.

4. Binning, Esterly, and Sracic, *Encyclopedia of American Parties*, 95–96.

5. Probus, "Letters from New York," 524; "The First Locomotive," 343; "Annihilation," 168; "Opening of the Baltimore," 302; Leo Marx, *The Machine*, 194.

6. For example, Gramling, *AP: The Story of News*, 24.

7. "Presidential Election," *Southport Telegraph* (Wisconsin Territory), November 10, 1840, 2. The use of the name "telegraph" for newspapers predated the invention of the electrical telegraph with which the word would later be associated.

8. Schwarzlose, *The Nation's Newsbrokers*, 142–45.

9. *Alton Telegraph*, November 19, 1848, 3, cited in Matheson, "Steam Packet," 87.

10. Nixon, "Henry W. Grady," 341–56, citing on page 354 the *Atlanta Constitution*, November 7, 8, and 9, 1882.

11. Kloeber, "The American Newspaper," 209.

12. "Their Sphere Enlarging," *New York Times*, November 28, 1896, 1; "Increased Use," 20.

13. Matheson, "Steam Packet," 80.

14. "Telegraphic Election Returns," *New York Daily Times*, October 20, 1852, 1. Similar requests in subsequent election years include, "Important to Those who Send Election Returns," *New York Daily Times*, October 30, 1856, 1.

15. "News of the Morning," *New York Daily Times*, November 10, 1852, 4; this article reported the results of the voting in Tennessee and Kentucky.

16. "California and Oregon; Arrival of the Overland Express," *New York Times*, November 26, 1860, 1.

17. "Later from the Pacific; Arrival of the Overland Express," *New York Times*, December 11, 1860, 5.

18. "The Telegraph—The Annihilation of Distance," *Weekly Wisconsin* (Milwaukee), November 22, 1848, 2.

19. "The Great Election," 2.

20. Abbot, "How the Returns," 876.

21. "To Politicians," *New York Tribune* advertisement, *New York Times*, November 3, 1860, 3.

22. "A Few Interesting Figures from City Election Returns," *New York Times*, November 12, 1864, 4.

23. Morgan, *Charles H. Taylor*, 123–29; Lyons, *Newspaper Story*, 104–6.

24. Morgan, *Charles H. Taylor*, 123–29.

25. Littlewood, *Calling Elections*, 12–14.

26. The system used by Chester S. Lord, managing editor of the *New York Sun* from 1880 to 1913, is described by Stoddart, "How the Newspapers," 566.

27. Woodbury, "Model Making Problems," 16–19.

28. Lyons, *Newspaper Story*, 105.

29. Abbot, "How the Returns," 876.

30. "How the Herald Gets Election Returns," *New York Herald*, November 9, 1890, 16.

31. See, for example, Kidwell and Ceruzzi, *Landmarks in Digital Computing.*
32. Stone, "The Associated Press," 379.
33. Burroughs Adding Machine Company advertisement, "The Back of the Book": originally in *Fra: A Journal of Affirmation,* January 1911, reproduced in *Fra Magazine: Exponent of American Philosophy, January 1911 to June 1911,* 2003.
34. *Illinois State Journal,* November 7, 1912, 2, cited by Matheson, "Steam Packet," 131.
35. "Thousands Phone to Learn Result," *Duluth News-Tribune* (MN), September 17, 1913, 2.
36. The *Daily Missouri Republican,* for example, reported on November 2, 1840, that "all returns sent to us will be spread on the Bulletin Board"; cited by Kelly, *Election Day,* 87.
37. Littlewood, *Calling Elections,* 40; Carlson, *The Man Who Made News,* 264.
38. "The Stereopticon," *Arthur's Home Magazine,* 253; "Lanterns Arranged," advertisement, *Scientific American* 4, no. 18 (May 4, 1861): 287; "The Stereopticon," *Saturday Evening Post,* 2.
39. "The Finale: The Scene around the Herald Office," *New York Herald,* November 7, 1860, 3; Littlewood, *Calling Elections,* 47, cites election night 1860 as the first use by papers in New York of a "primitive version of the stereopticon projector to enlarge their election bulletins across the entire side of a building."
40. "Our Bulletin," *New York Times,* October 10, 1872, 1.
41. "Receiving the News," *New York Times,* November 6, 1872, 8.
42. "In Front of the Bulletins," *New York Times,* November 3, 1897, 5.
43. "How the Herald Gets Election Returns," *New York Herald,* November 9, 1890, 16.
44. "News Promptly Given," *New York Times,* November 6, 1895, 8.
45. Marvin, *When Old Technologies Were New,* 217–18.
46. "Contest of the Wires; Will Compete in Obtaining Election Returns," *New York Times,* October 29, 1896, 16.
47. Marvin, *When Old Technologies,* 186; Marvin, "Dazzling the Multitude," 211–12; Littlewood, *Calling Elections,* 58–59; Meyer Berger, "Old Times Square Tradition Dies; Usual Election Night Uproar Gone," *New York Times,* November 5, 1952, 24.
48. "Election Results by Times Building Flash," *New York Times,* November 6, 1904, 3. The same code was repeated in a story the day before the election and in an advertisement, including a diagram, that ran on Election Day: "Tonight; Election Returns at Times Building, Times Square," advertisement, *New York Times,* November 8, 1904, 9.

49. "Election Results by Times Building Flash," *New York Times*, November 6, 1904, 3.

50. "Times Will Flash the Result," *New York Times*, November 4, 1906, 2.

51. "Signals in the Sky," *New York Tribune*, November 1, 1896, 1; "Flashing Out the Tidings," *New York Tribune*, November 3, 1896, 7; "Vast Crowds Cheer," *New York Tribune*, November 4, 1896, 5.

52. "Signals in the Sky," 1.

53. Buckley, "Whistles, Crowds, and Free Silver," 13–17.

54. Enthusiasm for technology as a major element in national development in that period has been documented by Thomas J. Misa, *A Nation of Steel*, and Thomas P. Hughes, *American Genesis*.

55. "The Great New York Aquarium," advertisement, *New York Times*, November 7, 1876, 7.

56. "P. T. Barnum's," advertisement, *New York Times*, November 7, 1876, 7.

57. "Olympia Theatre," advertisement, *New York Times*, November 3, 1896, 7.

58. See, for example, "Amusements," advertisement, *New York Times*, November 7, 1894, 7.

59. This sheet appears next to a Woodrow Wilson campaign poster that is the subject of a photograph in Bowman, *The History of the American Presidency*, 119.

60. Marvin, *When Old Technologies*, 221; Littlewood, *Calling Elections*, 55; Young, "Media on Display," 239.

61. "Times Will Flash the Result," *New York Times*, November 4, 1906, 2.

62. "The Times to Flash Election Results," *New York Times*, November 3, 1908, 3; "Jam Times Square for Election News," *New York Times*, November 4, 1908, 5.

63. Stories outlining the themes here appear in the editions of November 1 through 4, 1920. My attention was first drawn to the *Post-Dispatch* election-night arrangements by an anecdote in Kelly, *Election Day*, 187–88.

64. "Wireless Telephone to Carry Vote Returns" and "Post-Dispatch Election Bulletins to Be Furnished on 12th Street, at Armories and Public Schools," *St. Louis Post-Dispatch*, November 2, 1920, 1; "Post-Dispatch Furnished Returns to Record Outdoor Crowd and at 23 Buildings," *St. Louis Post-Dispatch*, November 3, 1920, 1; "30,000 Got Election Returns at 20 Schools by Post-Dispatch Service," 3; "Amusements" and "Photo Play Theaters," *St. Louis Post-Dispatch*, November 2, 1920, 22; advertisement, *St. Louis Post-Dispatch*, November 3, 1920.

65. "Post-Dispatch Furnished Returns," 1.

66. In the *Post-Dispatch* on November 3, 1920: "Post-Dispatch Furnished Returns," 1; "30,000 Got Election Returns," 3; "Wireless Phone Relays," 3; "Immense Throngs in Twelfth Street," 29.

67. "Wireless Phone Relays," 3.

68. After this phenomenon of "the story of the story" became apparent to me from my initial survey of election stories in the nineteenth and twentieth centuries, I discovered that Matheson had used the phrase at the very end of his 1967 dissertation, "Steam Packet to Magic Lantern," 170. In suggesting areas for further research, Matheson noted that while the systematic study of election-returns coverage had been neglected by journalism historians, the record left in the "the story of the story" is a means of understanding how election-returns coverage was produced. I am expanding that notion here to comment on the cultural significance of this phenomenon.

69. "How the Herald Gets Election Returns," *New York Herald*, November 9, 1890, 16.

70. The ad—"Tomorrow's Sunday Herald"—ran in a competing paper, the *New York Times*, November 8, 1890, 8.

71. "How the Herald," 16.

72. Ralph, "Election Night," *Scribner's Magazine*, 531–44. Excerpts appeared in Ralph, "Election Night," *Outlook*, 829, and the article was reprinted as a richly illustrated chapter, "Election Night," in Ralph, *The Making of a Journalist*, 145–73.

73. Abbot, "How the Returns," 876–77.

74. "The Finale," 3.

75. "The Spectacle," *New-York Daily Tribune*, November 4, 1896, 4.

76. Whitman, "Election Day," 380.

77. "Scenes around the Herald Office," *New York Herald*, November 9, 1864, 8.

78. "The Herald Building," *New York Herald*, November 4, 1868, 10.

79. "Election Excitement," *New York Times*, November 11, 1876, 8.

80. "Immense Throngs," 29.

81. De Forest, *Father of Radio*, 338. The episode is also described in Carneal, *A Conqueror of Space*, 272–73; "Election Returns," 650; and in two articles in the *New York American* on the days following the election: "American's Returns Sent 200 Miles by Wireless Telephone," November 8, 1916, 5, and "American's Bulletins Win Praise," November 9, 1916, 4.

82. "An Air Paper," *Kingston Gleaner* (Jamaica), November 14, 1916, 4.

83. Davis, "The Early History of Broadcasting," 189–225.

84. "Thousands Watch Times Bulletins," *New York Times*, November 7, 1928, 17; "Huge Times Sign Will Flash News," *New York Times*, November 8, 1928, 30; Milton Bracker, "History of a Decade Told by a Ribbon of Light," *New York Times Magazine*, November 13, 1938, 12–13, 22.

85. "Huge Times Sign," 30.

86. For example: "Nation Swept by Hughes; New York Elects Whitman," *New*

York American, November 8, 1916, 1; "Mr. Hughes Is Elected with Majority of Forty Votes in the Electoral College; Mr. Whitman Wins; House of
Representatives Will Be Republican," *New York Herald*, November 8, 1916,
1; "Record Election Night; 100,000 in Streets See Bulletins Flash Hughes'
Election," *Washington Post*, November 8, 1916, 3.

87. "American's Bulletins Win Praise," 4.

88. "American's Returns Sent," 5; "American's Bulletins Win Praise," 4.

89. "Newspaper in Sky Flashes Bulletins to Crowds Tonight," *New York Ameri-
can*, November 1, 1916, 5; "American's Returns Sent," 5; "American's Bulle-
tins Win Praise," 4; "Election Returns of the New York American," *New York
American*, November 5, 1916, part 2, 1; "Election Returns of the New York
American; Where They Will Be Displayed on Election Night," *New York
American*, November 6, 1916, 9.

90. Two other newspapers called attention to the historic broadcast: "Returns
by Wireless; De Forest Radio Laboratories Flashed Bulletins at High-
bridge," *New York Times*, November 8, 1916, 6; "Herald Spreads Election
News by Wireless," *New York Herald*, November 8, 1916, 11.

91. Douglas, *Inventing American Broadcasting*, 276.

92. See, for example, the discussion by Sterling and Kittross, *Stay Tuned*, 63–
67; Aitken, *The Continuous Wave*, 469; Greb and Adams, *Charles Herrold*,
150; Archer, *History of Radio to 1926*, 207.

93. Barnouw, *A History of Broadcasting*, 1:62–64; Sterling and Kittross, *Stay
Tuned*, 66; Emery, Emery, and Roberts, *The Press and America*, 272; Radio
Staff of the Detroit News, *WWJ-Detroit News*, 7–9; Archer, *History of Radio
to 1926*, 208; and the following articles in the *Detroit News*: "The News
Radiophone to Give Vote Results," August 31, 1920, 1; "Radio Operators!
Attention!" August 31, 1; "Land and Water Hear Returns by Wireless," September 1, 1920, 1; "Operators of Telephone and Wireless Sets!" September 1,
1920, 1; "Wireless Stations Praise News Radiophone Service," September 2,
1920, 1, 21; "Voice by Radio Clearly Heard by Night Listeners," September
3, 1920, 1–2.

94. Sterling and Kittross, *Stay Tuned*, 66; De Forest, *Father of Radio*, 356.

95. "The News Radiophone," 1.

96. "Land and Water Hear Returns," 1.

97. "Land and Water Hear Returns," 1; "Wireless Stations Praise," 1, 21; "Voice
by Radio Clearly Heard," 1–2.

98. See Archer, *History of Radio to 1926*; Barnouw, *A History of Broadcasting*,
vol. 1; Aitken, *Continuous Wave*; Emery, Emery, and Roberts, *The Press
and America*; Douglas, *Inventing American Broadcasting*; Balk, *The Rise
of Radio*; Greb and Adams, *Charles Herrold*; Simaan, "An Introduction,"

1273–78; Sterling and Kittross, *Stay Tuned*, 65–66; KDKA NewsRadio, "It All Started in Pittsburgh," https://web.archive.org/web/20060414233340 /http://www.kdkaradio.com/pages/15486.php; Davis, "The Early History of Broadcasting"; Kintner, "Pittsburgh's Contribution," 1849–62; Little, "The Reminiscences of Donald G. Little"; Little, "Dr. Conrad," 71–73.

99. Davis, "The Early History of Broadcasting," 197.

100. "Radio Broadcasting Started at KDKA Four Years Ago Today," *New York Times*, November 2, 1924, section 8, 16.

101. U.S. Department of Commerce, *Radio Service Bulletin*, 12–21.

102. "Election Returns by Radio," *Fitchburg Sentinel* (MA), November 4, 1924, 11; "Radio Party at the High School," *Marysville Evening Tribune* (OH), November 4, 1924, 1.

103. "New Fall Edition Ziegfeld Follies," *New York Times*, November 2, 1924, section 7, 4.

104. "Latest Improvements in Radio to Be Displayed This Week," *New York Times*, November 2, 1924, section 8, 12; "Marconi, by Flash, Opens Radio Show," *New York Times*, November 4, 1924, 12.

105. Although this figure appears in a *New York Times* article in advance of the election ("National Audience to Hear Election Returns by Radio," October 26, 1924, 14), a *Times* commentary following the election pointed out that "just how large the audience was nobody knows, for there are no trustworthy statistics of the number of receiving sets made by amateur radiologists, and the figures of the regular manufacturers do not include the achievements of this non-small army" ("Topics of the Times," November 6, 1924, 18).

106. Archer, *History of Radio to 1926*, 347.

107. "Topics of the Times," 18.

108. Avery Marks, NBC memo to John W. Elwood, October 24, 1932, box 9, folder 38, Central Files, NBC Records, WHS.

109. "Topics of the Times," 18.

110. "Election Returns on Radio over Nationwide Network," *New York Times*, November 4, 1928, 154.

111. Marks to Elwood, October 24, 1932, WHS.

112. For example, Niles Trammell, letter to F. A. Pearson, November 14, 1940, box 76, folder 75, Central Files, NBC Records, WHS.

113. Bohn, "Broadcasting National Election Returns," 267–86.

114. A comprehensive study is provided by Jackaway, *Media at War*. See also chapter 3, "Growing Pains: The Story of the Press-Radio War," in White, *News on the Air*, 31–42, and chapter 5, "The Press-Radio War," in Bliss, *Now the News*, 39–44.

115. "Transcript of Press-Radio Election Results and Special Election Broad-casts as Presented Over NBC-Red Network," November 3, 1936, box 49, folder 10, Central Files, NBC Records, WHS.

116. "Election Data Fill Programs on Air," *New York Times*, November 6, 1940, 5.

117. Bohn, "Broadcasting," 279.

118. "All-Night Returns by Radio Planned," *New York Times*, November 8, 1932, 15; Orrin E. Dunlap Jr., "Elaborate Plans for Tuesday," *New York Times*, November 6, 1932, section 8, 6.

119. Smith, *The Great Mental Calculators*, 283–88; Weinland, "The Memory of Salo Finkelstein," 243–57; Bousfield and Barry Jr., "The Visual Imagery," 353–58; Weinland and Schlauch, "An Examination," 382–402; "Human Cal-culator Demonstrates Skill," *New York Times*, October 22, 1932, 17.

120. "Magician," *New Yorker*, September 17, 1932, 9.

121. For example, "Calculating Genius to Speak at EHS Thursday Morning," *Elyria Chronicle-Telegram* (OH), May 12, 1936; Paul Harrison, NEA (News-paper Enterprise Association) service writer, penned a syndicated news story, "A Second Is a Long Time!" *Sheboygan Press* (WI), November 14, 1932, 3, that also ran in other newspapers around the country.

122. Trout and White, "What to Look for," 22–24.

123. "Election Returns," *Electrical Review*, November 19, 1892, 151, cited in Marvin, *When Old Technologies*, 218.

124. "For Radio Election Returns You Must Have Tally Sheets," advertisement, *New York Times*, November 1, 1924, 18.

125. "Test Your Skill in Election Forecasting," *Florence Morning News* (SC), November 3, 1936, 3.

126. This Associated Press feature, "The ABC of Interpreting Election Bulletins," appeared on November 3, 1940, in such papers as the *Cumberland Times* (MD), 2; *Montana Standard* (Butte), 28; and the *Oakland Tribune* (CA), 44.

127. "Here's your TABULATION SHEET for keeping posted on election night—NOVEMBER 3rd," undated, box 49, folder 10, Political Broadcasts and Elec-tion–1936, Central Files, NBC Records, WHS.

128. Marks to Elwood, October 24, 1932, WHS.

129. Marks to Elwood, October 24, 1932, WHS.

130. "Election Data Fill Programs on Air," 5.

131. "Helen Sioussat: Photos—Election Night," box 36, folder 6, Helen Sioussat Papers, series 7, subseries 3, LAB.

132. "WCBS Coverage of New York Elections On Radio, TV, to Be Sponsored," press release, CBS, November 4, 1949, box 29, folder 5, Helen Sioussat Papers, series 5, subseries 2, LAB.

133. For example, Stoddart, "How Newspapers," 566; Ralph, "Election Night," *Scribner's Magazine*, 531–44.

134. Gelb, *City Room*, 70–71.

135. Sid James, "Election Night Television" memo to Mr. Heiskell, September 24, 1948, box 300, folder 34, William Garden Papers, NBC Records, WHS.

136. See, for example, Orrin E. Dunlap Jr., "Lessons of the Campaign," *New York Times*, November 13, 1932, 6.

137. James to Heiskell, September 24, 1948, WHS.

138. Robert J. Wade, "Life-NBC Election Returns" memo to A. W. Reibling, October 15, 1948, box 300, folder 34, William Garden Papers, NBC Records, WHS.

139. Sid James, "LIFE-NBC Visual Material" memo, October 28, 1948, box 300, folder 34, William Garden Papers, NBC Records, WHS; Associated Press, "Election Day Activities to Be Televised; Night-Long Programs Planned on Four Hookups November 2," *Hartford Courant*, October 17, 1948, 15.

140. James memo, October 28, 1948, WHS.

141. "Life-NBC Television–Election Night," broadcast plan, October 27, 1948, box 115, folder 32, Niles Trammell Papers, NBC Records, WHS.

142. "Election Returns Radioed to World," *New York Times*, November 9, 1932, 17.

143. "All-Night Returns by Radio Planned," *New York Times*, November 8, 1932, 15.

144. "Election Returns Radioed," 17.

145. The description of audience inclusion in vaudeville is from Snyder, "Vaudeville and the Transformation of Popular Culture," 143.

146. Bianco, *Ghosts of 42nd Street*, 26–27.

147. "Thousands Watch Times Bulletins," *New York Times*, November 7, 1928, 17; "Huge Times Sign Will Flash News," *New York Times*, November 8, 1928, 30; Milton Bracker, "History of a Decade Told By a Ribbon of Light," *New York Times Magazine*, November 13, 1938, 12–13, 22; Michael Chabon, "1851: The First Issue," *New York Times*, November 14, 2001, H1; Cressman, "News in Lights," 198–208.

148. Bracker, "History of a Decade," 12–13, 22.

149. "Huge Times Sign," *New York Times*, November 8, 1928, 30.

150. Bracker, "History of a Decade," 12–13, 22.

151. "Election Results to Be Signaled from Times Tower," *New York Times*, November 6, 1928, 3; "Election Returns to Be Broadcast," *New York Times*, October 17, 1928, 24; "Election Night Is Climax for Politics on the Radio," *New York Times*, October 28, 1928, 16; "Election Returns on Radio over Nationwide Network," *New York Times*, November 4, 1928, 16; "Election Returns on Radio Tonight," *New York Times*, November 6, 1928, 38; "100 Stations Radio Election Returns," *New York Times*, November 7, 1928, 7.

152. "Election Night Is Climax," 16; "Vital Statistics in the Vote in Last Three Presidential Elections," *New York Times*, November 4, 1928, section 10, 3.

153. R. L. Duffus, "Our Radio Battle for the Presidency," *New York Times*, October 29, 1928, section 10, 1.

154. See, for example: "Times Sq. Is Packed by Election Crowd," *New York Times*, November 5, 1924, 6; "Huge Night Crowds Flock into Streets," *New York Times*, November 7, 1928, 16; "Great Throngs in Times Square Take the Election Result Quietly," *New York Times*, November 9, 1932, 8; Meyer Berger, "Roosevelt Crowd in Times Square Quiet, Very Young, Middle-Aged," *New York Times*, November 8, 1944, 7. In 1936, when Franklin Roosevelt won reelection in a landslide, *New York Times* reported a "crowd estimated by police at 'a million' persons"; "Election Crowd in a Merry Mood," November 4, 1936, 5.

155. "Election Returns Radioed to World," 17.

156. "Transcript of Press-Radio Election Results and Special Election Broadcasts as Presented Over NBC–Red Network," November 3, 1936, box 49, folder 10, Central Files, NBC Records, WHS.

157. "Transcript of Press-Radio Election Results," November 3, 1936, 32–33, WHS.

158. Charles R. Denny, memo to S. N. Strotz, October 13, 1948, box 115, folder 32, Niles Trammell Papers, NBC Records, WHS. Also: F. A. Wankel, assistant director of Television Engineering Operations (NBC), letter to J. Guetter, Rockefeller Center, October 26, 1948, box 115, folder 32, Niles Trammell Papers, NBC Records, WHS.

159. James to Heiskell, September 24, 1948, WHS.

160. Reuven Frank, "1948: Live . . . from Philadelphia. . . . It's the National Conventions," *New York Times Sunday Magazine*, April 17, 1988, 36.

161. Denny to Strotz, October 13, 1948, WHS.

162. Wankel to Guetter, October 26, 1948, WHS.

163. Meyer Berger, "Election Night Crowd in Times Sq. Is Thin," *New York Times*, November 3, 1948, 16.

164. Election preview, radio recording, CBS News, November 2, 1948, courtesy of A. R. Hogan.

165. "Election Night on CBS Radio and Television," October 21, 1948, box 309, folder 2, Francis C. McCall Papers, NBC Records, WHS.

166. Jack Gould, "Programs in Review: Radio and Television Cover the Election," *New York Times*, November 7, 1948, 11.

167. Conway, *The Origins of Television News in America*, 277.

168. Gould, "Programs in Review," 11.

169. See Nye, *American Technological Sublime*. Nye (on page xv) credits the term "technological sublime" to Perry Miller and notes elaborations by other scholars.

170. Nye, *American Technological Sublime*, xiv, 41–43.

171. "The Finale," 3.

172. "The Spectacle," 4.

173. "Immense Throngs," 29.

174. "Transcript of Press-Radio Election Results," November 3, 1936, 32–33, WHS.

3. ARE COMPUTERS NEWSWORTHY?

1. Jack Gould, "Pupils' Time Spent at TV Rivals Hours in Classes," *New York Times*, March 6, 1950, 1, 14; Campbell, Gurin, and Miller, "Television and the Election," 46–48.

2. Sterling and Kittross, *Stay Tuned*, table 6-A, 862, and table 7-A, 864.

3. Mickelson, *The Decade that Shaped Television News*; Baughman, *Same Time, Same Station*; Baughman, *The Republic of Mass Culture*; Sterling and Kittross, *Stay Tuned*; Barnouw, *Tube of Plenty*; Gomery, *A History of Broadcasting in the United States*; Bliss, *Now the News*.

4. Mickelson, *The Decade that Shaped Television News*, 33–41.

5. Boddy, *Fifties Television*, 53.

6. Sterling and Kittross, *Stay Tuned*, table 7-A, 864–65.

7. Barnouw, *Tube of Plenty*, 114; Sterling and Kittross, *Stay Tuned*, table 2-D, 834–35.

8. Beville, *Audience Ratings*, 62–64.

9. Sterling and Kittross, *Stay Tuned*, table 8-A, 867.

10. Gomery, "Talent Raids and Package Deals," 153, 156; Richard S. Paige, "Top Programs, '50–'51 and '51–'52," memo to Merritt Barnum, October 3, 1952, box 131, folder 11, William F. Brooks Papers, NBC Records, WHS.

11. Sterling and Kittross, *Stay Tuned*, 231–32, 259.

12. Sperber, *Murrow*, xii.

13. Spigel, *Make Room for TV*, 45–60; Bogart, *The Age of Television*, 245–89.

14. Ely, *The Adventures of Amos 'n' Andy*, 213–37; Barnouw, *A History of Broadcasting*, 2:297; Pondillo, "Racial Discourse and Censorship"; United States Commission on Civil Rights, *Window Dressing on the Set*, 4–5.

15. United Press, "Talmadge Raps TV Shows with No Segregation," *Corpus Christi Caller-Times* (TX), January 6, 1952, 13; Associated Press, "Talmadge Hits TV for Mixing Races," *New York Times*, January 6, 1952, 59.

16. "TV's Hottest Problem: Public Relations," *Sponsor*, June 16, 1952, cited by Boddy, *Fifties Television*, 102.

17. Boddy, *Fifties Television*, 102; Murray, "Establishment of the U.S. Television Networks," 37; Menand, *American Studies*, 120; Friendly, *Due to Circumstances Beyond Our Control*, 196.

18. For example: Michael Dann, "Responsibility Report, April 1–April 30," memo to Sylvester L. Weaver Jr., May 14, 1952, box 121, folder 33, Sylvester L. Weaver Jr. Papers, NBC Records, WHS.

19. Columbia Broadcasting System, *1952 Annual Report to the Stockholders*, LAB.

20. Merrill "Red" Mueller, "Election Coverage," part 1, NBC Radio, November 4, 1952, Disc 45A, Script and Recording Library, NBC Records, WHS.

21. *Official Philco Guide to the National Political Conventions and Presidential Elections, 1952*, Philco Corporation, 1952, box 136, folder 6, Office Files, NBC Records, WHS; Mueller, "Election Coverage," November 4, 1952, WHS.

22. Campbell, Gurin, and Miller, "Television and the Election," 46–48; Sterling and Kittross, *Stay Tuned*, 862, 864; Editors of *Broadcasting* Magazine, *The First 50 Years of Broadcasting*, 109–13.

23. Sterling and Kittross, *Stay Tuned*, table 5-c, 856–57.

24. Jack Gould, "Video News Coverage," *New York Times*, November 25, 1951, 11.

25. Sperber, *Murrow*, 350.

26. Barnouw, *A History of Broadcasting*, 3:40.

27. Gross, *I Looked and Listened*, 285, 298–300.

28. For example: Jack Gould, "What TV Is—and What It Might Be," *New York Times Magazine*, June 10, 1951, 18, 22–24; Frank, *Out of Thin Air*, 80–82.

29. Cronkite, *A Reporter's Life*, 177; Frank, *Out of Thin Air*, 11; Mickelson, *The Decade that Shaped Television News*, 2; Baughman, *Same Time, Same Station*, 23.

30. Mickelson, *From Whistle Stop to Sound Bite*, 48–49.

31. Mickelson, *From Whistle Stop to Sound Bite*, 52.

32. Mickelson, *From Whistle Stop to Sound Bite*, 49–52; Schoenbrun, *On and Off the Air*, 86–92.

33. Frank, *Out of Thin Air*, 69; Bogardus, "Television and the Conventions," 115–21.

34. Gould, "Programs in Review"; Frank, *Out of Thin Air*, 78; Gould, *Watching Television Come of Age*, 11.

35. Mosteller et al., *The Preelection Polls of 1948*; "Poll Errors Laid to Poor Judgment," *New York Times*, December 27, 1948, 23; Odegard, review of *The Preelection Polls*, 459–64.

36. Tim Jones, "Dewey Defeats Truman," *Chicago Tribune*, October 31, 2020, http://www.chicagotribune.com/news/politics/chi-chicagodays-deweydefeats-story,0,6484067.story.

37. Robert G. Whalen, "Our Forecast: What Went Wrong?" *New York Times*, November 7, 1948, E4.

38. Kaltenborn joked about it two years later in his autobiography, *Fifty Fabulous Years*, 297.

39. Bliss, *Now the News*, 215 and 493 (notes 18–19).

40. Frank, *Out of Thin Air*, 28.

41. Mickelson, *The Decade that Shaped Television News*, 53. The italics in this passage are Mickelson's.

42. Mickelson, *The Decade that Shaped Television News*, 51–59.

43. Hewitt, *Tell Me a Story*, 49–52.

44. Mickelson, *The Decade that Shaped Television News*, xviii.

45. Mickelson, *From Whistle Stop to Sound Bite*, 137–38.

46. See, for example: T. R. Kennedy Jr., "Electronic Computer Flashes Answers, May Speed Engineering," *New York Times*, February 15, 1946, 1; Robert K. Plumb, "Great Gains Seen in 'Brain' Machine," *New York Times*, November 18, 1949, 30; Associated Press, "Electronic Computers; Sarnoff Says They Should Be Available to Business Soon," *New York Times*, May 29, 1952, 33.

47. Many works address the early history of computers, including Haigh and Ceruzzi, *A New History of Modern Computing*; Williams, *A History of Computing Technology*; Kidwell and Ceruzzi, *Landmarks in Digital Computing*; Campbell-Kelly and Aspray, *Computer*; Cortada, *The Computer in the United States*; Augarten, *Bit by Bit*.

48. Debate has raged for decades—including an epic court battle—over who should be given credit for inventing the computer, in general, and who should get credit for inventing the ENIAC (Electronic Numerical Integrator and Computer). It is not my intent here to review that ground. It is simply worth noting that Eckert and Mauchly proposed the ENIAC project and led the team that developed it. Overviews of the ENIAC project and its context include Kidwell and Ceruzzi, *Landmarks in Digital Computing*, 63–66; Williams, *A History of Computing Technology*, 266–83; Stern, *From ENIAC to UNIVAC*.

49. Marguerite Reardon, "Net History Buffs Find Bargains at Christie's," *CNET News*, February 23, 2005.

50. "Outline of Plans for Development of Electronic Computors [*sic*]," draft business plan, March 13, 1946, viewed at Christie's in New York in February 2005. A scan of the document was subsequently made available by the purchaser, computer software pioneer Mitch Kapor, to the Computer History Museum in Mountain View CA, posted at http://archive.computerhistory .org/resources/text/Eckert_Mauchly/EckertMauchly.BusinessPlan.1946 .102660910.pdf. The spelling of computer as "Computor" is indicative of the lack of fixed meaning or even spelling at that time. The provenance and background of the document are described in a volume coauthored by Jeremy Norman, the collector who put the document up for auction at Christie's: Hook, Norman, and Williams, *Origins of Cyberspace*, 548–49.

51. In addition to accounts in general histories of computing in this era, useful histories of Eckert and Mauchly's commercial ventures include Norberg, *Computers and Commerce*; Stern, *From ENIAC to UNIVAC*; Lukoff, *From Dits to Bits*; Yates, *Structuring the Information Age*.

52. Cortada, *Before the Computer*, 156.

53. For the role of meetings and conferences in spreading and sharing ideas about computers, see Mowery and Rosenberg, *Paths of Innovation*, 138–39. Accounts and lists of speakers and attendees from early computer conferences include a number of individuals whose association with election-night forecasting in 1952 appear in this book. Among these were: the 1949 Institute of Radio Engineers National Convention; the 1950 Rutgers Conference on Automatic Computing Machinery; the 1951 Joint American Institute of Electrical Engineers–Institute of Radio Engineers Computer Conference in Philadelphia; and a 1952 meeting of the Association for Computing Machinery in Pittsburgh. Sources: Institute of Radio Engineers, "1949 IRE National Convention Program," 160–78; Rutgers Conference on Automatic Computing Machinery, March 27–29, 1950, list of registrants, box 3:C:6, folder 140, John W. Mauchly Papers, UP-RBML; American Institute of Electrical Engineers, *Review of the Electronic Digital Computers*; "Proceedings of the Association for Computing Machinery," May 2 and 3, 1952, Pittsburgh PA, box 122, Computer Documents, NMAH.

54. The two documents appear as 1955 reprints that include notes in parentheses and footnotes, which were identified as having been added after the original memos were drafted. The documents—John W. Mauchly, "Company Confidential, Reprint of 'Are Computers Newsworthy?'" written in 1951 and revised in 1955, and "Company Confidential, Reprint of 'A Scientific Research Bureau Is Needed,'" written July 19, 1952, and revised May 1955—are in box 5:B:28, folder 383, John W. Mauchly Papers, UP-RBML. The term "Company Confidential" does appear in 1956 as the name of a typewritten newsletter of the Remington Rand UNIVAC division of the Sperry Rand Corporation, successor to Remington Rand. A copy of at least one edition of this newsletter, dated November 1956, listed as vol. 1, no. 6, is included in Mauchly's papers in the same archive (box 3:C:8, folders 190–91). There is no indication whether there is any connection between Mauchly's "Company Confidential" documents and the "Company Confidential" newsletter, though the five items in the two-page newsletter are each just a paragraph in length—much shorter than Mauchly's documents.

55. Mauchly, "Are Computers Newsworthy?" UP-RBML.

56. Watson's son, Thomas J. Watson Jr., who would become IBM's president in January 1952, referred to the Selective Sequence Electronic Calculator as a

"technological dinosaur," a "weird gigantic hybrid of electronic and mechanical parts, half modern computer and half punched-card machine"; Watson and Petre, *Father, Son, & Co.*, 90. The development of the SSEC is described in Bashe, Johnson, Palmer, and Pugh, *IBM's Early Computers*, 47–58.

57. Mauchly, "Are Computers Newsworthy?" UP-RBML.

58. Mauchly, "A Scientific Research Bureau Is Needed," UP-RBML.

59. Evidence of Mauchly's difficulties inside Remington Rand appears in a file of personal notes in his papers at the University of Pennsylvania. There is a typed page labeled "CONFIDENTIAL" and identified in a typed notation at the top as "Copy of draft of letter composed in May, 1952, but never sent." It is addressed "Dear Mr. Rand," which, from the context, is Remington Rand head James H. Rand Jr. Although the document does not have the name of the author, the context makes clear that the writer is Mauchly. He notes that in the more than two years since Remington Rand bought the Eckert-Mauchly Computer Corporation, Mauchly and Rand had met several times but never for "earnest discussion," and that Mauchly's "situation at present very much requires your personal attention." He continues, "I am distinctly unhappy," and explains that his "usefulness" to the company "has not expanded but has become severely circumscribed." While asserting that the jobs he would "most like to tackle could be of immense benefit to Remington Rand," Mauchly complained, "at present, I am just punching an adding machine on a problem which deserves a UNIVAC. That isn't progress." Mauchly also suggested that if he could not be effectively used within the company, he would like to arrange to a "fair termination . . . without embarrassment to Remington Rand." The document is in box 3:C:6, folder 140, John W. Mauchly Papers, UP-RBML.

60. Mauchly, "A Scientific Research Bureau Is Needed," UP-RBML.

61. John Mauchly, datebook, 1952, box 3:D:2, John W. Mauchly Papers, UP-RBML.

62. The show aired from 8:30 to 9:00 p.m. on Monday nights. The broadcast schedule for *The Johns Hopkins Science Review* is in box 3:C:6, folder 142, John W. Mauchly Papers, UP-RBML.

63. The Peabody Awards, *The Johns Hopkins Science Review* awards for 1952 and 1950, University of Georgia, Athens, https://peabodyawards.com/?s=%22johns+hopkins+science+review%22.

64. Gould, "What TV Is—And What It Might Be," 18, 22–24.

65. Mauchly could have come to the attention of the host of *The Johns Hopkins Science Review* in any number of ways, but two months earlier, the UNIVAC inventor had been featured in a *New York Times* "Science in Review" piece. The article reported on a talk Mauchly had given to the American Meteorological Society on the connection between solar activity and the weather;

Waldemar Kaempffert, "Sun Does 'Make' Our Weather from Day to Day, According to Mathematician's Findings," *New York Times*, June 8, 1952, E11.

66. "Teletogram," Remington Rand, October 20, 1952, box 3:C:6, folder 142, John W. Mauchly Papers, UP-RBML.

67. "Can Machines Think?" Lynn Poole, producer; original broadcast date October 27, 1952; Johns Hopkins Television Programs, 1948–1960, Special Collections, JHU-EL.

68. "Can Machines Think?" JHU-EL.

69. Luther Harr, Remington Rand, memo to John Mauchly, "UNIVAC; Johns Hopkins Television Show," October 31, 1952, box 3:C:11, folder 240, John W. Mauchly Papers, UP-RBML. The memo is addressed from Harr at the Washington DC, sales office. Harr is identified as UNIVAC sales manager in Washington in an oral history of Willis K. Drake (founder of Data Card Corporation and formerly of Remington Rand), conducted by James Ross, February 3, 1983, CBI, https://conservancy.umn.edu/handle/11299/107248.

70. Edward A. McCormick, letter to Lynn Poole, October 30, 1952, box 3:B:1, folder 7, John W. Mauchly Papers, UP-RBML. Warren Wightman from the Office of the Director of Public Relations at Johns Hopkins University also wrote to Mauchly that "some very critical people here said they thought our show was excellent"; Warren Wightman, letter to John Mauchly, November 4, 1952, box 3:B:1, folder 7, John W. Mauchly Papers, UP-RBML. Wightman is also listed in a finding aid for the collection of Johns Hopkins television programs as the assistant producer for "Can Machines Think?"; "Johns Hopkins Television Programs 1948–1960," Special Collections, JHU-EL, archived by the Internet Archive Wayback Machine at https://web.archive.org/web/20051111143840/http://www.library.jhu.edu/collections/specialcollections/jhuxmlkineFind.frame.html.

71. John Mauchly, "Kinescope of JHU TV Show for Census" memo to A. N. Seares (Remington Rand), New York, November 6, 1952, box 3:C:11, folder 240, John W. Mauchly Papers, UP-RBML. Mauchly made the argument inside Remington Rand that the company should acquire a copy of the show and provide it to the census at no charge to the government as a return for the favor the census granted in allowing some of the show's film footage to be shot there.

72. "Tele Followup Comment," 34.

73. For example: A. N. Seares, "Systems Magazine Editorial Policy" memo to Arch Hancock and others, October 8, 1952; and John W. Mauchly, "Systems Magazine Editorial Policy" memo to A. N. Seares, Arch Hancock, and others, October 8, 1952; both in box 3:C:11, folder 240, John W. Mauchly Papers, UP-RBML.

74. Seares, memo to Hancock and others, UP-RBML.

75. The history of the Mark I is recounted in a number of works. See, for example, Cohen, *Howard Aiken*; Bashe et al., *IBM's Early Computers*, 26–33; Kidwell and Ceruzzi, *Landmarks in Digital*, 56–57.

76. Bashe et al., *IBM's Early Computers*, 161.

77. Works that describe the IBM Card-Programmed Electronic Calculator and discuss its place in the history of IBM and the development of the computing industry include Bashe et al., *IBM's Early Computers*, 68–72; Pugh, *Building IBM*, 143, 152–55; Ceruzzi, *A History of Modern Computing*, 18–20; Williams, *A History of Computing Technology*, 251–53; Aspray, *Computing Before Computers*, 244–46; Sheldon and Tatum, "The IBM Card-Programmed Electronic Calculator," 30–36; Hurd, "The IBM Card-Programmed Electronic Calculator," 37–41; Rosen, "Electronic Computers," 12–13; Columbia University Computing History, "The IBM Card-Programmed Calculator," July 17, 2003, http://www.columbia.edu/acis/history/cpc.html; "Card Programmed Electronic Calculator, " IBM products description, IBM-CA; Hurd, "Computer Development at IBM," 389–418.

78. Ceruzzi, *A History of Modern Computing*, 20.

79. "Office Robots," 3–4.

80. "Office Robots," 8.

81. Watson and Petre, *Father, Son, & Co.*, 194–95.

82. Watson and Petre, *Father, Son, & Co.*, 198.

83. Navy Mathematical Computing Advisory Panel, *A Symposium*, box 95, Computer Documents, NMAH; also at http://ed-thelen.org/comp-hist/Computers-1952-hand.html.

84. A review of the symposium report indicates that more than 250 persons attended; Gammon, "Review: The Automatic Handling of Paper Work," 63–73.

85. Navy Mathematical Computing Advisory Panel, *A Symposium*, ii, NMAH.

86. "Announcing a General-Purpose Digital Computer," advertisement, *Scientific American* 187, no. 3 (September 1952), 123.

87. "3 Important New Electronic Digital Computers," advertisement, *Scientific American* 187, no. 3 (September 1952), 131.

88. "Bendix Digital Computers," advertisement, *Scientific American*, September 1952, 121.

89. For a detailed account of this period, see Bashe et al., *IBM's Early Computers*.

90. Bashe et al., *IBM's Early Computers*, 99.

91. "IBM Calculator Program," report of the Future Demands Department, prepared by Stephen W. Dunwell, September 30, 1952, Technical History Proj-

ect, Book References, IBM's Early Computers, chapters 3 and 4, box 272, footnotes 70–80, IBM-CA. The initial resistance at IBM to using the term "computer"—a word that referred to a person who carried out calculations before it became permanently associated with a machine through the terminology employed by IBM competitors—is discussed by Pugh, *Building IBM*, 142–43.

92. John C. McPherson, "Competitive Situation re Drum Calculators," memo, November 12, 1952, box 272, chapters 3 and 4, folder: footnotes 70–80, Technical History Project, IBM-CA. For the dates of McPherson's positions at IBM, see the entry for "John C. McPherson" in Lee, *Computer Pioneers*, 465–66.

93. John C. McPherson, "Competitive Drum Computers," memo, November 20, 1952, box 272, chapters 3 and 4, footnotes 70–80, Technical History Project, IBM-CA.

94. B. E. Phelps, "Notes on Meeting at Kenyon Laboratory," November 18, 1952, box 272, chapters 3 and 4, footnotes 81–90, 70–80, Technical History Project, IBM-CA. The context for this meeting is described in Bashe et al., *IBM's Early Computers*, 98–101.

95. Bashe et al., *IBM's Early Computers*, 101, 165.

96. Bashe et al., *IBM's Early Computers*, 165–72; Ceruzzi, *A History of Modern Computing*, 43–44; Cortada, *Information Technology as Business History*, 67.

97. A history of Aiken and Chase's interactions and efforts to interest Monroe in Aiken's ideas appears in Cohen, *Howard Aiken*, 39–44. Sources for that account include an oral history with Aiken and an account written by Chase. Howard Aiken, oral history, interviewed by Henry Tropp and I. B. Cohen, February 26–27, 1973, Computer Oral History Collection, 1969–1973, 1977, Archives Center, NMAH, https://www.si.edu/media/NMAH/NMAH-AC0196_aike73027.pdf. Cohen indicated that he had a booklet written by Chase with a history of calculating methods and machines. In addition, in the records of the Monroe Calculating Machine Company archives at its successor, MSB, I came across the text of a speech Chase gave to the American Society of Tool Engineers on March 10, 1953. It is titled "History of Mechanical Computing Machinery," and it included a slide show. The last two of sixty slides are listed as images of Aiken and the Mark I, and his text includes a description of meeting with Aiken in April 1937 and hearing about Aiken's idea for what became the Mark I. After eventually seeing the Mark I, wrote Chase, he knew that a new era in the "development of computing machinery" was "well underway." Chase is also listed as having given a talk with the same title at the opening banquet of the spring

meeting of the Association for Computing Machinery, May 2, 1952, held at the Mellon Institute, Pittsburgh PA; "News," 186–90.

98. In the letter Burkhart referenced his conversation with Aiken, which he said took place "upon returning from the IRE meeting in New York last March"; William H. Burkhart, letter to director of research at Monroe Calculating Machine Company, July 31, 1949, William H. Burkhart Papers, WBP. The letter also explains Aiken's role in making the connection between Aiken and Monroe. The volume on which Burkhart was working when he left Harvard in 1949 was later published as Staff of the Computation Laboratory, *Synthesis of Electronic Computing and Control Circuits*. In the preface Aiken noted that he worked with Burkhart and fellow student Theodore Kalin on sections on "control-circuit theory" before Burkhart left in August 1949 to join Monroe. Also listed as a member of the staff working on the project was An Wang, who went on to found Wang Laboratories, notable as a manufacturer of computers and early word processors.

99. Burkhart to Monroe Calculating Machine Company, July 31, 1949, William H. Burkhart Papers, WBP.

100. Burkhart's résumés list him as a "research engineer" and "senior project engineer" at Monroe between 1949 and 1952, and then starting in 1952 as "director of electronic research," or similar titles. In these documents he indicated that the Monrobot and several later computers were developed under his direction. These résumés are in Burkhart's papers. Burkhart's oversight role in the development of the Monrobot—including the one used on election night and several later models—is listed in his résumés. The *Newsweek* article quoting Burkhart as Monrobot's "manager" was "The Machine Vote," 63–64. In a company publication from November 1952 reporting on Monroe's election-night role ("Monrobot Flashes Election Trends," *Keynote*, November 1952, 10–11, MSB), Burkhart is identified as "electronics supervisor," while his boss, E. J. Quinby, is identified as "director." Quinby's supervisory responsibilities and Burkhart's leading role in early computer design at Monroe are mentioned in author interviews with Burkhart's widow, Dorothy Burkhart (January 14–15, 2005), and coworkers Richard LaManna (December 14–15, 2004), Vincent Pogorzelski (April 20, 2005), and Irving Gardoff (January 4, 2005). Copies of the patents for which Burkhart applied, as William Henry Burkhart or William H. Burkhart, between his arrival at Monroe and the 1952 election (and for which patents were eventually granted) are in his papers: "Switching Circuit," with co-applicant Amir Hassan Sepahban, patent no. 2,603,746; "Keyboard Operated Translating Circuit," with Howard M. Fleming Jr., patent no. 2,610,243; "Shift Register Circuit," patent no. 2,601,089; "Electronic Com-

puter," patent no. 2,872,107; "Magnetic Storage Systems for Computers and the Like," patent no. 2,739,299; "Magnetic Tape Error Control," patent no. 2,628,346; "Keyboard Checking Circuit," patent no. 2,700,755; "Operating Controls for Electronic Computers," with Joseph F. McCarroll Jr., patent no. 2,855,584; "Decimal Point Locator," with Howard M. Fleming Jr. and Frederick W. Pfleger, patent no. 2,769,592; "Antikey-Bounce Circuit," patent no. 2,735,091; "Multiplying and Dividing Means for Electronic Calculations," patent no. 2,834,543; and "Switching Circuits," patent no. 2,844,8111.

101. This comes from a set of autobiographical sketches that Burkhart began drafting after he retired, according to his wife, Dorothy, who made them available to me; these are referred to hereafter as "Burkhart autobiographical sketches."

102. Burkhart autobiographical sketches, William H. Burkhart Papers, wbp.

103. The account here is developed from the following sources: Berkeley, *Giant Brains*, 144–66, which is the first published and most complete account of the Kalin-Burkhart machine; Gardner, *Logic Machines and Diagrams*, 128–30, which provides additional detail and was completed with input from Burkhart, who is acknowledged in the preface, vii; Bowden, *Faster Than Thought*, 186; Burkhart autobiographical sketches; William Burkhart's Harvard College transcript, provided by his wife, Dorothy Burkhart; Dorothy Burkhart, in discussion with the author, January 14–15, 2005.

104. Berkeley, in *Giant Brains*, gives the date of Burkhart's course in mathematical logic as 1946 and construction of the Kalin-Burkhart machine between March and June 1947. Gardner, in *Logic Machines and Diagrams*, identifies the professor as Quine, as does Burkhart in his autobiographical sketches. Burkhart's transcript lists him as taking the course "Math. 19, Mathematical Logic" in the spring term of the 1946–47 academic year.

105. Dorothy Burkhart (in discussion, January 14–15, 2005) recalled that at one point, in fact, Kalin did have the device stored under a bed.

106. Berkeley, *Giant Brains*, 165–66; "Edmund C. Berkeley," in Lee, *Computer Pioneers*, 85–88.

107. Berkeley, *Giant Brains*, 156. In the book Berkeley does not name the life insurance company. But a typescript for the book with marked revisions identified it as Prudential in Newark nj. The prepublication version was included in a large collection titled the "The Origins of Cyberspace," assembled by Jeremy Norman and put up for auction at Christie's in New York on February 23, 2005. The documents in this collection were available for inspection before the auction. Berkeley was a mathematician and actuary who had worked for Prudential and, as early as 1941 and 1942, had looked

into ways that symbolic logic might be put to use by Prudential; see Yates, *Structuring the Information Age*, 120.

108. Berkeley, *Giant Brains*, 166.

109. Gardner, *Logic Machines and Diagrams*, 130.

110. Burkhart wrote that he ended up working for Aiken after approaching Aiken for permission to take a graduate course in computing; Burkhart autobiographical sketches, William H. Burkhart Papers, WBP.

111. The Mark III was being designed and built for the Navy; Cohen, *Howard Aiken*, 203.

112. Burkhart autobiographical sketches, William H. Burkhart Papers, WBP.

113. Staff of the Computation Laboratory, *Synthesis of Electronic Computing*, preface.

114. Burkhart to Monroe Calculating Machine Company, July 31, 1949, William H. Burkhart Papers, WBP.

115. "Monroe's Annual Report to Employees," *Keynote*, March 1953, 7, MSB.

116. *Keynote*, March 1950, 17, MSB.

117. *Keynote*, March 1950, 17, MSB.

118. "The Open Book of a 'Closed' Corporation," 1951 annual report, Monroe Calculating Machine Company, 1952, 5, MSB.

119. "Presenting Information on Facilities for Military Production for the Consideration of Armed Forces Procurement Authorities," brochure, Monroe Calculating Machine Company, June–July 1953, 17–21, MSB.

120. These details in the Monroe report are consistent with brief mentions of Quinby's work at RCA and the Navy in a memoir dealing primarily with an earlier part of his life; Quinby, *Ida Was a Tramp—and Other Reflections*, 247–60.

121. His patents from this era can be found at https://patents.google.com/.

122. Quinby, *Ida Was a Tramp*, 260.

123. "Presenting Information on Facilities for Military Production," 17–21, MSB.

124. "Presenting Information on Facilities for Military Production," 19, MSB.

125. LaManna, discussion.

126. Gardoff, discussion.

127. E. J. Quinby, Monroe Calculating Machine Company, "The MONROBOT Electronic Calculators," in *A Symposium on Commercially Available General-Purpose Electronic Digital Computers of Moderate Price*, 7–11, NMAH. The Monrobot III is typically the first Monrobot model listed in a number of surveys of early computers done in the 1950s and 1960s. Among these surveys are: *A Survey of Automatic Digital Computers*, Office of Naval Research, Washington DC, 1953, box 252, Computer Documents, NMAH; Martin H. Weik, *A Survey of Domestic Electronic Digital Comput-*

ing Systems, Ballistic Research Laboratories Report No. 971, December 1955, http://ed-thelen.org/comp-hist/BRL.html. One exception to the surveys showing the Monrobot III as Monroe's first working Monrobot is a list of early computers that appeared in a computer textbook published in 1963: Chapin, *An Introduction to Automatic Computers*, 190. In a four-page chronology of "automatic computers," Chapin includes Monrobot I as being commercially available, as being installed first at Fort Monmouth NJ, and with March 1953 as the "estimated date" that it "passed [its] acceptance test." The source of this information is not cited, and I have not to date encountered any direct references elsewhere to a Monrobot I at Fort Monmouth or to a viable Monrobot model before the Monrobot III. However, as noted earlier, Monroe's annual report covering 1950 referred to a Monrobot I as a "study model." A Monroe brochure from mid-1953 ("Presenting Information on Facilities for Military Production for the Consideration of Armed Forces Procurement Authorities," brochure, Monroe Calculating Machine Company, June–July 1953, records of the Monroe Calculating Machine Company, MSB) mentions, under the heading "Military Production at Present," two "Prime Contracts," both for an "Electronic Computer, Digital Type." One was listed as being for the "Air Force Cambridge Mass. Research Laboratory," which did get a Monrobot III (per other documentation: "Monrobot Electronic Calculator Model III—Manual of Operating Instructions, Prepared for Air Force Cambridge Research Center, Cambridge MA," instruction manual, Monrobot Corporation [subsidiary of Monroe Calculating Machine Company], 1953, William H. Burkhart Papers, WBP). The other of these two computers mentioned in the mid-1953 Monroe brochure was listed as being for "Army Engineers Research and Development Laboratory," with no location given. This is consistent, however, with the ultimate destination of the next Monrobot model under development, the Monrobot V, which was delivered to the Army Corps of Engineers' Research and Development Laboratory at Fort Belvoir in Maryland in 1955 ("Monrobot V Goes to Uncle Sam," *Keynote*, April 1955, 5, records of the Monroe Calculating Machine Company, MSB). There is no mention of a Monrobot I or II in William Burkhart's résumés, which do include references to the Monrobot III and later models. His coworker Richard LaManna, who arrived at Monroe in 1951 to work in the unit developing computers, said he believed there had been two early iterations of the Monrobot before he came but that he did not see them, and that at the time of the election, the Monrobot III was the computer on which his unit was working (LaManna, discussion). The next Monrobot model, the Monrobot V, got its debut in 1955 for use by the Army in mapmaking (reported in various places, includ-

ing "Monroe Machine for Improvement of Army Mapmaking Is Unveiled,"
Orange Transcript [New Jersey], March 10, 1955, news scrapbook, 1955–
1957, records of the Monroe Calculating Machine Company, MSB).

128. Quinby, "The MONROBOT Electronic Calculators," 7, NMAH.

129. Quinby, "The MONROBOT Electronic Calculators," 8, NMAH.

130. LaManna, discussion.

131. Sources for Monrobot specifications in the William H. Burkhart Papers,
WBP, include "Monroe Electronic Calculator—MONROBOT—A New Tool for
Business and Science," brochure, Monroe Calculating Machine Company,
April 1952; and "Monrobot Electronic Calculator Model III—Manual of
Operating Instructions, Prepared for Air Force Cambridge Research Center,
Cambridge MA," instruction manual, Monrobot Corporation, 1953. Another
source includes Quinby, "The MONROBOT Electronic Calculators," in *A
Symposium on Commercially Available General-Purpose Electronic Digital Computers of Moderate Price*, 8, NMAH. The 1953 Monrobot operating
manual indicated that the Monrobot's drum memory could hold up to one
hundred operational orders. The April 1952 brochure and Monroe's May
1952 presentation at the Pentagon symposium reported that the Monrobot's
drum memory could store up to two hundred operational orders.

132. "Election Coverage," part 1, CBS Television News, New York: PCM, November 4, 1952.

133. "Monrobot Electronic Calculator Model III—Manual of Operating Instructions," William H. Burkhart Papers, WBP.

134. "Monroe Electronic Calculator—MONROBOT," William H. Burkhart Papers,
WBP. A small notation on the last page includes the words "Printed in
U.S.A." and "4–52," apparently the date, judging from the reference in the
brochure to a computer having been under development for three years.

135. "Monroe Electronic Calculator—MONROBOT," William H. Burkhart
Papers, WBP.

4. PROJECT X VERSUS OPERATION MONROBOT

1. Gould, "Programs in Review," 11.

2. For examples of specific contracts, see Morgan and Draper, "Evolution of
the Office Machine Industry," 29–39.

3. Morgan and Draper, "Evolution of the Office Machine Industry," 29–39.

4. Norberg, *Computers and Commerce*, 214.

5. The paper—A. F. Draper, "UNIVAC on Election Night; for AIEE Meeting January 22, 1953"—was found in two archives: box 382, file: "Sperry
UNIVAC—History—1950's," Sperry-UNIVAC Company Records, HML; and
box 3:C:8, folder 191, John W. Mauchly Papers, UP-RBML. The document

carries this note: "Revised text of a conference paper presented at the AIEE Winter General Meeting, New York NY, January 19–23, 1953." This account also appeared as an article in a trade publication later in 1953: Draper, "UNIVAC on Election Night," 291–93. Herman Lukoff, a senior engineer working on UNIVAC at the Eckert-Mauchly division of Remington Rand, wrote in a 1979 memoir that this idea of using a computer to forecast the election was raised by Draper. Lukoff, *From Dits to Bits*, 127.

6. Lukoff, *From Dits to Bits*, 127.

7. Draper, "UNIVAC on Election Night," 291–93.

8. Lukoff, *From Dits to Bits*, 127; Draper, "UNIVAC on Election Night," 291–93.

9. Max A. Woodbury, in discussion with the author, September 30, 2004. Mauchly's datebook does not provide clear clues about the start of the election-night effort, but an entry for September 5 indicates that Mauchly and his wife, Kay, had dinner with Max Woodbury while the couple were on an out-of-town trip to Michigan, perhaps to attend a conference. John Mauchly, datebook, 1952, box 3:D:2, John W. Mauchly Papers, UP-RBML.

10. Max A. Woodbury and Herbert F. Mitchell Jr., "How UNIVAC Predicted the Election for CBS-TV," December 15, 1952, box 263, Sperry-UNIVAC Company Records, HML.

11. Mickelson, *From Whistle Stop to Sound Bite*, 137–38. CBS press releases dealing with election-night coverage in 1952 identified Levitan as "Producer of Special Events for CBS-TV"; see CBS, "CBS-TV's Plans for Nationwide Election Day Coverage," press release, September 25, 1952, CBS-AS.

12. Lower, "Use of Computers in Projecting Presidential Election Results, 1952–1964."

13. "Election Night Coverage," part 1, CBS Television, New York: PCM, November 4, 1952.

14. In addition to the accounts noted here, there are additional references either to the birth of the idea of using a UNIVAC on election night or to the start of work on the project, though not definitive. "New Device to Be Used to Give Public Election Returns," transcript of interview with Walter Cronkite by Dorothy Fuldheim at 6:30 p.m. over WEWS-TV (Cleveland), October 16, 1952, prepared by Radio Reports, for Remington Rand, box 6, folder 8, Charles Collingwood Papers, WHS. Harry Wulforst, who was later a publicist for Remington Rand's successor company, Sperry Rand, dates the initial contact between CBS and Remington Rand to April 1952, but without citing his sources, in Wulforst, *Breakthrough to the Computer Age*, 163.

15. Mickelson, *From Whistle Stop to Sound Bite*, 138.

16. Mickelson, *From Whistle Stop to Sound Bite*, 148–49.

17. CBS, "CBS-TV's Plans," press release.

18. CBS, "CBS-TV to Use Giant Electronic 'Brain' Election Night," press release, October 14, 1952, CBS-AS.

19. For example, the Associated Press story ran on page one of the *Syracuse Post-Standard* (NY) ("Electronic Robot to Forecast Election Results on TV Nov. 4"), the *Titusville Herald* (PA) ("Electronic Robot Will Forecast Vote Results for TV Viewers"), the *Baltimore Sun* ("Electronic Brain to Be Used to Forecast Election Results"), and the *Oneonta Star* (NY) ("Machine with Memory; Electronic Robot to Forecast Election Data"). One of the most complete versions of the AP story ran in the *Hartford Courant* ("UNIVAC, Electronic Robot, Fattened for Election Duty," 21B). Three-paragraph versions ran in such papers as the *Los Angeles Times* ("Electronic Robot to Forecast Election Results for CBS-TV," 25) and the *New York Times* ("UNIVAC the Brain Unafraid to Be Out on Limb November 4," 27). Papers running the United Press story included the *Capital Times* in Madison WI ("'Ten-Minute Job'; Electronic Brain to Spot Vote Trends," 12).

20. These included "Vote Forecast by Machine," *Philadelphia Inquirer*, October 15, 1952, 38, and "CBS to Use Electronic Robot to Forecast Election Results," *Philadelphia Evening Bulletin*, October 15, 1952, 9.

21. The photograph appeared under the heading "Network 'Drafts' UNIVAC for Election Coverage" and ran with the story "CBS to Use Electronic Robot to Forecast Election Results," *Philadelphia Evening Bulletin*, October 15, 1952. The clipping was part of an online exhibit, "John W. Mauchly and the Development of the ENIAC Computer," Department of Special Collections, Van Pelt Library, University of Pennsylvania, Philadelphia, archived at https://web.archive.org/web/20190415090614/http://www.library.upenn .edu/exhibits/rbm/mauchly/. This photo and similar photos of the same scene have been widely circulated over the years with brief accounts of the 1952 election appearing in news stories, websites, and books that deal with the history of computing.

22. This phrase also appears in the *Philadelphia Evening Bulletin* story. The account of the AP story here is from the version that appeared in the *Hartford Courant*: "UniVac, Electronic Robot, Fattened for Election Duty," October 15, 1952, 21B.

23. AP, "UNIVAC, Electronic Robot, Fattened for Election Duty."

24. "CBS and Remington Rand Tell of Election-Night Experiment in which UNIVAC Will Predict Election Results," transcript of broadcast by Eric Sevareid at 11:00 p.m. over WTOP (Washington) and the CBS Network, October 14, 1952, prepared by Radio Reports, for Remington Rand, box 6, folder 8, Charles Collingwood Papers, WHS.

25. "New Device to Be Used to Give Public Election Returns," transcript of

broadcast hosted by Dorothy Fuldheim at 6:30 p.m. over WEWS-TV (Cleveland), October 16, 1952, prepared by Radio Reports, for Remington Rand, box 6, folder 8, Charles Collingwood Papers, WHS.

26. For Fuldheim profiles and obituaries, see: Associated Press, "Dorothy Fuldheim, 96, A News Commentator," *New York Times*, November 4, 1989, 10; Charles Hillinger, "Newscaster Still with Original Station; TV Pioneer Gets Her Share of Air Time," *Los Angeles Times*, December 26, 1982, C6; United Press International, "Newswoman, 82, 'Just Warming Up,'" *Hartford Courant*, January 14, 1976, 35.

27. "New Device to Be Used to Give Public Election Returns," Fuldheim transcript, WHS. In the transcript "gimmickry" is misspelled as "gimmitry."

28. CBS, "CBS-TV to Use Giant," press release.

29. These included at least two radio broadcasts: Charles Collingwood, "Report to the West," radio scripts, October 15 and 22, 1952, box 5, folder 12, Collingwood Papers, WHS. Collingwood also described his and UNIVAC's upcoming tandem election-night role during at least one television broadcast: "UNIVAC to Help CBS on Election Night," transcript of television broadcast by Charles Collingwood over WCBS-TV, New York, and the CBS Television Network, 9:45 a.m. [approximate time], October 28, 1952, transcribed by Radio Reports, for Remington Rand, box 6, folder 8, Charles Collingwood Papers, WHS.

30. Collingwood, "Report to the West," October 15, 1952, WHS.

31. Collingwood, "Report to the West," October 22, 1952, WHS.

32. "UNIVAC to Help CBS On Election Night," WHS.

33. "Starting at 8 Tonight See Your Vote Count," advertisement, the *New York World Telegram and The Sun*, November 4, 1952, 10; "Starting at 8 P.M. and All through the Night," advertisement, *Washington Post*, November 4, 1952, 15.

34. "Fast—Authentic Local & National Election Returns on Channel 2," advertisement, *Baltimore Sun*, November 4, 1952, 8.

35. "NBC Set to Cover '52 Political Drive; Philco Is $3,800,000 Sponsor in 100-Station TV-Radio Link, Starting with Conventions," *New York Times*, January 1, 1952, 30.

36. John H. Carmine, Philco executive vice president, cited in "NBC Set to Cover '52 Political Drive."

37. Charles C. Barry, memo to Sylvester L. Weaver Jr., August 8, 1952, box 121, folder 29, Papers of Sylvester L. Weaver Jr., NBC Records, WHS.

38. NBC News, "Most Elaborate Radio and TV News Center—with 'Electronic Brain'—to Be Installed by NBC for Election Night Headquarters," press release, September 12, 1952, NBC News, Office Files, NBC Records, WHS. A

small part of the press release was also excerpted in NBC *Chimes*, a publication for network employees: "NBC to Install 'Brain' for Election Night," NBC *Chimes*, October 1952, LAB.

39. "Operation Election Night," *Radio Age* 11, no. 5 (October 1952), 3–4, DSL.

40. "Minutes of Election Meeting held 4 PM Friday, October 10, 1952," box 314, folder 33, Joseph O. Meyers Papers, NBC Records, WHS. No mention of Monrobot appears in minutes of earlier election-planning meetings in this file, which are from the following dates in 1952: September 16; September 17; September 22; September 24; September 25; September 30; and October 3. There is a reference in the October 3 minutes to the next meeting being scheduled for October 7, but the next set of minutes in the file are from October 10.

41. LaManna, discussion.

42. Quinby, *Ida Was a Tramp*, 248.

43. Quinby, *Ida Was a Tramp*, 248–49.

44. Photograph of David Sarnoff and Franklin Folsom, RCA president, at NBC studios, November 4, 1952, David Sarnoff Business 5, 1952–1953, 20, DSL.

45. LaManna, discussion.

46. "Minutes—Election Meeting—October 14," October 14, 1952, box 314, folder 33, Joseph O. Meyers Papers, NBC Records, WHS.

47. Martin H. Weik, *A Survey of Domestic Electronic Digital Computing Systems*, Ballistic Research Laboratories Report no. 971, December 1955, http://ed-thelen.org/comp-hist/BRL.html.

48. "Minutes—Election Meeting—October 14th," WHS.

49. NBC, "Meet Mr. Mike Monrobot," press release.

50. These are ubiquitous in that era. See, for example, "Flexible Improved New VARGLAS SILICONE Tubing and Sleeving," in *Electronics* 25, no. 12 (December 1952), 198; "Instrument Makers Stabilize Lines," *Electronics* 25, no. 10 (October 1952), 20.

51. NBC, "Meet Mr. Mike Monrobot," press release.

52. Harriet Van Horne, "Robots Will Analyze TV Election Returns," *New York World-Telegram and The Sun*, October 22, 1952.

53. NBC, "NBC Brings the Nation Complete, Accurate Results," press release, November 5, 1952, NBC Trade Releases, LAB.

54. "The Machine Vote," 63–64.

55. Sources for information about Marilyn Mason come from an interview with her daughter, Wendy Friedman, on May 4, 2018, in Bethesda MD, and in documents Mason held on to and were provided by her daughter for this book. They include "Meet Mr. Machine," *Prudential Home Office News*, November 1952, cover and 8–11; "Promotions," *Prudential Home Office*

News, November 1952, 20; "People in the News," *Mirror*, December 1952; internal memos and promotions, Prudential Insurance, October 16, 1952, June 11, 1953, July 12, 1954, March 21, 1955; letter from E. J. Quinby, director of research at Monroe, to Bruce Moncrieff, methods division, Prudential Life Insurance Company, Newark NJ, October 20, 1952; letter form E. J. Tiffany Jr., vice president, H. B. Humphrey, Alley & Richards, New York, to Marilyn Mason, methods department, Prudential Insurance Company, Newark NJ, October 30, 1952; E. J. Quinby, Monroe Radio-TV Broadcast, memo to W. H. Burkhart and others, October 31, 1952; letter, from "Carole & Bob," to Marilyn Mason, November 4, 1952; letter from "Eve" to Marilyn Mason, November 4, 1952; letter, W. H. Burkhart, Monroe Calculating Machine Company, Orange NJ, to Marilyn Mason, East Orange NJ, November 25, 1952; paystub for Marilyn Mason, Monroe Calculating Machine Company, Orange NJ, November 24, 1952; ID badge, Miss M. Mason— Monroe, NBC-Philco, Election Night, November 14, 1952; letter and photograph, H. Brown, Newark Manager, IBM, to Mrs. F. T. David (Marilyn Mason's married name), Prudential Insurance Company, Newark NJ, September 8, 1954.

56. For example: Beyer, *Grace Hopper*; Kleiman, *Proving Ground*; Koss, "Programming on the UNIVAC 1," 48–59.

57. NBC, "Meet Mr. Mike Monrobot," press release.

58. "NBC Radio and TV Networks, with Staff of 250 Plus 'Electronic Brain' and Mobile Units," NBC Trade Releases, October 30,1952, LAB.

59. NBC also kept its own employees informed about the Monrobot, which was touted in a network newsletter: "'Mike Monrobot' . . . The Brain," *NBC Chimes*, November 1952, LAB.

60. Election Preview, NBC Radio, October 23, 1952, nos. 317–18, disc 45A, Script and Recording Library, NBC Records, WHS.

61. See, for example, "Follow the Returns on NBC," advertisement, *Chicago Daily Tribune*, November 4, 1952, 10; *New York Times*, November 4, 1952, 52; *Washington Post*, November 4, 1952, 30.

62. The Monroe ad "Many Happy Returns of the Day" appeared the day before the election in newspapers around the country, including the *Chicago Daily Tribune* (B4), *Los Angeles Times* (13), *New York Times* (20), and *Washington Post* (2).

63. "Election 'Robot,'" advertisement, *New York Herald Tribune*, October 30, 1952, 18. This clipping was also pasted into a scrapbook of news coverage kept by the Monroe Calculating Machine Company, MSB. The scrapbook page notes that this ad also ran in at least two other New York newspapers, the *Daily News* and the *Journal-American*.

64. "TV . . . Radio Tonight," advertisement, *New York Times*, November 4, 1952, 36. This ad also appeared in other newspapers around the country, including the *New York World-Telegram and The Sun*, November 4, 1952, 10, and the *Washington Post*, November 4, 1952, 31.

65. Sources checked for any evidence of IBM promotion of its role included the ProQuest Historical Newspapers database and the NewspaperArchives.com database, as well as microfilm of several major urban newspapers at the beginning of election week, when widespread ads and coverage did appear for UNIVAC's role on CBS and Monrobot's role on NBC.

66. Ben Gross, "Televiewing and Listening in with Ben Gross," *New York Daily News*, November 3, 1952, 79.

67. Larry Wolters, "Television News and Views," *Chicago Daily Tribune*, October 27, 1952, E6.

68. "Radio-TV Set for '99% Coverage' on Election Nite," 1, 44.

69. These include an Associated Press item by Wayne Oliver (published as "This Week on Air" in the *Sun*, Baltimore MD, October 26, 1952, L19); "TV Nets Plan Full Election Coverage," *Washington Post*, November 2, 1952, L6; "Radio: UNIVAC and Monrobot"; Henry, "By the Way with Bill Henry"; Wolters, "Television News and Views."

70. "Starting at 8 P.M.," advertisement, *New York Times*, November 4, 1952, 37.

71. Merrill Panitt, "Networks' Full Resources Tuned for Election Night," *Philadelphia Inquirer*, November 2, 1952, 23 and 28. Within months of the election, Panitt became the first managing director of *TV Guide* and was later its editor; "Merrill Panitt, 76, Ex-TV Guide Editor," obituary, *New York Times*, March 31, 1994.

72. Harriet Van Horne, "Ballot Brains Train on Election Picture," *New York World-Telegram and The Sun*, October 31, 1952, 25.

73. "Univac & Monrobot," 52.

74. Gross, *I Looked and Listened*, 246–47.

75. John Charles Daly, letter to John Madigan, Station WMTW, Poland Springs ME, September 20, 1956, box 11, folder 2, John Charles Daly Papers, WHS. The recipient of the letter, John T. Madigan, who was working in 1956 at a television station in New England, had been ABC's television news director in 1952.

76. "IBM Machines Play Key Parts in Elections," *Business Machines*, November 18, 1952, IBM-CA.

77. The use of computation equipment at Lockheed in connection with the election is also mentioned at: Robert J. Bemer, "Lockheed Aircraft—California Division; Computer History Vignettes," archived at https://web.archive.org/web/20090131123217/http://www.trailing-edge.com/

~bobbemer/LOCKHEED.HTM; Walter Ames, "Networks, Local Stations to Use All Facilities Covering Presidential Election Tonight," *Los Angeles Times*, November 4, 1952, 20.

78. "Electronic Computers Call the Shots on Election Night 1952," *Hopper* 3, no. 6 (November–December 1952), 3, CBI.

79. "IBM Machines Play Key Parts in Elections," IBM-CA.

80. These include Maney, *The Maverick and His Machine*; Rodgers, THINK: A Biography of the Watsons and IBM; Tedlow, *The Watson Dynasty*; Watson and Petre, *Father, Son, & Co.*; Cortada, *Before the Computer*; Bashe et al., IBM's Early Computers; Pugh, *Building IBM*; Fisher, McKie, and Mancke, IBM and the U.S. Data Processing Industry; Belden and Belden, *The Lengthening Shadow*.

81. See, for example, Maney, *The Maverick and His Machine*, 397–404; Tedlow, *The Watson Dynasty*, 186; Rodgers, THINK, 176–77 (note 3), 199; Watson and Petre, *Father, Son, & Co.*, 228–29; Pugh, *Building IBM*, 159.

82. "The Courant Prepares for Operation Election," *Hartford Courant* Sunday magazine, November 2, 1952, 3.

83. A story that ran after the election referred to the "special IBM tabulator" used by "the *Courant*'s team of election experts." "The Dispatch that Heralded Ike's Landslide," *Hartford Courant*, November 9, 1952, 18. The photograph that accompanied the preelection story resembled one of a sequence of IBM accounting machines of the models 402, 403, or 419. When combined with several other pieces of equipment, such accounting machines served as one component of the Card-Programmed Electronic Calculator. Sources for photographs and descriptions of IBM equipment of that era include Frank da Cruz, Columbia University, "Columbia University Computing History: A Chronology of Computing at Columbia University," updated October 7, 2022, http://www.columbia.edu/acis/history/; IBM Archives, http://www-03.ibm.com/ibm/history/index.html; Bashe et al., IBM's Early Computers.

84. "The Courant Prepares," 3.

85. The *Courant* would boast about this after the election in a story about its conclusion, less than an hour after the polls closed, that Eisenhower had taken Connecticut: "The Dispatch that Heralded."

86. "Lightning-Fast IBM Devices to Help Speed W-T&S Televised Vote Count," *New York World-Telegram and The Sun*, October 31, 1952, 25.

87. William Michelfelder, "W-T&S and Video to Team in All-Night Election Coverage," *New York World-Telegram and The Sun*, October 22, 1952, 27.

88. "Lightning-Fast IBM Devices to Help Speed."

89. Ames, "Networks, Local Stations to Use All Facilities."

90. Van Horne, "Ballot Brains Train on Election Picture."

91. Henry, "By the Way With Bill Henry."

92. Bill Henry's background in this chapter comes from the following: Val Adams, "How Much Commentary Is Necessary?" *New York Times*, July 20, 1952, x9; Henry, "By the Way With Bill Henry"; "The Man Who Doesn't Take Sides," 9; "Henry for Hedda," 55; "One Big Stage," 38, 41; Frank, *Out of Thin Air*, 58–59.

93. Henry was to be such a critical part of the coverage for NBC and Philco that when they announced their plans more than six months earlier, he was the only reporter named in the thirteen-paragraph story in the *New York Times*; "NBC Set to Cover '52 Political Drive." Some details about Henry's choice and role as anchor are provided by Frank, *Out of Thin Air*, 68–69.

94. Henry, "By the Way With Bill Henry."

95. At the dinner of presidential electors in January 1949, Truman's mimicking of Kaltenborn's tenacity in holding to a Dewey victory prediction on election night was deemed a highlight of the event; Dixon Jr., "Electoral College Procedure," 220. Kaltenborn also mentioned it in his autobiography, *Fifty Fabulous Years*, 297.

96. The parenthetical reference is Henry's.

97. Wayne Oliver, Associated Press, "Robots on Video: Man vs. Machine on Election Night," *Washington Post*, October 29, 1952, 35. The story apparently moved on the wire several days earlier; a version with no byline and an October 25 dateline appeared as "Men, Machines Will Relay Ballot Tallies" in the *Los Angeles Times* on October 26, 1952, E11.

98. Wolters, "Television News and Views."

99. Wolters, "Television News and Views."

100. Van Horne, "Robots Will Analyze TV Election Returns."

101. See, for example, Ames, "Networks, Local Stations to Use All Facilities"; Jack Fitzgerald, "All Night Election Returns Week's Big TV Attraction," *Hartford Courant* Sunday magazine, November 2, 1952, 15.

102. "Electronic 'Brain,'" 46. The comparison here was made with the previously discussed October 14 CBS release, "CBS-TV to Use Giant Electronic 'Brain' Election Night."

103. Sources for this account of the methodology employed in generating predictions with a UNIVAC on election night include, Woodbury and Mitchell, "How UNIVAC Predicted the Election for CBS-TV," HML; Draper, "UNIVAC on Election Night," *Electrical Engineering*. Sources also include the following from John W. Mauchly Papers, box 3:C:8, folders 190–91, UP-RBML: Draper, "UNIVAC on Election Night," paper for AIEE meeting, January 22, 1953; P. S. Vincent, "UNIVAC and Election Predictions" (speech made to

Stamford Engineering Society, Norwalk CT, October 18, 1956); John Diebold and Associates staff, *Methods Report*; "UNIVAC and the 1956 Election,"
source identified as "Information prepared by Dr. Max Woodbury," date
stamped July 20, 1956; "Management Controller #831, Application of the
UNIVAC Fac-tronic System to Election Prediction." Other sources include,
Max A. Woodbury, in discussion with the author, September 30, 2004; Stephen E. Wright, in discussion with the author, April 10, 2006; Lukoff, *From
Dits to Bits*; Mickelson, *From Whistle Stop to Sound Bite*. Not all sources
are consistent—especially in terms of the chronology and results of election
night itself—but the account here captures the common and generally consistent elements from these sources.

104. Draper, "UNIVAC on Election Night," 291–93.
105. Woodbury and Mitchell, "How UNIVAC Predicted the Election for CBS-TV,"
HML.
106. Wright, discussion.
107. Woodbury and Mitchell, "How UNIVAC Predicted the Election for CBS-TV,"
HML.
108. These key metropolitan areas were listed as: San Francisco County CA;
Cook County IL; Boston MA; Hennepin, Ramsey, and St. Louis counties
MN; St. Louis MO; Bronx, Kings, New York, Queens, and Richmond Counties NY; Cuyahoga County OH; Allegheny and Philadelphia Counties PA.
109. Woodbury and Mitchell, "How UNIVAC Predicted the Election for CBS-TV,"
HML.
110. CBS, "Specially Designed and Constructed Visual Aids," press release, October 28, 1952, CBS-AS.
111. AP, "UNIVAC, Electronic Robot, Fattened for Election Duty"; "CBS to Use
Electronic Robot to Forecast Election Results."
112. Lukoff, *From Dits to Bits*, 128.
113. LaManna, discussion; this interview is the source of the account that
follows.
114. Letter from E. J. Tiffany Jr., vice president, H. B. Humphrey, Alley & Richards, New York, to Marilyn Mason, Methods Department, Prudential
Insurance Company, Newark NJ, October 30, 1952. The letter survives in
papers kept by Marilyn Mason, courtesy of Wendy Friedman.
115. Quinby to W. H. Burkhart and others, October 31, 1952, records of Marilyn
Mason.
116. LaManna, discussion.
117. NBC, "Meet Mr. Mike Monrobot," press release.
118. Burkhart mentioned this when he was quoted in a postelection *Newsweek* article about computer use on election night ("The Machine Vote,"

63–64). The account does not reveal much about just what else the Monrobot did, but it does include this line: "Instead of basing its calculations on breakdowns of previous elections, Monrobot was told by its manager William Burkhart to assume that 'the most you can say about the past is it's crazy.'" No documents have turned up to date that detail the methodology used. LaManna (discussion) said that Irving Gardoff, a mathematician and programmer who worked on the program, could have played a role in developing the election-night algorithms. But Gardoff, whom the author interviewed by telephone on January 4, 2005, indicated that he did not have a detailed recollection of the method used.

119. Samuel Lubell, "The Voters Speak: Grassroots Poll Favors Ike; Switch from 1948 Found by Analyst," *New York World-Telegram and The Sun*, October 27, 1952, 1–2.

120. Associated Press, "Stevenson May Hold Lead—Gallup," *Brainerd Daily Dispatch* (MN), November 4, 1952, 1; Associated Press, "Gallup Says Ike Has Edge," *Bismarck Tribune* (ND), November 4, 1952, 1; Associated Press, "Gallup Poll Notes Possibility of 50–50 Popular Vote," *Northwest Arkansas Times* (Fayetteville), November 4, 1952, 1.

121. Associated Press, "Gallup Poll Notes Possibility of 50–50 Popular Vote."

122. See, for example, United Press, "Samplers of Public Opinion See Photo-Finish for U.S. White House," *Panama City News* (FL), November 4, 1952, 2.

123. Princeton Research Service, "The U.S. Poll—Ike Holds Lead in Popular Vote," *Post-Standard* (NY), November 4, 1952, 1.

124. Tankard Jr., "Public Opinion Polling," 361–65; Smith, "The First Straw?" 21–36.

125. Associated Press, "Smokers' Poll Gives Ike 3,000,000 Pack Edge," *Brainerd Daily Dispatch* (MN), November 4, 1952, 1.

126. *U.S. News and World Report*, October 31, 1952, 14, cited by Lower, "Use of Computers," 21.

127. Associated Press, "October Survey Showed Eisenhower as Victor," *Philadelphia Inquirer*, October 26, 1952, 10.

128. Brown, "Ike Press Support 67%," 9–10, 69–71.

129. See "Odds Facts," *Florence Morning News* (SC), November 4, 1952, 3; "Reno Bookie Quotes Ike 2–1 Choice," *Syracuse Post-Standard* (NY), November 4, 1952, 16.

130. "Straws in the Wind Hit Dead Center," *Long Beach Press-Telegram* (CA), November 4, 1952, A8.

131. "BE SURE AND VOTE TODAY," *Florence Morning News* (SC), November 4, 1952, 1.

132. Photo caption, *Florence Morning News* (SC), November 4, 1952, 3.

133. Arthur Krock, "In the Nation: If It Is as Close as 'They' Say," *New York Times*, November 4, 1952, 28.

134. James A. Hagerty, "Election Outcome Highly Uncertain, Survey Indicates," *New York Times*, November 3, 1952, 1, 16–17.

135. Associated Press, "Instantaneous Computing Machine 'Thinks' 20,000 Times in a Second," *New York Times*, December 13, 1951, 53; Associated Press, "New Machine Revealed for Computing," *Indiana Evening Gazette* (PA), December 13, 1951, 2. The story also appeared in other media, including magazines, for example, "Whirlwind, Ultra-Fast 'Brain,' Now Operating," 387–88.

136. "See It Now: Interview with the Whirlwind," television recording, CBS, Accession 102651641, CHM. Other sources give the date of this broadcast as December 16, 1951, including an online catalog of *See It Now* episodes at the Paley Center for Media, http://www.paleycenter.org.

137. Arthur L. Norberg provides a brief list of the innovative features of the Whirlwind in "The Shifting Interests of the U.S. Government," 30. Histories of the Whirlwind include Redmond and Smith, *Project Whirlwind*.

138. Sources for this account include Kennedy Jr., "Electronic Computer Flashes Answers," 1; Frank E. Carey, Associated Press, "Huge Calculator One Thousand Times More Rapid Than Others," *Syracuse Post-Standard* (NY), February 15, 1946, 15; "ENIAC," 90; Arthur Burks, "Who Invented the General-Purpose Electronic Computer?" speech, box 42, folder 1, series 8, John Vincent Atanasoff Papers, ISU. Original documents, including press releases, information sheets, guest lists, speeches, and correspondence, are in the folder "ENIAC (Electronic Numerical Integrator and Computer); Dedication Ceremony, 15 February 46, Philadelphia," entry 646A, box A770, "R&D: Coordinating Research Council to Foreign Correspondence," Military Historical Files, Historical Branch, Executive Division, Series: Military Historical Files, 1917–1962, Record Group 156: Records of the Office of the Chief of Ordnance, 1797–1968, Post World War I Division, NARA. A portion of the MovieTone newsreel can be seen at http://www.youtube.com/watch?v=OSYpYFEwr4o&feature=related.

139. Morgan W. Huff, a 1950 University of Maryland graduate who was present at the UNIVAC factory in Philadelphia on election night 1952 early in his career in computers, recalled in a February 13, 2009, interview with the author that he would have available for demonstrations a computer program that would do card tricks and another that would play music. He also recalled that when demonstrations were to be run on live data, tapes from the successful operation of a particular program would be prepared as a backup.

140. At Prudential Insurance, Marilyn Mason was on the circulation list for a pair of such letters that came to the company from Monroe and Remington Rand alerting recipients to watch on election night: D. V. Savidge, sales manager, UNIVAC, Remington Rand, Manhattan, letter to Fred Haumacher, Prudential Insurance, Newark NJ, October 28, 1952; E. J. Quinby, director of research, Monroe, letter to Bruce Moncrieff, Methods Division, Prudential Life Insurance Company, Newark NJ, October 20, 1952; letters courtesy of Wendy Friedman.

141. "Tele Followup Comment."

142. Charles Collingwood, "Report to the West," script, October 22, 1952, Collingwood Papers, WHS. Collingwood repeated this story four years later when he was a featured speaker at a national computer symposium in Chicago: Collingwood, "The Election and the UNIVAC," 9–15.

143. Collingwood, "Report to the West," October 22, 1952, WHS.

5. STIRRED UP BY THE CAMPAIGN

1. Associated Press, "Shots Persuade Some Convicts to Halt Rioting," *Oneonta Star* (NY), November 4, 1952, 1; "Ohio Fellows Offer Surrender in Riots; Militia in Charge," *New York Times*, November 4, 1952, 1.

2. Associated Press, "Bloody Battle of Ridges in Korea Rages On," *Oneonta Star* (NY), November 4, 1952, 1; Lindesay Parrott, "Red Shells Repel Three Korean Attacks Up 'Triangle Hill,'" *New York Times*, November 4, 1952, 1.

3. Associated Press, "U.S. Pollsters Remember 1948," *Oneonta Star* (NY), November 4, 1952, 1; Associated Press, "Cautious Pollsters Refuse to Predict 'Sure Fire' Victor," *Albuquerque Journal*, November 4, 1952, 1.

4. Leo Egan, " 55,000,000 Are Expected to Vote Today," *New York Times*, November 4, 1952, 1; Arthur Edson, Associated Press, "Record 55 Million Vote Expected in Close '52 Presidential Race," *Oneonta Star* (NY), November 4, 1952, 1; "Record County Vote Expected," *Kalispell Daily Inter Lake* (MT), November 4, 1952, 1.

5. "Early Vote Is Record," *Bismarck Tribune* (ND), November 4, 1952, 1.

6. "Valparaiso Early Vote Heavy," *Valparaiso Vidette-Messenger* (IN), November 4, 1952, 1.

7. Lyle C. Wilson, United Press Staff Correspondent, "Residents All Over U.S. Swarm to Polls," *Valparaiso Vidette-Messenger* (IN), November 4, 1952, 1.

8. Egan, "55,000,000 Are Expected to Vote Today," 1.

9. Wilson, "Residents All Over U.S. Swarm to Polls," 1.

10. Associated Press, "Absentee Votes Could Delay Election Results Two Weeks," *Syracuse Herald-Journal* (NY), November 4, 1952, 20.

11. "Election Night: Test for Polls and Robot Brains," 30.

12. See, for example, "Starting at 8 P.M.," advertisement, *New York Times*, November 4, 1952, 37, and *New York World-Telegram and The Sun*, November 4, 1952, 11.

13. See, for example, "Starting at Tonight," advertisement, *New York Times*, November 4, 1952, 36.

14. "Follow the Returns on NBC," advertisement, *New York Times*, November 4, 1952, 52.

15. "Follow the Returns on NBC," advertisement, *Washington Post*, November 4, 1952, 30.

16. Master Broadcast Reports for *Today*, *The Kate Smith Hour*, and *Advancing Human Frontiers*, November 4, 1952, in NBC Television Master Books, Microfilm box MT-286, NBC Collection, LOC. The "Master Broadcast Forms" include this language at the bottom when a script is included: "Master script attached represents as accurately as possible the verbal, musical, and visual content of this program as actually broadcast." The Marilyn Mason documents are referenced in chapter 4.

17. Master Broadcast Report for *Today*, LOC.

18. "Monrobot Flashes Election Trends," *Keynote*, November 1952, 10–11, MSB.

19. Master Broadcast Report for *The Kate Smith Hour*, LOC.

20. Master Broadcast Report for *Advancing Human Frontiers*, LOC.

21. Master Broadcast Report for *Advancing Human Frontiers*, LOC; "Monrobot Flashes Election Trends," *Keynote*, 10–11, MSB.

22. "UNIVAC to Be Used in CBS Election Coverage," transcript prepared for Remington Rand from CBS television broadcast, box 6, folder 8, Charles Collingwood Papers, WHS.

23. "Daily Northwestern to Bulletin Returns," *Oshkosh Daily Northwestern* (WI), November 4, 1952, 1.

24. "Listen to 1400; Star, WDOS to Bring Returns on Today's Election," *Oneonta Star* (NY), November 4, 1952, 1.

25. "Evening Telegraph Will Be Open through Night," *Dixon Evening Telegraph* (IL), November 4, 1952, 1.

26. "Daily News, WMIK, Plan to Give Voting Results," *Middleboro Daily News* (KY), November 4, 1952, 1.

27. Stories include "1952 Presidential Election Wordiest in All History," *Brainerd Daily Dispatch* (MN), November 4, 1952, 1, 7; International News Service, "Wordage Record Set," *Syracuse Herald-Journal* (NY), November 4, 1952, 2.

28. International News Service, "Wordage Record Set," 2.

29. "1952 Presidential Election Wordiest in All History," 1, 7.

30. Front-page placement of the United Press story included: "Big Audience Will Watch the Big Show," *Hayward Daily Review* (CA), November 4, 1952,

1; "Biggest Audience Ever to Receive Election Results," *Valparaiso Vidette-Messenger* (IN), November 4, 1952, 1.

31. United Press, "Big Audience Will Watch the Big Show," 1.

32. Examples on Election Day include United Press, "Big Audience Will Watch the Big Show," 1; Terry Vernon, "Tele-Vues," *Long Beach Independent* (CA), November 4, 1952, 18; "Local Returns Will Be Late," *Portsmouth Times* (OH), November 4, 1952, 1; "Big Story of 1952 Now Up to Voters," advertisement, *Reno Evening Gazette*, November 4, 1952, 3; and a CBS station break heard at about 3:45 p.m. over WCBS-TV (NY) and the CBS Television Network, documented as "UNIVAC to Be Used in CBS Election Coverage," transcript prepared for Remington Rand, November 4, 1952, box 6, folder 8, Charles Collingwood Papers, WHS.

33. Vernon, "Tele-Vues," 18. Those celebrities who had indicated they would take part included Anne Baxter, Dana Andrews, Edward Arnold, Zsa Zsa Gabor, and Dorothy Lamour.

34. Vernon, "Tele-Vues," 18.

35. Young and Young, *The 1950s*, 223; Vernon, "Tele-Vues," 18.

36. Sidney Lohman, "News and Notes Gathered from the Studios," *New York Times*, November 2, 1952, 11.

37. Marling, *As Seen on TV*, 58, 60, 63, 203–6.

38. This Associated Press scorecard, "You Can Keep Your Own Record of Returns," ran in many communities, including, *Zanesville Signal* (OH), November 4, 1952, 2; *Austin Daily Herald* (MN), November 4, 1952, 12; *Hagerstown Daily Mail* (MD), November 4, 1952, 4; *Kerrville Times* (TX), November 4, 1952, 1.

39. "Guide and Tally Sheet for the Presidential Election," *New York Times*, November 4, 1952, 22.

40. See, for example, Associated Press, "Vote Counters Tonight Have 2 Systems to Follow," *Brainerd Daily Dispatch* (MN), November 4, 1952, 2.

41. "Poll Experts Eye Limaland for Vote Trend," *Lima News* (OH), November 4, 1952, 1.

42. Associated Press, "Handy Guide in Wisconsin Vote Watching," *Oshkosh Daily Northwestern* (WI), November 4, 1952, 10.

43. "Official Philco Guide to the National Political Conventions and Presidential Elections, 1952," Philco Corporation, 1952, box 136, folder 6 Office Files, NBC Records, WHS; a copy of this document was also obtained via eBay.

44. Trout and White, "What to Look for on Election Night," 22–24.

45. United Press, "Biggest Audience Ever to Receive Election Results," *Valparaiso Vidette-Messenger* (IN), November 4, 1952, 1; United Press, "World to Hear Vote Returns," *Traverse City Record-Eagle* (MI), November 4, 1952, 9; United Press, "Big Audience Will Watch the Big Show," 1.

46. Berger, "Roosevelt Crowd," 7.

47. "Times Square Is Quiet, Crowd Apathetic," *New York Times*, November 7, 1945, 2; Meyer Berger, "Crowds Apathetic in Times Sq. Area," *New York Times*, November 6, 1946, 5; Meyer Berger, "No Crowds Flock to Times Square," *New York Times*, November 5, 1947, 3.

48. "Times Square Is Quiet, Crowd Apathetic," 2; Berger, "Crowds Apathetic," 5.

49. Berger, "Election Night Crowd in Times Square Is Thin," 16; Meyer Berger, "Times Sq. Crowds Muster Thin Line," *New York Times*, November 9, 1949, 3; Berger, "Dwindling Crowd Threads Times Sq.," *New York Times*, November 8, 1950, 6.

50. Berger, "Election Night Crowd in Times Sq. Is Thin," 16.

51. *Time* magazine also took note after the 1948 election of the notably diminished Times Square activity: "Election Sidelights," 24.

52. Berger, "Times Sq. Crowds," 3; Berger, "Dwindling Crowd Threads Times Square," 6.

53. "How Times Will Flash Election Results by Lights from Tower in Times Square," *New York Times*, November 2, 1952, 76.

54. "Times Sq. Getting Vote Result Sign," *New York Times*, October 24, 1952, 25. Other stories promoting the new election indicator appeared on November 3 and November 4 ("Times' New Election Indicator Will Give Returns at a Glance," November 3, 16, and a story with the same headline and a photograph on November 4, 14). The *Times* in-house publication, *Times Talk*, reported that "initial plans for the new Times Square bulletin board had been drafted by the mechanical department last January": "Sweep Coverage Leaves Nothing for Sweeper," *Times Talk* 6, no. 3 (November 1952), 1, NYPL.

55. "Times Sq. Getting Vote Result Sign," 25. The story included a plug for the firm constructing the sign, the Artkraft Strauss Sign Company.

56. "Sweep Coverage Leaves Nothing for Sweeper," NYPL.

57. "Get the New York Times Election Returns Vote by Vote over WQXR," advertisement, *New York Times*, November 2, 1952, 110; "How Times Will Flash Election Results," 76; "WQXR to Provide Election Returns," *New York Times*, November 2, 1952, 66; "Sweep Coverage Leaves Nothing for Sweeper," NYPL.

58. These themes are explored in Taylor, *Inventing Times Square*.

59. I have found no comprehensive studies of the history of election night in Times Square, a subject that also tends to get little attention in book-length works on the history of Times Square and its environs.

60. It had been more than a century, for example, since the *Alton Telegraph* reported following the 1848 presidential election that, due to the "facilities afforded by the magnetic telegraph," the paper received returns from as far

away as Boston, New York , and Richmond several hours before returns came in from nearby precincts: *Alton Telegraph*, November 19, 1848, 3, cited in Matheson, "Steam Packet to Magic Lantern," 87.

61. Mitchell and Woodbury, "How UNIVAC Predicted the Election for CBS-TV," 2, HML.

62. "To: All persons participating in Project 'Election Return' at Ridge Avenue Plant, November 4, 1952," memo, Eckert-Mauchly Division, Remington Rand, box 5, folder 3, Herman Lukoff Papers, UP-UARC.

63. Vincent, "UNIVAC and Election Predictions," speech, UP-RBML.

64. "Minutes–Election Meeting," October 14, 1952, box 314, folder 33, Joseph O. Meyers Papers, NBC Records, WHS.

65. C. K. Sullivan, "Preliminary Report on Election Night," memo to Edward D. Madden, November 7, 1952, box 569, folder 19, Edward D. Madden Papers, NBC Records, WHS; NBC, "NBC Brings the Nation Complete, Accurate Results," press release.

66. Sullivan to Madden memo, November 7, 1952, WHS.

67. "Information for Guidettes Working Election Coverage," memo, box 163, folder 55, Sidney H. Eiges Papers, NBC Records, WHS.

68. Election preview, WNBC radio, New York NY, November 4, 1952, no. 319, DISC 45A, Recordings, Script, and Recording Library, NBC Records, WHS.

69. "Election Night: Test for Polls and Robot Brains," 30.

6. THIS IS NOT A JOKE OR A TRICK

1. "Election Coverage," part 1, CBS Television Network, November 4, 1952, PCM.

2. Alan J. Gould, "Election Instructions," memo to Associated Press domestic bureaus, October 8, 1952, AP 02A, General Files, Subject Files, box 57, APCA.

3. "Election Coverage," part 1, CBS, November 4, 1952, PCM.

4. Mickelson, *From Whistle Stop to Sound Bite*, 139.

5. "Election Coverage," part 1, CBS, November 4, 1952, PCM.

6. "Election Coverage," parts 1 to 8, CBS Television Network, November 4–5, 1952, PCM.

7. "Election Coverage," part 1, CBS, November 4, 1952, PCM.

8. Associated Press, "Stassen behind-Scenes Worker for Eisenhower," *Baltimore Sun*, October 21, 1952, 2.

9. "Election Coverage," part 1, CBS, November 4, 1952, PCM.

10. "Election Coverage," part 2, CBS Television Network, November 4, 1952, PCM.

11. "Election Coverage," part 3, CBS Television Network, November 4, 1952, PCM.

12. "The Dispatch that Heralded Ike's Landslide."

13. "Election Coverage," part 2, CBS, November 4, 1952, PCM.

14. "Election Coverage," part 3, CBS, November 4, 1952, PCM.

15. "Lubell Gets Ahead of UNIVAC," transcript prepared for Remington Rand from CBS radio broadcast, November 4, 1952, box 6, folder 8, Charles Collingwood Papers, WHS.

16. There will be more details later in this chapter.

17. The developments on NBC will be detailed in the next chapter.

18. "Election Coverage," part 3, CBS, November 4, 1952, PCM.

19. "Election Coverage," part 4, CBS Television Network, November 4, 1952, PCM.

20. Jack Gould, "C.B.S. Television Coverage of Election Returns Resulted in Landslide Victory for Network," *New York Times*, November 7, 1952, 31.

21. "UNIVAC Correctly Predicts GOP Sweep in Connecticut," transcript of segment of CBS radio election coverage, November 4, 1952, box 6, folder 8, Charles Collingwood Papers, WHS.

22. "The Dispatch that Heralded Ike's Landslide."

23. "Election Coverage," part 4, CBS, November 4, 1952, PCM.

24. "Election Coverage," part 5, CBS Television Network, November 4–5, 1952, PCM.

25. For example, "Remington Rand Man Regrets Lack of Faith in UNIVAC," transcript for Remington Rand of broadcast on station KNX, Los Angeles, November 5, 1952, box 6, folder 8, Charles Collingwood Papers, WHS; Associated Press, "Electric Brain's Aberration Is All Its Masters' Fault," *Baltimore Sun*, November 5, 1952, 6:00 a.m. edition, 8.

26. "Election Coverage," part 5, CBS, November 4–5, 1952, PCM.

27. "Election Coverage," parts 4 and 5, CBS, November 4–5, 1952, PCM.

28. "Election Coverage," part 5, CBS, November 5, 1952, PCM.

29. Woodbury and Mitchell, "How UNIVAC Predicted the Election for CBS-TV," 20–21, HML.

30. Lukoff, *From Dits to Bits*, 127–31; Mickelson, *From Whistle Stop to Sound Bite*, 137–41; Mickelson, *The Electric Mirror*, 80–82; Draper, "UNIVAC on Election Night," 291–93; A. F. Draper, "UNIVAC on Election Night," paper presented at AIEE Meeting, January 22, 1953, HML; Woodbury and Mitchell, "How UNIVAC Predicted the Election for CBS-TV," HML; John W. Mauchly Papers, UP-RBML; Computer Documents, NMAH; A. C. Hancock, "UNIVAC Beats Statisticians on Election Night," *Systems Magazine*, December 1952, reprint in box 185, file: "UNIVAC I/UNIVAC, Election Night 1952," Computer Documents, NMAH; Vincent, "UNIVAC and Election Predictions," speech, UP-RBML; Wulforst, *Breakthrough to the Computer Age*, 161–71.

31. Versions of this document were found in these locations: as a copy reproduced in Woodbury and Mitchell, "How UNIVAC Predicted the Election for CBS-TV," HML; as a copy in box 388, Sperry-UNIVAC Company Records,

HML; in Lukoff, *From Dits to Bits*, 130; as a copy in box 3:C:8, folder 191, John W. Mauchly Papers, UP-RBML; "Original UNIVAC Printout of Election '52 Prediction," including the handwritten notation "property of Grace M. Hopper," in box 5, folder 10, series 5, Eckert-Mauchly Computer Corporation, 1949–1965, Grace Murray Hopper Papers, collection 324, Archives Center, NMAH; Sperry-UNIVAC promotional poster, oversize materials, Herman Lukoff Papers, UP-UARC; an original computer printout was made available by Thomas J. Bergin from his collection of artifacts in the history of computing; Unisys promotional film, CHM.

32. Lukoff, *From Dits to Bits*, 130–31.

33. The 8:30 time is given in: Draper, "UNIVAC on Election Night," paper, January 22, 1953, HML; Draper, "UNIVAC on Election Night," 291–93; Lukoff, *From Dits to Bits*, 130; Mickelson, *From Whistle Stop to Sound Bite*, 140; "Script as Broadcast," KYW, November 5, 1952, 6:15 p.m., Sperry-UNIVAC Company Records, box 382, file "Sperry UNIVAC–History–1950s," HML. The 9:15 time is given in: George Staab, "Electronic Brain Whirs and Purrs: 'Landslide,'" *Philadelphia Evening Bulletin*, November 5, 1952, 3; Hancock, "UNIVAC Beats Statisticians on Election Night," *Systems Magazine*, NMAH.

34. The 8:30 time appears in the version of Woodbury and Mitchell, "How UNIVAC Predicted the Election for CBS-TV" in the Sperry-UNIVAC Company Records at HML and UP-RBML; the account giving the 9:15 time is in a version of the Woodbury-Mitchell report in Computer Documents, NMAH.

35. In an account he prepared after the election, Draper said that at 8:30 p.m. "slightly over three million" scattered returns were in and were used to generate the first prediction: Draper, "UNIVAC on Election Night," 292.

36. Woodbury and Mitchell reported that five minutes were needed for the program to run: "How UNIVAC Predicted the Election for CBS-TV," 15, HML.

37. See, for example, Draper, "UNIVAC on Election Night," 292.

38. "Election Coverage," part 1, CBS, November 4, 1952, PCM.

39. "Election Coverage," part 2, CBS, November 4, 1952, PCM.

40. Dewey L. Fleming, "Ike Out in Front in 23 States with Stevenson Holding Advantage in 11," *Baltimore Sun*, November 5, 1952, edition B*, 1.

41. International News Service, "UNIVAC, Electronic Brain, Figured Ike 4-to-1," *Hartford Courant*, November 5, 1952, 2.

42. Woodbury and Mitchell, "How UNIVAC Predicted the Election for CBS-TV," 19, 2, HML.

43. Lukoff, *From Dits to Bits*, 130–31.

44. Vincent, "UNIVAC and Election Predictions," speech, 5, UP-RBML.

45. Draper, "UNIVAC on Election Night," 293.

46. Woodbury and Mitchell, "How UNIVAC Predicted the Election for CBS-TV," 19, HML; Draper, "UNIVAC on Election Night," 293.

47. Woodbury and Mitchell, "How UNIVAC Predicted the Election for CBS-TV," 19–20, HML; Draper, "UNIVAC on Election Night," 291–93; Lukoff, *From Dits to Bits*, 131; Mickelson, *From Whistle Stop to Sound Bite*, 140; Mickelson, *The Electric Mirror*, 82; Wulforst, *Breakthrough to the Computer Age*, 167–70.

48. For example: Draper, "UNIVAC on Election Night," 291–93; Woodbury and Mitchell, "How UNIVAC Predicted the Election for CBS-TV," HML; Lukoff, *From Dits to Bits*; Vincent, "UNIVAC and Election Predictions," UP-RBML.

49. Mickelson, *The Electric Mirror*, 82.

50. Mickelson, *From Whistle Stop to Sound Bite*, 140.

51. Charles Collingwood, "Report to the West," script, November 5, 1952, box 5, folder 12, Charles Collingwood Papers, WHS.

52. "The Dispatch that Heralded."

53. Cornell, "Okay, Okay, Election 'Brain'—but Can It Write Leads Too?" *AP World*, LOC.

54. "Election Coverage," parts 1–2, NBC Radio, November 4–5, 1952, no. 320, disc 45A, Recordings, Script, and Recording Library, NBC Records, WHS.

55. "Sweep Coverage Leaves Nothing for Sweeper," NYPL.

56. "Election Night," 22–25.

57. "Election Coverage," part 2, CBS, November 4, 1952, PCM.

58. D. V. Savidge, Sales Manager, UNIVAC, Remington Rand, New York, letter to Fred Haumacher, Prudential Insurance, Newark NJ, October 28, 1952, from the papers of Marilyn Mason, courtesy of Wendy Friedman.

59. "Election Coverage," part 2, CBS, November 4, 1952, PCM.

60. Draper, "UNIVAC on Election Night," 293.

61. "Election Coverage," part 8, CBS, November 5, 1952, PCM.

62. "Election Coverage," part 8, CBS, November 5, 1952, PCM.

7. THE MECHANICAL GENIUS

1. "Buick Circus Hour," advertisement, *New York Times*, November 4, 1952, 36.

2. For the accounts in this chapter of NBC television: "Presidential Election Coverage," parts 1–12, NBC Television News, 9:00 p.m., November 4, to 3:00 a.m., November 5, 1952, NBC-NA; Program Analysis Cards, November 4–5, 1952, NBC-NA. For NBC Radio: "Presidential Election Coverage," parts 1–13 and 15, NBC Radio, November 4–5, 1952, nos. 320–26, disc 45A, Recordings, Script, and Recording Library, NBC Records, WHS.

3. "Presidential Election Coverage," part 1, NBC Radio, November 4, 1952, WHS.

4. "Presidential Election Coverage," part 3, NBC Radio, November 4, 1952, WHS.

5. "Presidential Election Coverage," part 4, NBC Radio, November 4, 1952, WHS.

6. "Presidential Election Coverage," part 1, NBC Television, November 4, 1952, NBC-NA.

7. Henry, "By the Way With Bill Henry."

8. "Presidential Election Coverage," part 1, NBC Television, November 4, 1952, NBC-NA.

9. "Presidential Election Coverage," part 2, NBC Television, November 4, 1952, NBC-NA.

10. "Presidential Election Coverage," part 3, NBC Television, November 4, 1952, NBC-NA.

11. LaManna, discussion.

12. Associated Press, "Morgan Beatty, Broadcaster, Newsman for 50 Years, Dead," *New York Times*, July 7, 1975, 28.

13. "Presidential Election Coverage," part 3, NBC Television, November 4, 1952, NBC-NA.

14. "Presidential Election Coverage," part 9, NBC Radio, November 4, 1952, WHS.

15. "Presidential Election Coverage," part 7, NBC Radio, November 4, 1952, WHS.

16. "Presidential Election Coverage," part 4, NBC Television, November 4, 1952, NBC-NA.

17. "Presidential Election Coverage," part 5, NBC Television, November 4, 1952, NBC-NA.

18. "Presidential Election Coverage," part 6, NBC Television, November 4, 1952, NBC-NA.

19. "Presidential Election Coverage," part 7, NBC Television, November 5, 1952, NBC-NA; Associated Press, "Farley Becomes Export Head of Coca-Cola Firm," *St. Petersburg Evening Independent* (FL), August 10, 1940, 1, 2.

20. "Presidential Election Coverage," part 7, NBC Television, November 5, 1952, NBC-NA.

21. "Presidential Election Coverage," part 8, NBC Television, November 5, 1952, NBC-NA.

22. "Presidential Election Coverage," part 9, NBC Television, November 5, 1952, NBC-NA.

23. "Presidential Election Coverage," part 9, NBC Television, November 5, 1952, NBC-NA.

24. "Presidential Election Coverage," part 12, NBC Television, November 5, 1952, NBC-NA.

25. Berger, "Roosevelt Crowd," 7.

26. Postelection stories by Meyer Berger from 1946 to 1951 in the *New York Times*: "Crowds Apathetic," 5; "No Crowds Flock to Times Square," 3; "Elec-

tion Night Crowd in Times Sq. Is Thin," 16; "Times Sq. Crowds," 3; "Dwindling Crowd Threads Times Sq." 6. In 1951 there was just a three-paragraph item with no byline: "Times Square Police Find Election Night 'Dullest Yet,'" *New York Times*, November 7, 1951, 21.

27. "Times' New Election Indicator Will Give Returns at a Glance," *New York Times*, November 3, 1952, 16; "How Times Will Flash Election Results," 76.

28. "Sweep Coverage Leaves Nothing for Sweeper," NYPL.

29. "Eisenhower Landslide," outtakes, November 4–5, 1952, no. 411, Universal International Newsreel, Record Group 200 UN, Motion Picture, Sound and Video Division, NARA.

30. Berger, "Old Times Square Tradition Dies," 24.

31. "The Times Square Trend," editorial, *New York Herald Tribune*, November 6, 1952, 22.

32. Trout and White, "What to Look for on Election Night," 22–24.

33. Scammon, *America Votes*, 82–83, 421.

34. *Congress and the Nation, 1945–1964*, 30.

35. "The Machine Vote," 63.

36. Frank, "The Great Coronation War," 74; Frank also spoke of this in a telephone interview by the author on October 29, 2005.

37. "Election Night: Test for Polls and Robot Brains," 30.

8. THE TROUBLE WITH MACHINES

1. "NBC-TV's Election Night Coverage Had More Viewers Than Any Other Network, Trendex Reports in 10-City Survey," December 7, 1952, NBC Trade Releases, LAB; "Tele Topics," *Radio Daily–Television Daily*, November 10, 1952, 7.

2. NBC, "NBC Brings the Nation Complete, Accurate Results," press release.

3. NBC, "NBC-TV's Election Night Coverage," press release, November 7, 1952, NBC Trade Releases, LAB.

4. Davidson Taylor, memo to Joseph McConnell, November 13, 1952, box 29, folder 121, Sylvester L. Weaver Jr. Papers, NBC Records, WHS.

5. NBC, "'Who's Winning?'" press release, October 27, 1954, NBC Trade Releases, LAB.

6. NBC, "Vice President Nixon Telephones NBC," press release, November 3, 1954, NBC Trade Releases, LAB.

7. "Monrobot Flashes Election Trends," *Keynote*, November 1952, 10–11, MSB.

8. "Monroe Calculating Machine Company: Presenting Information on Facilities for Military Production for the Consideration of Armed Forces Procurement Authorities," brochure, Monroe Calculating Machine Company, June–July 1953; "Monroe Calculating Machine Company: A Presentation

of Its Facilities for Precision Production," brochure, Monroe Calculating Machine Company, December 1953, MSB.

9. Records of the Monroe Calculating Machine Company, MSB.

10. "Monrobot Electronic Calculator Model III—Manual of Operating Instructions, Prepared for Air Force Cambridge Research Center, Cambridge MA," instruction manual, Monrobot Corporation [subsidiary of Monroe Calculating Machine Company], 1953, William H. Burkhart Papers, WBP; this Monrobot III installation is also listed in *A Survey of Automatic Digital Computers*, Office of Naval Research Washington DC, 1953, 67, box 252, Computer Documents, NMAH.

11. "Monrobot V Goes to Uncle Sam," *Keynote*, April 1953, 5–7, MSB; Clarence W. Kitchens, "Monrobot V Electronic Survey Computer," paper presented at the joint meeting of the American Society of Photogrammetry and the American Congress of Surveying and Mapping, Washington DC, March 10, 1955, reprint, courtesy of Vincent Pogorzelski, and archived at box 81, Computer Documents, NMAH.

12. "Continued Growth," Monroe Systems for Business, archived on the Internet Archive Wayback Machine at https://web.archive.org/web/20101231003512/http://www.monroe-systems.com/SWAPPID/74/SubPageID/23453; Rodengen, *The Legend of Litton Industries*, 34, 37, 44.

13. "Portable Robot," 34–36.

14. "Monrobot History," fact sheet, MSB.

15. "Rapid Change over the Next 40 Years," Monroe Systems for Business, archived on the Internet Archive Wayback Machine at https://web.archive.org/web/20080622170826/https://monroe-systems.com/SWAPPID/74/SubPageID/23454.

16. The *New Yorker* article from November 1956 is reprinted as chapter 13, "Brain," in Hamburger, *Matters of State*, 93–96.

17. "Company History," Unisys, http://www.unisys.com/unisys/about/company/history.jsp?id=209&pid=201.

18. CBS, "CBS-TV Sets Pace in Covering Eisenhower Victory," press release, November 5, 1952, CBS-AS.

19. Lukoff, *From Dits to Bits*, 131.

20. Sig Mickelson, letter to Phil Vincent, November 14, 1952, box 3:B:1, folder 7, John W. Mauchly Papers, UP-RBML.

21. "Election 1952," excerpts of television broadcast, CBS Television Network, November 4–5, 1952, WJB.

22. Collingwood, "Report to the West," November 5, 1952, WHS.

23. Part of Collingwood's line—"The trouble with machines is people"—would

also be attributed to Edward R. Murrow in a postelection magazine article: "The Machine Vote," 64.

24. Collingwood, "Report to the West," November 5, 1952, WHS.

25. For example: "Radio-TV First with Full Returns," *Radio Daily–Television Daily*, November 5, 1952, 1, 3; Bob Foster, "TV Sets New Mark with Election Night Coverage," *San Mateo Times*, November 6, 1952, 29.

26. For example: Gould, "C.B.S. Coverage of Election Returns Resulted in Landslide Victory for Network"; C. E. Butterfield, "Election on TV: Were the Robots Fully Successful?" *Washington Post*, November 8, 1952, 25; "Machine vs. Man," 25.

27. "Script as Broadcast," radio script, KYW, Westinghouse Radio Stations, Philadelphia PA, November 5, 1952, box 6, folder 8, Charles Collingwood Papers, WHS.

28. Alistair Cooke, "'UNIVAC' Forecast the Landslide," *Manchester Guardian*, November 13, 1952.

29. "UNIVAC Has Given Us a Glimpse of the Future," transcript prepared for Remington Rand, Barbara Hall's Scrapbook, Rural Radio Network, November 5, 1952, box 6, folder 8, Charles Collingwood Papers, WHS.

30. "Machine vs. Man," 25.

31. Van Horne, "Robots Will Analyze TV Election Returns."

32. Harriet Van Horne, "TV Brought Rivals Close to the People," *New York World-Telegram and The Sun*, November 5, 1952.

33. "Kollmars Think UNIVAC Made Poor Showing," transcript prepared for Remington Rand, Dorothy and Dick Kollmar, WOR, November 5, 1952, box 6, folder 8, Charles Collingwood Papers, WHS.

34. Gould, "C.B.S. Television Coverage of Election Returns."

35. Butterfield, "Election on TV: Were the Robots Fully Successful?"

36. Merrill Panitt, "Screening TV: Electronic Brains Prove They Need Smart Men," *Philadelphia Inquirer*, November 6, 1952, 26.

37. Ben Gross, "Televiewing and Listening in," *New York Daily News*, November 6, 1952, 80.

38. Foster, "TV Sets New Mark with Election Night Coverage."

39. Associated Press, "Electric Brain's Aberration Is All Its Masters' Fault."

40. "Network Reporting," 27, 85, 112–13.

41. Wolters, "Television News and Views."

42. "Computers Sweat Out Election Results," *Electronics*, December 1952, 14, 16.

43. "Unhappy UNIVAC," *Washington Post*, November 8, 1952, 8.

44. Stanton Delaplane, "Short Circuit," *San Francisco Chronicle*, November 14, 1952, 32.

45. "Remington Rand Man Regrets Lack of Faith in UNIVAC," partial transcript of radio broadcast prepared for Remington Rand, KNX, Los Angeles, November 5, 1952, box 6, folder 8, Charles Collingwood Papers, WHS.

46. "UNIVAC Proves Correct Despite Human Doubts," partial transcript of radio broadcast prepared for Remington Rand, KNX, Los Angeles, November 5, 1952, box 6, folder 8, Charles Collingwood Papers, WHS.

47. "Godfrey Explains Secret of UNIVAC," transcript prepared for Remington Rand, WCBS, New York, November 5, 1952, box 6, folder 8, Charles Collingwood Papers, WHS.

48. "Godfrey Apologizes to UNIVAC," transcript prepared for Remington Rand, WCBS, New York, November 7, 1952, box 6, folder 8, Charles Collingwood Papers, WHS.

49. "Scientist to Unveil Rival to UNIVAC," transcript prepared for Remington Rand by Radio Reports, WCBS-TV, New York, November 5, 1952, box 6, folder 8, Charles Collingwood Papers, WHS.

50. "Koviac May Outdo Union," transcript prepared for Remington Rand by Radio Reports, WCBS-TV, New York, November 6, 1952, box 6, folder 8, Charles Collingwood Papers, WHS.

51. "The Koviac Slips Up on Simple Question," transcript prepared for Remington Rand by Radio Reports, WCBS-TV, New York, December 1, 1952, box 6, folder 8, Charles Collingwood Papers, WHS.

52. Walter Cronkite Papers, DB-CAH.

53. Viewer Mail and Other Materials, Fall 1952–53, call no. 2M406, DB-CAH; Fan Mail, 1952–53, call no. 2M485, DB-CAH.

54. Viewer Mail and Fan Mail, Walter Cronkite Papers, DB-CAH.

55. Stephen P. Parke, letter, November 7, 1952, Viewer Mail, and Allen Dibble, letter, November 10, 1952, Fan Mail, Walter Cronkite Papers, DB-CAH.

56. Albert and Helen Ehringer, letter, November 5, 1952, Walter Cronkite Papers, DB-CAH.

57. J. S. Meroney, letter, November 5, 1952, Fan Mail, Walter Cronkite Papers, DB-CAH.

58. Robert L. Tiffany, letter, November 5, 1952, Viewer Mail, Walter Cronkite Papers, DB-CAH.

59. John F. Flynn, letter, November 8, 1952, Fan Mail, Walter Cronkite Papers, DB-CAH.

60. Cecily Feder, letter, November 6, 1952, Fan Mail, Walter Cronkite Papers, DB-CAH.

61. Box 87, Fan Mail, November–December 1952, Morgan Beatty Papers, AHC.

62. Emmett Durrett, letter, November 9, 1952, box 87, Fan Mail, November–December 1952, Morgan Beatty Papers, AHC.

63. Letter to H. W. Hansen from "Secretary to Morgan Beatty," November 21, 1952, box 87, Fan Mail, November–December 1952, Morgan Beatty Papers, AHC.

64. Ed Beattie, letter to Edward R. Murrow, November 6, 1952, Edward R. Murrow Papers, 1927–1965, microform, reel 40, no. 356.

65. Sperber, *Murrow*, 161, 177, 186.

66. Sperber, *Murrow*, 177, 191–92.

67. Beattie letter, Edward R. Murrow Papers.

68. "A Machine Makes a Monkey Out of Man," editorial, *Jacksonville Journal* (FL), November 11, 1952, 4, microfilm available at the Jacksonville Public Library.

69. "Kovacs Improves on UNIVAC," transcript prepared for Remington Rand by Radio Reports, WCBS-TV, New York, November 13, 1952, box 6, folder 8, Charles Collingwood Papers, WHS.

70. Mary Hornaday, "UNIVAC–Conversation Piece: An Intimate Message from New York," *Christian Science Monitor*, November 15, 1952, 20.

71. Hornaday's role as a pioneering female correspondent covering Washington politics can be found in Beasley, *Eleanor Roosevelt and the Media*, 43, and Beasley, Shulman, and Beasley, *The Eleanor Roosevelt Encyclopedia*, 249–50.

72. Hornaday, "UNIVAC–Conversation Piece."

73. Hancock, "UNIVAC Beats Statisticians on Election Night," NMAH.

74. Draper, "UNIVAC on Election Night," paper presented at AIEE Meeting, January 22, 1953, HML.

75. IBM founder, Thomas J. Watson Sr., launched the motto "THINK" when he worked as general sales manager for the National Cash Register Company before it became an IBM motto and the title of an IBM magazine: "Thomas J. Watson," IBM, https://web.archive.org/web/20061104060008/http://www-03.ibm.com/press/us/en/biography/10152.wss; Rodgers, *THINK*, 87.

76. Woodbury, discussion.

77. Warren Wightman, letter to John Mauchly, November 11, 1952, box 3:B:1, folder 7, John W. Mauchly Papers, UP-RBML.

78. Vincent, "UNIVAC and Election Predictions," speech, UP-RBML; archived with Vincent's written speech is a newsletter with an item taking note of the event: James J. Land, ed., *Company Confidential* 1, no. 6 (November 1956), Remington Rand UNIVAC, Sperry Rand Corporation, box 3:C:8, folders 190–91, John Mauchly Papers, UP-RBML.

79. Vincent, "UNIVAC and Election Predictions," 5–6, UP-RBML.

80. Berkeley's role in linking the insurance and computer industries is explored by Yates, *Structuring the Information Age*, 113–32; for the public Edmund C. Berkeley wrote *Giant Brains, or Machines that Think* in 1949.

81. Murphy and Berkeley, "Automatic Computers on Election Night," 26.

82. The pioneering role of Berkeley in publishing *Computers and Animation* and its predecessor, *The Computing Machinery Field*, is described in Hook, Norman, and Williams, *Origins of Cyberspace*, 323–24.

83. Berkeley and Wainwright, *Computers, Their Operation and Applications*, 291–92.

9. A HAZARD OF BEING DISCREDITED

1. R. M. Bury, memo to L. H. LaMotte, "Subject: Election Forecasting," February 21, 1955, from the Cuthbert C. Hurd Papers, Election Forecasting, 1955–56, box 8, folder 7, IBM-CA.

2. John Creacy, "Use of Computer 'First' for Times," *Detroit Times*, November 4, 1954, 1, 8.

3. "Hearst Folds *Detroit Times*, Sells Its Assets to News; Knight's Free Press Steps Up 'Fiercely Competitive' Enterprise," *Editor & Publisher*, November 12, 1960, 11–12.

4. Robert L. Wells, "Pair's Future Darkened by Red Shadow," *Detroit News*, May 21, 1952.

5. Harold Jackson, "Professor Lives Down His 1933 Role as Red," *Detroit News*, May 21, 1952; James S. Pooler, "Dr. Jacobson's Life Devoted to Others," *Detroit Free Press*, May 22, 1952, 22.

6. Jackson, "Professor Lives Down His 1933 Role as Red."

7. "American Arrested as Spy in Finland," *New York Times*, October 28, 1933, 18; "American Pardoned by Finnish President," *New York Times*, July 3, 1936, 7.

8. James S. Pooler, "Wayne Kept Ex-Red on Faith," *Detroit Free Press*, May 23, 1952, 12.

9. De Toledano and Lasky, *Seeds of Treason*, 91–104; Pooler, "Wayne Kept Ex-Red on Faith."

10. "Wayne U. Defends Ex-Red," *Detroit Times*, May 21, 1952, 3; Pooler, "Wayne Kept Ex-Red on Faith." The university's response is described in part in two memos in the Wayne State University Archives (hereafter cited as WSUA) from Victor A. Rapport, dean of the Wayne University College of Liberal Arts: Rapport to Pres. David D. Henry, June 29, 1950, and Rapport to Pres. Clarence B. Hilberry, September 21, 1954, subseries D, box 14, folder 19, Arvid Jacobson (Communism), 1952–54, 1958, Files of the Office of the President: Clarence Beverly Hilberry, WSUA.

11. Chambers, *Witness*, 295, 387; James S. Pooler, "Wayne Professor Revealed as Ex-Red; 20 Years' Fear of Betrayal of Post Ends with Identification in Chambers's Book," *Detroit Free Press*, May 21, 1952, 1.

12. "Wayne U. Defends Ex-Red"; Pooler, "Wayne Kept Ex-Red on Faith."

13. "Backers Vote for Jacobson; Industrialists Hold Faith in Former Red," *Detroit News*, May 22, 1952.

14. "Burroughs Laboratory and Wayne University Computers," 9–10; Fisher, McKie, and Mancke, *IBM and the U.S. Data Processing Industry*, 83.

15. Jacobson, *Proceedings of the First Conference on Training Personnel for the Computing Machine Field*; the conference was reviewed or noted in the following: Kircher, review of *Proceedings of the First Conference on Training Personnel for the Computing Machine Field*, 725–26; Hohn, "The First Conference on Training Personnel for the Computing Machine Field," 8–15; "New Books," 503.

16. Jacobson, *Proceedings of the First Conference*.

17. Problem logbook, problems 41–52, 1953–55, box 5, folders 5–23, Records of the Wayne State Computation Laboratory/Computer Center, WSUA.

18. "#45 Election Problem," problem logbook, 157–58, WSUA.

19. Rosen Center for Advanced Computing, "Saul Rosen 1922–91," Purdue University, https://www.rcac.purdue.edu/about/saul-rosen.

20. "#45 Election Problem," WSUA.

21. Creacy, "Use of Computer 'First' for Times."

22. Rosen, "Election Forecasting on UDEC," 49–52.

23. "'Brain' Set for Election," *Detroit Times*, November 5, 1956; "'Brain' to Cover Election," *Detroit Times*, November 2, 1956; John Creacy and Lou Arkles, "E101 Gives Detroit Times Six-Hour Lead in Election Returns," *Detroit Times*, November 8, 1956, reprinted in *The B Line*, Burroughs Corporation, December 17, 1956, Burroughs Corporation Records, CBI.

24. "Detroit Times Uses Electric Brain on Polls," *Editor & Publisher*, November 20, 1954, 64.

25. "The Tough One," 75; "Counting the Votes," 89.

26. "The Tough One," 75.

27. "'Brain' Set for Election"; "'Brain' to Cover Election"; Creacy and Arkles, "E101 Gives Detroit Times Six-Hour Lead."

28. "The Dispatch that Heralded"; Douglas Cornell, "Okay, Okay, Election 'Brain'—but Can It Write Leads Too?" *AP World*, Winter, 1952–53, 6, LOC; Edward Ellis, "Television Tells Election Story From W-T&S," *New York World-Telegram and The Sun*, November 5, 1952, 12; "IBM Machines Play Key Parts in Elections," IBM-CA.

29. This account is derived from documents in the papers of Louis H. LaMotte and Cuthbert C. Hurd at the IBM Corporate Archives, Somers NY. From the Louis H. LaMotte Papers, Subject Files: Election Returns, folder 11, box 46: H. T. Rowe, memo to L. H. LaMotte, November 24, 1954; T. V. Learson,

memo to L. H. LaMotte, "Subject: Election Coverage–1956," November 26, 1954; L. H. LaMotte, memo to T. J. Watson Jr., "Subject: Election Coverage–1956," December 13, 1954; R. M. Bury, memo to T. V. Learson, "Subject: Election Coverage–1956," January 11, 1955; L. H. LaMotte, memo to R. M. Bury, "Subject: Election Coverage, 1956," January 26, 1955; Gordon Smith, memo to T. J. Watson Jr., "Subject: Election Coverage," October 31, 1956, with attachments of two NBC press releases: "Electronic Computing Wizardry and Instantaneous Communications Setup Pace Swifter Election Returns than Ever Before on NBC-TV and Radio," and "Here's How NBC's Electronic Election Computing and Reporting System Will Work," October 30, 1956. From the Cuthbert C. Hurd Papers, Election Forecasting, 1955–56, folder 7, box 8: C. C. Hurd, memo to R. M. Bury, "Subject: Election Forecasting," February 16, 1955; R. M. Bury, memo to L. H. LaMotte, "Subject: Election Forecasting," February 21, 1955; W. H. Johnson, memo to R. M. Bury, "Subject: Election Coverage 1956," March 1, 1955; R. M. Bury, memo to T. V. Learson, "Subject: Election Forecasting," March 11, 1955; H. T. Rowe, memo to R. M. Bury, March 25, 1955; R. M. Bury, memo to T. V. Learson, "Subject: Election Coverage," April 5, 1955; Liston Tatum, memo to F. G. Smith, "Dr. Max Woodbury," September 22, 1952; H. T. Rowe, memo to T. V. Learson, October 5, 1955. Identification of these individuals as being executives and managers in the areas of media relations, image, sales, customer relations, technology, and overall management comes from contemporary news items about executive promotions, new products, and computer issues, along with obituaries, in the *New York Times*, the *Wall Street Journal*, the *Hartford Courant*, and the *Christian Science Monitor*; biographical sketches in Lee, *Computer Pioneers*; biographical information provided by the IBM Corporate Archives website and reference staff.

30. Rowe to LaMotte, November 24, 1954, IBM-CA. The announcement of Learson's promotion as vice president in charge of sales appeared in "I.B.M. Sales Executive Elected Vice President," *New York Times*, November 29, 1954, 35. A few days earlier LaMotte, who had previously held that position, was promoted to executive vice president, as reported in "I.B.M. Elevates Two Officers," *New York Times*, November 24, 1954, 37. A news item the same month reported that Rowe, who had been director of advertising and information at IBM since 1952, was going to focus exclusively on the director of information role as part of a reorganization of the advertising and information department; "News in the Advertising and Marketing Fields," *New York Times*, November 18, 1954, 52.

31. The device is described in "'Windows' for Computers," *Wall Street Journal*, November 18, 1954, 10.

32. Bury to Learson, January 11, 1955, IBM-CA.

33. Hurd to Bury, February 16, 1955, IBM-CA. Mickelson's name is spelled "Michelson" in the memo; the context and his description as a CBS vice president make clear that the subject is Sig Mickelson.

34. Hurd to Bury, February 16, 1955, IBM-CA. In a November 1954 reorganization of IBM's advertising and information department, Bury, the director of sales promotion, was to be given authority for "advertising and information programs and applications, business shows, display and exhibit and special activities departments"; "News in the Advertising and Marketing Fields."

35. Hurd to Bury, February 16, 1955, IBM-CA.

36. Johnson to Bury, March 1, 1955, IBM-CA, contains the reference to "Dr. Kullback of the NSA" and "Dr. Tokey of Princeton." Solomon Kullback's career is described in the National Security Agency's "Hall of Honor"; see National Security Agency, "Dr. Solomon Kullback (1903–94); 1999 Inductee," https://www.nsa.gov/History/Cryptologic-History/Historical-Figures/Historical-Figures-View/Article/1623043/dr-solomon-kullback/. John W. Tukey's career is described in a *New York Times* obituary that deemed him "one of the most influential statisticians of the last 50 years" upon his death in 2000; David Leonhardt, "John Tukey, 85, Statistician; Coined the Word 'Software,'" *New York Times*, July 28, 2000, A19.

37. Bury to LaMotte, February 21, 1955, IBM-CA.

38. Rowe to Bury, March 25, 1955, IBM-CA.

39. Bury to Learson, April 5, 1955; Tatum to Smith, September 22, 1955; Rowe to Learson, October 5, 1955, IBM-CA.

40. Smith to Watson, October 31, 1956, IBM-CA. The memo identifies the attachments as copies of the "NBC press kit given to reporters" on the afternoon of October 30. The two attached NBC releases—"Electronic Computing Wizardry" and "Here's How NBC's"—are dated October 30, 1956. The same two releases with the same date are in the archival collection of the papers of a director of information at NBC: box 179, folder 13, Michael Horton Papers, NBC Records, WHS. One of these two press releases— "Electronic Computing Wizardry"—appears with the same content but a different date, October 23, 1956, in a collection of NBC trade releases at the Library of American Broadcasting, College Park MD. The second of these releases is not in the LAB collection.

41. Smith to Watson, October 31, 1956, IBM-CA.

42. NBC, "Electronic Computing Wizardry," press release, October 23, 1956, LAB.

43. NBC, "NBC Mobilizes Men and Machines to Present Fastest and Most Complete Returns on TV and Radio Tuesday, November 6," press release, October 2, 1956; NBC, "Electronic Computing Wizardry," press release.

44. NBC, "NBC Mobilizes," press release.

45. NBC, "Electronic Computing Wizardry," press release.

46. NBC, "NBC Mobilizes," press release.

47. For example, the ad—"See it All, Tonight on NBC!"—ran on Election Day, November 6, 1956, in the *New York Times* (71), *Los Angeles Times* (A7), and *Chicago Daily Tribune* (A6).

48. "Find Out First on NBC!" advertisement, *Life*, November 5, 1956, 134–35.

49. Val Adams, "TV-Radio Notes: Networks Announce Plans for Coverage of the Elections—Other Items," *New York Times*, November 4, 1956, 13.

50. Sid Shalit, "Machines Plus Humans Make for Fast Returns," in the "TV-Radio—What's On?" column, *New York Daily News*, November 7, 1956.

51. NBC, "NBC Mobilizes," press release.

52. NBC, "Electronic Computing Wizardry," press release.

53. "No Gadgets," *New York Times*, November 4, 1956, section 2, 13.

54. ABC, "ABC Election Night Coverage Team," press release, October 30, 1956, box 11, folder 16, John Charles Daly Papers, WHS.

55. John Charles Daly, letter to John Madigan, Station WMTW, Poland Springs ME, September 20, 1956, box 11, folder 2, John Charles Daly Papers, WHS.

56. Charles Mercer, Associated Press, "Machines to Mastermind TV Election Coverage," *Hartford Courant*, November 3, 1956, 4G.

57. ABC, "ABC to Have Exclusive Use" and "ABC Election Night Coverage Team," press releases, October 30, 1956, box 11, folder 16, John Charles Daly Papers, WHS.

58. "Elecom 125 Meets the Press," *Elecom Pulse*, Underwood Corporation, Autumn 1956, 1, box 80, Computer Documents, NMAH.

59. Langman, "Television," 374–75.

60. "Eisenhower Landslide Forecast by Elecom," *Elecom Pulse*, Underwood Corporation, Autumn 1956, 4–5, box 80, Computer Documents, NMAH.

61. Bean's role is mentioned in ABC, "ABC Election Night Coverage Team," press release.

62. Harris, "Be Your Own 'Armchair Expert,'" 28–31.

63. "Eisenhower Landslide Forecast by Elecom," NMAH.

64. Jack Gould, "Election Projection: A Great Click-Clack in the Back of the Sacred UNIVAC," *New York Times*, November 5, 1954, 30.

65. "Counting the Votes," 89.

66. Hamburger's *New Yorker* article about use of the UNIVAC for the 1956 election is reprinted as chapter 13, "Brain" in Hamburger, *Matters of State*, 93–96.

67. Jack Gould, "TV: Landslide on C.B.S.; Cronkite and Crew Outpace the Other Networks in Election Returns," *New York Times*, November 8, 1956, 79.

68. "Who Won the Computer Battle Last Night?" advertisement, *New York Times*, November 9, 1960, 57.

69. "Election Nite: The Scoop & Scope," 28.

70. Jack Gould, "TV: Election Coverage; Electronic Computers Prove Value in Forecasting Results—C.B.S. Excels," *New York Times*, November 8, 1962, 61.

71. Jack Gould, "TV and Press Wed by Computers," *New York Times*, May 31, 1964, 11.

72. A brief summary of the key figures in television criticism of this area can be found in James A. Brown, "Television Criticism (Journalistic)," Museum of Broadcast Communications, archived at https://web.archive .org/web/20020628191901/http://www.museum.tv/archives/etv/T/htmlT /televisioncr/televisioncr.htm.

73. Lawrence Laurent, "Radio and Television; Machinery Seemed to Cast Final Vote," *Washington Post*, November 8, 1962, B15.

74. Jack Gould, "TV: Emphasis on Scoops Befogs Election Results," *New York Times*, November 10, 1966, 95.

75. Jack Gould, "TV: The Election as a 17-Hour Color Spectacular; Reliance on Computers Produces Confusion," *New York Times*, November 7, 1968, 95.

76. See, for example, Russo, "CBS and the American Political Experience."

77. Sources for this history of exit polling and collaborative vote tallies are: Robin Sproul, "Exit Polls: Better or Worse Since the 2000 Election?" Joan Shorenstein Center on the Press, Politics and Public Policy, Harvard Kennedy School of Government, 2008, https://shorensteincenter.org/exit-polls -better-or-worse-since-the-2000-election/; Best and Krueger, *Exit Polls: Surveying the American Electorate, 1972–2010*, 1–25; Campbell, *Lost in a Gallup*, 105–6, 142–46, 150–60, 186–87; Mitofsky and Edelman, "Election Night Estimation," 165–80; Littlewood, *Calling Elections*, 151–65.

78. Joan Konner, James Risser, and Ben Wattenberg, *Television's Performance on Election Night 2000*, CNN.com, January 29, 2001, https://www.cnn.com /2001/ALLPOLITICS/stories/02/02/cnn.report/cnn.pdf.

79. Sproul, "Exit Polls," 7.

80. Sproul, "Exit Polls," 8.

81. Sources include Russert, *Big Russ and Me*, ix–xi; NBC News, "NBC News: Decision 2000," transcripts, November 7 and 8, 2000, Nexis Uni; MSNBC, "Countdown with Keith Olbermann," June 12, 2009, Nexis Uni.

82. NBC, "NBC News: Decision 2000," November 7, 2000, 10:00 p.m. segment, via Nexis Uni.

83. NBC, "NBC News: Decision 2000," November 8, 2000, 4:00 a.m. segment, via Nexis Uni; MSNBC "Countdown with Keith Olbermann," June 12, 2009.

84. MSNBC, "Countdown with Keith Olbermann," June 12, 2009.

85. Mitofsky and Edelman, "Election Night Estimation," 167.

10. TRULY THE QUESTION OF OUR TIME

1. Nick Corasaniti, Karen Yourish, and Keith Collins, "How Trump's 2020 Election Lies Have Gripped State Legislatures," *New York Times*, May 22, 2022, https://www.nytimes.com/interactive/2022/05/22/us/politics/state -legislators-election-denial.html; Chris Canipe and Jason Lange, "The Republicans Who Voted to Overturn the Election," *Reuters Graphics*, February 4, 2021, https://graphics.reuters.com/USA-TRUMP/LAWMAKERS /xegpbedzdvq/; Harry Stevens et al., "How Members of Congress Voted on Counting the Electoral College Vote," *Washington Post*, January 7, 2021, https://www.washingtonpost.com/graphics/2021/politics/congress -electoral-college-count-tracker/.

2. Ben Collins, Ryan J. Reilly, and Jacob Ward, "In Harvard Study of January 6 Rioters, Top Motivation Is Clear: Trump," NBC News, July 20, 2022, https://www.nbcnews.com/politics/politics-news/harvard-study-jan-6 -rioters-top-motivation-clear-trump-rcna38794.

3. Karen Yourish, Larry Buchanan, and Denise Lu, "The 147 Republicans Who Voted to Overturn Election Results," *New York Times*, January 7, 2021, https://www.nytimes.com/interactive/2021/01/07/us/elections/electoral -college-biden-objectors.html.

4. Jon Greenberg, "Most Republicans Still Falsely Believe Trump's Stolen Election Claims. Here Are Some Reasons Why," Poynter Institute, June 16, 2022, https://www.poynter.org/fact-checking/2022/70-percent -republicans-falsely-believe-stolen-election-trump/.

5. Ben Kamisar, "Two-Thirds of Republicans Still Don't Believe Biden Was Elected Legitimately," NBC News, October 25, 2022, https://www.nbcnews .com/meet-the-press/meetthepressblog/two-thirds-republicans-still-dont -believe-biden-was-elected-legitimate-rcna53880; Greenburg, "Most Republicans Still Falsely Believe"; Lane Cuthbert and Alexander Theodoridis, "Do Republicans Really Believe Trump Won the 2020 Election? Our Research Suggests that They Do," *Washington Post*, January 27, 2022, https://www.washingtonpost.com/politics/2022/01/07/republicans-big-lie -trump/.

6. David Siders, "Why Many Republicans Believe the Big Lie," *Politico*, June 9, 2022, https://www.politico.com/newsletters/politico-nightly/2022/06/09 /why-many-republicans-believe-the-big-lie-00036384.

7 . Jeremy W. Peters and Katie Robertson, "Fox Stars Privately Expressed Disbelief about Election Fraud Claims. 'Crazy Stuff,'" *New York Times*, Feb-

ruary 16, 2023, updated February 22, 2023, https://www.nytimes.com
/2023/02/16/business/media/fox-dominion-lawsuit.html; Jeremy W.
Peters and Katie Robertson, "'The Whole Thing Seems Insane': New Documents on Fox and the Election," *New York Times*, March 7, 2023, https://
www.nytimes.com/2023/03/07/business/media/fox-dominion-2020
-election.html.

8. Sarah Longwell, "Trump Supporters Explain Why They Believe the Big
Lie," *The Atlantic*, April 18, 2022, https://www.theatlantic.com/ideas
/archive/2022/04/trump-voters-big-lie-stolen-election/629572/.

9. John Danforth et al., "Lost, Not Stolen: The Conservative Case that
Trump Lost and Biden Won the 2020 Presidential Election," July 2022,
lostnotstolen.org; Canon and Sherman, "Debunking the 'Big Lie,'" 546–81.

10. Danforth et al., "Lost, Not Stolen"; Canon and Sherman, "Debunking the 'Big Lie,'" 546–81; Bernard Grofman and Jonathan Cervas, "Fal-
lacies in Statistically-Based Claims about Massive Election Fraud in
2020: A Compendium," September 3, 2022, https://ssrn.com/abstract=
3794738; Hope Yen, "AP Fact Check: Yes, Trump Lost Election Despite
What He Says," Associated Press, May 6, 2021, https://apnews.com
/article/donald-trump-michael-pence-electoral-college-elections-health
-2d9bd47a8bd3561682ac46c6b3873a10.

11. Brennan Center for Justice, "Voting Laws Roundup: October 2022," October 6, 2022, https://www.brennancenter.org/our-work/research-reports
/voting-laws-roundup-october-2022.

12. Keith A. Spencer, "Trump Is Defeated. Trumpism Is More Alive than Ever,"
Salon, November 11, 2020, https://www.salon.com/2020/11/11/trumpism
-the-dead-end-of-neoliberalism/; Terry Gross, "How Did the Republican Party Become the Party of Trump?" Fresh Air, NPR, February 8, 2022,
https://www.npr.org/2022/02/08/1079191067/how-did-the-republican
-party-become-the-party-of-trump; David Leonhardt and Ian Prasad Phil-
brick, "The Party of Trump," *New York Times*, August 17, 2022, https://www
.nytimes.com/2022/08/17/briefing/liz-cheney-gop-donald-trump.html.

13. Ryan Lizza, Rachael Bade, and Eugene Daniels, "Politico Playbook:
Trump's Pre-Runoff Message: Terminate the Constitution," *Politico*, December 3, 2022, https://www.politico.com/newsletters/playbook/2022/12/03
/trumps-pre-runoff-message-terminate-the-constitution-00072059.

14. Ken Meyer, "Trump Threatens Journalists with Prison Rape in Bizarre
Rant about Supreme Court Leaker," *Mediaite*, October 23, 2022, https://
www.mediaite.com/trump/trump-threatens-journalists-with-prison-rape
-in-bizarre-rant-about-supreme-court-leaker-if-they-dont-give-them-up
-theyll-be-the-bride-of-another-prisoner/.

15. Linley Sanders, "The Difference between Which News Outlets Republicans and Democrats Trust," YouGovAmerica, June 18, 2020, https://today .yougov.com/topics/entertainment/articles-reports/2020/06/18/trust -news-republican-democrat-poll; Linley Sanders, "Trust in Media 2022: Where Americans Get Their News and Who They Trust for Information," YouGovAmerica, April 5, 2022, https://today.yougov.com/topics/politics /articles-reports/2022/04/05/trust-media-2022-where-americans-get -news-poll; Washington Post-University of Maryland Poll, December 2021, cited in Phillip Bump, analysis, "The Unique, Damaging Role Fox News Plays in American Media," *Washington Post*, April 4, 2022, https://www .washingtonpost.com/politics/2022/04/04/unique-damaging-role-fox -news-plays-american-media/.
16. Kovach and Rosenstiel, *The Elements of Journalism*, xxvii.
17. "Scenes around the Herald Office," *New York Herald*, November 9, 1864, 8.
18. Whitman, "Election Day, November, 1884."
19. "Presidential Election Coverage," part 1, NBC Radio, November 4, 1952, WHS.
20. Email, Margaret Sullivan to the author, June 9, 2022.
21. Megan Brennan, "Americans' Trust in Media Remains Near Record Low," Gallup, October 18, 2022, https://news.gallup.com/poll/403166/americans -trust-media-remains-near-record-low.aspx.
22. Washington Post-University of Maryland Poll, December 2021, cited by Phillip Bump, *Washington Post*.
23. Stirewalt, *Broken News*, 8.
24. AP-NORC Center for Public Affairs Research, "AP VoteCast 2018," https:// apnorc.org/projects/ap-votecast-2018/.
25. AP-NORC Center for Public Affairs Research, "AP VoteCast 2020," May 2021, https://apnorc.org/projects/ap-votecast-2020-general-elections/.
26. Stirewalt, *Broken News*, 218.
27. Penny Abernathy, "The State of Local News 2022," Local News Initiative, Medill School of Journalism, Northwestern University, June 29, 2022, https://localnewsinitiative.northwestern.edu/research/state-of-local-news /report/#executive-summary.
28. The Media Insight Project, "The Personal News Cycle: A Focus on African American and Hispanic News Consumers," 2014, American Press Institute and the AP-NORC Center for Public Affairs Research, https://apnorc .org/projects/the-personal-news-cycle-a-focus-on-african-american-and -hispanic-news-consumers/.
29. Hayes and Lawless, *News Hole*, 3.
30. Solutions Journalism, "Transforming News Is Critical to Building a More

Equitable and Sustainable World," https://www.solutionsjournalism.org
/about.

31. The American Journalism Project, "Empowering Communities. Preserving Democracy. Rebuilding Local News," https://www.theajp.org/.

32. MacArthur Foundation, "Press Forward Will Award More Than $500 Million to Revitalize Local News," Sept. 7, 2023, https://www.macfound.org /press/press-releases/press-forward-will-award-more-than-500-million-to -revitalize-local-news.

33. Philip Merrill College of Journalism, "Local News Network," https://merrill.umd.edu/why-merrill/local-news-network; this Local News Network is supported by the Andrew and Julie Klingenstein Family Fund, and in full disclosure, Merrill College is my home base, and I was involved in initial discussions with Andrew and Julie Klingenstein about creating this initiative.

34. Capital News Service, "Board of Education Voter Guide," https:// cnsmaryland.org/board-of-education-maryland/.

35. For example: Ali Velshi, "#Velshi Across America: The Damage of Election Lies," MSNBC, October 30, 2022, https://www.msnbc.com/ali-velshi/watch/ -velshiacrossamerica-the-damage-of-election-lies-151958085761.

36. Washington Post-University of Maryland Poll, December 2021, cited by Phillip Bump, *Washington Post*.

37. The Media Insight Project, "A New Way of Looking at Trust in Media: Do Americans Share Journalism's Core Values?" American Press Institute, April 14, 2021, https://www.americanpressinstitute.org/publications /reports/survey-research/trust-journalism-values/.

38. Email, Tom Rosenstiel to the author, January 2, 2023; Tom Rosenstiel, "News as Collaborative Intelligence: Correcting the Myths about News in the Digital Age," Center for Effective Public Management at Brookings, June 30, 2015, https://www.brookings.edu/research/news-as-collaborative -intelligence-correcting-the-myths-about-news-in-the-digital-age/; Kovach and Rosenstiel, *Elements of Journalism*, 18–19, 22–25, 59–61, 331–37.

39. Ahler and Sood, "The Parties in Our Heads," 964–81; the authors used other surveys of party composition for the numbers to compare to the stereotypes they found.

40. Washington Post-University of Maryland Poll, December 2021, cited by Phillip Bump, *Washington Post*.

41. Amanda Ripley, "Complicating the Narratives," The Whole Story, Solutions Journalism, updated January 11, 2019, https://thewholestory .solutionsjournalism.org/complicating-the-narratives-b91ea06ddf63.

42. Ripley, *High Conflict*, 7.

43. See Guzmán, *I Never Thought of It That Way*.

44. Trusting News, "Trusting News: A Project of RJI and API," https://trustingnews.org/about-us/; RJI and API are the Donald W. Reynolds Journalism Institute and the American Press Institute.

45. The Media Insight Project, "A New Way of Looking at Trust in Media."

46. See Haidt, *The Righteous Mind*.

47. The Media Insight Project, "A New Way of Looking at Trust in Media."

48. Ipsos, "Americans' Views on the Media," August 7, 2018, https://www.ipsos.com/en-us/news-polls/americans-views-media-2018-08-07.

49. The Media Insight Project, "A New Way of Looking at Trust in Media."

50. Margaret Sullivan, "Polls Show Americans Distrust the Media. But Talk to Them, and It's a Very Different Story," *Washington Post*, December 28, 2017, https://www.washingtonpost.com/lifestyle/magazine/polls-show-americans-distrust-the-media-but-talk-to-them-and-its-a-very-different-story/2017/12/27/ed9bbabe-ce3b-11e7-81bc-c55a220c8cbe_story.html?noredirect=on&utm_term=.87b6f5cb874d.

51. James Kimmel Jr., "What the Science of Addiction Tells Us about Trump," *Politico*, December 12, 2020, https://www.politico.com/amp/news/magazine/2020/12/12/trump-grievance-addiction-444570.

52. Guzmán, *I Never Thought of It That Way*, 34.

53. Ripley explores the role of conflict entrepreneurs in *High Conflict*.

54. Jeffrey M. Jones, "Confidence in U.S. Institutions Down; Average at New Low," Gallup, July 5, 2022, https://news.gallup.com/poll/394283/confidence-institutions-down-average-new-low.aspx; Fried and Harris, *At War with Government*, 1–20, 197–217; Fried and Harris, "In Suspense," 527–33.

55. McIntyre, *Post-Truth*, 1.

56. The 2010 book was updated in 2019 as Oreskes and Conway, *Merchants of Doubt: How a Handful of Scientists Obscured the Truth on Issues from Tobacco Smoke to Climate Change*.

57. Dan Friedman, "New Evidence Shows How Trump Planned to Falsely Declare Victory and Steal the Election," *Mother Jones*, October 13, 2022, https://www.motherjones.com/politics/2022/10/january-6-committee-trump-falsely-declare-victory/.

58. Yevgeny Prigozhin, quoted by Josh Kovensky, "Russian Mercenary Leader Commits to More Meddling in U.S. Elections," Talking Points Memo, November 7, 2022, https://talkingpointsmemo.com/news/russian-mercenary-leader-commits-to-more-meddling-in-us-elections.

59. Michael Golebiewski and Danah Boyd, "Data Voids: Where Missing Data

Can Be Easily Exploited," *Data & Society*, May 11, 2018, https://datasociety .net/library/data-voids-where-missing-data-can-easily-be-exploited/.

60. This is explored by Francesca Tripodi in "Searching for Alternative Facts: Analyzing Scriptural Inference in Conservative News Practices," *Data & Society*, May 16, 2018, https://datasociety.net/library/searching-for -alternative-facts/; Tripodi, *The Propagandists' Playbook*.

61. Draper, *Weapons of Mass Delusion*, 5.

62. The Election Integrity Partnership, "The Long Fuse: Misinformation and the 2020 Election," 2021, https://stacks.stanford.edu/file/druid: tr171zs0069/EIP-Final-Report.pdf, 241.

63. The Election Integrity Partnership, "The Long Fuse," 233–42.

64. Anne Applebaum, "The Reason Liz Cheney Is Narrating the January 6 Story," *The Atlantic*, June 29, 2022, https://www.theatlantic.com/ideas /archive/2022/06/jan-6-hearings-fact-check-trump-supporters-2020 -election/661428/.

65. Lehigh University, "Predicting the Likelihood People Will Believe in Con- spiracy Theories," May 30, 2018, https://neurosciencenews.com/conspiracy -theory-believers-9192/; Vitriol and Marsh, "The Illusion of Explanatory Depth and Endorsement of Conspiracy Beliefs," 955–69.

66. Lehigh University, "Predicting the Likelihood People Will Believe in Con- spiracy Theories."

67. Tom Rosenstiel, in discussion with the author, June 1, 2022; Margaret Sul- livan, "Three Ways the Media Can Vanquish the Big Lie that Will Linger Even After Trump Is Gone," *Washington Post*, January 17, 2021, https:// www.washingtonpost.com/lifestyle/media/media-fight-trump-big-lie/2021 /01/15/d3cafa3c-5745-11eb-a08b-f1381ef3d207_story.html.

Bibliography

ARCHIVES

AHC: American Heritage Center, University of Wyoming, Laramie

APCA: Associated Press Corporate Archives, New York NY

CBI: Charles Babbage Institute, University of Minnesota, Minneapolis

CBS-AS: CBS Audience Services, New York NY

CHM: Computer History Museum, Mountain View CA

DB-CAH: Dolph Briscoe Center for American History, University of Texas at Austin

DSL: David Sarnoff Library, Princeton NJ

HML: Hagley Museum and Library, Wilmington DE

IBM-CA: IBM Corporate Archives, Somers NY

ISU: Iowa State University Archives, Special Collections Department, Ames

JHU-EL: Johns Hopkins University, Milton S. Eisenhower Library, Baltimore MD

LAB: Library of American Broadcasting, University of Maryland, College Park

LOC: Library of Congress, Washington DC

MSB: Records of the Monroe Calculating Machine Company, Monroe Systems for Business, Levittown PA

NARA: National Archives, College Park MD

NBC-NA: NBC News Archives, New York NY

NMAH: National Museum of American History, Washington DC

NYPL: New York Public Library, New York NY

PCM: Paley Center for Media, New York NY

UP-RBML: University of Pennsylvania, Annenberg Rare Book and Manuscript Library, Philadelphia

UP-UARC: University of Pennsylvania, University Archives and Records Center, Philadelphia

WBP: William H. Burkhart Papers, private collection, courtesy of Dorothy Burkhart, Los Altos CA

WHS: Wisconsin Historical Society, University of Wisconsin–Madison

WJB: Walter J. Brown Media Archives and Peabody Awards Collection, University of Georgia, Athens

WSUA: Wayne State University Archives, Detroit MI

PUBLISHED WORKS

Abbot, Willis John. "How the Returns Come In: Election Night in a Great Newspaper Office." *Christian Union*, November 12, 1892.

Abernathy, Penny. *The State of Local News: The 2022 Report*. Evanston IL: Medill School of Journalism, 2022. https://localnewsinitiative.northwestern.edu /research/state-of-local-news/report/#executive-summary.

Ahler, Douglas J., and Gaurav Sood. "The Parties in Our Heads: Misperceptions about Party Composition and Their Consequences." *Journal of Politics* 80, no. 3 (July 2018): 964–81. http://dx.doi.org/10.1086/697253.

Aitken, Hugh G. J. *The Continuous Wave: Technology and American Radio, 1900–1932*. Princeton: Princeton University Press, 1985.

American Institute of Electrical Engineers. *Review of the Electronic Digital Computers Joint AIEE-IRE Conference, Philadelphia PA, December 10–12, 1951*. New York: American Institute of Electrical Engineers, 1952.

"Annihilation of Space and Time." *Dwight's American Magazine, and Family Newspaper* 3, no. 11 (March 13, 1847): 168.

Archer, Gleason L. *History of Radio to 1926*. New York: American Historical Society, 1938.

Aspray, William, ed. *Computing Before Computers*. Ames: Iowa State University Press, 1990.

Augarten, Stan. *Bit by Bit: An Illustrated History of Computers*. New York: Ticknor and Fields, 1984.

Balk, Alfred. *The Rise of Radio, from Marconi through the Golden Age*. Jefferson NC: McFarland and Company, 2006.

Barnouw, Erik. *A History of Broadcasting in the United States*. 3 vols. New York: Oxford University Press, 1966–70.

——. *Tube of Plenty: The Evolution of American Television*. Rev. ed. New York: Oxford University Press, 1990.

Bashe, Charles J., Lyle R. Johnson, John H. Palmer, and Emerson W. Pugh. *IBM's Early Computers*. Cambridge: MIT Press, 1986.

Baughman, James L. *The Republic of Mass Culture: Journalism, Filmmaking, and Broadcasting in America Since 1941*. 3rd ed. Baltimore: Johns Hopkins University Press, 2006.

——. *Same Time, Same Station: Creating American Television, 1948–1961*. Baltimore: Johns Hopkins University Press, 2007.

Beasley, Maurine H. *Eleanor Roosevelt and the Media: A Public Quest for Self-Fulfillment*. Chicago: University of Illinois Press, 1987.

Beasley, Maurine H., Holly Cowan Shulman, and Henry R. Beasley, eds. *The Eleanor Roosevelt Encyclopedia*. Westport CT: Greenwood Press, 2001.

Belden, Thomas, and Marva Belden. *The Lengthening Shadow: The Life of Thomas J. Watson*. Boston: Little, Brown, and Company, 1962.

Berger, Meyer. *The Story of the New York Times, 1851–1951*. New York: Simon and Schuster, 1951.

Berkeley, Edmund C. *Giant Brains, or Machines that Think*. New York: John Wiley & Sons, 1949.

Berkeley, Edmund Callis, and Lawrence Wainwright. *Computers, Their Operation and Application*. New York: Reinhold Publishing, 1956.

Best, Samuel J., and Brian S. Krueger, eds. *Exit Polls: Surveying the American Electorate, 1972–2010*. Washington DC: CQ Press, 2012. https://dx.doi.org/10.4135/9781452234410.

Beville, Hugh Malcolm, Jr. *Audience Ratings: Radio, Television, Cable*. Rev. ed. Hillsdale NJ: Lawrence Erlbaum Associates, 1988.

Beyer, Kurt W. *Grace Hopper and the Invention of the Information Age*. Cambridge: MIT Press, 2009.

Bianco, Anthony. *Ghosts of 42nd Street: A History of America's Most Infamous Block*. New York: Harper Perennial, 2005.

Binning, William C., Larry E. Esterly, and Paul A. Sracic. *Encyclopedia of American Parties, Campaigns, and Elections*. Westport CT: Greenwood Press, 1999.

Bliss, Edward, Jr. *Now the News: The Story of Broadcast Journalism*. New York: Columbia University Press, 1991.

Boddy, William. *Fifties Television: The Industry and Its Critics*. Chicago: University of Illinois Press, 1990.

Bogardus, Emory S. "Television and the Conventions." *Sociology and Social Research* 37, no. 2 (November–December 1952): 115–21.

Bogart, Leo. *The Age of Television: A Study of Viewing Habits and the Impact of Television on American Life*. 3rd ed. New York: Frederick Ungar Publishing, 1972.

Bohn, Thomas W. "Broadcasting National Election Returns: 1916–1948." *Journal of Broadcasting* 12, no. 3 (1968): 267–86.

Bousfield, W. A., and H. Barry Jr. "The Visual Imagery of a Lightning Calculator." *American Journal of Psychology* 45, no. 2 (April 1933): 353–58.

Bowden, B. V., ed. *Faster Than Thought: A Symposium on Digital Computing Machines*. London: Sir Isaac Pitman and Sons, 1953.

Bowman, John. *The History of the American Presidency*. Rev. ed. North Dighton MA: World Publications Group, 2002.

Brennan Center for Justice. "Voting Laws Roundup: October 2022." October 6, 2022. https://www.brennancenter.org/our-work/research-reports/voting -laws-roundup-october-2022.

Brewin, Mark. *Celebrating Democracy: The Mass-Mediated Ritual of Election Day*. New York: Peter Lang, 2008.

———. "The History and Meaning of the Election Night Bonfire." *Atlantic Journal of Communication* 15, no. 2 (2007): 153–69.

Brown, Robert U. "Ike Press Support 67%; Stevenson Backed by 14%; More Than 18% of Dailies Not Supporting Either." *Editor & Publisher*, November 1, 1952.

Buchanan, William, and Virginia V. S. Zerenga. *County Chairmen as Election Forecasters*. Starkville: Social Science Research Center, Mississippi State College, 1952.

Buckley, Thomas C. "Whistles, Crowds, and Free Silver: St. Paul's Noisy Election Night in 1896." *Ramsey County History* 27, no. 3 (Fall 1992): 13–17.

"Burroughs Laboratory and Wayne University Computers." *Digital Computer Newsletter* 5, no. 4 (October 1953): 9–10.

Campbell, Angus, Gerald Gurin, and Warren E. Miller. "Television and the Election." *Scientific American* 188, no. 5 (May 1953): 46–48.

Campbell, W. Joseph. *Lost in a Gallup: Polling Failure in U.S. Presidential Elections*. Oakland: University of California Press, 2020.

Campbell-Kelly, Martin, and William Aspray. *Computer: A History of the Information Machine*. New York: BasicBooks, 1996.

Canon, David T., and Owen Sherman. "Debunking the 'Big Lie': Election Administration in the 2020 Presidential Election." *Presidential Studies Quarterly* 51, no. 3 (September 2021): 546–81.

Carlson, Oliver. *The Man Who Made News, James Gordon Bennett*. New York: Duell, Sloan, and Pearce, 1942.

Carneal, Georgette. *A Conqueror of Space: An Authorized Biography of the Life and Work of Lee De Forest*. New York: Horace Liveright, 1930.

Ceruzzi, Paul E. *A History of Modern Computing*. 2nd ed. Cambridge: MIT Press, 2003.

Chambers, Whittaker. *Witness*. New York: Random House, 1952.

Chapin, Ned. *An Introduction to Automatic Computers*. 2nd ed. Princeton NJ: D. Van Nostrand Company, 1963.

Cohen, I. Bernard. *Howard Aiken: Portrait of a Pioneer*. Cambridge: MIT Press, 2000.

Collingwood, Charles. "The Election and the UNIVAC." *Proceedings of the Third*

Annual Computer Applications Symposium, October 9–10, 1956. Chicago: Armour Research Foundation of Illinois Institute of Technology, 1956, 9–15.

"Computers Sweat Out Election Results; Nonpartisan Electronic Machines Vie with Human Experts to Predict Outcome." *Electronics* 25, no. 12 (December 1952): 14–16.

Congress and the Nation, 1945–1964, Vol. 1-A: A Review of Government and Politics in the Postwar Years. Washington: Congressional Quarterly Service, 1965.

Conway, Michael. *The Origins of Television News in America: The Visualizers of CBS in the 1940s*. New York: Peter Lang, 2009.

Cortada, James W. *Before the Computer: IBM, NCR, Burroughs, and Remington Rand and the Industry They Created, 1865–1956*. Princeton: Princeton University Press, 1993.

——. *The Computer in the United States: From Laboratory to Market, 1930 to 1960*. Armonk NY: M. E. Sharpe, 1993.

——. *Information Technology as Business History: Issues in the History and Management of Computers*. Westport CT: Greenwood Press, 1996.

"Counting the Votes." *Time*, November 15, 1954.

Cressman, Dale. "News in Lights: The Times Square Zipper and Newspaper Signs in an Age of Technological Enthusiasm." *Journalism History* 43, no. 4 (Winter 2018): 198–208.

Cronkite, Walter. *A Reporter's Life*. New York: Ballantine Books, 1996.

Davis, H. P. "The Early History of Broadcasting in the United States." In *The Radio Industry: The Story of Its Development*, 189–225. Chicago: A. W. Shaw Company, 1928.

Dayan, Daniel, and Elihu Katz. *Media Events: The Live Broadcasting of History*. Cambridge: Harvard University Press, 1992.

De Forest, Lee. *Father of Radio*. Chicago: Wilcox and Follett, 1950.

De Toledano, Ralph, and Victor Lasky. *Seeds of Treason: The True Story of the Hiss-Chambers Tragedy*. New York: Funk and Wagnalls, 1950.

"Detroit Times Uses Electric Brain on Polls." *Editor & Publisher*, November 20, 1954.

Dixon, Robert G., Jr. "Electoral College Procedure." *Western Political Quarterly* 3, no. 2 (June 1950): 214–24.

Douglas, Susan J. *Inventing American Broadcasting, 1899–1922*. Baltimore: Johns Hopkins University Press, 1987.

Draper, A. F. "UNIVAC on Election Night." *Electrical Engineering*, April 1953.

Draper, Robert. *Weapons of Mass Delusion: When the Republican Party Lost Its Mind*. New York: Penguin Press, 2022.

Editors of *Broadcasting* Magazine. *The First 50 Years of Broadcasting: The Running Story of the Fifth Estate*. Washington DC: Broadcasting Publications, 1982.

"Election Night." *Time*, November 10, 1952.

"Election Night: Test for Polls and Robot Brains." *Business Week*, November 1, 1952.

"Election Nite: The Scoop & Scope." *Variety*, November 16, 1960.

"Election Returns Flashed by Radio to Seven Thousand Amateurs." *Electrical Experimenter* 45, no. 9 (January 1917): 650.

"Election Sidelights." *Time*, November 8, 1948.

"Electronic 'Brain' Will Turn Election Reporter." *Editor & Publisher*, November 1, 1952.

Ely, Melvin Patrick. *The Adventures of Amos 'n' Andy: A Social History of an American Phenomenon*. New York: Free Press, 1991.

Emery, Michael, Edwin Emery, and Nancy L. Roberts. *The Press and America: An Interpretive History of the Mass Media*. 9th ed. Boston: Allyn and Bacon, 2000.

"ENIAC." *Time*, February 25, 1946.

"The First Locomotive." *Knickerbocker; or New York Monthly Magazine* 13, no. 4 (April 1839): 343.

Fisher, Franklin M., James W. McKie, and Richard B. Mancke. *IBM and the U.S. Data Processing Industry: An Economic History*. New York: Praeger Publishers, 1983.

Frank, Reuven. "The Great Coronation War." *American Heritage* 44, no. 8 (December 1993): 74.

———. *Out of Thin Air: The Brief Wonderful Life of Network News*. New York: Simon and Schuster, 1991.

Fried, Amy, and Douglas B. Harris. *At War with Government: How Conservatives Weaponized Distrust from Goldwater to Trump*. New York: Columbia University Press, 2021.

———. "In Suspense: Donald Trump's Efforts to Undermine Public Trust in Democracy." *Society* 57, no. 5 (October 2020): 527–33.

Friendly, Fred W. *Due to Circumstances Beyond Our Control*. New York: Times Books, 1995. First published 1967 by Random House (New York).

Gallup, George. "We Won't Be Red-Faced This Time!" *Cosmopolitan*, November, 1951.

Gammon, Howard. "Review: The Automatic Handling of Paper Work." *Public Administration Review* 14, no. 1 (Winter 1954): 63–73.

Gardner, Martin. *Logic Machines and Diagrams*. New York: McGraw-Hill Book Company, 1958.

Gelb, Arthur. *City Room*. New York: Putnam, 2003.

Gomery, Douglas. *A History of Broadcasting in the United States*. Malden MA: Blackwell Publishing, 2008.

———. "Talent Raids and Package Deals; NBC Loses Its Leadership in the 1950s." In *NBC: America's Network*, edited by Michele Hilmes, 153–68. Berkeley: University of California Press, 2007.

Gould, Jack. *Watching Television Come of Age: The* New York Times *Reviews*. Edited by Lewis L. Gould. Austin: University of Texas Press, 2001.

Gramling, Oliver. *AP: The Story of News*. New York: Farrar and Rinehart, 1940.

Gray, George. "UNIVAC I: The First Mass-Produced Computer." *Unisys History Newsletter* 5, no. 1 (January 2001).

"The Great Election." *Massachusetts Ploughman and New England Journal of Agriculture* 8, no. 6 (November 11, 1848): 2.

Greb, Gordon B., and Mike Adams. *Charles Herrold, Inventor of Radio Broadcasting*. Jefferson NC: McFarland and Company, 2003.

Gross, Ben. *I Looked and Listened: Informal Recollections of Radio and TV*. New York: Random House, 1954.

Grundy, Pamela, and Susan Shackelford. *Shattering the Glass: The Remarkable History of Women's Basketball*. New York: New Press, 2005.

Guzmán, Mónica. *I Never Thought of It That Way: How to Have Fearlessly Curious Conversations in Dangerously Divided Times*. Dallas: BenBella Books, 2022.

Haidt, Jonathan. *The Righteous Mind: Why Good People Are Divided by Politics and Religion*. New York: Vintage Books, 2013.

Haigh, Thomas, and Paul E. Ceruzzi. *A New History of Modern Computing*. Cambridge: MIT Press, 2021.

Hamburger, Philip. *Matters of State: A Political Excursion*. Washington DC: Counterpoint, 2000.

Hancock, A. C. "UNIVAC Beats Statisticians on Election Night." *Systems Magazine*, December 1952.

Harris, Louis. "Be Your Own 'Armchair Expert'—A TV Game for Election Night." *Collier's*, November 9, 1956.

Hayes, Danny, and Jennifer L. Lawless. *News Hole: The Demise of Local Journalism and Political Engagement*. Cambridge UK: Cambridge University Press, 2021.

"Hearst Folds Detroit Times, Sells Its Assets to News; Knight's Free Press Steps Up 'Fiercely Competitive' Enterprise." *Editor & Publisher*, November 12, 1960.

"Henry for Hedda." *Time*, August 18, 1941.

Hewitt, Don. *Tell Me a Story: Fifty Years and Sixty Minutes in Television*. New York: PublicAffairs, 2001.

Hilmes, Michele, ed. *The Television History Book*. London: British Film Institute, 2003.

———. *NBC: America's Network*. Berkeley: University of California Press, 2007.

Hohn, Franz. "The First Conference on Training Personnel for the Computing Machine Field." *American Mathematical Monthly* 62, no. 1 (January 1955): 8–15.

Hook, Diana H., Jeremy Norman, and Michael R. Williams. *Origins of Cyberspace: A Library on the History of Computing, Networking, and Telecommunications*. Novato CA: historyofscience.com, 2002.

Hughes, Thomas P. *American Genesis: A History of the American Genius for Invention*. New York: Penguin, 1989.

Hurd, Cuthbert C. "Computer Development at IBM." In *A History of Computing in the Twentieth Century: A Collection of Essays*, edited by N. Metropolis, J. Howlett, and Gian-carlo Rota, 389–418. New York: Academic Press, 1980.

———. "The IBM Card-Programmed Electronic Calculator." In *Proceedings, Seminar on Scientific Computation, November 1949*, edited by the IBM Applied Science Department, 37–41. New York: International Business Machines Corporation, 1950.

"Increased Use of Homing Pigeons." *Scientific American* 76, no. 2 (January 9, 1897): 20.

Institute of Radio Engineers. "1949 IRE National Convention Program." *Proceedings of the IRE* 37, no. 2 (February 1949): 160–78.

"Instrument Makers Stabilize Lines." *Electronics* 25, no. 10 (October 1952): 20–22.

"It's a Free Country." *Time*, September 1, 1952.

Jackaway, Gwenyth L. *Media at War: Radio's Challenge to the Newspapers, 1924–1939*. Westport CT: Praeger, 1995.

Jacobson, Arvid W., ed. *Proceedings of the First Conference on Training Personnel for the Computing Machine Field*. Detroit: Wayne University Press, 1955.

John Diebold and Associates staff. *Methods Report: The Use of Computers and Data Processing Equipment in the 1956 Election*. Chicago: Cudahy Publishing Company, 1956.

Johns, Albert. "Presidential Candidates that Won't Get Elected." *Cosmopolitan*, August 1952.

Kaltenborn, H. V. *Fifty Fabulous Years, 1900–1950*. New York: G. P. Putnam's Sons, 1950.

Kelly, Kate. *Election Day: An American Holiday, an American History*. New York: Facts on File, 1991.

Keyssar, Alexander. *The Right to Vote: The Contested History of Democracy in the United States*. New York: Basic Books, 2000.

Kidwell, Peggy A., and Paul E. Ceruzzi. *Landmarks in Digital Computing*. Washington DC: Smithsonian Institution Press, 1994.

Kintner, S. M. "Pittsburgh's Contribution to Radio." *Proceedings of the Institute of Radio Engineers* 20, no. 12 (December 1932): 1849–62.

Kircher, Paul. Review of *Proceedings of the First Conference on Training Personnel for the Computing Machine Field*, by Arvid W. Jacobson. *Accounting Review* 30, no. 4 (October 1955): 725–26.

Kleiman, Kathy. *Proving Ground: The Untold Story of the Six Women Who Programmed the World's First Modern Computer*. New York: Grand Central Publishing, 2022.

Kloeber, Charles Edward, Jr. "The American Newspaper; IX: The Press Association." *The Bookman: A Magazine of Literature and Life*, November 1904.

Knoll, Erwin. "Evangelist Billy Graham to Write Daily Column." *Editor & Publisher*, November 15, 1952.

Koss, Adele Mildred. "Programming on the UNIVAC 1: A Woman's Account." *IEEE Annals of the History of Computing* 25, no. 1 (January–March 2003): 48–59. https://doi.org/10.1109/MAHC.2003.1179879.

Kovach, Bill, and Tom Rosenstiel. *The Elements of Journalism: What Newspeople Should Know and What the Public Should Expect*. 4th ed. New York: Crown, 2021.

Langman, Anne W. "Television." *The Nation*, November 10, 1956.

Lee, J. A. N. *Computer Pioneers*. Los Alamitos CA: IEEE Computer Society Press, 1995.

Little, Donald G. "Dr. Conrad Founds KDKA." *American Heritage* 6, no. 5 (August 1955): 71–73.

———. "The Reminiscences of Donald G. Little." Columbia University Oral History Collection, New York NY, 1984.

Littlewood, Thomas B. *Calling Elections: The History of Horse-Race Journalism*. Notre Dame: University of Notre Dame Press, 1998.

Lower, Elmer W. "Use of Computers in Projecting Presidential Election Results, 1952–1964." Master's thesis, Columbia University, 1970.

Lukoff, Herman. *From Dits to Bits: A Personal History of the Electronic Computer*. Portland OR: Robotics Press, 1979.

Lyons, Louis M. *Newspaper Story; One Hundred Years of the Boston Globe*. Cambridge: Belknap Press of Harvard University Press, 1971.

"The Machine Vote." *Newsweek*, November 17, 1952.

"Machine vs. Man." *Variety*, November 12, 1952.

"Magician." *New Yorker*, September 17, 1932.

Maney, Kevin. *The Maverick and His Machine: Thomas Watson Sr. and the Making of IBM*. Hoboken NJ: John Wiley and Sons, 2003.

"The Man Who Doesn't Take Sides." *Time*, December 25, 1964.

Marling, Karal Ann. *As Seen on TV: The Visual Culture of Everyday Life in the 1950s*. Cambridge: Harvard University Press, 1994.

Marvin, Carolyn. "Dazzling the Multitude: Imagining the Electric Light as a Communication Medium." In *Imagining Tomorrow: History, Technology, and the American Future*, edited by Joseph J. Corn, 202–17. Cambridge: MIT Press, 1986.

———. *When Old Technologies Were New: Thinking about Electric Communication in the Late Nineteenth Century*. New York: Oxford University Press, 1988.

Marx, Leo. *The Machine in the Garden: Technology and the Pastoral Ideal in America*. New York: Oxford University Press, 1964.

Matheson, John M. "Steam Packet to Magic Lantern: A History of Election-Returns Coverage in Newspapers of Four Illinois Cities, 1836–1928." PhD diss., Southern Illinois University Carbondale, 1967.

McCartney, Scott. *ENIAC: The Triumphs and Tragedies of the World's First Computer*. New York: Walker and Company, 1999.

McIntyre, Lee. *Post-Truth*. Cambridge: MIT Press, 2018.

Menand, Louis. *American Studies*. New York: Farrar, Straus, and Giroux, 2002.

Metropolis, N., J. Howlett, and Gian-carlo Rota, eds. *A History of Computing in the Twentieth Century: A Collection of Essays*. New York: Academic Press, 1980.

Mickelson, Sig. *The Decade that Shaped Television News: CBS in the 1950s*. Westport CT: Praeger, 1998.

———. *The Electric Mirror: Politics in an Age of Television*. New York: Dodd, Mead, and Company, 1972.

———. *From Whistle Stop to Sound Bite: Four Decades in Politics and Television*. New York: Praeger, 1989.

Misa, Thomas J. *A Nation of Steel: The Making of Modern America, 1865–1925*. Baltimore: Johns Hopkins University Press, 1995.

Mitofsky, Warren J., and Murray Edelman. "Election Night Estimation." *Journal of Official Statistics* 18, no. 2 (2002): 165–80.

Morgan, James. *Charles H. Taylor, Builder of the Boston Globe*. Published by the author, 1923.

Morgan, W. E., and Arthur F. Draper. "Evolution of the Office Machine Industry." *The Analysts Journal* 8, no. 1 (January 1952): 29–39. https://www.jstor.org/stable/40796930.

Mosteller, Frederick, Herbert Hyman, Philip J. McCarthy, Eli S. Marks, and David B. Truman. *The Preelection Polls of 1948: Report to the Committee on Analysis of Preelection Polls and Forecasts*. New York: Social Science Research Council, 1949.

Mowery, David C., and Nathan Rosenberg. *Paths of Innovation: Technological Change in 20th-Century America*. New York: Cambridge University Press, 1998.

Murphy, Eugene F., and Edmund C. Berkeley. "Automatic Computers on Election Night." *Computing Machinery Field* 2, no. 1 (January 1953). Reprint, *Computers and Automation* 16, no. 12 (December 1967): 26.

Murray, Matthew. "Establishment of the U.S. Television Networks." In *The Television History Book*, edited by Michele Hilmes, 35–39. London: British Film Institute, 2003.

Navy Mathematical Computing Advisory Panel. *A Symposium on Commercially Available General-Purpose Digital Computers of Moderate Price*. Washington DC: Department of the Navy, Office of Naval Research, 1952.

"Network Reporting." *Broadcasting–Telecasting*, November 10, 1952.

"New Books." *Science* 121, no. 3145 (April 8, 1955): 503.

"News." *Mathematical Tables and Other Aids to Computation* 6, no. 39 (July 1952): 186–90.

Nixon, Raymond B. "Henry W. Grady, Reporter; A Reinterpretation." *Journalism Quarterly* 12, no. 4 (December 1935): 341–56.

Norberg, Arthur L. *Computers and Commerce: A Study of Technology and Management at Eckert-Mauchly Computer Company, Engineering Research Associates, and Remington Rand, 1946–1957*. Cambridge: MIT Press, 2005.

——. "The Shifting Interests of the U.S. Government in the Development and Diffusion of Information Technology since 1943." In *Information Technology Policy: An International History*, edited by Richard Coopey, 24–53. New York: Oxford University Press, 2004.

Nye, David E. *American Technological Sublime*. Cambridge: MIT Press, 1994.

Odegard, Peter. Review of *The Pre-Election Polls of 1948*, by Frederick Mosteller, Herbert Hyman, Philip J. McCarthy, Eli S. Marks, and David B. Truman, and *The Polls and Public Opinion*, by Norman C. Meier and Harold W. Saunders. *American Political Science Review* 44, no. 2 (June 1950): 459–64.

"Office Robots." *Fortune*, January 1952.

"One Big Stage." *Time*, July 21, 1952.

"Opening of the Baltimore and Philadelphia Railroad." *Catholic Telegraph* 6, no. 38 (August 24, 1837): 302.

Oreskes, Naomi, and Erik M. Conway. *Merchants of Doubt: How a Handful of Scientists Obscured the Truth on Issues from Tobacco Smoke to Climate Change*. New York: Bloomsbury Publishing, 2019.

Pondillo, Bob. "Racial Discourse and Censorship on NBC-TV, 1948–1960." Paper presented at the Association for Education in Journalism and Mass Com-

munication, San Antonio TX, August 2005. http://list.msu.edu/cgi-bin/wa
?A2=ind0602a&L=aejmc&P=14191.

"Portable Robot." *New Yorker*, March 19, 1960.

Probus. "Letters from New York." *Southern Literary Messenger* 5, no. 8 (August 1839): 524.

Pugh, Emerson W. *Building IBM: Shaping an Industry and Its Technology.* Cambridge: MIT Press, 1995.

Quinby, E. J. *Ida Was a Tramp—and Other Reflections.* Hicksville NY: Exposition Press, 1975.

Radio Staff of the Detroit News. *WWJ-Detroit News: The History of Radiophone Broadcasting by the Earliest and Foremost of Newspaper Stations; Together with Information on Radio for Amateur and Expert.* Detroit: Evening News Association, 1922.

"Radio-TV First with Full Election Returns." *Radio Daily–Television Daily*, November 5, 1952.

"Radio-TV Set for '99% Coverage' on Election Nite." *Variety*, October 29, 1952.

Ralph, Julian. "Election Night in a Newspaper Office." *Outlook* 50, no. 20 (November 17, 1894): 829.

———. "Election Night in a Newspaper Office." *Scribner's Magazine* 16, no. 5 (November 1894): 531–44.

———. *The Making of a Journalist.* New York: Harper and Brothers, 1903.

Redmond, Kent C., and Thomas M. Smith. *Project Whirlwind: The History of a Pioneer Computer.* Bedford MA: Digital Press, 1980.

Ripley, Amanda. *High Conflict: Why We Get Trapped and How to Get Out.* New York: Simon and Schuster, 2021.

Rodengen, Jeffrey L. *The Legend of Litton Industries.* Fort Lauderdale FL: Write Stuff Enterprises, 1999.

Rodgers, William. *THINK: A Biography of the Watsons and IBM.* New York: Stein and Day, 1969.

Rosen, Saul. "Election Forecasting on UDEC." *Industrial Mathematics* 6 (1955): 49–52.

———. "Electronic Computers: A Historical Survey." *Computing Surveys* 1, no. 1 (March 1969): 7–36.

Russert, Tim. *Big Russ and Me: Father and Son—Lessons of Life.* New York: Hyperion, 2004.

Russo, Michael Anthony. "CBS and the American Political Experience: A History of the CBS News Special Events and Election Units, 1852–1968." PhD diss., New York University, 1983.

Scammon, Richard M., ed. *America Votes: A Handbook of Contemporary Ameri-*

can Election Statistics. New York: Macmillan and the Governmental Affairs Institute, 1956.

Schoenbrun, David. On and Off the Air: An Informal History of CBS News. New York: E. P. Dutton, 1989.

Schwarzlose, Richard A. The Nation's Newsbrokers. Vol. 1, The Formative Years, from Pretelegraph to 1865. Evanston IL: Northwestern University Press, 1989.

Sheldon, John W., and Liston Tatum. "The IBM Card-Programmed Electronic Calculator." In Review of the Electronic Digital Computers Joint AIEE-IRE Conference, Philadelphia PA, December 10–12, 1951, 30–36. New York: American Institute of Electrical Engineers, 1952.

Simaan, Marwan A. "An Introduction to D. G. Little's 1924 Classic Paper 'KDKA.'" Proceedings of the IEEE 86, no. 6 (June 1998): 1273–78.

Smith, Steven B. The Great Mental Calculators; The Psychology, Methods, and Lives of the Calculating Prodigies, Past and Present. New York: Columbia University Press, 1983.

Smith, Tom W. "The First Straw? A Study of the Origins of Election Polls." Public Opinion Quarterly 54, no. 1 (Spring 1990): 21–36.

Snyder, Robert W. "Vaudeville and the Transformation of Popular Culture." In Inventing Times Square: Commerce and Culture at the Crossroads of the World, edited by William R. Taylor, 133–46. Baltimore: Johns Hopkins University Press, 1996.

Sperber, A. M. Murrow: His Life and Times. New York: Bantam Books, 1986.

Spigel, Lynn. Make Room for TV: Television and the Family Ideal in Postwar America. Chicago: University of Chicago Press, 1992.

Staff of the Computation Laboratory. Synthesis of Electronic Computing and Control Circuits. Cambridge: Harvard University Press, 1951.

"The Stereopticon." Arthur's Home Magazine, April 1861.

"The Stereopticon." Saturday Evening Post, January 5, 1861.

Sterling, Christopher H., and John M. Kittross. Stay Tuned: A History of American Broadcasting. 3rd ed. Mahwah NJ: Lawrence Erlbaum Associates, 2002.

Stern, Nancy. From ENIAC to UNIVAC: An Appraisal of the Eckert-Mauchly Computers. Bedford MA: Digital Press, 1981.

"Stevenson Backed by 14%; More than 18% of Dailies Not Supporting Either." Editor & Publisher, November 1, 1952.

Stirewalt, Chris. Broken News: Why the Media Rage Machine Divides America and How to Fight Back. New York: Center Street, 2022.

Stoddart, Alexander McD. "How the Newspapers Tell the Story of Election Day." Outlook, November 8, 1916.

Stone, Melville E. "The Associated Press." Century Illustrated Magazine 70, no. 3 (July 1905): 379.

"Sweep Coverage Leaves Nothing for Sweeper." *Times Talk* 6, no. 3 (November 1952): 1–6.

Tankard, James W., Jr. "Public Opinion Polling by Newspapers in the Presidential Election Campaign of 1824." *Journalism Quarterly* 49, no. 2 (Summer 1972): 361–65.

Taylor, William R., ed. *Inventing Times Square: Commerce and Culture at the Crossroads of the World.* Baltimore: Johns Hopkins University Press, 1996.

Tedlow, Richard S. *The Watson Dynasty: The Fiery Reign and Troubled Legacy of IBM's Founding Father and Son.* New York: HarperCollins, 2003.

"Tele Followup Comment." *Variety*, October 29, 1952.

"Tele Topics." *Radio Daily–Television Daily*, November 10, 1952.

"Theatres in Pitch for Election Nite TV-ers." *Variety*, October 29, 1952.

"The Tough One." *Time*, November 15, 1954.

Tripodi, Francesca. *The Propagandists' Playbook: How Conservative Elites Manipulate Search and Threaten Democracy.* New Haven: Yale University Press, 2022.

Trout, Robert, and Paul W. White. "What to Look for on Election Night." *Collier's*, November 8, 1952.

United States Commission on Civil Rights. *Window Dressing on the Set: Women and Minorities in Television.* Washington DC: Government Printing Office, 1977.

"UNIVAC & Monrobot." *Time*, October 27, 1952.

U.S. Department of Commerce, Bureau of Navigation. *Radio Service Bulletin* no. 83 (March 1, 1924): 12–21.

Vitriol, Joseph A., and Jessecae K. Marsh. "The Illusion of Explanatory Depth and Endorsement of Conspiracy Beliefs." *European Journal of Social Psychology* 48, no. 7 (May 12, 2018): 955–69.

Watson, Thomas J., Jr., and Peter Petre. *Father, Son, & Co.: My Life at IBM and Beyond.* New York: Bantam Books, 1990.

Weik, Martin H. *A Survey of Domestic Electronic Digital Computing Systems, Report No. 971.* Aberdeen Proving Ground MD: Ballistic Research Laboratories, Department of the Army, 1955.

Weinland, James D. "The Memory of Salo Finkelstein." *Journal of General Psychology* 39 (October 1948): 243–57.

Weinland, James D., and W. S. Schlauch. "An Examination of the Computing Ability of Mr. Salo Finkelstein." *Journal of Experimental Psychology* 21, no. 3 (1937): 382–402.

"Whirlwind, Ultra-Fast 'Brain,' Now Operating." *Science News Letter* 60, no. 25 (December 22, 1951): 387–88.

White, Paul W. *News on the Air.* New York: Harcourt, Brace, and Company, 1947.

Whitman, Walt. "Election Day, November 1884." In *The Complete Poems of Walt Whitman*. With an introduction and notes by Stephen Matterson, 380. Hertfordshire UK: Wordsworth Editions Limited, 2006.

Whittier, John G. "The Poor Voter on Election Day." In *The Chapel of the Hermits and Other Poems*, 93–94. Boston: Ticknor, Reed, and Fields, 1853.

Williams, Michael R. *A History of Computing Technology*. 2nd ed. Los Alamitos CA: IEEE Computer Society Press, 1997.

Woodbury, Max A. "Model Making Problems in Election Forecasting." *Proceedings of the Third Annual Computer Applications Symposium*, October 9–10, 1956, 16–19. Chicago: Armour Research Foundation of Illinois Institute of Technology, 1956.

Wulforst, Harry. *Breakthrough to the Computer Age*. New York: Harry Scribner's Sons, 1982.

Yates, JoAnne. *Structuring the Information Age: Life Insurance and Technology in the Twentieth Century*. Baltimore: Johns Hopkins University Press, 2005.

Young, Paul. "Media on Display: A Telegraphic History of Early American Cinema." In *New Media, 1740–1915*, edited by Lisa Gitelman and Geoffrey B. Pingree, 229–64. Cambridge: MIT Press, 2003.

Young, William H., with Nancy K. Young. *The 1950s*. Westport CT: Greenwood Press, 2004.

Index

Chicago IL, 105, 144

Christian Science Monitor (newspaper), 207

cigarette poll, 117

Closter NJ, 205

CNN, 228, 229

coast-to-coast broadcasting, 39, 55, 127

coded returns, 27–29

collaborations, 19, 54, 84–86, 212, 215–16, 228–29, 236–37, 239–40

collating returns, 22

collective activity, 32–34

Colledge, Charles H. "Joe," 93, 95, 192, 196

Collier's (magazine), 130–31, 191, 222

Collingwood, Charles: and CBS's election night 1952 broadcast, 86, 140, 144–48, 151–63, 167, 169–71; in election-night lineup, 87, 126; and human-machine comparisons, 118, 161–63, 198–99, 223–24; and letter from Ed Beattie, 206; and the NBC-IBM plan, 218; and newspaper ads, 124; and postelection reactions, 198–99, 202; and rehearsals held on Election Day 1952, 134; and *Report to the West* (radio news program), 12, 90–92, 121; and UNIVAC, 12, 82, 90–92, 112, 118, 121, 124, 134, 140, 144–48, 151–63, 167, 169–71, 181, 206, 223–24

Collins, Ted, 125–26

Columbia Broadcasting System, 42

Columbia University, 144

commentators, 124, 128, 135, 164, 184, 186, 230

commercial computers, 54, 70–72, 75–76, 103, 195, 211

"Commercially Available General-Purpose Electronic Digital Computers of Moderate Price," 72–73

Commodore Hotel, 154

Common Sense (Paine), 246

Communist Party, 11, 213

"Company Confidential" documents, 65–69

comparative data, 12–13, 22, 23–24, 39, 89, 91, 103, 115, 170, 181, 185–86, 214, 216

competition: over computers, 74–75; and election night at Times Square, 46–50; and exit polling, 228; Jack Gould on, 201; between networks, 55–56, 84, 95–96, 125, 139; between newspapers, 25–26, 28–29; and postelection reactions, 196; between radio networks, 55–56; and responses to computer use on election night, 139, 204–5; and special guests, 43–45

comptometers, 110

computer-generated timestamp, 166

Computer History Museum, California, 140

Computer Research Corporation of California, 73

computers, 1–8, 12–13, 15, 17–18, 51, 54–83, 233, 235–36; and ABC's debut of the Elecom computer, 221–22; acceptance in election-night broadcasting, 88–90, 134, 136, 139, 174, 192–93, 220, 222–26; and accounts on Election Day, 128; Bill Henry on, 105–8; and CBS's election night 1952 broadcast, 137–73; and collaboration, 84–86; and commercial computers, 54, 70–72, 75–76, 103, 195, 211; as commodities, 84; and "Company Confidential" documents, 65–69; and computer use on election night 1962, 226–27; and the *Detroit Times* project, 212–16; and early history of television news, 60–61; and election night 1956, 215–22, 224–25; and election-night computing plans in 1952, 120–21; Jack Gould on, 158, 200–201, 225–27; and lessons of 1948, 169–70; and lessons of 1952, 211; and magnetic drum technology, 73–75; and the NBC-IBM plan, 216–20; and NBC's election night 1952 broadcast, 174–93; not an all-or-nothing gamble on, 123–24; Philip Hamburger on, 224–25; and responses to computer use, 105–9, 194–207; in the service of many agendas, 209–10; and stored-program development, 62; and theory needed for UNIVAC, 108–9; versus veteran political reporters, 229–30; and William H. Burkhart, 76–79; and women, 99. *See also* human-machine comparisons

Computers and Automation (Murphy and Berkeley), 210

The Computing Machinery Field (journal), 210

Con Edison, 100

conflict entrepreneurs, 234, 243–44

Congress, 20, 228, 231, 244

Connecticut, 103–4, 142, 150, 152, 159, 169–70, 176, 178, 182–83, 209

conspiracy theories, 232, 243–45

continuity, 34, 191

control-circuit theory, 79

Conway, Erik M., 244

Cooke, Alistair, 199

Cornell, Douglas, 170

corrective information, 241, 244

correspondence with listeners or viewers, 204–7

Cosmopolitan (magazine), 9, 17

cost of exit polling, 228, 240

couriers on horseback, 21

Cox, James M., 38

CPCS (Card-Programmed Electronic Calculators), 66, 71, 74, 103

crisis of credibility, 1–2, 236, 242

Cronkite, Walter: and CBS's election night 1952 broadcast, 2, 18, 137–38, 141–44, 148, 150–61, 163–64, 167, 169, 171–73; and confidence in UNIVAC plan, 89–90; and correspondence with listeners or viewers, 204–5; in election-night lineup, 5, 87; and postelection reactions, 201

Crossley, Archibald, 17, 58

cultural icons, 128

culture of demonstration, 120

Daly, John Charles, 59, 102, 124, 200, 221–22

data voids, 244

David Sarnoff Library, Princeton NJ, 94

Davis, Elmer, 101–2

Davis, Harry P., 34

daytime programs, 194

Defense Calculator, 70–71

de Forest, Lee, 34–37

democracy, 20, 33, 51, 57, 230, 231–36, 240, 244–46

Detroit MI, 37, 212–15, 217

over computers, 74–75; and computing plans in 1952, 120–21; and conspiracy theories, 243–45; and cultural icons, 128; and David Nye, 51; and the *Detroit Times* project, 212–16; and displays in Times Square, 34, 46–50, 52, 131–33, 189–91; and distant audiences, 26–27; and do-it-yourself scorecards, 128–29; and early history of television news, 54–61; and election night 1896, 28, 32–33; and election night 1928, 47; and election night 1936, 52; and election night 1952, 1–6, 8–18, 32, 54, 57, 60, 61, 73–75, 137–73, 174–93, 194–210, 211; and election night 1954, 211–16; and election night 1956, 215–22, 224–25; and election night 1960, 225; and election night 1962, 226–27; and election night 2000, 229–30; and election night 2020, 51, 139, 227, 231–34, 236–37, 245; and election-night choices, 133–34; and election-night excitement, 43–45; and election-night mathematics, 24, 145; evolution of, 20–21; and historical data, 23–24; and IBM, 101–5; Jack Gould on, 7, 225–27; and mass action, 51–52, 175; and the NBC-IBM plan, 216–20; and not an all-or-nothing gamble on computers, 123–24; and postelection reactions, 33–34, 189, 194–204; processing and analysis of data on, 111–12, 119–21; public exposure on, 92; and publicity, 66–70, 99–102, 104, 109, 120, 197–204, 207–8, 220;

and public participation, 20; and radio journalism, 37–42; and showmanship, 25, 27–28, 45, 60, 68, 114, 120–21, 131, 219, 221; and significance of election night for newspapers, 22–38; and special guests, 43–45; and speed versus accuracy, 20–22, 96, 141–42; and standards for broadcasting returns, 39–40; and stereopticons, 25–26; and street scenes, 25–26; and sublime of the crowd, 52–53; and television ownership, 54–55; and theory needed for UNIVAC, 109; and trust in journalism, 235–37, 241–42; and use of experts outside the newsroom, 19, 24–25, 42; and the Wayne computation lab, 212–15. *See also* 1948 election

"Election Night Estimation" (Mitofsky and Edelman), 230

Electoral College, 116

electoral votes, 9, 129–30, 141, 151, 156, 158, 167, 178, 184, 190–91, 198

electric election indicator, 131–32

electronic calculators, 65–66, 70–72, 74, 103–4

Electronic Computer Corporation, 73

Electronic Discrete Variable Automatic Computer (EDVAC), 62

Electronic Numerical Integrator and Computer (ENIAC), 61–62, 72, 78, 120

Electronics (magazine), 202–3

Emerson, Faye, 136

ENIAC (Electronic Numerical Integrator and Computer), 61–62, 72, 78, 120

Evening Bulletin (newspaper), 89

journalism and journalists (*cont.*)
computers, 229–30; and post-election reactions, 198–200; risks for, 21, 115; and technologists, 36, 54, 61, 120, 216, 219; and values, 242; versus showmanship, 121. *See also* collaborations; human-machine comparisons; story of the story

Kalin, Theodore, 77–78
Kalin-Burkhart Logical-Truth Calculator, 78
Kaltenborn, H. V., 59, 106, 176–77, 179–80, 184–86, 200
The Kate Smith Hour (television show), 125–26
KDKA, 34, 38
KECA, 43, 128
Keenoy, Charles L., 93
Kennedy, John F., 191, 225
Kentucky, 142, 179, 191, 227–28
Keokuk IA, 205
Keynote (magazine), 125, 197
"key precincts," 23–24
KFI, 43
Kilgallen, Dorothy, 200
Kimmel, James Jr., 243
King, John, 236
Knight Foundation, 239
Kollmar, Dick, 200
Kornacki, Steve, 236
Kovacs, Ernie, 5, 204, 207
Koviac, 204, 207
Krock, Arthur, 118
Kullback, Solomon, 217

La Conca d'Ora restaurant, 14
LaManna, Richard, 80–82, 94–95, 113–15, 181

Landon, Alf, 48
landslide prediction, 6–7, 153–54, 166–70, 172–73, 177, 186, 198, 207–8, 233
Laramie WY, 206
Lasswell, Harold, 128
Laurent, Lawrence, 226
Lawrence, David, 118
Lawrence, William H., 133, 201
League, Margery K., 110
letters from listeners and viewers, 204–7
Levitan, Paul, 85–87
Library of American Broadcasting, 7
Life (magazine), 45, 49, 219
Lima News (newspaper), 130
Lincoln, Abraham, 22–23
Lincoln AR, 13–14
literacy, 10
Literary Digest (magazine), 16, 115–16
Littlejohn, Fritz, 87
Littlewood, Thomas, 23
Litton Industries, 197
local journalism, 238–39
Local News Network, 239
Lockheed Aircraft, 102–4
Lodge, Henry Cabot Jr., 191
Logic Machines and Diagrams (Gardner), 78
Long Beach CA, 117
long-distance telephone lines, 26–27
Longwell, Sarah, 232
Los Angeles Times (newspaper), 104–5, 107
Louisville Tobacco Blending Corporation, 117
Lower, Elmer W., 86
Lubell, Samuel, 116, 128, 153–54
Lukoff, Herman, 112, 168, 198
lynching, 12

Lynn MA, 153

MacArthur, Douglas, 9
MacArthur Foundation, 239
Madigan, John, 102
magic lanterns. *See* stereopticons
Magnavox telemegaphone, 29
Magnetic Drum Calculator (MDC), 75
magnetic drum technology, 73–75
mail ballots, 232
Maine, 153
major party candidates, 9–10
man-bites-dog tale, 164, 199, 208–9
man versus machine. *See* human-
    machine comparisons
Marion County IN, 150
Mark I. *See* Harvard Mark I
Mark III, 79
Marks, Avery, 40
Marlow Theater, 14
Marvin, Carolyn, 26
Maryland, 142–43, 178, 239
Mason, Marilyn, 98–99, 114, 125, 179–
    80, 182–83, 186–87
Massachusetts, 14, 152–53, 156, 163–
    64, 191
Massachusetts Institute of Technol-
    ogy, 118–19
*Massachusetts Ploughman and Jour-
    nal of Agriculture*, 22
mass action, 51–52, 175
Master Broadcast Reports, 125–26
mathematics, 24, 145
Mauchly, John W., 61–70, 85, 120, 209,
    213, 224–25
McAndrew, William R., 196, 220
McCaffrey, Joseph F., 196
McClellan, George B., 23
McConnell, Joseph, 196
McCrary, Jinx Falkenburg, 136

McNamara, Patrick V., 214–15
MDC (Magnetic Drum Calculator), 75
media events, 15–16
Media Insight Project, 242
memo on speed versus accuracy,
    141–42
Mercer, Charles, 221
merchants of doubt, 244
Merton, Robert K., 128
Miami Herald (newspaper), 170
Michigan, 212–17
Mickelson, Sig, 58–61, 85–87, 92, 146,
    149–50, 169, 198, 217
Middleboro KY, 127
"Mike" persona of Monrobot, 7–8,
    12, 96–99, 125, 179, 188. *See also*
    human-machine comparisons;
    Monrobot
Minnesota, 25
minor parties, 8–9
misinformation, 239, 243–45
Mississippi, 10–11
Mississippi State College, 16
Missouri, 130, 161, 191
Mitchell, Herbert F. Jr., 110–11, 166–68
Mitofsky, Warren, 227–28, 230
mobile units, 48–50, 52
Modesto CA, 14–15
Mondale, Walter, 228
Monrobot: attractiveness of, 96–97;
    background of, 79–83; Bill Henry
    on, 105–8; and competition, 113–
    14; and competition over com-
    puters, 74–75, 95; disappeared
    from accounts of election night
    1952, 209–10; and election-night
    choices, 133; and election-night
    role in 1952, 3–4, 7–8, 13, 174–92,
    194–97, 200–203; featured on
    daytime programs, 125; and

2020, 229–30; and election-night lineup, 126; and election-night party, 43–44; and Jack Gould on networks' arrangements, 223; and Marilyn Mason, 98–99; Master Broadcast Reports of, 125–26; and mobile units, 48–49, 52; and the NBC-IBM plan, 216–20; and newspaper ads, 99–101, 124–25; and not an all-or-nothing gamble on computers, 123–24; and origin of plan to deploy a computer on election night, 92–94; and Philco, 57, 92–93, 100–101, 130, 175; and postelection reactions, 199–200; and publicity, 92, 220; and radio broadcast 1952, 99, 135–36, 170, 175–77, 234; and rehearsals held on Election Day 1952, 114, 135; and Richard LaManna, 94–95; and self-regulation, 57; and standards for broadcasting returns, 40; and Television Code, 57; and trade releases, 7–8, 12. *See also* Monrobot

NEP (National Election Pool), 229
NES (News Election Service), 228
Nevada, 117
Newark NJ, 98, 220
New Hampshire, 131
New Jersey, 153
New Orleans LA, 12
Newport Daily News (newspaper), 15
news deserts, 238
News Election Service (NES), 228
news organizations, 237, 246; at the center of attention, 18, 189; and collaboration, 19, 54, 84–86, 212, 215–16, 228–29; and election-night culture, 93; and election-night excitement, 43–45; and local journalism, 238–39; and official counts, 123; and preelection guides, 43

Newspaper Printing Corporation, 102
newspapers: and blank score sheets, 43; as center of attention on election night, 18, 20; and collective activity, 32–34; and the *Detroit Times*, 195, 212–16; and election-night advances, 25–29; and election-night excitement, 44–45; and IBM, 103–4; and journalism about journalism, 126–27; and the Lee de Forest method, 34–37; and mass action, 51–52; and meaning from early returns, 40; and news deserts, 238; and newspaper ads, 92, 99–101; and photography, 33–34; and polls, 117; and the Press-Radio War, 41–42; and radio, 38, 41; and responses to computer use on election night, 204–5; and segregation, 56; and significance of election night for, 22–38; and size of election-night audiences, 19; and standards for broadcasting returns, 39–40; and story of the story, 30–33, 103–4; and use of experts outside the newsroom, 24–25, 189; as venues for live election-night news, 15, 19, 43. *See also individual newspapers*
Newsweek (magazine), 98
New York, ABC headquarters. *See* Studio 1 in New York
New York, CBS headquarters, 44, 112, 134, 167

New York, NBC headquarters. *See*
Studio 8-H at Rockefeller Center
New York American (newspaper), 35–
36, 37
New York City, 15, 23, 25–27,
38–39, 128
New York Daily News (newspaper),
201, 220
New York Daily Times (newspaper), 21
New-York Daily Tribune (newspaper),
32–33
New Yorker (magazine), 42, 197
New York Herald (newspaper), 24, 25–
26, 30–31, 32, 33, 52, 234
New York Herald Tribune (newspaper), 191
New York State, 144, 154, 185, 186
New York Sun (newspaper), 43
New York Times (newspaper), 15;
and the 1876 election, 33; and
coded returns, 27; and coverage
of radio, 38–41; and displays in
Times Square, 34, 47–48, 131–
33, 189–90; and do-it-yourself
scorecards, 129; and early voting,
170; and election-night analysis, 23, 29, 58–59; and election-
night excitement, 44–45; and the
Electronic Numerical Integrator
and Computer (ENIAC), 120; and
minor-party candidates, 9; and
newspaper ads, 124, 220; and
publicity, 92; and recall, 215; and
responses to computer use on
election night, 200–201, 205; and
stereopticons, 25–26; and survey
research, 16; and waiting for concession, 187; and the "zipper,"
34, 47–48, 132, 189–90. *See also*
Gould, Jack

New York Tribune (newspaper), 22,
27, 52
*New York World-Telegram and The
Sun* (newspaper), 102–5, 216
Nidecker, Hildegard, 110
Nielsen, A. C., 55
Nixon, Richard M., 9, 11, 225
NORC (National Opinion Research
Center), 237, 242
Norman, Jeremy, 63
Northern Steamship Company, 28
North West (ship), 28
Norwalk CT, 85
novelty, 204
Nye, David, 51

Oakland CA, 14
Ochs, Adolph S., 47
O'Dowd, Jack, 118
Ohio, 25, 122, 130, 143, 178, 179
Oklahoma, 150, 179, 191
Olbermann, Keith, 230
Oliver, Wayne, 107–8
on-air celebrities, 203–4
Oneonta NY, 13
Oneonta Star (newspaper), 126
Operation Monrobot, 114, 135
Operation No Sleep, 127
Orange NJ, 79. *See also* Monroe Calcu-
lating Machine Company
Oreskes, Naomi, 244
oscilloscopes, 119
Oshkosh Daily Northwestern (newspa-
per), 126, 130
Oshkosh WI, 14
outcomes based on early returns, 1, 23–
24, 87, 107, 150, 182, 205–6, 212,
220. *See also* landslide prediction
outdoor displays. *See* displays in Times
Square

Quinby, E. J. "Jay," 80–81, 94–95, 114
Quine, Willard V., 77

race, 10–11
radio: and beginning of radio jour-
    nalism, 37–38; and CBS's election
    night 1952 broadcast, 153–54,
    158–59, 169; and coast-to-coast
    broadcasting, 39; and commer-
    cial broadcasting, 34, 36–37; and
    competition, 55–56; and displays
    in Times Square, 46–50, 52, 189–
    91; as dominant platform for
    broadcast news, 12; and election-
    night dilemma, 39–40; and
    election-night excitement, 43–45;
    invention of, 34; and listener-
    friendly reports, 40–41; Mon-
    robot featured on, 194; and NBC's
    election night 1952 broadcast,
    170, 175–77, 182–84; and post-
    election reactions, 198–201, 203;
    and the Press-Radio War, 41–42;
    and publicity, 99; and regulation,
    56–57; and Salo Finkelstein, 42;
    and size of radio audiences, 54–
    55, 128; and standards for broad-
    casting returns, 39–40; UNIVAC
    featured on, 158–59
Radio Age (magazine), 93
Radio Corporation of America (RCA),
    49, 55
radiophone, 37
radiotelephone, 34
Ralph, Julian, 31–32
ratings, 55–56, 60, 194, 196
RCA (Radio Corporation of America),
    49, 55, 93–94
RCA Laboratories, 80
Reagan, Ronald, 228

recordings, 138–39
red mirage, 232, 244
Rees, Mina, 73
Reeves, Rosser, 11
regulation, 56–57
Remington Rand: and IBM, 13, 64–67,
    71, 73–74, 208, 211; and market
    for commercial computers, 162,
    211; and Paul Levitan, 85–86;
    and postelection reactions, 200;
    and Prudential Insurance, 170;
    and publicity, 68–70, 120, 207–
    8; and public relations, 89, 103;
    transcript made for, 203–4; and
    Unisys, 7, 197. *See also* Eckert-
    Mauchly Computer Corporation;
    UNIVAC (Universal Automatic
    Computer)
Remington Typewriter Company,
    24–25
Report to the West (radio news pro-
    gram), 12, 90–92, 121
Republican National Convention in
    1952, 60
reputations, 13, 115, 123–24
responses to computer use on election
    night, 105–9, 194–207
returns, reporting on, 12–15; and
    coded returns, 27–29; and col-
    lating returns, 22; and displays
    in Times Square, 34, 46–50, 52,
    131–33, 189–91; and election-
    night choices, 133–34; and IBM,
    101–3; Jack Gould on, 58–59,
    225–27; and journalism about
    journalism, 126–27; and the Lee
    de Forest method, 34–37; and
    media events, 15; and NBC's elec-
    tion night 1952 broadcast, 175–
    89, 219; and preelection guides

in newspapers, 43; and the Press-Radio War, 41–42; and radio journalism, 37–42; and reputations, 13, 115, 123–24; and significance of election night for newspapers, 22–38; and standards for broadcasting returns, 39–40; and stereopticons, 25–26; and survey research, 16–17; and visual presentations, 27–28, 45–46. *See also* studio arrangements

reviews. *See* postelection reactions

Rhode Island, 15, 179

Richmond VA, 21

The Righteous Mind (Haidt), 242

Ripley, Amanda, 241

Rockefeller Center, 49, 75, 94–95, 105, 131. *See also* Studio 8-H at Rockefeller Center

Rogers, Will, 39

Rome NY, 170

Roosevelt, Franklin Delano, 10, 48, 192

Roper, Elmo, 17, 58, 128, 184, 186

Rosen, Saul, 214–15

Rosenstiel, Tom, 240, 245–46

Rural Radio Network, 199

Russert, Tim, 229–30

San Francisco CA, 218

San Francisco Chronicle (newspaper), 203

Sarnoff, David, 94–95

Scientific American (magazine), 73

"A Scientific Research Bureau Is Needed" (Mauchly), 67–68

Scribner's Magazine, 31–32

Scripps, William E., 37

Scripps-Howard newspapers, 116

searchlights, 27, 132, 189–90

Seares, Al, 70

Seeds of Treason (De Toledano and Lasky), 213

See It Now program, 57, 118–19, 140

Selective Sequence Electronic Calculator (SSEC), 66, 70–71

Senate, 10, 191–92, 214–15, 223, 231

Sevareid, Eric, 5, 89, 153, 158, 160–61, 171–73, 201, 206

Shannon, Claude, 77

sheets pasted alongside campaign posters, 28–29

showmanship, 15, 25, 27–28, 45, 60, 68, 96, 114, 120–21, 131, 219, 221

Solutions Journalism Network, 239

South Carolina, 10, 117–18, 143, 177, 178

Sparkman, John J., 9–10

special guests, 43–45

speed versus accuracy, 20–22, 96, 141–42

Sperber, A. M., 56

split screens, 196

Sponsor (magazine), 56

sponsors, 41–42, 57

SSEC (Selective Sequence Electronic Calculator), 66, 70–71

Stamford Engineering Society, 209

Standard (establishment in St. Louis), 29

standards for broadcasting returns, 39–40

Stassen, Harold, 150

statistical sampling, 16

Stereopticon Advertising Company, 25–26

stereopticons, 25–26

stereotypes, 8, 56, 240–41

Stevenson, Adlai: and campaign trains, 127; and CBS's election

Stevenson, Adlai (*cont.*)
  night 1952 broadcast, 3, 141–72;
    and do-it-yourself scorecards,
    129; and the Gallup poll, 17; and
    minor-party candidates, 9; and
    NBC's election night 1952 broad-
    cast, 178–91; and polls in news-
    papers, 116–17; and preelection
    polls, 122
Stirewalt, Chris, 237
St. Louis MO, 29
St. Louis Post-Dispatch (newspaper),
  29–30, 33–34, 52
"Stop the Steal," 231–32, 236, 244
stored-program computers, 13, 62, 64,
  74, 103. *See also* Defense Calculator; Electronic Discrete Variable
  Automatic Computer (EDVAC)
story of the story, 19; and Bill Henry's
  column, 105–8; and CBS's election night 1948 broadcast, 49–
  50; and collective activity, 32–34;
  and Ed Herlihy radio broadcast,
  135–36; and election nights, 45,
  133–34; and the Harold Arlin
  feature, 151–52; and the *Hartford Courant*, 103–4; and Julian
  Ralph's account, 31–32; and NBC's
  election night 1952 broadcast,
  189; and radio broadcasts, 41–42,
  175–77; and studio arrangements,
  148–50, 178–79; and sublime
  of the crowd, 52–53; and television in 1952, 127–28. *See also*
  gimmickry
St. Paul Dispatch (newspaper), 28
St. Paul MN, 28
straw polls, 16, 115–17
street scenes, 15, 25–26, 30, 32–33,
  48–50, 52, 131, 189

Studio 1 in New York, 102
Studio 8-H at Rockefeller Center, 3,
  18, 44, 96, 113–14, 125–26, 135–36,
  174–93, 219
studio arrangements, 148–50, 178–79
sublime of the crowd, 52–53
suffrage, 20, 22
Sullivan, Margaret, 234–35, 242–43,
  246
Sulzberger, Arthur Hays, 44–45, 190
Summerfield, Arthur, 150, 170
supervisory control panel, UNIVAC, 2,
  112, 137
survey research, 16–17, 115–18, 240–41.
  See also pollsters
Swayze, John Cameron, 3, 177–79,
  182, 185
Syracuse NY, 129
Systems Magazine, 208

tabulating machines, 135, 176
Taft, Robert, 173
tally boards, 50, 219, 223
Tarrant County TX, 151
Taylor, Charles H., 23
Taylor, J. Davidson, 196, 218–19
technologists, 36, 54, 61, 120, 216,
  219–20
telautograph, 29
telegraph and telegraph companies,
  20–22, 26–27, 30, 39, 127, 240
Teleregister Corporation, 219, 220
teletype machines, 14, 111, 134–35, 138,
  167, 176, 178–79
Television Code, 56–57
television networks, 4; and access to
  television, 12; and challenges of
  election nights, 230; competition between, 84, 125, 139; and
  computers, 192–93; and early

history of television news, 54–
61; and election night 1948, 1–2;
and election-night crowds, 189–
90; and exit polling, 227–29; and
Jack Gould on networks' arrangements, 50–51, 223; and newspaper ads, 124–25; and opinions
about use of computers, 105–8;
and regulation, 56–57; speeches
and appearances on, 11; and story
of the story in 1952, 127–28; and
studio arrangements, 148–50,
178–79; and transparency, 236;
watching news on, 204–5; and
wire services, 141–42
television news, early history of, 54–61
television sets, 54–55, 100
Tennessee, 143, 178, 186, 224
Texas, 191, 233
theaters, 28–29
Thomas, Lowell, 87, 126, 148–50, 171–
72, 200
Thurmond, Strom, 9
Tiffany, E. J. Jr., 114
Tilden, Samuel, 33
Time (magazine), 8, 12, 102, 170, 215,
223–24
timeliness, 173, 230. *See also* accuracy
Times radio station, 133, 190, 201
Times Square, 27, 34, 46–50, 52, 131–
33, 189–91
Times Talk (television show), 190
Times Tower, 34, 46–47, 132, 190
Timesweek (newspaper publication),
45
Today show, 99, 114, 125, 194
total votes, 111. *See also* electoral votes;
popular votes
touch-screen graphics, 236
trade releases, 7–8, 12

transparency, 145, 236
Traverse City MI, 131
Trendex ratings service, 196
Trout, Robert, 42, 130–31, 154, 157
Truman, Harry S., 10, 17, 58–59, 84,
106, 116, 130, 153, 176–77, 181, 185
Trump, Donald J., 231–33, 235, 237,
242, 244–45
Trusting News, 241
truth tables, 77–78
Tukey, John W., 85, 217
Tulsa Tribune (newspaper), 102
Tulsa World (newspaper), 102

UDEC (Unitized Digital Electronic
Computer), 213–14
understory, 241
Underwood Corporation, 221–22
uniform voting day for president, 20
Unisys, 7, 197
United Press, 17, 89, 102, 116, 122–23,
127–28, 131, 206
United Press International, 228
Unitized Digital Electronic Computer
(UDEC), 213–14
UNIVAC (Universal Automatic Computer), 84–121, 194–210; attractiveness of, 96–97; Bill Henry on,
105–8; and CBS's election night
1952 broadcast, 2–3, 6, 137–72,
197–204; and Charles Collingwood's description of plan for,
12, 90–92; and competition, 95,
113–14; and correspondence with
listeners or viewers, 205–7; and
early prediction of a landslide,
153–54, 166–70, 198, 207–8; and
election-night choices, 133; and
election-night computing plans
in 1952, 84–93, 120–21; and

UNIVAC (*cont.*)

Grace Hopper, 99; and human-machine comparisons, 118–20, 160–64, 224–25; and IBM, 71, 73, 211; introduction of, 64–65; Jack Gould on, 158, 200–201, 223; and media events, 15; in newspaper ads, 124; not an all-or-nothing gamble on, 123; Philip Hamburger on, 224–25; postelection documents, 111; and postelection reactions, 194, 196, 197–204; promotional outing of, 126; and publicity, 66–70, 101–2, 109, 220; and public relations, 103; and rehearsals held on Election Day 1952, 134; and the remote tour, 145–47; speed of, 82; supervisory control panel of, 2, 112, 137; theory and methodology of for election night, 109–10; *Time* magazine on, 223–24; and the UNIVAC-only story, 209–10

Universal Automatic Computer. *See* UNIVAC (Universal Automatic Computer)

University of Chicago, 237, 242

University of Maryland's Philip Merrill College of Journalism, 239

University of Pennsylvania, 120

U.S. Census, 64, 69, 134

U.S. Supreme Court, 10, 56

Valparaiso IN, 131

Van Horne, Harriet, 98, 102, 105, 108, 200

Variety (magazine), 14, 69, 101, 120, 199–200, 225

Vegetarian Party, 9

Velshi, Ali, 239

Vermont, 21

Victor Adding Machine Company, 189

Victor Talking Machine Company, 94

Vidette Messenger (newspaper), 122

Vincent, Phillip S., 168, 209

Virginia, 143, 156, 178, 191

visual presentations, 27–28, 45–46, 50. *See also* displays in Times Square; studio arrangements

vitascopes, 29

VNS (Voter News Service), 228–29

Vonnegut, Kurt, 61

VoteCast, 237

vote counts, 2, 15, 25, 40, 58, 94, 103, 111–12, 115, 126, 129, 141, 142–43, 152–53, 160, 164, 166–67, 176, 219–20. *See also* electoral votes; returns, reporting on

Voter News Service (VNS), 228–29

Voter Research and Surveys (VRS), 228

voters: demographics of, 10; exit polling of, 227–29, 237, 240; gender breakdown of, 188; and minor-party candidates, 9; and mystery of deciphering, 172–73; and turn-out, 122–23, 141, 156, 228; and voter suppression, 10–12, 233; and voting rights, 10–12, 20

VRS (Voter Research and Surveys), 228

WABC, 42

Wall Street Journal (newspaper), 216

Washington Peace Party, 9

Washington Post (newspaper), 125, 200–201, 203

Watson, Thomas J. Jr., 72, 74–75, 216, 218

Watson, Thomas J. Sr., 66

Wayne University, 195, 212–15, 217

WCBS, 44